Helping America's Homeless

Martha Burt
Laudan Y. Aron
and Edgar Lee
with Jesse Valente

Other Urban Institute Press books by Martha Burt

America's Homeless: Numbers, Characteristics, and Programs That Serve Them
(Martha Burt and Barbara E. Cohen)

Helping America's Homeless

Emergency shelter or affordable housing?

THE URBAN INSTITUTE PRESS
Washington, D.C.

THE URBAN INSTITUTE PRESS
2100 M Street, N.W.
Washington, DC 20037

Library of Congress Cataloging-in-Publication Data

Helping America's Homeless: Emergency shelter or affordable housing? /
Martha Burt ... [et al.]..
p. cm.
Includes bibliographical references.
ISBN 0-87766-701-2 (pbk. : alk. paper)
1. Homelessness—United States. 2. Homeless persons—United States.
3. Homelessness—Government policy—United States. 4. Homeless persons—Services for—United States. I. Burt, Martha R.
HV4505 .H4 2001
363.5′96942—dc21
2001001363

Printed in the United States of America

THE URBAN INSTITUTE is a nonprofit policy research and educational organization established in Washington, D.C., in 1968. Its staff investigates the social and economic problems confronting the nation and evaluates the public and private means to alleviate them. The Institute disseminates its research findings through publications, its Web site, the media, seminars, and forums.

Through work that ranges from broad conceptual studies to administrative and technical assistance, Institute researchers contribute to the stock of knowledge available to guide decisionmaking in the public interest.

Conclusions or opinions expressed in Institute publications are those of the authors and do not necessarily reflect the views of officers or trustees of the Institute, advisory groups, or any organizations that provide financial support to the Institute.

"In his inaugural address last January, President George W. Bush pledged that, 'When we see that wounded traveler on the road to Jericho, we will not pass by to the other side.' Using the best study of homeless Americans ever conducted, with information on both client needs and the services available to meet those needs, *Helping America's Homeless*, Martha Burt's latest book, shows who these wounded travelers are, what we have done for them so far, and what we have yet to do to end their homelessness. This landmark study should end pointless ideological bickering and provide a rock-solid foundation for finally ending this national disgrace."

—Dr. Robert Rosenheck, Professor of Psychiatry and Public Health, Yale Medical School, National Director of Evaluation of VA Homeless Programs

"Every person seeking to affect public policy—whether as a public official, professional, or advocate—should not only read this book but use it daily to create real change in their communities. This is the most comprehensive, thorough, and practical material to date on homelessness. The authors take a more holistic look at homelessness than ever before by including both the rural and suburban homeless, as well as urban, and by comparing the homeless to other poor Americans. This is not just a review of statistical data but a real analysis of the effects of public policy and ways to improve strategies to address the needs of our country's poorest citizens."

—Natalie Hutcheson, Director of Specialized Housing Resources, Kentucky Housing Corporation

"*Helping America's Homeless* offers a rich and informative overview of who is homeless and why, and what is now being done, based on an unprecedented national survey. The conclusions make a compelling call for reinvigorating homeless policy and programs with a much sharper focus on affordable and supportive housing as the way to permanently end homelessness in America, coupled with prevention efforts focused in hospitals and jails and other settings to end the practice of routinely discharging people into homelessness."

—Carla I. Javits, President and CEO, Corporation for Supportive Housing

Contents

1 Introduction 1

2 How Many Homeless People Are There? 23

3 Homeless Families, Singles, and Others 55

4 Effects of Alcohol, Drug, and Mental Health Problems on Characteristics and Circumstances of Homeless People 97

5 Issues in Child and Youth Homelessness 137

6 Patterns of Homelessness 161

7 Comparing Homeless Subgroups within Community Types 187

8 Factors Associated with Homeless Status 219

9 Homeless Assistance Programs in 1996, with Comparisons to the Late 1980s 241

10 Program Structures and Continuums of Care 267

11 Conclusions 319

References 335

Appendix 343

Index 357

About the Authors 365

Figures

1.1 Factors Influencing Homelessness .9

3.1 Family Status, by Sex Subgroups .60

5.1 Residence of Minor Children Who Do Not Live with a Homeless Parent .147

6.1 Base and Net Spell Lengths of Currently Homeless Clients .177

9.1 Number of Homeless Assistance Programs in the United States, 1996 .247

9.2 Number of Program Contacts Expected at Programs of Different Types on an Average Day in February 1996 .251

9.3 Distribution of Programs and Program Contacts across Community Types, by Program Type .254

9.4 Size of Homeless Assistance Programs .256

9.5 Proportion of Daily Program Contacts Provided by Larger Programs .257

9.6 Types of Agencies Operating Housing, Food, Health, and Other Programs .260

9.7 Program Reliance on Government Funding .262

10.1 Program Contacts in Primary Sampling Areas, by Overall Population, per 10,000 Population, and per 10,000 Living in Poverty .271

10.2 Program Contacts in Primary Sampling Areas, by Program Type .275

10.3 Rate of Shelter/Housing Program Contacts per 10,000 Poor People, by Type of Housing Program .277

10.4 Soup Kitchen Weekday Service Units and Meals Served per 10,000 Poor People: Low, High, and Average Estimates .281

Tables

2.1 Program Contacts at Homeless Assistance Programs during a Four-Week Period in October/November 1996 .32

2.2 Number of Clients Using Homeless Assistance Programs during an Average Week in October/November 1996 .33

2.3 Children in Homeless Families Using Homeless Assistance Programs during an Average Week in October/November 1996 34

2.4 Comparing Daily and Weekly Estimates of Households and People Using Homeless Assistance Programs 35

2.5 Family and Urban-Rural Status of Homeless Households and People Using Homeless Assistance Programs during an Average Week in the October/November 1996 Target Period 36

2.6 Estimates for February vs. October/November 1996 of All and Homeless Users of Homeless Assistance Programs . . . 40

2.7 Comparison of NSHAPC and 1987 Urban Institute Estimates of Homeless People Identified for Interview in Shelters and Soup Kitchens in Central Cities 41

2.8 Comparing 1987 Urban Institute and 1996 NSHAPC Estimates of Homelessness Rates, by Community Type 43

2.9 Projections from NSHAPC Data to the Number of People Homeless during a Year's Period, Adjusted for Duplication: Using October/November and February 1996 Base Estimates, for Homeless Clients, and for Homeless Clients Plus Children 47

3.1 Basic Demographic Characteristics of Homeless Clients, by Family Status and Sex 58

3.2 Conditions of Homelessness, by Family Status and Sex 64

3.3 Top Four Reasons for Leaving Last Regular Place to Stay, by Family Status and Sex 67

3.4 Current Living Situation and Use of Homeless Assistance Programs, by Family Status and Sex 71

3.5 Income Levels, Income Sources, and Employment of Homeless Clients, by Family Status and Sex 75

3.6 Physical Health and Nutrition Status of Homeless Clients, by Family Status and Sex 81

3.7 Adverse Experiences of Homeless Clients, by Family Status and Sex 87

3.8 Childhood Out-of-Home Experiences of Homeless Clients, by Family Status and Sex 90

4.1 Alcohol, Drug, and Mental Health Problems among Homeless Clients, by Family Status and Sex 103

4.2 Drug Use Patterns Reported by NSHAPC and NHSDA Clients 108

4.3 Percentage of NSHAPC and NHSDA Clients Reporting Treatment for Alcohol, Drug, and Mental Health Problems 110

4.4 Basic Demographic Characteristics of Homeless Clients, by ADM Status 113

4.5 Conditions of Homelessness, by ADM Status 117

4.6 Income Levels, Income Sources, and Employment of Homeless Clients, by ADM Status 120

4.7 Physical Health and Nutrition Status of Homeless Clients, by ADM Status 123

4.8 Adverse Childhood Experiences of Homeless Clients, by ADM Status 127

4.9 Childhood Out-of-Home Experiences of Homeless Clients, by ADM Status 130

4.10 Federal Poverty Thresholds and Corresponding Household Income Categories for Low-Income NHSDA Adults 134

5.1 Parenting Status of Homeless Clients 141

5.2 Minor Children of Homeless Clients: Demographic Characteristics and Living Situations 143

5.3 Minor Children of Homeless Clients: Age, Parent's Gender, and Child's Age and Living Situation 145

5.4 Basic Demographic Characteristics of Young Homeless Clients 151

5.5 Childhood Neglect, Abuse, and Out-of-Home Experiences of Young Homeless Clients 154

5.6 History of Alcohol, Drug, and Mental Health Problems among Young Homeless Clients 157

6.1 Classification of Homeless Clients by Length of and Number of Homeless Spells 166

6.2 Characteristics of Crisis, Episodic, and Chronically Homeless Clients, Using Two Methods of Deriving Categories 168

6.3 Base and Net Spell Lengths, and Number of Times Homeless 176

6.4 Types of Places Where Homeless Clients Spent Time during Their Current Homeless Spell 179

6.5 Mean Number of Places Clients Have Spent Time during Their Current Homeless Spell, by Base Spell Length 180

6.6 Net Spell Length: Base Spell Length, Less Time Spent in Other Places 181

7.1 Basic Demographic Characteristics of Homeless Clients, by Homeless Status within Community Type 191

7.2 Homeless Histories and Use of Homeless Assistance Programs, by Homeless Status within Community Type 194

7.3 Income Levels, Income Sources, and Employment of Homeless Clients, by Homeless Status within Community Type 199

7.4 Physical Health and Nutrition Status of Homeless Clients, by Homeless Status within Community Type 204

7.5 Alcohol, Drug, and Mental Health Problems among Homeless NSHAPC Clients, by Homeless Status within Community Type 207

7.6 Adverse Experiences of Homeless Clients, by Homeless Status within Community Type 210

7.7 Childhood Out-of-Home Experiences of Homeless Clients, by Homeless Status within Community Type 213

8.1 Demographic Characteristics of Currently, Formerly, and Never Homeless Clients 225

8.2 Risk Factors among Currently, Formerly, and Never Homeless Clients 226

8.3 Characteristics Associated with Ever Being Homeless: Results from Logistic Regressions 230

8.4 Characteristics Differentiating Currently from Formerly Homeless Clients: Results from Logistic Regressions 234

9.1 Changes in Shelter and Soup Kitchen Capacity in the United States, as Registered by Five Studies 244

9.2 Distribution of NSHAPC Programs, by Urban/Rural Location 248

9.3 Distribution of Estimated Program Contacts, by Urban/Rural Status 252

10.1 Statistics for Program Contacts in Primary Sampling Areas 273

10.2 Provider Perceptions of Service Availability 284

10.3 Geographic Distribution of NSHAPC Service Locations . . .289

10.4 Stand-Alone Programs 291

10.5 Programs and Services Attached to Emergency Shelters 294

10.6 Programs and Services Attached to Transitional Housing Programs 298

10.7 Programs and Services Attached to Permanent Housing Programs 299

10.8 Programs and Services Attached to Soup Kitchens 300

10.A1 Total Service Units per Day 303

10.A2 Percent of Program Contacts in a Primary Sampling Area That Are Allocated to Different Types of Services 306

10.A3 Housing/Shelter Program Contacts by Primary Sampling Area 308

10.A4 Soup Kitchen Weekday/Weekend Program Contacts per 10,000 Poor People: Low, High, and Average Estimates 312

1

Introduction

Homelessness has now been on the American policy agenda for close to two decades. In 1989, when the Urban Institute published *America's Homeless* (Burt and Cohen 1989), policymakers and the public may have expected, or hoped, that we could end the crisis of homelessness relatively quickly. The decade of the 1990s has not fulfilled that expectation. Programs and services to help homeless people expanded dramatically in the 1990s, just as they did in the 1980s. At the same time, visible homelessness in many American communities does not seem to have diminished. How are we to think about the persistence of homelessness at the end of a decade of unprecedented prosperity, and at the dawn of a new millennium?

Answers to this question are complex, because homelessness itself is complex. In this chapter, we explore some of these complexities. They form the critical context within which we can begin to interpret the information presented in following chapters. We will look briefly at some of the historical fluctuations in types and levels of homelessness within the United States. These include moments when homelessness has assumed the stature of a "social problem" and moments when it has not. We also undertake a fairly extended discussion of the meanings or definitions of homelessness as a condition experienced by some people.

Given that homelessness stems, at base, from an inability to afford housing, we next consider the structural conditions of the economy, housing markets, labor markets, and related factors that influence people's ability to afford housing. We also consider how people with different individual characteristics may be affected. Finally, we look at the ways in which the United States has chosen to address homelessness from the federal level. We save for the concluding chapter a discussion of what societies may be willing to do to reduce the probability that their members will become homeless. Such a discussion will take us into the realm of cultural norms and expectations about individual and societal responsibility for the well-being of individuals and households, and consider their practical extensions in the form of stronger or weaker, publicly funded, "safety net" or "social assistance" programs and supports. This discussion is best approached after the reader has absorbed the information about homeless people and homeless assistance programs presented in the intervening chapters.

A Brief Historical Overview

Many essays have been written in the last decade and a half examining the historical meaning and experience of homelessness in the United States (Hoch and Slayton 1989; Hopper 1991; Hopper and Baumohl 1994, 1996; Rossi 1989). European countries have also recently focused on the existence and meaning of homelessness in their midst (Avramov 1999). All of these writings conclude that one of the essential characteristics of homelessness as a phenomenon is its transience, instability, and flux. In this, homelessness as a whole resembles the trajectories of its individual members, who enter and leave homelessness, sometimes repeatedly, sometimes only once, depending on their fortunes. We may distill the essence of these discussions to suggest that three elements, separately or in combination, characterize homelessness for some writers, with regard to some populations, at some times. These elements are the transience or instability of *place*, the instability or absence of connections to *family*, and the instability or absence of *housing*.

Without Place

In talking about homelessness, most writers have found it necessary and important to note that most societies have included larger or smaller groups of people who have no fixed place to live, and almost always are poor. Some have been cohesive groups for whom wandering is a way of life, such as nomadic tribes, circus and carnival workers, and many of today's migrant farm workers. They have families, and usually some form of housing, but no fixed place. Others have been individual wanderers, such as peddlers or tinkers, who move from community to community in their own van or wagon. They have housing, but no family or place.

Other collections of wanderers have been as changeable in their composition as they are in their location. In the United States, for instance, the last decades of the 19th century and first decades of the 20th saw an ever-changing population of single men following construction and industrial development opportunities across the country, and then returning to low-rent sections of cities when work was scarce. Most often, individuals in these groups were not "literally" homeless in today's sense of the word, because they usually could afford a room in a cheap hotel or boarding house. But they were unattached to a particular place, and without family, and thus without a home in the larger sense of the word.

Depending on economic conditions and cycles, these groups of transients swelled or diminished. In really bad times, local out-of-work laborers joined the itinerant core (houseless, but *not* placeless). During the Great Depression of the 1930s, when unemployment reached the astonishing level of one-quarter of the workforce, an official government survey in the United States estimated that at least 1.2 million people (or 1 percent of the total population) were homeless at a single point in time (mid-January 1933) (Crouse 1986). Further, the researchers felt this number was conservative. In addition to these patterns, intra- and international migration flows caused by war, famine, economic displacement (such as the failure of rural economies), and the economic draw of work in developed countries also contribute to houselessness, uprootedness, and large numbers of at least initially transient people flooding into receiving communities. Even homeless service systems can create this effect. For example, Milofsky and colleagues (1993) describe the effects on a small town of the influx of large numbers of homeless people relocating from nearby metropolises to obtain substance abuse recovery services.

Without Family

Studies of skid row populations in the 1950s and 1960s (Bahr and Caplow 1974; Bogue 1963; Wiseman 1970) provided a different lens on homelessness. The situations they studied were different. These studies described a population, mostly of single men, who were housed, lived steadily in a particular part of a particular city, but lived by themselves. That is, they did not live with any family members although they clearly lived in hotel rooms with many other people on the same and adjacent floors. Very few men in these communities would have been classified as literally homeless by today's formal government definition, yet they were considered homeless by the people who studied them. Even the U.S. Census Bureau, as late as the 1980 decennial census, identified people who lived by themselves and did not have a "usual home elsewhere" (i.e., with family) as "homeless." This way of thinking about homelessness reflects a cultural expectation that the "normal" way to live is in a family, and that something is wrong when people live by themselves. "Home" in this usage implies *people,* not physical shelter.

Homeless people, themselves, in the 1980s and 1990s drew a distinction between being sheltered or housed, and having a home. One of the great difficulties in gathering information about patterns and histories of homelessness comes from the distinction between "housing" and "home." A common question on homeless surveys, designed to determine how long a person has been homeless, asks in effect, "When was the last time you had a home or other permanent place to stay?" or "When was the last time you had a place of your own, such as a house, apartment, room, or other housing, for 30 days or more in the same place?"[1] It is not uncommon for people to respond that they last had such a place a very long time ago. Some people say "never." Yet further probing uncovers that people have spent significant periods of time living in conventional dwellings where their tenure was insecure and/or they did not feel "at home." This could include accommodations such as hotel rooms they had paid for themselves. Thus their experience of *literal* homelessness was much shorter, or much more intermittent, than would be implied by their answer to the survey question. But their answers accurately reflect how long they have been without significant attachments to people.

Without Housing

Writers struggling with the concept of homelessness also recognize that individuals and families may become homeless "in place," so to speak. Fire, flood, or natural disaster could render people homeless by destroying their dwelling. Or circumstances could change the ability of families and communities to accommodate certain of their members, causing them to eject the most burdensome. Or people's own behaviors may make it difficult for family and community to support them in housing. In the United States, official government definitions of homelessness focus exclusively on this "houseless" aspect.

If money were no problem, these temporary losses of a dwelling could easily be overcome, without risk of becoming an actual or potential social problem. Essential elements of homelessness as a social problem are a level of poverty so extreme that homeless people cannot remove their homeless condition themselves, and an unwillingness or inability of society either to do it for them or to establish conditions that would not make them so desperate in the first place. Finally, even so apparently clear a condition as being houseless is specific to particular times and places. Residents of shantytown dwellings under a bridge or along a roadside, for example, are considered homeless in New York City, where such structures are not allowed, but are well-housed in many cities in the developing world, where such structures are the norm for millions.

Today's homeless in the United States are houseless, and some are placeless (transient). Many are also without family. But some significant number bring at least part of their family with them into homelessness, and maintain some reasonable degree of connectedness with housed family members. Over time, these "connected" people comprise a larger proportion of people experiencing homelessness than the isolates, because "connected" people stay homeless for relatively shorter periods and are replaced by others like themselves. In this respect American homelessness of the 1980s and 1990s differs considerably from that of the 1950s and 1960s, but perhaps not so much from the homeless experiences of families in local communities during hard times in the 19th century or during the Great Depression of the 1930s.

Further Definitional Considerations

The foregoing discussion notes historical circumstances that have been considered part of the phenomenon of homelessness at different times. Definitions of a phenomenon such as homelessness usually embody one or more social purposes. They are not neutral, but, rather, are constructed to affect public concern and action. Thus they are "programmatic." They may be trying to make a phenomenon visible, to get it defined as a "problem," and thus make it worthy of intervention and amelioration. They may be trying to do the opposite. They may be trying to influence the scope of action expected or demanded. Or they may be trying to influence the value placed on one way of living compared to others.

Definitions are necessary, though, from several perspectives. From the perspective of immediate action, definitions identify who is eligible to receive whatever assistance is available specifically for homeless people. From a research perspective, definitions identify who should be counted and described. And from a policy perspective, definitions identify who should be planned for and what policies will be most relevant to the type of assistance needed.

However, definitions of a phenomenon such as homelessness are difficult, and frequently require balancing two horns of a dilemma. If the definitions are too inclusive, they become useless; the phenomenon becomes too diffuse, ultimately covering too many people. With homelessness, this tendency is manifested by definitions that threaten to include the entire population in poverty, or everyone who is poorly housed. But if the definitions are too specific, they focus too exclusively on the homelessness of the moment. They can lead to policies and practices that are ameliorative but not preventive, that fail to address the larger question of desperate poverty and the pool of people at high risk for periodic bouts of literal homelessness.

At present, United States government policy and access to particular kinds of government-supported assistance are driven by a clear but narrow definition of homelessness, based on a person's sleeping arrangements. "Literal" homelessness is defined on a day-by-day basis, and involves sleeping either in a facility serving homeless people, in accommodations paid for by a voucher from a program serving homeless people, or in places not meant for human habitation. This official definition narrows homelessness to a fairly small proportion of the precariously housed or unhoused population. About the only way to shrink the group further would be to exclude anyone in a shelter or transitional housing program, or using an emergency voucher, during the night of such use. The official definition is meant to help providers determine whom to serve, and to help planners calculate levels of service to provide.

While conveniently precise from some perspectives (it is relatively easy to ascertain where a person slept on the previous night, and therefore easy to determine whom to help), the official definition is overly precise and therefore misleading from other perspectives. For example, if people can afford to pay for a motel room three nights a week, but sleep in the park the other four, and this goes on week after week because they cannot afford a room, it seems relatively meaningless to say they are homeless only on the nights they sleep in the park. Truly helping them would mean helping them achieve stable housing. Similarly, if someone has no stable place to stay, but obtains housing from a relative for two or three days until space in a homeless shelter opens up, it seems relatively meaningless to say the person is housed (because sleeping in conventional housing) and therefore not eligible for the homeless service.[2] The ultimate failure of the official definition is that it does not help us address the larger issues of how to end homelessness for the long term. It only helps decide who should receive services at any particular time.

Structural Factors Affecting Levels of Homelessness

The "homeless population" will be larger or smaller depending on one's definition of homelessness, regardless of anything real happening in society to increase people's risk of being without *place*, without *family*, or without *housing*. But if we want to address the larger issue of ending homelessness, rather than just ameliorating the conditions of some homeless people for brief periods, then we need to try to understand why we have homelessness *now*, and why we have it *here*. Only then can we ask *who* will become homeless out of all the people vulnerable to the condition. Further, the answers should point toward solutions.

Early in the 1980s, two opposing explanations of homelessness quickly gained rhetorical prominence. As many have described before (e.g., Burt 1992; Koegel and Burnam 1992), one explanation emphasized structural factors, the other individual factors, as "the cause" of homelessness. The structural argument focused on the impact of changing housing markets for low-income families and singles, changing employment opportunities for people with a high school education or less, and changing institutional supports for persons with severe mental illness (epitomized by drastic reductions in the use of long-term mental hospitalization). The effects of persistent poverty and racial inequalities were also offered as structural explanations for homelessness in the 1980s. In general, liberal to radical activists and analysts were most likely to focus on structural factors.

The individual argument focused on personal problems and inadequacies, since homeless populations routinely report many more such problems than the general public. Individual factors include adult and childhood victimization, mental illness, alcohol and/or drug abuse, low levels of education, poor or no work history, and too-early childbearing. In general, conservative activists and analysts were most likely to focus on personal factors. But often joining them were clinicians and practitioners, who recognized the seriousness of the problems and wanted to help people deal with them.

Over the years, most people have come to recognize that both structural and individual factors play a role in producing homelessness. The structural factors set the stage, without which fewer people would be homeless. They help to answer the question, "Why more homelessness *now*?" (Koegel and Burnam 1992). Then the individual factors help to identify "*Who*?"—which particular people subject to the worst combinations of structural factors are most likely to lose their housing. However, as the structural conditions worsen, even people without personal vulnerabilities other than poverty may experience crises that precipitate a homeless episode.

The full effect of both structural and individual factors must be understood in the context still another set. That is the degree to which a society provides a safety net, in the form of social insurance (e.g., Social Security), social assistance (e.g., housing, food, child care, and other subsidies), and services (e.g., mental health services), intended to cushion the more-severe consequences of structural and individual factors. The better the safety net, the less effect either structural or individual factors will have on producing homelessness.

In Burt's work (1992) identifying causes of the growth of homelessness in the 1980s, she began with a model that incorporated structural and individual factors, along with safety net programs (figure 1.1), showing how all three may influence the ability to afford housing and, hence, the probability of homelessness. Housing affordability was, and still is, assumed to be the immediate cause of homelessness. If the cost of housing is too high for the incomes of households that need housing, then homelessness is likely to result for at least some of those households. Housing affordability is represented in the middle of figure 1.1 by the (potentially unequal) relationship between household resources and housing costs.

Factors affecting whether a household will have sufficient income include job opportunities (a structural factor); personal factors, both

Figure 1.1 *Factors Influencing Homelessness*

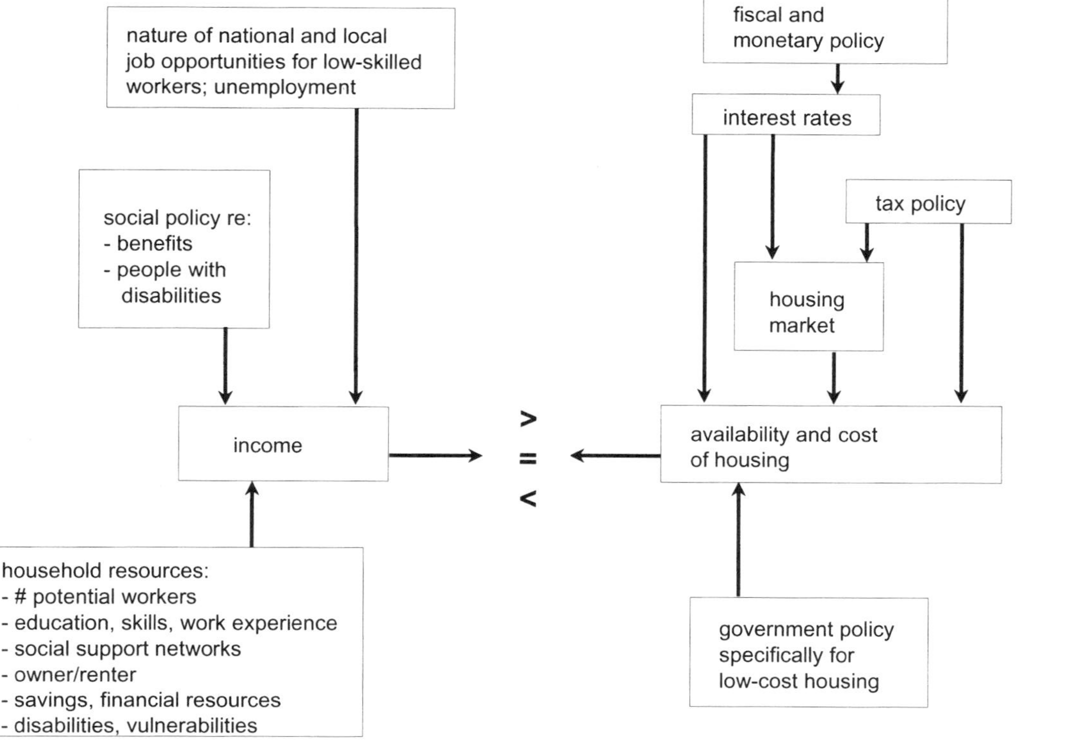

Source: A slightly different version of this figure was first published in Burt, M.R. 1992. *Over the Edge: The Growth of Homelessness in the 1980s.* New York and Washington D.C.: Russell Sage Foundation and the Urban Institute. Reprinted with permission.

individual and household, which appear in the box at the lower left of the figure; and government policy with respect to cash and non-cash benefit programs that are part of the safety net. Factors shown affecting the availability and cost of housing include fiscal and monetary policy, tax policy, interest rates, and government policy specifically affecting low-cost housing, including housing subsidies. The box labeled "housing market" incorporates policy influences plus the effects of personal incomes on the cost of housing. If the personal incomes of many people are stimulated by a booming economy, the housing market will be high, making it more difficult for people with lower incomes to afford housing.

In addition to addressing Koegel and Burnam's (1992) question, "Why more homelessness *now*?" structural factors can also address the question, "Why more homelessness *here* (as opposed to *there*)?" These, in turn, may shed some light on why we still have high levels of homelessness after a decade of significant economic expansion and a rising standard of living for most Americans. Burt's 1992 analysis of differences in levels of homelessness among U.S. cities with 100,000 or more people showed homelessness in cities with very depressed economies. But cities with extremely rapid population growth due to expanding economic opportunities also showed significant homelessness. Only in the latter cities was cost of living a factor in predicting homeless levels.

What appears to have happened in the latter cities, and in many parts of the United States in recent years, is that economically successful people put more pressure on housing markets, which drives up prices and increases housing's scarcity relative to households that want it. The effects of such pressures are felt particularly at the low end of the market. Many analyses (e.g., Dolbeare 1999) show dramatic reductions in the number of housing units low-income households can afford, if they spend no more than one-third of their income for housing. All other things being equal, the fewer such units there are in comparison to households with incomes at or below the level used in these analyses, the more likely some of the households are to become homeless. Under these circumstances, homelessness will happen even to people whose only personal vulnerability is poverty. Thus, paradoxically, the success of the many plays a role in creating conditions conducive to homelessness for the (relatively) few who have been left behind by boom times.

In 1996, 36.5 million people lived in poverty in the United States—13.7 percent of the population. Only 2 percent needed to be homeless at any given time to produce the level of homelessness we report in chapter 2. It is not hard to imagine that rising housing costs coupled with stable wage levels for low-skilled workers could, in turn, combine with the periodic crises that beset poor households to push this many people into homelessness at any given time. To illustrate, in 1996–1997, according to the National Survey of America's Families, 28 percent of families with children whose incomes were below 200 percent of the federal poverty level had been unable to pay their mortgage, rent, or utility bills at least once during the previous 12 months. This was true also for 17 percent of childless adults (Wigton and D'Orio 1999). This level of difficulty in affording housing, even among people with incomes up to twice the federal poverty level, bespeaks a large pool of people, including many households with children, who have some vulnerability to becoming homeless.

The Government Response to Homelessness in the United States

American government at all levels was active in the homeless arena during the 1980s and 1990s. In the mid-1980s, state and local governments greatly increased their commitments to homeless services. The Department of Housing and Urban Development's (HUD's) 1988 study, collecting data in the first quarter of 1988, before anything but a trickle of federal money was actually in use, found that the total dollars committed to shelter services in the United States had climbed to $1.6 billion, from $300 million in 1984. HUD also found that the share of this much larger figure coming from state and local governments had increased to 65 percent in 1988, from 37 percent in 1984 (HUD 1989).

In 1987, homelessness had been visible long enough, was extensive enough, and had been documented often enough through research, that Congress inaugurated a major federal effort to address it through the Stewart B. McKinney Homeless Assistance Act. Most McKinney Act programs required their recipients to match federal dollars with a certain percentage of other funds. For states and localities that had long been spending their own tax dollars to serve homeless people, the match was easy to meet and did not require a major change of policy. But for states and localities that had never committed any of their own money toward programs for the homeless, the McKinney matching requirement stimulated creation of new statewide homeless task forces, coordinating committees, and funding programs. Thus the McKinney Act generated significantly more money for homeless services from state and local governments than had previously been available.

Much of the McKinney Act money went, in the early years, toward fixing, renovating, or building structures that could serve as shelters. As a consequence, the number of shelter beds in the United States increased by about half in the Act's first three years (Burt 1992). Further, the types of shelter being built changed. McKinney funds made possible—for the first time—transitional shelters, primarily for families and the mentally ill, and specialized permanent housing with supportive services, for homeless people whose disabilities and handicaps made it unlikely they could ever house themselves. The act supported demonstration projects that established the feasibility of bringing mentally ill, alcoholic, or drug-abusing homeless people in off the streets and creating living environments that could keep them in stable housing.

As the years have passed, the uses of McKinney Act money have shifted. After building new shelters and expanding the national capacity to shelter homeless people, the need for more shelter beds has waned. However, the needs still are pressing to staff shelters and offer rehabilitation services to homeless people through shelters and other mechanisms. HUD, which generally uses its money to build structures rather than run them, has found its homeless dollars going more and more for services to run programs than for "bricks and mortar."

New Policy Orientations

For their first few years, during the Reagan administration, McKinney Act programs were funded significantly below their authorized levels. The Bush administration supported some additional funding, but it took the installation of a new Democratic administration in 1993 for homeless policy in Washington to take a new turn.

The first actions of the Clinton administration were to increase funding for McKinney Act programs. In 1995, funding hit more than $1 billion. A second major policy shift was initiated by the Department of Housing and Urban Development. HUD officials recognized that homeless services had grown and developed haphazardly, without providing assurance to homeless people in any community that needed services of a particular type would be available. The new administration promoted the related ideas of a "continuum of care" and "coordinated services." That is, the administration wanted communities to make care available at each level or stage on a continuum that might be needed by homeless people. This included intake and assessment, emergency shelter, transitional shelter, and specialized services such as alcohol and drug treatment. Further, the administration wanted homeless clients to be able to access the various services through a coordinated system—with all providers in a community knowing about available services and how to help their clients receive them.

As a result, new applications for funding under the various homeless programs run by HUD had to show how the new services fit into a continuum of care and how they would be coordinated with other services. These requirements pushed local communities and service providers to talk to each other and learn more about available community resources. Interaction and increased cooperation between local governments and community service providers in their communities was one result—to the benefit of both local service networks and their homeless clients. Chapter 10 explores the nature of these networks.

Another policy change in the early 1990s was increased attention to rural homelessness. In 1995, the Rural Economic and Community Development (RECD) administration of the Department of Agriculture sponsored four regional conferences on rural homelessness (Burt 1995). The conferences pursued several objectives. They were designed to identify the nature and needs of the rural homeless, and how they might differ from the urban homeless; to learn how available federal programs were being used, and barriers to their use; and to explore how RECD programs and initiatives, in particular, could be structured to fill gaps in the network of available services. In addition, the National Survey of Homeless Assistance Providers and Clients (NSHAPC) covered rural as well as urban areas, giving, for the first time, a systematic view of rural homelessness in relation to urban homelessness. This is described in chapter 7.

The 1990s also saw significant advances in knowledge about what does and does not work in helping people while they are homeless, and then to leave homelessness. In 1999, the Departments of Health and Human Services and Housing and Urban Development sponsored a symposium to summarize and synthesize a decade of learning from program evaluations (Fosburg and Dennis 1999). The chapters in the summary volume focus on a wide variety of program types, from street outreach, to case management, to permanent housing plus supportive services. They make clear there are some things we know how to do and do well, but other needs where we are only just beginning to think about what might work. The greatest successes have come in programs helping people with the longest histories of homelessness and the highest levels of disability. The answer, succinctly put, is "housing" (Shinn and Baumohl 1999). Subsidize their housing, and they become—and stay—housed. The greatest gaps lie in the areas of short-term homelessness and family homelessness, which overlap considerably but are not identical. These gaps may exist because only recently have we come to recognize that a very large number of people experience short-term homelessness in the course of a year or several years. Programs, and evaluation of them, are just beginning to grapple with the implications of these findings.

New Evidence for an Old Phenomenon

A final thrust of policy in the 1990s emerged because of new evidence that the number of people who experience homelessness during the course of a year or longer could be as much as six times the number homeless at any given time (Burt 1994; Culhane et al. 1994; Link et al. 1994, 1995). Further, these studies also documented that the proportion of the U.S. population experiencing homelessness in the past five years could be as high as 3 percent (7 to 8 million people—Link et al. 1995, 1994), and that even the proportion experiencing homelessness in the past year approaches 1 percent of all Americans and a higher proportion of poor Americans. We make our own estimates of annual homelessness in chapter 2, where we come quite close to those just described.

All this evidence has pushed policymakers to begin distinguishing between policies and services appropriate for alleviating short homeless episodes and those appropriate for people whose homelessness is long-term, and to recognize that the same set of policies and services might not be needed, or appropriate, for all homeless people. Some states and localities, for instance, have initiated "diversion" programs that help people experiencing short-term homelessness. These programs screen applicants for shelter services and identify those who could be helped to maintain or regain their housing with a little cash, negotiations with a landlord, or other immediate assistance.

Homeless-Specific versus Generic Services—The Weakness of the U.S. Safety Net

The vast majority of programs for homeless people discussed above, which have seen such growth in the last decade, are homeless-specific. That is, they are designed for homeless people, delivered to homeless people, and operated by programs and agencies focused on serving homeless people. Throughout the late 1980s and early and mid-1990s, services for homeless people were the only programming for poor people into which the federal government was putting, as opposed to cutting, money. Therefore, homeless-specific programs became something of a "growth industry." Homeless service providers argued that since they knew and worked with homeless people, they could help homeless people better than generic service providers. As a consequence, we now have health care, job training, GED preparation, substance abuse treatment, and even apartment complexes (transitional housing facilities) specifically for homeless people. We also have residential facilities for formerly homeless people with disabilities.

This structure has its advantages and disadvantages. There can be little question that generic services—those that serve the general population rather than focusing on a particular user group—have not been either interested in serving homeless people or easy for them to use. These generic services include various cash assistance programs (Aid to Families with Dependent Children, General Assistance, Social Security Income, Social Security Disability Insurance), in-kind benefit programs (Food Stamps; Medicaid and state medical assistance; federal, state, and local housing subsidies), and problem-focused services (mental health, alcohol, and drug treatment services). Most of their disinterest can be attributed to lack of resources to assist even their "usual" clientele. Many of these programs faced cuts in funding and/or restrictions on eligibility during the period we are considering, rendering them less able to provide a previous level of service. Applying for these programs can be prohibitively difficult for people who cannot readily acquire or maintain needed documentation, and agencies do not go out of their way to make the process any easier. Another part of the problem is that homeless people often are perceived as "hard to serve," and generic agencies do not take the trouble unless required to do so. Some generic programs actually changed rules in ways that reduced the eligibility of many homeless people. This included many state general assistance programs and

Supplemental Security Income at the federal level. Thus homeless people themselves, and people vulnerable to homelessness, have actually lost important sources of income, especially in the late 1990s.

On the other hand, homeless-specific services help people who are homeless now. The federal definition of homelessness and eligibility for assistance with federal homeless dollars make this specialization necessary. Only in rare instances have even the most far-reaching local "homeless plans" extended themselves to reduce homelessness, prevent homelessness, or change the conditions that push people into homelessness. Thus homeless programs usually remain Band-Aids, even though they make the homeless condition less onerous for a lot of people. When they are able to help people leave homelessness, it is often because they have succeeded in making up for failures of many systems in the past, including school systems, child welfare systems, juvenile and adult justice systems, mental health systems, and substance abuse treatment systems. Further, even though they absorb a good deal of money in the context of *homelessness*, their funding is small compared to the resources potentially available to generic services. And they have not stanched the flow of people *into* homelessness.

The obvious policy challenge still is, after a decade and a half, "What will we need to do to end homelessness?" The answer is at one level obvious—make housing affordable. But how do we get there, if we do? We return to this question in the concluding chapter, where we explore the pushes and pulls on the American political scene that will shape any approaches to solving homelessness.

Sources of Data for This Book

To help generate useful approaches to thinking about homelessness in the United States for the future, this book describes homeless people and homeless service systems across America toward the end of the 1990s. It is based on data from the National Survey of Homeless Assistance Providers and Clients (NSHAPC), conducted in 1996.[3] This survey builds upon and extends the methodology first employed in the Urban Institute's 1987 study, reported in *America's Homeless*. It offers the first opportunity in almost a decade to look at homelessness from a national perspective that is based on information collected directly from homeless assistance programs and the homeless—and other—people who use them.

NSHAPC is unique in its scope and coverage.[4] First, it covered the entire United States, offering a systematic view of suburban and rural homelessness as well as the more familiar homelessness found in central cities.[5] Second, it offers the only national data for the 1990s on which to base estimates of the size of the homeless population and changes since 1987. It also provides the opportunity to create national estimates of homelessness at a single point in time and over the course of a year. Third, it offers comparisons among currently homeless, formerly homeless, and never-homeless people who use homeless assistance programs other than shelters, such as soup kitchens or drop-in centers. Fourth, NSHAPC's rich information about client histories and characteristics lets us examine patterns of homelessness, childhood and adult antecedents of homeless episodes, and changes in the adult homeless population between 1987 and 1996.

Finally, NSHAPC offers a new and comprehensive look at homeless assistance programs nationally and in the 76 metropolitan and rural areas that comprise the study's sampling locations. This information lets us see the effects of public policy that encouraged organizing homeless service systems into continuums of care. Looking at this new evidence, and integrating it with other major advances in knowledge about homelessness gained in the 1990s, this book concludes with a discussion of implications for how we might want to think about and address homelessness in the future.

Sixteen types of homeless assistance programs were included (full definitions appear in the appendix):

- Emergency shelters
- Transitional housing programs
- Permanent housing programs
- Programs distributing vouchers to obtain emergency accommodation
- Programs accepting vouchers in exchange for giving emergency accommodation
- Food pantries
- Soup kitchens
- Mobile food programs
- Physical health care programs

- Mental health programs
- Alcohol/drug programs
- HIV/AIDS programs
- Outreach programs
- Drop-in centers
- Migrant labor camps used to provide emergency shelter for homeless people
- Other programs

Defining Homeless Status

Since homelessness is the core concept in the analyses in all subsequent chapters, it is important for the reader to understand how it was defined. Because NSHAPC sampled all clients—whether homeless or not—of the homeless assistance programs just described, it was necessary to classify the clients as currently, formerly, or never homeless, based on the answers they gave to survey questions. The following alerts the reader to the criteria used in differentiating homeless people from other program clients.

The definitions used closely follow the official federal definition of literal homelessness, except that they are based on experiences during a week rather than on a single day (chapter 2 explains the reason for this approach).

Currently Homeless. The following specific conditions were used to classify clients as *currently homeless:*

- The client stayed in any of the following places on the day of the survey or during the seven-day period prior to being interviewed for NSHAPC:
  1. An emergency or transitional shelter, or
  2. A hotel or motel paid for by a shelter voucher, or
  3. An abandoned building, a place of business, a car or other vehicle, or anywhere outside.
- Or:
  4. Reported that the last time they had "a place of [their] own for 30 days or more in the same place" was more than seven days ago, or
  5. Said their last period of homelessness ended within the last seven days, or

6. Were identified for inclusion in the NSHAPC client survey at an emergency shelter or transitional housing program, or
7. Reported getting food from "the shelter where you live" within the last seven days, or
8. On the day of the interview, said they stayed in their own or someone else's place but that they "could not sleep there for the next month without being asked to leave."

Use of the first criterion (shelter use) classifies 34.9 percent of the sample as currently homeless. Criteria two (voucher use) and three (places not meant for habitation) add 1.7 percent and 9.8 percent, respectively, for a total of 46.4 percent. The five remaining criteria together add another 7.1 percent, for a final total of 53.5 percent of the sample classified as currently homeless. All but the final criterion meet the McKinney Act definition of homelessness; the last criterion adds only 0.3 percentage points to the final proportion classified as currently homeless, and was included because the survey itself treats clients in this situation as homeless.

Formerly Homeless. Many clients who were not literally homeless reported having been homeless at some earlier time in their lives (22 percent of the sample). The circumstances used to classify clients as formerly homeless also meet the McKinney Act definition of homelessness. Clients were classified as *formerly homeless* if they:

- Did not meet any of the conditions qualifying them as currently homeless but at some point in their lives had stayed in any of the following:
  1. An emergency or transitional shelter, or
  2. A welfare/voucher hotel, or
  3. An abandoned building, a place of business, a car/other vehicle, or anywhere outside, or
  4. A permanent housing program for the formerly homeless, or
- Said they had previously had a period when they were without regular housing.

Never Homeless. The remaining 24 percent of NSHAPC clients had never been homeless at the time of the survey, according to the criteria used here, and also said they had never been homeless. They are referred to throughout this book as *never homeless*.

Weighting

All data reported in this book have been weighted to be nationally representative.[6] Without weighting, respondents to a survey such as NSHAPC represent only themselves. Weighting makes their responses representative of all people using homeless assistance programs in the United States in the fall of 1996.

All data describing client characteristics have been weighted to be nationally representative of *clients of homeless assistance programs during an average WEEK from October 18 through November 14, 1996;* that is, the week before the client was interviewed. The client weights were constructed to ensure that a person is not double-counted even if she or he used several homeless assistance programs during the course of the seven-day period. In addition, the client weight itself is used as the basis of estimates of population size, found in chapter 2.

Information describing programs and service locations is weighted to be nationally representative of *homeless assistance programs and service locations on an average day in February 1996.* In addition, the program and service location weights themselves have been used as the basis for estimating the total number of service locations, programs, and service contacts in the nation, as discussed in chapters 9 and 10.

The Plan of This Book

The remaining chapters explore issues pertaining to people who are homeless, and findings pertaining to homeless assistance programs and service systems in the United States. Chapters 2 through 8, analyzing the NSHAPC client data, include some that are purely descriptive and some that use statistical techniques to address complex questions such as population size or patterns of homelessness. Chapters 9 and 10 focus on the information collected through NSHAPC on homeless assistance programs and services. Specifically:

- Chapter 2 addresses the question, "How many homeless people are there?" presenting a variety of estimates that are useful for different policy purposes.
- Chapter 3 divides the homeless sample into subgroups based on family status (with children, alone, and with other adults) and sex,

and describes each subgroup in terms of demographic, economic, health, childhood, and other characteristics.

- Chapter 4 divides the homeless sample into subgroups based on history of alcohol, drug, and mental health problems, and describes each subgroup in terms of demographic, economic, health, childhood, and other characteristics.
- Chapter 5 examines the situation of children of homeless clients, whether or not they live with the client. It also looks at the characteristics of the youngest homeless adults (those younger than 20, and those age 20 to 24), and examines the role of childhood abuse, neglect, and out-of-home placement in their homeless careers.
- Chapter 6 examines homeless episodes, or spells, in several ways. It first looks at subgroups among the homeless, based on their pattern of homelessness, in two ways. It uses a simple cross-classification by length of current spell and number of homeless spells, and also uses cluster analysis to identify patterns. Three patterns of homelessness are identified by both methods: episodic (many spells, many of them relatively short), chronic (very long current spell, with relatively few other spells), and crisis/first-time homelessness. It then examines the meaning of "a spell," looking at continuity or breaks in clients' current homeless episode, and describing the places that clients report staying during a homeless episode that would not, in themselves, be classified as a literally homeless situation.
- Chapter 7 divides the entire NSHAPC sample into currently, formerly, and never homeless clients, and further divides these subgroups into those found in central cities, suburban/urban fringe areas, and rural areas. It then describes the subgroups in terms of many of the same characteristics as presented in chapters 3 and 4.
- Chapter 8 uses the entire NSHAPC sample, again divided into currently, formerly, and never homeless clients. It uses logistical regression analysis to estimate factors associated with homelessness by comparing those who have ever been homeless (currently and formerly homeless clients) to those who have never had a homeless episode. Then, within the ever-homeless group, it uses logistical regression analysis to identify factors that differentiate clients who are currently homeless from those who are not now homeless but have had at least one homeless episode in their past.

- Chapter 9 provides estimates of the number and types of homeless assistance programs in the United States in 1996, and compares these estimates to those from the late 1980s to identify the amount and type of change in homeless services during the 1990s. It also describes homeless assistance programs in terms of their size, geographic location, and populations served.
- Chapter 10 looks at the issue of *systems*. It explores the way in which homeless assistance programs are configured, whether standing alone or clustered together with other programs of different types. It also looks at the service offerings *by sampling area*, assessing the degree to which the policy goal of a continuum of care has been realized in communities of different sizes and types.
- Chapter 11 summarizes major findings, and draws out their implications for programs and policies in the coming decade. In doing so, it also examines American norms and values for personal and collective responsibility for individuals' well-being.

NOTES

1. The first wording was used in the 1987 Urban Institute study (Burt and Cohen 1989); the second wording was used on the National Survey of Homeless Assistance Providers and Clients (Burt et al. 1999).
2. These examples may seem extreme, but they have happened not infrequently in the course of applying the federal definition of homelessness.
3. Twelve federal agencies sponsored NSHAPC: the U.S. Departments of Housing and Urban Development, Health and Human Services, Veterans Affairs, Agriculture, Commerce, Education, Energy, Justice, Labor, and Transportation, the Social Security Administration, and the Federal Emergency Management Administration. The Bureau of the Census carried out the sample design and all aspects of the data collection. Martha Burt of the Urban Institute, along with representatives of the sponsoring agencies, was involved from the study's earliest stages in study design and development of the client survey instrument. She also directed the Urban Institute's work to analyze the NSHAPC data and write up the results for the sponsoring agencies, along with other authors of this book.
4. For a more complete description of the NSHAPC methodology, see the appendix.
5. The study used 76 primary sampling areas, including the 28 largest metropolitan statistical areas (MSAs) in the United States; 24 small and medium-sized MSAs, selected at random to be representative of geographical region (northeast, south, midwest, west) and size; and 24 rural areas (groups of counties), selected at random from a sampling frame defined as the catchment areas of Community Action Agencies, and representative of geographical regions. In New England the actual areas sampled were parts of counties.
6. A full explanation of weighting procedures may be found in Burt et al., 1999, *Homelessness—Programs and the People They Serve: Technical Report, Appendix D.*

2

How Many Homeless People Are There?

The first question most people ask about homelessness is, "How many people are homeless?" In asking, they really are probing, "Is this problem big enough for me to worry about?" Once assured that it is, they then usually go on to ask, "Who are they?" This seemingly simple question may really mask a number of others. They can range from, "Are they people I am likely to care about?" to, "What special needs might they have for which we should offer services?"

This chapter addresses the issue of numbers. It provides a variety of estimates of the number of people who experience homelessness during periods of a day, a week, and a year. It does not, in the end, propose a single "right" number. Indeed, in calculating a variety of numbers, the chapter raises important questions about whether we will ever *really* know precisely how many people are homeless. In addition, the search for precise numbers may divert us from recognizing the most important thing about homelessness in the 1990s: It has become far too common an experience in the lives of poor people, including many poor children.

Further, in searching for numbers, we are inclined to forget the great influence that definitions of homelessness have on any answer. For example, if staying in an emergency shelter or transitional housing program is one of the ways that a person's situation can be accepted as literal homelessness (which it is), and if the availability of such programs has grown (as it has), then it stands to reason that the population we are willing to call literally homeless, and are able to count with a service-based study methodology, should have grown along with service availability. In this sense we have "made" more people homeless by providing a service that allows desperately poor people to stay in places that will get them counted as homeless.

Estimates of the number of people homeless are always political footballs. Those who do not want to help homeless people will use a low number to suggest that the problem is not big enough to worry about, or a high number contingent in part on service availability to suggest that perhaps the amount of service should be decreased. Those who want to help homeless people will discount a low number, attacking the methodology used to produce it, and use a high number to argue for more services. Virtually everyone will concentrate on a point-in-time number and ignore the much larger proportion of the poor population that will probably experience some homelessness in the course of a year.

This chapter, we believe, will provide compelling evidence for the pervasiveness of homelessness, evidence bolstered by similar results from very different methodologies. Evidence of pervasiveness should push us toward rethinking our approach to homelessness, and to homeless assistance programs, as we discuss in the conclusion to this chapter and in chapter 11. But first, we must focus on the technicalities of numerical estimates.

Types of Numerical Estimates

In the past, most counts of homeless populations or studies that tried to estimate the size of the homeless population did so for a single night or single 24-hour period (Burt 1991; Burt and Taeuber 1991). They ranged in technique from basic one-night "blitz" counts to sophisticated block probability sampling approaches (Bray, Dennis, and Lambert 1993; Rossi, Fisher, and Willis 1986; Vernez et al. 1988). They also varied in where they went to find homeless people. Some focused entirely on shelters; others added more or less complete and thorough searches of street locations (see also Burt 1996 for a full discussion of counting methods and their relative advantages and disadvantages).

As a variation on calculating a number for a 24-hour period, the 1987 Urban Institute study (Burt and Cohen 1989) collected data over the course of a month, and created estimates of homeless population size for both one-day and one-week periods. The Urban Institute study contained several methodological innovations that expanded the opportunities to cover more of the homeless population and made a one-week estimate possible. First, it did *not* go to streets and other non-shelter locations, but *did* go to soup kitchens and other meal distribution programs, as well as to shelters. Everyone needs to eat, of course, whether or not they need to be inside to sleep. Thus, including meal programs in the sampling design let the study find and interview a significant number of homeless individuals who did not use shelters. Second, the interview asked where people slept (including in shelters or in places not meant for habitation) and where they got food (including meal programs), recording this information for each of the seven days before the interview. This gave analysts information to do two very important things—*eliminate duplication* among people who used both meal programs and shelters, and calculate a *per week* estimate of homelessness.[1]

Burt and Cohen (1989) argued (we still think conclusively) that it is very difficult to find most homeless people if you only give yourselves one day to do it. Further, the fewer homeless assistance services there are in a community, the longer it will probably take to get a good representation of homeless people based on their use of services. Not surprisingly, the one-week estimate derived by Burt and Cohen was significantly higher (by 75 percent) than their one-day estimate. The one-week estimate was 194,000 homeless adults and their 35,000 homeless children (229,000 total) who used soup kitchens and/or shelters in U.S. cities with populations of 100,000 or more during an average seven-day period in March 1987. This, in turn, compared to 110,000 homeless adults and their 26,000 homeless children (136,000 total) during an average one-day period in the same month. Burt and Cohen maintained that the one-week figure was a much truer estimate of how many were homeless *on a given day* than the one-day figure, because many people who use services only one or two days a week are still homeless the other days. To insist, as some purists have (Garfinkel and Piliavin 1994; Jencks 1994), that certain homeless people not be considered part of a one-day homeless count just because researchers failed to find them on the day they looked does not make any practical sense.

Other studies that have allowed more time for identifying and interviewing homeless people, coupled with a method for eliminating duplication, include statewide studies in Kentucky (Kentucky Housing Corporation 1993) and Hawaii (SMS Research 1990). The Hawaii studies covered a week. The 1993 Kentucky study covered two months, and a repeat, to be conducted in 2001, will do the same. A longer time period is important in studies that are trying to cover areas with few or no homeless assistance programs, and perhaps few other programs as well. This was true for rural Kentucky, and prompted the design created to study the state. Note, however, that the goal was still to learn the number of people homeless *on a given day*, for which the first day of the study was selected. These studies found homeless people on their first day, and additional homeless people on each subsequent day of their search. The 1993 Kentucky study found, for example, that most of the people who ultimately were identified as having been homeless on the first day of the study were actually contacted and interviewed later in the study period.

A different issue, but also an important one, is the number of people who experience homelessness over an extended period, such as a year. In recent years, two different approaches have been used for obtaining these numbers. One is the telephone survey of households conducted by Link and colleagues (1994, 1995). Their data reveal that 6.5 percent of American adults have had a lifetime experience of literal homelessness, with about 3 percent experiencing literal homelessness in the past five years. The second is the shelter tracking database, a system usually used to provide a continuous, unduplicated record of *every* use of *any* shelter throughout a whole community.

Culhane and his colleagues, using records from such databases for New York City and Philadelphia, found that the average number of days a person stayed in the shelter system during a year was 120 in New York and 60 in Philadelphia. Since the level of shelter use remained fairly constant throughout the year in both cities, these figures implied that in New York, three times as many people used the shelters in a year's time as were present at any given time. In Philadelphia, the corresponding figure was six times as many people. Using three years of data in Philadelphia, they documented that almost 3 percent (2.8 percent) of the city's population had been in a shelter in the years 1990 through 1992. In New York City, more than 3 percent (3.3 percent) of that city's population had been in shelters at least once over the five years 1988 through 1992. These findings provide strong corroboration for Link's findings based on household telephone surveys. In both cities, about 1 percent of the population had used a shelter during a single year.[2] Burt (1994) assembled and summarized similar or more startling figures for other jurisdictions, both large and small. These figures indicated that this level of homelessness over the course of a year was not confined just to the nation's largest cities.

These reports have revolutionized the concept of a "homeless count" for the last decade of the 20th century. They have made clear yet again that many more people experience homelessness during the course of a year than are reflected in any one-day or even one-week count, however accurate. They have further highlighted the issue of *flow* into and out of the condition of homelessness, and the extreme dynamism of the "population." That is, the idea of a relatively static "homeless population" implies that more or less the same people comprise it over time. However, data from shelter tracking systems bring us back to the reality, noted in homeless literature going back to the 1890s and even earlier (Anderson 1923, 1940; Hoch and Slayton 1989; Hopper and Baumohl 1996; Rossi 1989). The reality is that people move into and out of homelessness. Those who do so relatively quickly and do not return greatly outnumber those who stay homeless for a very long time or who experience repeated episodes of homelessness over many years.

The 1996 NSHAPC survey was, in one sense, an old-fashioned, cross-sectional, single-point-in-time study, albeit one that incorporated many different types of homeless assistance programs in its sampling frames. However, the survey did everything possible to collect information that could be used to approximate longer time periods. It asked people to report their history of living or staying in places that would get them classified as homeless. Those included emergency or transitional homeless shelters, on the streets, in cars or vans, in abandoned buildings, or in other places not meant for habitation. It also asked about the length and recentness of homeless experiences. The rest of this chapter uses different elements of the NSHAPC data to develop several estimates of how many people were homeless users of homeless assistance programs in the United States in 1996, including estimates focusing on periods of an average day, an average week, and a whole year.

The reader is warned at the outset that the estimates in this chapter vary widely, not just because the periods being covered change (e.g., from one week to one year), but even within periods of the same length at different times of year. At the end of the chapter, we will summarize and integrate the findings, after which we will discuss how these estimates may be used, and their implications in thinking about the problem of homelessness.

What Estimates Can the NSHAPC Data Produce?

NSHAPC was designed to collect information about the characteristics of homeless assistance programs and the people who use them. Understanding who turns to emergency assistance programs and the circumstances that lead them to do so should help us design more effective programs and service delivery strategies to end current, and prevent future, homelessness. As already noted, however, many people are first interested in learning about "the number of homeless people." Indeed, this phrase is often used as if there really were a single such number, and the meaning of "homeless" were clear. In reality, determining how many homeless people there are is quite complex. One should always ask several questions to clarify what any given number really represents (Burt 1991). These include when and where the data were collected, what time period the data cover, what or who was counted, and how the estimate was developed.

NSHAPC's sophisticated sample design and wealth of data allow it to support a variety of different estimates of the number of people who use homeless assistance programs and, of these, the number who are homeless. The implications of two related aspects of the NSHAPC design are important to understand before turning to actual estimates. As explained in chapter 1, every person interviewed for NSHAPC was identified through participation in a homeless assistance program. One issue, therefore, is the extent to which NSHAPC includes homeless "street people"—that is, people who do not use shelters. A second issue is NSHAPC's ability to include homeless people who live in communities that have few or no homeless assistance services.

NSHAPC differed from the common homeless study design of counting people in shelters and then conducting street searches to find non-sheltered homeless people. NSHAPC *did* go to shelters, but its approach to finding homeless people who do not use shelters relied on their contacts with non-shelter services. In communities with many non-shelter services, inclusion in NSHAPC of certain types of homeless assistance programs probably resulted in 85 to 90 percent of homeless people having a chance to be chosen for the study.[3] This is true because many non-shelter-using homeless people eat at soup kitchens, get their food from mobile food programs, use drop-in centers for homeless people, or are contacted by outreach programs that walk the local streets establishing relationships with more-elusive homeless people. All these types of programs were included in NSHAPC. Therefore, all the non-shelter-using homeless people who have any contact with any such program are represented in the 27 percent of NSHAPC's homeless subsample who said they did not use any shelter/housing programs on the day of, or in the week before, being interviewed.

There is no question that NSHAPC missed some homeless people, so any estimate made from NSHAPC data should be treated as a lower-bound estimate. That lower-bound estimate is still very good (probably as close to a full enumeration as we are ever likely to get) for communities with high levels of homeless assistance services. But what happens when a community has relatively few such services, or none at all? Basically, the less chance a community's homeless people have of using a service, the less accurately a service-based estimate will reflect the true number of homeless people in that community unless some adjustments are made.[4] This is an important caveat for rural areas, and for some parts of metropolitan areas that also have relatively few services. In fact, 2 of NSHAPC's 76 primary sampling areas, both rural, had *no* homeless assistance services, therefore NSHAPC *did not interview any homeless people in those areas.* But it would be unreasonable to maintain, based on NSHAPC, that those areas did not include a single homeless person. Because NSHAPC was a national study, having to use the same methods everywhere, it was unable to "do something different" to find homeless people in areas without homeless assistance services.

In addition to deriving estimates of the number of homeless and other people who use homeless assistance programs, NSHAPC also lets us examine the number of program contacts—meaning bed-nights of shelter, or meals, or contacts with an outreach worker—made by clients of homeless assistance programs. Finally, because the NSHAPC client survey, originally scheduled for February 1996, had to be postponed to autumn (following a late-1995 federal government shutdown), estimates can be calculated for each of two months in different seasons in 1996. Most estimates reported in this chapter refer to an average week during the four-week period, October 18 through November 14, 1996, when NSHAPC client interviews were actually conducted. But we have also calculated one-day estimates for October/November that are limited to information about an average day, and projected backward to produce both one-day and one-week estimates for February. Finally, we have used several approaches to calculate a one-year prevalence rate.

Units of Analysis

This chapter discusses three different units of analysis—*program contacts, clients/households,* and *people.* All NSHAPC estimates start from the base of the total number of *program contacts* made with all types of homeless assistance programs in the four-week period in fall 1996 when client data were collected. Many jurisdictions rely on homeless assistance programs to tell how many people they serve, after which the answers are compiled into an estimate of how many people are homeless in the jurisdiction. When the participating programs are all shelters and are asked to report for a single, pre-specified night (e.g., the first Monday in February), the probability of duplicate counting is small enough to justify simply adding all the numbers together. However, the NSHAPC client survey covered many types of homeless assistance programs (see chapter 9 and the appendix). When every homeless assistance program in a jurisdiction reports the number of people it served "on an average day," many individuals are probably being counted more than once. What the programs actually report are "program contacts," not distinct, individual people. If, for example, a homeless person goes to a soup kitchen for an evening meal and then walks across town to an emergency shelter for the night, the two service providers would each report having served one person. Totaling these reports would suggest that two people had been served, when in fact one person had simply received two services.

Clients/households and *people* are the other two units of analysis described in this chapter. All people in the NSHAPC sample, designated as *clients* hereafter, had to be either adults or under age 18 and *not with an adult.* Most clients in the sample were adults without accompanying children; they represent themselves as households of one person. Any other clients (adults) who might be with them (such as a spouse, partner, or aunt) had an equal chance of being selected into the sample, and thus are represented by all those who actually were selected. Therefore no adjustment to the client estimates is necessary to account for the people in households with more than one adult but no children.

Some clients, however, were with their own minor children, and these children *did not* have a chance to be selected into the NSHAPC sample. These clients/parents represent *family households.* As *household* representatives, they count as one household each, and are reflected as such in all estimates of *clients/households.* But some *people* in these family households, namely the minor children, *need to be added* to the estimates based on households to achieve an accurate sense of the number of *people* (adults and their accompanying children) using homeless assistance programs.

The reader is advised to carefully distinguish between estimates of *clients/households* and of *people* throughout this chapter, as the unit of analysis makes a big difference in the size of the estimates.

1996 NSHAPC Estimates

Program Contacts in a Month (October/November 1996)

The number of program contacts made through homeless assistance programs is a very important figure. It is discussed at length in chapters 9 and 10. It indicates the volume of services being delivered to people in need. These are the estimates most likely to correspond to service providers' perceptions of the size of the homeless population.[5] However, as a count of homeless people, they will be quite inaccurate. They do not take into account that people use more than one service and, even more important, they do not take into account that many people who use homeless assistance programs as defined by NSHAPC are not homeless. A very sophisticated study of homelessness in the Washington, D.C., metropolitan area in 1991 found, for example, that after eliminating duplication, the number of program contacts by homeless people on an average day was half again as high as the number of homeless people being served (about 15,000 program contacts versus about 10,000 people—Bray, Dennis, and Lambert 1993).

To derive the estimates of homelessness for this chapter, we started with program contacts by all clients using programs during the four-week target period in NSHAPC sampling areas. These estimates were supplied by the Census Bureau, based on information collected during sampling and data collection. We then eliminated duplication and identified the clients' homeless status. We present estimates mostly for those who were currently homeless, because this is the major population of interest. But we start with all clients and all program contacts.

The Census Bureau staff conducting the NSHAPC data collection estimated that a total of 10.9 million program contacts were made through homeless assistance programs during the target period (first column of table 2.1; all estimates have been rounded to the nearest

Table 2.1 *Program Contacts at Homeless Assistance Programs during a Four-Week Period in October/November 1996*

	Contacts Associated with All Clients	*Contacts Associated with Homeless Clients*
Program Contacts of All Types	10,932,000	7,996,000
Housing (bed-nights)	5,725,000	4,831,000
Food (meals)	3,912,000	2,268,000
Other (outreach contacts, etc.)	1,295,000	897,000

Source: Urban Institute analysis of 1996 NSHAPC client data.
Note: Estimates have a 95 percent confidence interval (margin of error) of ± 6 percent; they have been rounded to the nearest 1,000.

1,000 to avoid the impression of undue precision). Just over half these program contacts (5.7 million) occurred at housing programs (i.e., a night in a shelter, a night in a transitional housing program, a night in a permanent housing program for formerly homeless people, or a night in a hotel/motel paid for by a voucher). Another 36 percent (3.9 million) occurred at food programs (soup kitchen or mobile food van meals, or a bag of food from a rural food pantry). The remaining 12 percent (1.3 million) occurred at some other type of homeless assistance program, such as a contact with an outreach worker or a visit to a drop-in center.[6]

It is important to understand that not all clients of homeless assistance programs are homeless.[7] Some may have been homeless at some time in the past; others may rely on meal programs in an effort to save money and avert homelessness for the first time. Others may never experience homelessness, but still require assistance with food or other basic support services. Applying the definition of a currently homeless client (hereafter, *homeless client*) given in chapter 1, we found that homeless clients made 73 percent of all the program contacts during the target period (8.0 million—second column of table 2.1). Sixty percent of these occurred at housing programs, 28 percent at food programs, and the remaining 11 percent at other types of program.

Going from Program Contacts to Clients: Estimating the Number of Clients Using Homeless Assistance Programs During the Target Period

To get from program contacts to clients (households)—that is, to eliminate duplication—one needs to know how many programs each client

Table 2.2 *Number of Clients Using Homeless Assistance Programs during an Average Week in October/November 1996*

All Clients (Households)	*Homeless Clients (Households)*
646,000	346,000

Source: Urban Institute analysis of weighted 1996 NSHAPC client data.
Note: Estimates have a 95 percent confidence interval (margin of error) of ± 6 percent; they have been rounded to the nearest 1,000.

used on any given day or during a week's time. The NSHAPC client survey asked clients to report this information for the 11 types of homeless assistance programs where the study sampled clients.[8] Using information on all program contacts during the October/November 1996 target period, and clients' own reports of the number and types of services they used each day in the week preceding their NSHAPC interview, we are able to eliminate duplication, and estimate the number of *clients* and *people* who used homeless assistance programs during the target period.

The NSHAPC data reveal that, nationally, homeless assistance programs served 646,000 different clients during an average week in October/November 1996 (table 2.2), including currently, formerly, and never homeless clients. Of the total, 53.5 percent, or 346,000 clients, were homeless.

Children Living with Homeless Clients

As noted, NSHAPC only administered its client survey to adults over the age of 18 and *unaccompanied* youth under age 18. The estimates presented in table 2.2 are for the households represented by these adults or near-adults. However, almost half (48 percent) of all homeless clients had children under age 18, and almost one-third of these parents (15 percent of all homeless clients) had at least one of their children under age 18 *living with them in their homeless condition*. These households were considered to be homeless families.[9]

Clients in homeless families reported that 98,000 of their own minor children were living with them (table 2.3). Adding these children to the estimate of homeless clients brings the total estimated number of homeless *people* using homeless assistance programs (clients *plus* children) to 444,000 for an average week during the four-week target period in October/November 1996.

Table 2.3 *Children in Homeless Families Using Homeless Assistance Programs during an Average Week in October/November 1996*

Children in Homeless Families	*Total Number of Homeless People (Clients and Children)*
98,000	444,000

Source: Urban Institute analysis of weighted 1996 NSHAPC client data.

Note: Estimates have a 95 percent confidence interval (margin of error) of ± 6 percent; they have been rounded to the nearest 1,000.

This estimate of homeless people, combining homeless adults and their children who live with them, is considerably lower than the 500,000 to 600,000 estimate for the average number of homeless people (children and adults) that the Urban Institute developed from its 1987 study. Remember, however, that the NSHAPC estimate covers only users of homeless assistance programs, while the 1987 estimate was a projection meant to cover all homeless people, whether or not they used services. Such a large difference deserves further comment, of course. But we need to defer comment or interpretation until we also have presented estimates for February 1996 and looked at projections to all homeless people, as these are relevant to the discussion.

Day versus Week in October/November 1996

The NSHAPC survey asked clients detailed questions about their use of various homeless assistance programs during the week preceding their interview. We used this information, without differentiating on which day or days program use was reported, to develop the preceding estimates of the number of clients using such programs during an average week in the target period. One can also estimate the number of clients using homeless assistance programs on an *average day* during this period (although we think the weekly estimates give a more appropriate assessment of people homeless on an average day, since many will not use such services every day). Table 2.4 presents these results.

On an average day in the October/November 1996 target period, 291,000 clients are estimated to have used homeless assistance programs (45 percent of the corresponding weekly estimate). The number of *homeless* clients using programs on an average day was estimated at 203,000 (59 percent of the corresponding weekly estimate). When their

Table 2.4 *Comparing Daily and Weekly Estimates of Households and People Using Homeless Assistance Programs*

	October/November 1996	
	Users During an Average Week	*Users During an Average Day*
Clients (Households)	646,000	291,000
Homeless Clients (Households)	346,000	203,000
Homeless People (Clients plus Children)	444,000	267,000

Source: Urban Institute analysis of weighted 1996 NSHAPC client data.
Note: All estimates have a 95 percent confidence interval (margin of error) of ± 6 percent; they have been rounded to the nearest 1,000.

children are added, the figure increases to 267,000 (60 percent of the weekly estimate).

Note that the daily estimates are around three-fifths of the weekly estimates. This occurs because most clients use homeless assistance programs on several, but not all, days in a week. If every client used programs on only one day a week, then the daily estimate would be one-seventh the weekly estimate; and if every client used at least one program each day, then the two estimates would be equal. The reality lies in between. Some clients used programs infrequently (only once or twice a week), while others used them every day during the week preceding their interview.

Despite the great interest that usually surrounds the daily number, the weekly estimate is of much greater value in developing sound policies and effective services. It provides a more complete picture of the number of people in need of emergency assistance in what is still a relatively short period of time, one week. Further, it is most likely that the vast majority of homeless people using homeless assistance programs on Monday and Thursday are still homeless Tuesday and Wednesday, even though they do not use any homeless assistance programs those days. Undoubtedly, many reasons may exist for their intermittent use of these programs, but some might relate to an inadequate supply of services.

Subpopulations of Interest

Having developed an estimate of all homeless people in the United States who used homeless assistance programs during an average week in October/November 1996, many people will want to see how many are in family households (i.e., living with at least one of their own minor children) and how many are not. Also of interest is how homeless users of NSHAPC programs are distributed among central cities, the suburban/urban fringe, and rural areas. Table 2.5 provides the relevant statistics.

Fifteen percent of homeless clients in 1996 represented family households—that is, they were the parents of children who lived with them in their homeless condition. Adding the children in these families, however, to the total number of homeless clients of NSHAPC programs offers a notably different picture. With the children included, 33 percent of the *people* we estimate to be homeless were in families, two-thirds of them children.

About 7 in 10 service-using homeless households were found in central cities at the time of the NSHAPC survey. Two in 10 were found in

Table 2.5 *Family and Urban-Rural Status of Homeless Households and People Using Homeless Assistance Programs during an Average Week in the October/November 1996 Target Period*

	Homeless Clients (Households)		*Homeless People (Clients plus Children)*	
	Number	*Percent*	*Number*	*Percent*
All	346,000	100	444,000	100
Family Status[a]	50,000	15	148,000	
Living in family	296,000	85	296,000	33
All others				67
Urban-Rural Status	244,000	71	308,000	
Central city	71,000	21	94,000	69
Suburban/urban fringe (rest of MSAs)	30,000	9	41,000	21
Rural (outside of MSAs)				9

Source: Urban Institute analysis of weighted 1996 NSHAPC client data.

Note: All estimates have a 95 percent confidence interval (margin of error) of ± 6 percent; they have been rounded to the nearest 1,000. Percentages do not sum to 100 percent due to rounding.

[a] A homeless family is defined as one or more parents living with one or more of their own minor children. Every homeless child counted in this table is, by definition, in a homeless family. Everyone else is counted among "all others," even if they are under 18 (e.g., homeless youth) or do not live with a child but do live with one or more other adults, including a spouse.

suburban and urban fringe areas (specifically, in the parts of MSAs other than central cities). The remaining tenth were found in rural areas (defined as outside MSAs). These proportions are basically unchanged, regardless of whether the focus is on homeless *people* or on homeless *households*. In contrast, people living in poverty, who provide the most relevant housed comparison to the homeless population at a point in time, were distributed quite differently in 1990. Forty-three percent lived in central cities, 34 percent lived in suburban/urban fringe areas, and 23 percent in rural areas and towns outside MSAs.

Thus, whether one considers service-using *homeless households* or *homeless people*, they appear to be disproportionately found in central cities. Whether central cities *produce* more homelessness or simply are the ultimate refuge of people who became homeless elsewhere is a question with important implications for the development of homeless services. NSHAPC data indicate that 44 percent of homeless clients left the community where their current spell of homelessness began. Half the movers came to the place where they were interviewed for NSHAPC without staying anywhere else, while one-fourth had been in five or more different communities since becoming homeless. Only 28 percent began their current homeless spell in a central city. Two basic generalizations can be made about these movers. First, they tended to move from smaller communities to larger ones (hardly any went the other way). Second, the smaller the community they started in, the more likely they were to move to a larger one, rather than one the same size.

Central cities were the primary destination of most movers. Although *lack* of shelters and other programs was not a major reason for leaving where they became homeless (losing housing and needing work were more important), the availability of shelters, services, and programs for homeless people *was* a major reason why movers chose the community where they were selected for NSHAPC.

February versus October/November

The NSHAPC client survey was originally scheduled for February 1996. February is a month when use of emergency assistance such as that provided by NSHAPC programs is usually greater than in the fall. Indeed, many cities have shelter and feeding programs that operate only in winter or when the temperature drops below freezing. The client survey had to be postponed, however, due to a federal government shutdown in

December 1995. In pre-shutdown preparations for the February client survey, Census Bureau staff had conducted telephone interviews with service providers in NSHAPC's primary sampling areas, asking how many clients they expected to serve on "an average day in February." These reports formed the basis for the final client sampling plan, although they were subsequently adjusted to account for lower service levels in October/November. As a result of having information on, and/or expectations of, program contacts for both February 1996 and October/November 1996, the NSHAPC data can support estimates of program contacts and clients served in both periods.

Estimates for February 1996, however, are less reliable than those for October/November 1996, for several reasons. Our February NSHAPC estimates, for example, may be *higher* than the true numbers of people homeless in February. The most important reason is that providers consistently overestimate how many people they serve. As an illustration, one expert on NSHAPC's advisory panel noted that the estimates given by shelter providers in her state's major metropolitan area for the number of people they expected to serve on an average day in February were significantly greater than the total shelter *capacity* (*not* occupancy) regularly reported to government agencies *for the entire state*. Further, the February figures derived from NSHAPC are uncorroborated, since Census staff never actually appeared to observe program-use patterns firsthand while conducting client interviews. (Providers of non-shelter services also are not very accurate in their estimates of the proportion of their clients who are homeless, but that error would not affect an overall estimate of program contacts such as we are after here.)

Another reason why our estimates may *exceed* true February figures has to do with variations in patterns of service use over time. Estimates of the number of people served rely on information about clients' service-use patterns during the week preceding their interview. Clients were interviewed only in October/November, and service-use patterns may differ from season to season. If service use is more intensive during colder months, then estimates based on NSHAPC's October/November data will overestimate the true number of clients and homeless clients served in February.

Unfortunately, we cannot even say with certainty that our NSHAPC-based estimates for February 1996 are higher than reality, because one important source of bias probably makes our estimates *lower* than their true value. Many homeless assistance programs are open only a few months a year (during winter). There is also a great deal of turnover among these programs, irrespective of their regular schedule of operation. The Census Bureau found this out when it had to determine which programs were actually serving clients in October/November, based on a list compiled for February. None of the programs open in February 1996 that were closed (either permanently or seasonally) in October/November 1996 are included in our February estimates. These omitted programs are likely to be ones whose clientele is almost entirely homeless, and that may serve a significant number of people. They include emergency shelters in armories, fire houses, or churches; drop-in programs such as warming centers; and emergency outreach programs in many northern cities that contact street people on very cold nights and urge them to use available shelters. Unfortunately, the confounding effects of several sources of bias prevent us from saying definitively whether our estimates for February are likely to over- or underestimate the "true" February figures. The different sources of bias, in fact, may cancel each other out.

Despite these limitations, the February estimates are of great interest, because there is little question that more people use homeless assistance programs in February than in October/November (which is why NSHAPC was originally planned for February). Overall, estimates based on the NSHAPC data for February show that homeless assistance programs expected to receive approximately 19.6 million program contacts in February 1996. This estimate is almost 80 percent higher than the corresponding estimate for October/November 1996 (table 2.6). Of these, we estimate that 13.8 million (71 percent) were made by *homeless* clients. This numerical estimate is 73 percent higher than the corresponding estimate for October/November 1996.

As was done for the October/November estimates, client reports of their service-use pattern were used to estimate the distinct (unduplicated) number of clients contacting homeless assistance programs (table 2.6). These estimates indicate that 1.3 million households were served through homeless assistance programs during an average week in February 1996. Of these households, 637,000 (47 percent) were homeless (as with the estimates of number of program contacts, these two figures are considerably higher than those for October/November 1996, 108 percent and 84 percent, respectively). When one considers service-using homeless *people* rather than *households*, the weekly February estimate increases to 842,000 (86 percent higher than the same

Table 2.6 *Estimates for February vs. October/November 1996 of All and Homeless Users of Homeless Assistance Programs*

	Month and Time Period of Estimate					
	October 18– November 14, 1996			*February 1996*		
	Month	*Average Week*	*Average Day*	*Month*	*Average Week*	*Average Day*
Program Contacts Made by						
All clients (households)	10,932,000	2,733,000	390,000	19,619,000	4,736,000	677,000
Homeless clients (households)	7,996,000	1,999,000	286,000	13,849,000	3,343,000	478,000
Number of Clients (households)		646,000	291,000		1,342,000	508,000
Homeless clients (households)		346,000	203,000		637,000	334,000
Homeless People (clients plus children)		444,000	267,000		842,000	462,000

Source: Urban Institute analysis of weighted 1996 NSHAPC client data.

Note: All estimates have a 95 percent confidence interval (margin of error) of ± 6 percent; they have been rounded to the nearest 1,000.

estimate for October/November). Finally, table 2.6 presents February estimates of all households and homeless households using homeless assistance programs on an *average day*. In general, these estimates also are 65 to 75 percent higher than the corresponding estimates for October/November.

Changes since 1987

The only other study to collect data nationwide from homeless people using a systematic sampling strategy was conducted by the Urban Institute in March 1987. This study was limited to large cities with populations greater than 100,000, went only to shelters and soup kitchens, and interviewed only homeless clients. Estimates comparable to the Urban Institute 1987 study can be developed from NSHAPC data by limiting the sample to clients identified in shelters and soup kitchens in large central cities.[10] Table 2.7 compares the 1987 Urban Institute estimates to estimates for an average seven-day period in February 1996 and the four-week target period in October/November 1996.

The 1987 Urban Institute study (Burt and Cohen 1989) estimated there were 194,000 adult homeless users of shelters and soup kitchens in cities of 100,000 or more in the United States during an average week in March 1987. This figure increased to 229,000 when children homeless with their parents were included.[11] The October/November 1996 estimates derived from NSHAPC data using an equivalent subsample (homeless people found in shelters and soup kitchens in central cities), 197,000 and 234,000, respectively, are surprisingly close to the Urban Institute estimates from nearly a decade ago (table 2.7). However, the February 1996 NSHAPC estimates are more than double the 1987 Urban Institute estimates. Although the February 1996 estimates derived from NSHAPC data are less reliable than the October/November estimates, they are more seasonally comparable to the March 1987 Urban Institute estimates, both being for a winter month. The winter-month-to-winter-month comparison suggests that the population of homeless people using central city homeless assistance programs has grown considerably since 1987, along with the growth in homeless assistance programs themselves.

Another way to think about changes between 1987 and 1996 is to examine the *rate of homelessness per 10,000 population*. Even more than

Table 2.7 *Comparison of NSHAPC and 1987 Urban Institute Estimates of Homeless People Identified for Interview in Shelters and Soup Kitchens in Central Cities*

		NSHAPC	
	Urban Institute March 1987	*February 1996*	*Oct./Nov. 1996*
Homeless clients (households)	194,000	404,000	197,000
Homeless people (clients plus children)	229,000	516,000	234,000

Source: Urban Institute analysis of 1996 NSHAPC client data, and M. R. Burt and B. E. Cohen, *America's Homeless: Numbers, Characteristics, and Programs that Serve Them*, Urban Institute Press, Washington, D.C., July 1989.

Note: All NSHAPC estimates have a 95 percent confidence interval (margin of error) of ± 6 percent; estimates from the 1987 Urban Institute study have a 95 percent confidence interval of ± 42 percent. All have been rounded to the nearest 1,000.

the absolute numbers already discussed, *rates* take into consideration population growth and shifts from one type of community to another. Further, if rates can be calculated for communities of different types, they also provide a point of comparison that allows communities to estimate what their own homeless population might be if it conformed to the average for the United States.

Table 2.8 offers several comparisons, but it is important to understand the assumptions that underlie each. The issues have to do with service-using versus non-service-using homeless people, and communities of different types. For 1987, the *only* estimates and rates that are *based on actual data* are those for service-using homeless people in cities with 100,000 or more population. To project to the total homeless population, including non-service users, and to the United States as a whole, assumptions had to be made about the ratio of service-using to non-service-using homeless people, and about the probable rates of homelessness outside the cities in the 1987 study. Burt (1991) assumed that the service-using homeless population rate in suburban/urban fringe areas (balance of MSAs) was one-third of that in the cities, and that the *overall* (not just service-using) rate for rural areas (outside of MSAs) was 9/10,000. She projected rates to the total homeless population based on two different assumptions: that the study had captured 80 percent of all homeless people in central cities, and thus the observed rates needed to be multiplied by 1.2 to estimate the total homeless population, and that the study had captured only two-thirds of all homeless people, producing a multiplier of 1.5. The 1987 U.S., cities, and balance-of-MSA rates for the total homeless population are thus projections based on these multipliers. In contrast, the service-using homeless rate for rural areas is the opposite, dividing 9/10,000 by both 1.2 and 1.5.

For the 1996 estimates, NSHAPC provides estimates of the service-using homeless population in all three community types, so no assumptions are necessary to calculate rates per 10,000. We use the multiplier of 1.2 to project rates for all homeless people, based on the assumption that the expanded level of homeless assistance programs and services in 1996 assures that a higher proportion of the homeless population will be in contact with one or more services.

Looking first at the rates for service-using homeless people, shown in the left three columns of table 2.8, several things are obvious. First, the 1996 figures based on the October/November estimates are very close to those for 1987, while those based on the February estimates are almost

Table 2.8 *Comparing 1987 Urban Institute and 1996 NSHAPC Estimates of Homelessness Rates, by Community Type*
(rate of homeless persons per 10,000 population)

	Users of Homeless Assistance Programs Only			*Projections to Entire Homeless Population, Including Non-Service Users*			
	1987	*1996*		*1987*		*1996*	
	Using 600,000 Estimate	*Using October/ November Estimates (444,000)*	*Using February Estimates (842,000)*	*Using Assumption of 20 Non-Service-Using Homeless to 100 Service-Using Homeless*	*Using Assumption of 50 Non-Service-Using Homeless to 100 Service-Using Homeless*	*Using October Estimate and Assumption of 20 Non-Service-Using Homeless to 100 Service-Using Homeless*	*Using February Estimate and Assumption of 20 Non-Service-Using Homeless to 100 Service-Using Homeless*
Total: United States	16.2	16.7	31.6	19.4	24.3	20.0	38.0
Cities over 100,000/ central cities	37.4	36.8	69.8	44.9	56.1	44.2	83.7
Suburban/urban fringe areas (balance of MSAs)	12.3	7.2	13.6	14.8	18.5	8.6	16.3
Rural areas (outside of MSAs)	6–7.5	7.3	13.9	9.0	9.0	8.8	16.7

Source: Urban Institute analysis of 1996 NSHAPC client data, and M. R. Burt and B. E. Cohen, *America's Homeless: Numbers, Characteristics, and Programs that Serve Them,* Urban Institute Press, Washington, D.C., July 1989.

Note: All NSHAPC estimates have a 95 percent confidence interval (margin of error) of ± 6 percent; estimates from the 1987 Urban Institute study have a 95 percent confidence interval of ± 42 percent. All have been rounded to the nearest 1,000. Shaded cells are based on assumptions, not on actual data. For 1987, Burt (1991) assumed that balance of MSAs had a rate 1/3 that of cities over 100,000, and that the overall rate for rural areas was 9/10,000. The rates of 6–7.5 for service users is based on the assumption that there are 210–250 non-service-using homeless for every 100 service-using homeless.

twice as high. Thus, if one believes that the October/November estimates are the right ones, then one will assume that the homeless population has neither grown nor shrunk since 1987. On the other hand, if one believes that the February estimates come closer to capturing the true size of the homeless population, then one will conclude that the proportion of the population in most communities that is homeless at any given time has grown considerably.

Second, suburban/urban fringe areas are the exception to this generalization, indicating that the 1987 assumption that suburban rates would be one-third the central city rates was not true in 1996 and probably not true in 1987. Third, the suspicion that 9/10,000, the somewhat arbitrary rate used for rural areas in 1987 (based on what little data were available), was too high is *not* supported by NSHAPC data. It appears, in fact, to be either low or about right.

Looking next at the projections to the total homeless population (including both service-using and non-service-using homeless people), one can see again the similarities between the 1987 projections (especially those based on a ratio of 1.2 total to service-using population) and the 1996 projections based on the October/November estimates. Projections based on the February 1996 estimates are, of course, higher.

Going from a Weekly to an Annual Estimate

Evidence from shelter tracking databases and telephone surveys of housed populations emphasizes the importance of getting estimates of the number of people who experience homelessness or go through the homeless service system both during extended periods of time and on an average day or week. The point-in-time numbers, which most of this chapter has focused on, are very important for planning the total capacity of a service system. But how should that system be configured? How much of its shelter/housing resources should be bare-bones emergency shelter, how much should be transitional or permanent, and how many and what kinds of ancillary services should be available? The answers may come, in part, from counts and characteristics of people who might need to use a homeless service system sometime during a year. They paint a very different picture of homeless people from one painted at a single point in time. It's a picture that may challenge communities to give their homeless service system renewed scrutiny.

Like so many other efforts to describe homeless people, NSHAPC data were collected from homeless assistance program clients at only one point in time, albeit a point stretched over 28 days rather than focused on one. Even so, such a process does not provide annual data, nor can any other point-in-time study do so definitively. However, knowing the policy importance of data covering a longer period, the designers of NSHAPC proposed asking clients enough about their experiences of homelessness to support projections for longer periods. When the relevant questions were included, we still did not know how well the resulting projections would approximate real data on annual counts from shelter tracking databases (e.g., Culhane et al. 1994) or household surveys (Link et al. 1994, 1995). But we thought it was important at least to try. The rest of this section indicates that we came pretty close.

The Technique We Used

The technique we used relies on information reported by homeless clients about when their current period of homelessness began. We assume that the NSHAPC sample is representative of homeless people who use homeless assistance programs in the United States at a given point in time, and that the length of their current homeless episode is likewise representative. Therefore, we further assume that we can use information about how many homeless episodes began during the past week, two weeks, or month as the basis for a multiplier to project to a year.[12] For example, if we know we have 1,000 homeless people right now, and 10 of them became homeless during the past week, we can multiply 10 by 51 (the number of weeks remaining in a 12-month period) to obtain 510. This figure, 510, is the number of people *in addition to the 1,000 people who are homeless right now* who can be expected to become homeless during the remaining 51 weeks of the year. The projected annual total would thus be 1,510.

By extension, if 15 of the 1,000 people homeless this week became homeless in the last *two* weeks, we can multiply 15 by 25.5 (the number of two-week periods in a year minus the week of the original estimate of 1,000) to get 383 additional people becoming homeless, for a projected annual total of 1,383. Also by extension, if we know that 20 of our original 1,000 people became homeless during the past month, we could multiply 20 by 11.75 to get 235 additional people, for a projected annual total of 1,235.

Notice in our examples that the projected annual total gets *smaller* as the base period gets longer. We get the largest projected annual total using one week as the basis, and the smallest using one month. This is because, knowing what *actual* homeless episode lengths at the short end of the distribution look like in NSHAPC and other homeless databases, we did not assume an even distribution of episode lengths.[13] Rather, we assumed that among people with relatively short spells (under three months), more people have the shortest episodes, and the number with longer episodes shrinks pretty quickly. Thus, in our hypothetical sample we had 10 people becoming homeless within the past week, another 5 who became homeless between 8 and 14 days ago, and 5 more who became homeless between 15 and 30 days ago.

Two caveats are important when looking at these annual projections. First, the technique we use forces us to assume that the rate of entry into homelessness is constant over 12 months—that is, that the same number of people will become homeless during each base time period throughout the year. This assumption is almost certainly not true, but we have no basis for making any other assumption, as NSHAPC collected data only during a four-week period in fall 1996. Second, without adjustment, the technique does not account for exit and re-entry during the year, with its implied duplicate counting. That is, some proportion of our in-flow statistic (clients reporting becoming homeless during the past week/two weeks/month) represents people who will leave homelessness within a few weeks or months and then become homeless again within the year. We should not be recounting people who end one homeless spell and begin another within the same year. We use NSHAPC data to estimate and adjust for this duplication.

Results

We applied this projection technique to the NSHAPC data; the results are reported in table 2.9. Since making these projections is a relatively untried technique, and since quite a bit may depend on the outcome, we decided to present all three base periods, rather than choose just one. In addition, we have estimates for two different 1996 seasons, an adjustment for multiple spells, and an interest in both homeless adults, who were the actual NSHAPC respondents, and the total homeless population, which included minor children living with them. Therefore, we present a relatively complicated, but very interesting, table. The first two

Table 2.9 *Projections from NSHAPC Data to the Number of People Homeless During a Year's Period, Adjusted for Duplication: Using October/November and February 1996 Base Estimates, for Homeless Clients, and for Homeless Clients Plus Children*

	Base Estimate	*In-Flow*	*Multiplier*	*Annual Projection*	*Percent of In-Flow with a Prior Spell Beginning in Past Year*	*Annual Projection, Adjusted for Multiple Spells*	*Ratio of Annual Projection to Base Estimate, Adjusted for Multiple Spells*
			Projections Based on Estimates for October/November 1996				
Homeless Clients (Households)							
1 week	346,000	25,800	51.00	1,662,000	17.4	1,433,000	4.14
2 weeks	346,000	31,200	25.50	1,142,000	16.5	1,010,000	2.92
1 month	346,000	52,200	11.75	959,000	14.6	870,000	2.51
Homeless People (Clients Plus Children)							
1 week	444,000	42,000	51.00	2,586,000	12.2	2,325,000	5.24
2 weeks	444,000	51,200	25.50	1,750,000	12.3	1,589,000	3.58
1 month	444,000	85,000	11.75	1,443,000	13.6	1,307,000	2.94
			Projections Based on Estimates for February 1996				
Homeless Clients (Households)							
1 week	637,000	38,700	51.00	2,611,000	23.7	2,143,000	3.36
2 weeks	637,000	52,700	25.50	1,981,000	19.8	1,715,000	2.69
1 month	637,000	98,300	11.75	1,792,000	18.0	1,584,000	2.49
Homeless People (Clients Plus Children)							
1 week	842,000	66,000	51.00	4,208,000	21.2	3,494,000	4.15
2 weeks	842,000	91,900	25.50	3,185,000	17.3	2,781,000	3.30
1 month	842,000	161,000	11.75	2,735,000	17.8	2,398,000	2.85

Source: Urban Institute analysis of weighted 1996 NSHAPC client data.

panels show results based on the October/November 1996 estimates; the second two cover results based on the February 1996 estimates. Within each *set*, the first panel shows results just for homeless (adult) clients; the second shows results for homeless clients and their minor children living with them. Finally, within each *panel*, we show the results using all three base periods: one week, two weeks, and one month.

Table 2.9's *columns* show, in order, (1) the base period; (2) the base estimate of how many people are currently homeless; (3) the in-flow, which is how many currently homeless people became homeless within the base period; (4) the multiplier corresponding to the base period; (5) the projected annual total, given the base period; (6) the proportion of the in-flow who had at least one prior spell of homelessness within the 12 months prior to being interviewed; (7) the annual projection corrected for multiple spells; and (8) the ratio of the corrected annual projection to the base estimate of current homelessness.

Looking at the first row of the first panel (for homeless clients, using a one-week base period and the October/November NSHAPC estimates), we see that the base estimate of currently homeless clients is 346,000, that the in-flow for the one-week period is 25,800, and that multiplying 25,800 by 51 and adding 346,000 yields 1,662,000. However, the in-flow group should be reduced by 17.4 percent to account for multiple spells (duplication), so the adjusted annual projection is 1,433,000. Thus 1.4 million adults are projected to have been homeless at some time during the year beginning with a week in October/November 1996. This figure is more than four times the number of adults estimated to be homeless during our base period in October/November 1996, and is within the range of point-in-time to annual multipliers reported by Burt (1994) and Culhane et al. (1994).

Projections for homeless clients plus their minor children, which total 2.6 million using the one-week base period without adjustment for duplication, and 2.3 million adjusted for duplication, are larger than those for homeless clients alone, because they start from a larger base (444,000 rather than 346,000). In addition, the in-flow for any given base period is a greater percentage of the base estimate when children are included than when they are not. The one-week in-flow of 25,800 for homeless clients is 7.5 percent of the base estimate of 346,000, while the one-week in-flow of 42,000 for homeless clients plus their children is 9.5 percent of the corresponding base estimate of 444,000. The same pattern holds for the two-week and one-month base periods.

The larger proportion that is in-flow for the "homeless clients plus children" analysis results in projections that are higher in relation to their base estimates than the "homeless clients" projections. Thus 5.24, the ratio of the one-week duplication-adjusted annual projection to the base estimate for homeless clients plus children, is substantially higher than the corresponding ratio of 4.14 for homeless clients alone. These figures tell us that homeless households with children are more likely than other homeless households to have very short spells, and that more can expect to experience homelessness during a year, if our assumptions are correct. In addition, the reduction for prior spells within the past 12 months is substantially smaller for homeless clients plus children than it is for homeless clients alone (12.2 versus 17.4). This indicates that homeless families are more likely to be in their first spell, or at least their only recent one.

Table 2.9 also reveals that the annual projection gets smaller as the in-flow base period gets longer. Thus the estimate using a one-month base period is only 58 percent of the estimate using the one-week base period. People captured by the one-week base period represent more than four in five of those captured by the two-week base period and one in two of those captured by the one-month base period.[14] The October/November 1996 estimates thus produce relatively sharp differences, depending on the base period. This suggests that households homeless and using homeless assistance programs in the October/November period included a relatively high proportion with very short spells. Because those represented in the one-week base period comprise such high proportions of those found in the two-week and one-month base periods, and because people with very short spells could already have left homelessness and been replaced in the course of a month, we believe the one-week base period is the most reasonable one in making these projections.

The annual numbers projected by this method, using the October/November 1996 estimates, are very large. The annual projection for homeless clients plus their children of 2.3 million (using the one-week base period) represents 0.9 percent of the entire population of the nation in 1996 (266.2 million), and 6.3 percent of its population living in poverty (36.5 million) (Committee on Ways and Means, 1998, tables H-1 and H-3). As large as these numbers are, however, the corresponding projections based on NSHAPC's February 1996 estimates are even larger. They show that a total of 3.5 million adults and children may have been homeless at some time during a year starting in February 1996 (again using the one-week base period). This figure is 1.3 percent of the nation's population and 9.6 percent of its poor population. Such very large numbers may be startling, but they are not out of line with the one-year findings from shelter tracking databases for Philadelphia and New York (Culhane et al. 1994). They do have very serious implications for how we think about homelessness and what to do about it.

Concluding Thoughts

The question everyone asks about homelessness—whether the number of homeless people has grown from the widely accepted 500,000 to 600,000 estimate for 1987—does not appear to have a simple answer. First, remember that 500,000 to 600,000 was a projection to the *total* homeless population at any given time, and not just to the service-using homeless population. At 444,000, estimates of the service-using homeless population based on October/November 1996 data are somewhat smaller than the low end of the 1987 range, but still within its very large confidence limits (± 42 percent). Projecting the total homeless population based on the October/November estimates and the rate of 20/10,000 calculated in this chapter yields 532,000, which again is within the confidence limits of the 1987 estimates. From this we can feel quite confident that the number of people homeless at any given time has definitely not shrunk in the past decade.

However, at 842,000 for the service-using homeless population and 1.0 million for the total homeless population, using the rate of 38.0/10,000 calculated earlier, estimates based on February 1996 projections are more than 60 percent higher than the high end of the 1987 range.

It is possible that both estimates reflect a part of the truth—that the number of people homeless at any given time *and using homeless assistance programs* is highly variable, and probably greatly affected by the season. However, we are inclined to place more credence in the February than the October/November numbers as reflections of the true size of the homeless population at any given time in 1996, based on two convergences. The first is a calculation based on available shelter resources, as reported in chapter 9; the second is the convergence of our projections to annual numbers with those derived from two quite different methods.

We look first at calculations based on expected shelter usage as reported in chapter 9. There we learn that emergency shelters, transitional housing programs, and voucher distribution programs expected 511,000 program contacts in February 1996.[15] Let us take these expectations as indicators of program *capacity* rather than *occupancy*, just to be conservative. To determine occupancy, and therefore the number of homeless shelter users, we multiply 511,000 by 70 percent (reflecting the average level of occupancy reported for emergency shelters and transitional housing), getting 358,000 people using these shelter/transitional/voucher programs on an average single day in February.

Next, let us suppose that one-third of those people were in family households, and assume that they stayed in their shelter/transitional/voucher programs for all seven days in a week, as homeless families tend to do. That is 118,000 people. Then let us suppose that two different people occupied each of the remaining two-thirds of shelter/transitional/voucher beds during the same seven days, staying 3.5 days each (this, also, is a conservative assumption). That is 479,000 people. Adding these two figures together, we get 597,000 people using shelter/transitional/voucher programs during a week's time, and automatically being considered homeless as a consequence. We also know, however, that 27 percent of NSHAPC's homeless sample *did not* use shelter/housing programs at all during a week's time, although they did use other homeless assistance programs. So we also have to account for them. If we consider 597,000 to be 73 percent of all service-using homeless people, we arrive at 818,000 as the final figure for the service-using homeless population during a week's time in February 1996. This is within the ± 6 percent confidence interval for the estimate of 842,000 homeless service users in February that we reported earlier. Thus one convergence supports the higher February estimate.

A second is equally important. The annual projections made in this chapter, of approximately 1 percent of the total U.S. population experiencing homelessness at least once during a year's time, yield a picture similar to that obtained from both shelter tracking databases and national surveys of housed individuals (Culhane et al. 1994; Link et al. 1994, 1995). Further, the projections based on the February figures come closest to the estimates from these other sources. Both convergences thus lend credence to the February figures.

What emerges is a reality containing a very large pool of poor people living such precarious lives that, at any given moment, enough will need to use homeless assistance programs to support the validity of our estimates. If the facilities are available, the combination of structural and economic factors coupled with personal vulnerabilities consistently produces enough people who need facilities to keep them in business.

More facilities, in particular more shelter/housing facilities, mean that more people are likely to be *counted* as homeless, because the definition of homelessness depends in part on use of such facilities. But the existence of facilities does not create the need that presses people into using them; it only illuminates a level of need that already exists. Because there were many more homeless assistance programs in 1996 than in 1987, including shelter/housing programs whose occupants are, by definition, homeless, people in desperate circumstances had recourse to more help. As a consequence, we estimated that more people were homeless, both during a given week and over the period of a year.

However, the focus of concern should not be on the numbers of literally homeless people, because they can be made to vary considerably, depending on service capacities and definitions. Instead, the estimates presented in this chapter suggest, we believe, that policymakers and practitioners should adopt a different focus. They need to rethink their ideas about the nature of homelessness and the homeless services and programs that make the most sense, in light of ample evidence of major levels of short-term homelessness and even higher levels of long-term misery. Rather than discuss these implications here, however, we will save that discussion for chapter 11. Meantime, we will present more evidence that also should be considered in developing policies and programs for the future.

NOTES

1. Details of these procedures may be found in Burt et al. 1996b, appendix D.
2. These figures are unduplicated. That is, each person is counted only once, regardless of how many times he or she used the shelter system in either New York or Philadelphia. Therefore, the figures given for the proportion of the city population who experienced homelessness are accurate, and are not inflated by counting people in shelters more than once.
3. Bray, Dennis, and Lambert (1993) provide the best evidence for this level of population coverage. Their study of the Washington, D.C., metropolitan area went to shelters and soup kitchens/meal programs, as did the 1987 Urban Institute study, and also conducted systematic street searches. They found that 85 to 90 percent of all the homeless people they found would have been found without the street searches, just by going to shelters and meal programs. The meal programs picked up 84 percent of the total estimated homeless population who did *not* use shelters.

4. For example, the Kentucky studies already mentioned faced this dilemma. To compensate, they extended the time frame to two months, and also greatly expanded the types of program included as places to interview people, including a large array of generic services and agencies, and screened their clients for homelessness.
5. Program contacts are a measure of service *availability*, but not necessarily a measure of service *need*. We may assume that the services delivered were needed, but without knowing how many people who needed services were *not* able to get them, we cannot consider program contacts as indicating anything but the lowest possible amount of need that exists in a community.
6. The 95 percent confidence interval for all estimates in this and subsequent paragraphs is ± 6 percent unless specifically noted.
7. Remember that "client" is used in the sense of "household" to refer to the adults who were eligible to be interviewed. A client who has children with her/him is treated as one household in any analysis referring to "clients."
8. The four types of health programs and migrant housing used for homeless people in the off-season were not included in client sampling, nor were outreach or "other" programs unless they afforded access to clients not already covered by the shelter/housing and food program sampling frames.
9. The other children live away from their homeless parent in various settings, including with their other parent or with other relatives or in foster care. None of these children of adult NSHAPC clients have been included in our estimates of children living with homeless clients (chapter 4 describes the characteristics and whereabouts of the children of homeless clients who do not live with them).
10. These estimates required developing a unique set of weights for the NSHAPC client sample. The public use files of NSHAPC data do not include these weights, nor can they be developed from the NSHAPC variables that have been made publicly available.
11. The 95 percent confidence interval for the 1987 Urban Institute figures was ± 42 percent.
12. For these very short periods of time, we feel confident that we can count on people to report the beginning of their current homeless spell with acceptable accuracy. Of course, we are relying on each client's own personal definition of homelessness in asking when their current spell of homelessness began. Relying on personal definitions has its problems, but so does relying on shelter use data. The former involves recall problems and also whether the experience being reported would meet a definition of literal homelessness. The latter, by equating homelessness with nights in a shelter, gives the research a perhaps false sense of precision, in that it also entails an inability to capture any type of homeless experience other than that involving a shelter stay.
13. If we *had* assumed an even distribution, the examples in the previous paragraph would look like this: 20 of the 1,000 homeless people became homeless in the last *two* weeks, multiply 20 by 25.5 to get 510; or, 40 of our original 1,000 people became homeless during the past month, multiply 40 by 11.75 to get 510. Thus it would not matter what time period we chose as the basis of the annual projection.
14. 25,800/31,200 = 83 percent; 25,800/53,000 = 49 percent.
15. Counting 111,100 for voucher distribution programs, assuming that one-third of vouchers (22,000 vouchers) go to families and that each family includes three people.

3

Homeless Families, Singles, and Others

After the numbers, the next question asked about homeless people is, "What are they like?" Basic demographic characteristics such as sex, age, family status, and race have always been of interest. This is in part because the homeless population appears to be very different from the general public on these characteristics, and even from most poor people who are housed. Because the differences are so dramatic, demographic characteristics often are overinterpreted as representing *reasons* for homelessness. But as chapter 8 will show later, demographic factors quickly disappear as proximate causes when other factors representing extreme poverty, by itself or coupled with personal vulnerabilities, are examined. Of course, the *underlying* causes of homelessness, those structural conditions that turn individual vulnerabilities into lost housing, do not lie within individuals at all, as we discussed in chapter 1.

The Urban Institute's 1987 study of homeless service users in large American cities (those with a population of more than 100,000) provided the first opportunity to examine the characteristics of homeless people at the national level.[1] Prior to that, policymakers, researchers, advocates, and others had to content themselves with trying to generalize from single-city studies. Differences in methodologies, plus differences in local population characteristics and conditions of homelessness, made this a relatively unrewarding task. Yet everyone retains an interest in asking, "Who are homeless people?" because the answers provide keys to designing appropriate short- and long-term remedies.

NSHAPC offers only the second opportunity to understand the characteristics of homeless people at the national level, since homelessness became a visible national problem in the early 1980s. It can provide comparisons that match the 1987 Urban Institute data (homeless people in central cities found in soup kitchens and shelters). But it offers a significantly expanded scope, since it also includes people who were homeless in suburban and urban fringe areas and in rural areas (outside of MSAs). The 1996 study also asked many more detailed questions on a wider range of topics.

In this chapter, we present findings for currently homeless people on many different factors. They include demographic, human capital, income and work, and health characteristics, and adverse childhood experiences. We also look at homeless clients' history of homelessness and use of homeless assistance services.[2] We focus on similarities and differences among important subgroups, defined by the family status and sex of the homeless client. Findings for all currently homeless people are offered for comparison, as well as statistics for adults living in households with incomes below the poverty level in the United States in 1996, when available. Discussion focuses on differences between male and female clients within each family status, and also on differences among family statuses for men and women. Most findings confirm results reported over the years from many local studies. The chapter concludes with thoughts on the implications of these findings for public policy. These include the service-using propensities of the different subgroups (high for families, lowest for male and female other clients), their available financial resources (highest for families, lowest for single men), their histories of homelessness (shortest for families, longest for singles, whether men or women), and their adverse childhood experiences (high for everyone). Family statuses used throughout the chapter include the following:

- "Clients with children" = clients who reported that at least one of their own minor children was living with them;
- "Single clients" = clients who reported that they were alone; and
- "Other clients" = clients who reported being with one or more persons, none of whom were their own minor children.

Demographic Characteristics

Before turning to the main focus of this chapter, namely the differences among subgroups of homeless people, it may be helpful to place the entire population of service-using homeless people in October/November 1996 in the context of poor, housed adults in 1996. Using *poor* adults is more appropriate than using *all* U.S. adults, because the vast majority of homeless people come from the ranks of the poor, and their demographic characteristics differ considerably from the overall adult population.

The first two columns of table 3.1 provide the relevant statistics, calculated from the March 1997 Current Population Survey for all persons age 18 and older who lived in households with income below the federal poverty level for 1996 (the year of NSHAPC). As can be seen, homeless people were less likely to be white or Hispanic, and more likely to be African-American, than the housed, poor adult population.[3] The homeless population was far less likely to include people 65 and older, and more likely to include people in their middle years. Homeless service users were much more likely than poor people in general to be found in central cities.[4] Educational attainment did not differ significantly, but marital status was very different. Far fewer homeless than poor housed adults were currently married, and more had never married or were divorced or separated.

Relative Size of Subgroups

We begin our examination of subgroups with an overview of how many clients are members of each (figure 3.1). For the sample as a whole, male clients with children comprised only 2.3 percent, while female clients with children comprised 12.2 percent. Single men were 60.7 percent of the whole sample, while single women were only 14.9 percent. Among other clients, men and women represented more equal proportions (5.3 and 4.6 percent, respectively) of the sample as a whole.

There were important differences in the proportion of men and women in the three family status subgroups. Among homeless women, those homeless with children and those by themselves comprised large and roughly equal proportions (38 and 47 percent, respectively), but female other clients were 15 percent. Among homeless men, 89 percent were single, those with children were a very small fraction (3 percent), and male other clients also were a relatively insignificant share (8 percent).

Table 3.1 *Basic Demographic Characteristics of Homeless Clients, by Family Status and Sex*
(weighted percentages)

	U.S. Poor Adult Population (1996)	All Currently Homeless Clients (UN = 2,938)	Clients with Children		Single Clients		Other Clients	
			Men (UN = 58)	Women (UN = 405)	Men (UN = 1,798)	Women (UN = 444)	Men (UN = 129)	Women (UN = 101)
Proportion of All Homeless Clients	NA	100	2	12	61	15	5	5
Race/Ethnicity[a]								
White non-Hispanic	52	41	58	34	37	52	36	67
Black non-Hispanic	23	40	32	45	43	36	26	23
Hispanic	20	11	8	16	9	10	30	5
Native American	2	8	1	6	11	2	7	3
Other	4	1			1	1	1	3
Age[a]								
Under 18	—	1	1	12	3	9	18	22
18 to 21 yrs.	12	6						
22 to 24 yrs.	8	5	16	15	2	9	3	1
25 to 34 yrs.	23	25	29	46	21	23	19	34
35 to 44 yrs.	20	38	42	25	44	29	37	22
45 to 54 yrs.	11	17	11	2	21	16	16	19
55 to 64 yrs.	10	6			8	7	6	3
65 or more yrs.	16	2			1	8		

Urban/Rural Status[b]								
Central cities	31	71	64	70	74	68	78	38
Suburban/urban fringe	46	21	31	19	16	30	18	55
Rural	23	9	5	11	11	3	4	7
Education/Highest Level of Completed Schooling[a]								
Less than high school	42	38	54	53	34	44	29	35
High school graduate/G.E.D.	33	34	25	20	36	30	38	51
More than high school	25	28	21	27	30	26	33	14
Marital Status[a]								
Married	31	9	63	15	3	4	31	46
Widowed	12	3	0	0	2	13	1	3
Divorced	15	24	21	39	26	31	17	8
Separated	6	15			16	8	5	13
Never married	37	48	15	46	53	45	46	31
People Homeless with Client								
Spouse	NA	6	62	11	NA	NA	29	44
Partner/boyfriend/girlfriend	NA	4	12	7	NA	NA	36	31
Other relative	NA	2	5	9	NA	NA	16	8
Other person(s)	NA	2	0	1	NA	NA	20	16

Source: Urban Institute analysis of weighted 1996 NSHAPC client data; *N*s given at top of table are unweighted (designated "UN").

Note: Percentages do not sum to 100 due to rounding. NA = not applicable. Shaded cells have been grouped due to small *N*s.

Family Status: "Clients with Children" = client reported that at least one of his/her minor children was living with client; "Single Clients" = client reported that s/he was alone; "Other Clients" = client reported being with one or more persons, none of whom were their minor children.

[a]Statistics for the poor adult (ages 18 and older) population in the United States calculated from March 1997 Current Population Survey using Unicon, with poverty status determined for 1996.

[b]Geographic distribution of the poor U.S. population in 1996 taken from Lamison-White (1997), P60-198, table A.

Figure 3.1 *Family Status, by Sex Subgroups*

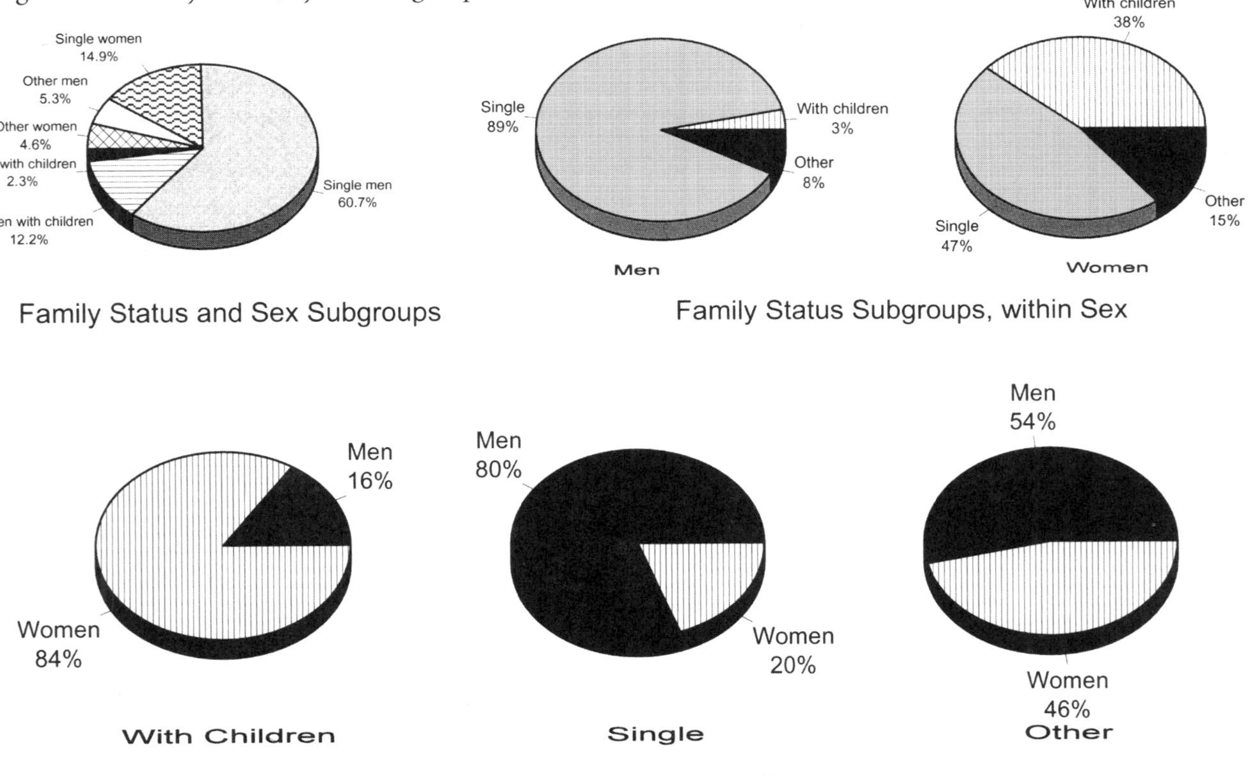

Source: Urban Institute analysis of weighted 1996 NSHAPC client data.

These patterns seem to carry into homelessness the greater tendency of women to stay connected and maintain responsibility for children and of men for separation.

In terms of family status categories, men and women comprised very different proportions of clients with children and single clients. Women predominated among clients with children, while men predominated among single clients. Men represented only 16 percent of clients with children, but 80 percent of single clients and 54 percent of other clients.

Differences by Sex within Family Status

Relatively few differences exist among the men and women in NSHAPC who were with children, but the differences that do exist are striking (table 3.1). Men who were homeless with their children were much more likely than similar women to be white (58 versus 34 percent) and married (63 versus 15 percent). They were also less likely to be very young (21 or younger) or never married. Men and women homeless with their children did not differ by educational attainment or by urban-rural status. They did, however, differ significantly in saying they were with a spouse or partner. Sixty-two percent of men with children said they were with their spouse, and another 12 percent said they were with a partner or girlfriend. Comparable figures for women with children were 11 percent with a spouse and 7 percent with a partner or boyfriend. Thus homeless households with children in the NSHAPC sample represented by women were mostly single-parent families, while three in four of those represented by men were two-parent (or at least two-adult) households.

Single clients were the biggest subgroup. Within this subgroup, men were less likely than women to be white (in contrast to homeless families), to be found in suburban/urban fringe areas, and to be widowed. But they were more likely to be separated.

Other clients, those who reported being with another adult but not with one or more of their own children, were a relatively small subgroup. Among them, men were less likely than women to be white (36 versus 67 percent) and more likely to be Hispanic (30 versus 5 percent). Men were much more likely to be found in central cities; women in suburban/urban fringe areas. Educational attainment also differed, with men being more likely to have had some education beyond high school. There were no differences by age or marital status. Male and female other clients were equally likely to be homeless with a spouse or partner, and proportions reporting these relationships were very high (65 and 75 percent, respectively).

Differences by Family Status among Women and among Men

Changing the focus to differences within gender groups across family status, male clients with children were significantly more likely to be white than single male clients (58 versus 37 percent). They were also marginally more likely to be white than male other clients. Male clients with children reported lower educational attainment than single male clients (54 versus 34 percent with less than a high school education). They also were marginally less likely than male other clients to have a high school diploma. Males with children were much more likely to report being married at the time of their NSHAPC interview (63 percent) and less likely to say they had never married (15 percent) than either single or male other clients (3 and 31 percent were currently married; 53 and 46 percent had never married). Notably, male other clients were also more likely than single male clients to be currently married, and 29 percent said they were with a spouse. Another 36 percent said they were homeless with a partner or girlfriend.

Among women, those with children were the *least* likely to be white (34 percent), and female other clients were the *most* likely to be white (67 percent), with single women falling in between (52 percent). Female other clients were less likely than either female clients with children or single female clients to have been found in a central city. They were more likely to have been found in a suburban/urban fringe area.

Educational differences also exist among the different subgroups of homeless women. Female other clients were most likely to have a high school diploma, and marginally less likely than women with children to have dropped out of high school. However, they were marginally less likely than single women to have some education beyond high school. Female other clients were also the most likely to report being currently married (46 versus 15 and 4 percent for women with children and single women, respectively). In addition, more women with children than single women were currently married. Many more female other clients were with a spouse (44 percent) or partner (31 percent), especially when compared to women with children, 11 percent of whom reported being with a spouse and 7 percent a partner or boyfriend.

These findings confirm the importance of looking at subgroups among homeless populations. Otherwise, one might draw inaccurate conclusions, applying the characteristics of the whole, or even the dominant group, to particular subgroups. Even within subgroups, characteristics may differ considerably, as they do in this study for homeless men and women with children.

Conditions of Homelessness

If basic demographic characteristics differ considerably among homeless subgroups, one might also expect that the subgroups' experience with homelessness itself would differ. For each subgroup, this section examines the number of homeless spells, their length, and reasons why clients had to leave the last place they called "home."

Among clients with children, men were more likely than women to have spells at the two extremes; either a very short spell that was their first, or a longer spell that was not (table 3.2). Women with children were more spread out over the various possibilities, but tended toward spells of six months or less that were equally likely to be their first or a subsequent spell.

Among single clients, women were more likely than men to be in their first homeless spell. However, these women's first spells were more likely than those of men to exceed six months. For single men and women whose current spell was *not* their first, more men had spells that had lasted over six months. Among other clients, no differences emerged in the number of spells and their length. But female other clients were more likely than male other clients to be in a first spell (of any length), and more likely to be in a spell of one to six months. Male other clients were more likely than female other clients to be in a very short spell—lasting less than a month. Male other clients stood out among all the subgroups as having the greatest likelihood of reporting 11 or more spells of homelessness. (Obviously, there is a tradeoff between the length and number of spells, with those reporting very long spells less likely to report very high numbers.)

Looking at men's and women's homelessness across family status, both men with children and male other clients were more likely than single men to be in a first homeless spell lasting less than six months (50 and 31 percent, respectively, versus 13 percent). On the other hand,

Table 3.2 *Conditions of Homelessness, by Family Status and Sex*
(weighted percentages)

		Clients with Children		*Single Clients*		*Other Clients*	
	All Currently Homeless Clients (UN = 2,938)	*Men (UN = 58)*	*Women (UN = 405)*	*Men (UN = 1,798)*	*Women (UN = 444)*	*Men (UN = 129)*	*Women (UN = 101)*
Spell History and Current Spell Length							
First time homeless							
6 months or less	18	50	30	13	15	31	14
More than 6 months	31	6	18	34	45	18	25
Not first time homeless							
Current spell 6 months or less	21	7	29	19	20	24	19
Current spell more than 6 months	30	37	22	34	21	27	43
Length of Current Period of Homelessness							
< 1 week	5	43	18	4	4	26	4
≥ 1 week and < 1 month	8			6	9		
1–3 months	15	14	43	12	12	26	47
4–6 months	11			10	10		
7–12 months	15	23	34	14	18	32	38
13–24 months	16			19	9		
25–60 months	10			11	14		
5 or more years	20	20	5	24	24	15	11

Number of Times Homeless or without Regular Housing for 30 Days or More							
1	49	56	49	47	60	46	46
2	17	9	31	16	11	10	11
3	12	35	21	11	12	10	21
4–10	18			21	15	21	22
11 or more	4			5	1	13	*
Kind of Place Lives Now (Today)							
Emergency shelter/welfare hotel	30	13	37	30	27	36	30
Transitional shelter/housing	33	72	44	28	48	21	20
House/apt./room paid for by client	16	14	18	16	14	6	26
Space not meant for habitation, plus other[a]	21	1	2	26	11	37	24
While Respondent Was Homeless							
People stole money or things directly from respondent while respondent was there	38	19	23	42	43	38	21
People stole money or things from respondent's bags, locker, etc., while respondent was gone	41	20	33	45	37	43	36
People physically assaulted respondent, beat respondent up	22	16	13	24	28	21	23
People sexually assaulted respondent, raped respondent	7	*	9	4	16	5	17

Source: Urban Institute analysis of weighted 1996 NSHAPC client data; *N*s given at top of table are unweighted (designated "UN").

Note: Percentages do not sum to 100 due to rounding. Shaded cells have been grouped due to small *N*s.

*Denotes values that are less than 0.5 percent but greater than 0. *Family Status:* "Clients with Children" = client reported that at least one of his/her minor children was living with client; "Single Clients" = client reported that s/he was alone; "Other Clients" = client reported being with one or more persons, none of whom were their minor children.

[a]Includes the following types of locations: car or other vehicle, abandoned building, transportation site, place of business, anywhere outside, and other place.

single men had a higher likelihood of being in a first homeless spell lasting more than six months than either men with children or male other clients (34 versus 6 and 18 percent, respectively). Single men were the least likely to report spells lasting less than a month (10 percent versus 43 and 26 percent of men with children and male other clients, respectively).

Among women, those with children were more likely than either single or female other clients to be in a first spell lasting six months or less (30 versus 15 and 14 percent), while single women were more likely than those with children or female other clients to be in a first spell lasting more than six months (45 versus 18 and 25 percent). Finally, female other clients were the most likely to be in a spell that was not their first and already had lasted more than six months.

Reasons for Leaving One's Last Residence

Table 3.3 gives the top four reasons why people left the last regular place they had and became homeless. It provides some insight into why people in different subgroups might fall into these different patterns of homelessness. People's reasons for leaving concentrated in a very few categories, although the interview listed 31 and also offered "other." In every subgroup, only two or three reasons were selected by at least 10 percent of homeless clients. "Couldn't pay the rent" was the most consistent. At least 10 percent of clients in every subgroup offered it. It was the most-frequent reason for both men and women with children (33 and 20 percent) and single women (20 percent). In addition, men with children gave a related reason, "landlord made us leave," about as frequently (28 percent). Women with children also cited this reason in their top four, but did so marginally less frequently (with only 8 percent doing so).

"Lost job or job ended" was in the top four reasons for all three male subgroups and for single women. It was the most frequent reason for single men and male other clients. One reason was important only for women: "I or my children were abused, beaten, and/or I was afraid of the violence in the household." It was among the top four reasons given by women with children and single women (the difference between women with children and single women was also significant). "Was doing drugs" figured in the top four only for single clients, both men and women. "Was drinking" was also in the top four for single men. Female other clients cited their top reason as becoming sick or disabled with some

Table 3.3 *Top Four Reasons for Leaving Last Regular Place to Stay, by Family Status and Sex*
(weighted percentages)

	All Currently Homeless Clients	Clients with Children		Single Clients		Other Clients	
		Men	*Women*	*Men*	*Women*	*Men*	*Women*
	(UN = 2,938)	*(UN = 58)*	*(UN = 405)*	*(UN = 1,798)*	*(UN = 444)*	*(UN = 129)*	*(UN = 101)*
Main Reason Left Last Regular Place to Stay (Just Before This Period of Homelessness): Top Four Reasons for Each Group							
Couldn't pay rent	15	33	20	13	20	10	15
Lost job or job ended	14	6	—	17	9	40	—
Client or children abused, beaten/violence in the household	4	—	16	—	10	—	—
Pushed out, kicked out	4	—	—	—	—	12	—
Was drinking	4	—	—	7	—	*	—
Was doing drugs	7	—	—	7	13	—	—
Became sick or disabled (other than HIV/AIDS)	2	—	—	—	—	*	27
Left town	4	—	—	—	—	8	9
Landlord made client leave	6	28	8	—	—	—	—
Displaced because building was condemned, destroyed or urban renewal, fire	3	—	—	—	—	—	9
Problem with residence or area where residence is located	3	6	8	—	—	—	—

Source: Urban Institute analysis of weighted 1996 NSHAPC client data; *N*s given at top of table are unweighted (designated "UN").
Note: Percentages do not sum to 100 due to rounding.
*Denotes values that are less than 0.5 percent but greater than 0. *Family Status:* "Clients with Children" = client reported that at least one of his/her minor children was living with client; "Single Clients" = client reported that s/he was alone; "Other Clients" = client reported being with one or more persons, none of whom were their minor children.

condition other than HIV/AIDS (27 percent). No more than 1 or 2 percent of any other group gave this reason, suggesting that these female other clients may have a unique set of problems that help explain their likelihood (greater than for single women or women with children) for having relatively many homeless spells and for their current one being relatively longer. They are also the only group to select condemnation or destruction of residence among its top four reasons for homelessness.

Where Clients Were Living on Day of Interview

Given all the other differences among the subgroups, it should not be surprising that they also have differential access to, or at least a different propensity to use, a variety of places where they might sleep or live. The bottom panel of table 3.2 shows the locations in which NSHAPC clients said they were living when they were interviewed. The categories have been collapsed because many of them were used very infrequently. They include emergency shelters, including voucher hotels and motels; transitional housing, including houses, apartments, and rooms that are part of such programs; self-pay arrangements, including hotel and motel rooms and other rooms, apartments, and houses; and locations not meant for habitation, including any place outdoors, cars and other vehicles, abandoned buildings, bus, train, and subway stations and other transportation sites, businesses (e.g., laundromats, all-night movies, or restaurants), and other miscellaneous locations.

Among clients with children, both men and women were most likely to be living in a transitional housing program at the time they were interviewed for NSHAPC, but this is more true for men than for women (71 versus 44 percent). Women with children were more likely than men with children to be living in an emergency shelter. Hardly any of either subgroup were living in places not meant for habitation (2 percent each). Among single clients, women were more likely than men to be in transitional housing programs, and less likely to be living in places not meant for habitation. Female other clients were more likely than male other clients to be living in accommodations that they paid for themselves.

Among men, those with children were more likely than men in the other groups to be living in transitional housing, and least likely to be outside or in places not meant for habitation. Women with children were the least likely of all the groups of women to be living in places not meant for habitation, while female other clients were the least likely to be in transitional housing. This pattern confirms the sense of providers and researchers who do street searches that very few homeless families with children are literally "on the streets." Because homeless families arouse relatively more sympathy than some other subgroups of homeless people, development of shelter and housing arrangements to accommodate them has been relatively rapid. Of course, an unknown number of homeless families may be living in their vehicles, moving from place to place and not using any homeless assistance programs. NSHAPC could not include such people who did not make any service contacts. But to the best of the study's ability to judge, the homeless service system appears able to help homeless families with children to avoid staying in places not meant for habitation.

Victimization while Homeless

Among the many hazards of homelessness, victimization through criminal attack is one that epitomizes the vulnerability of not having four walls and a door. Needing to be constantly on guard contributes even more stress to circumstances that already are extremely stressful. Victimization while homeless is not a minor event; the evidence indicates the majority of homeless people have experienced it in one form or another during their current spell of homelessness (table 3.2).

Robbery and theft were among the most-common forms of victimization among the homeless people in NSHAPC. Thirty-eight percent reported robbery (stealing from a person while the person is present); 41 percent reported theft (stealing in the victim's absence). Violations of one's person are also quite common, including both physical and sexual assault.

Within family status, the only type of victimization on which men and women differed was sexual assault. Significantly more women than men reported this crime in every family status (marginally so for other clients). Overall, about one in every eight homeless women reported being raped during their current homeless spell, with no significant differences among different family statuses. Homeless men were not immune to rape either, although their rate overall was considerably lower, at 1 in every 25 men. Men with children were less likely than single men to report a sexual assault. This relative immunity to criminal victimization among men with children also appeared with respect to robbery and theft; they reported lower levels than either single men or male other clients. Their residence in shelters may help explain this difference.

Among women, the only crime differentiating the three groups was robbery. More single women than either women with children or female other clients reported having money or things stolen from them in their presence. Their very aloneness undoubtedly increased their vulnerability. Women in the other two groups had other people with them, who may have offered some protection; women with children also obtained some protection from their shelter residence and infrequent resort to sleeping on the streets.

Use of Homeless Assistance Programs

Continuing our description of service use patterns, we turn now to service use in both the immediate past (during the week before the interview as well as on the day of it), and the lifetime of homeless clients. The information available through NSHAPC on service use patterns may be quite important, because it reveals which subgroups are being reached and helped, and which may need further efforts. Table 3.4 presents the relevant statistics. They appear, first, for where people slept or ate, then for combinations of service use, then for specific types of shelter/housing and other programs used within the past seven days, and, finally, for lifetime use of various homeless assistance programs.

Table 3.4 reveals some fairly consistent patterns, regardless of which panel is examined. Basically, households with children did not report many differences, regardless of whether they were headed by a man or a woman. Among singles, women were more likely than men to use shelters at all, and to use shelters but not soup kitchens. Men showed the opposite pattern, being more likely to have slept in places not meant for habitation in the past week, to have used a soup kitchen at all, and to have used soup kitchens but not shelters. Single men thus were receiving less than single women of what the homeless assistance network had to offer.

Single men were also more likely than single women to report that over their lifetime they had used emergency shelters, soup kitchens, outreach programs, and drop-in centers; the last three reflect programs oriented toward people who are not frequenting shelters. Male other clients showed the same propensities toward "the streets" and soup kitchens, compared to female other clients. Female other clients, for their part, stood out as having had more contact with outreach programs than

Table 3.4 *Current Living Situation and Use of Homeless Assistance Programs, by Family Status and Sex*
(weighted percentages)

	All Currently Homeless Clients	*Clients with Children*		*Single Clients*		*Other Clients*	
	(UN = 2,938)	*Men (UN = 58)*	*Women (UN = 405)*	*Men (UN = 1,798)*	*Women (UN = 444)*	*Men (UN = 129)*	*Women (UN = 101)*
Pattern of Program Use within Last Seven Days or on Day of Interview							
Shelter and soup kitchen, with or without other programs	15	5	6	20	12	15	5
Shelter but no soup kitchen, with or without other programs	50	64	71	43	69	42	31
Soup kitchen but no shelter, with or without other programs	21	23	7	26	5	30	21
Other program type, with no shelter or soup kitchen use	14	8	16	11	15	14	43
Where Slept or Ate within Last Seven Days or on Day of Interview							
Street[a]	32	4	7	39	15	66	31
Shelter[b]	73	87	82	69	86	60	63
Soup kitchen[c]	40	29	14	49	20	67	28
Other[d]	27	15	28	27	28	20	31

(Continued)

Table 3.4 *Current Living Situation and Use of Homeless Assistance Programs, by Family Status and Sex (Continued)*

(weighted percentages)

		Clients with Children		*Single Clients*		*Other Clients*	
	All Currently Homeless Clients (UN = 2,938)	*Men (UN = 58)*	*Women (UN = 405)*	*Men (UN = 1,798)*	*Women (UN = 444)*	*Men (UN = 129)*	*Women (UN = 101)*
Type of Shelter/Housing Programs Clients Reported Using in the Seven Days before Being Interviewed							
Emergency shelter	28	13	36	28	24	30	10
Transitional housing	26	53	36	23	34	17	14
Shelter[e]	3	0	*	4	3	5	1
Permanent housing	3	0	1	3	7	2	0
Shelter vouchers	1	*	2	1	*	1	*
Other Programs Clients Reported Using within the Seven Days before Being Interviewed							
Soup kitchen	31	20	9	41	16	33	20
Food pantry	5	2	11	4	2	3	7
Mobile food program	5	1	1	6	5	6	8
Outreach	7	1	5	7	5	6	25
Drop-in center	9	5	3	10	9	16	10
Programs Ever Used							
Emergency shelter	65	38	74	68	53	59	56
Transitional housing	40	58	44	40	41	27	39

Permanent housing	10	12	8	8	17	7	23
Shelter vouchers	15	25	17	15	11	16	31
Soup kitchen	62	46	38	75	45	45	43
Food pantry	40	59	64	36	37	22	41
Mobile food program	21	9	14	24	17	17	22
Outreach	17	14	12	18	9	20	34
Drop-in center	26	22	17	30	20	34	22

Source: Urban Institute analysis of weighted 1996 NSHAPC client data; *N*s given at top of table are unweighted (designated "UN").

Note: Percentages do not sum to 100 due to rounding.

*Denotes values that are less than 0.5 percent but greater than 0. *Family Status:* "Clients with Children" = client reported that at least one of his/her minor children was living with client; "Single Clients" = client reported that s/he was alone; "Other Clients" = client reported being with one or more persons, none of whom were their minor children.

[a]This includes clients who reported staying in the streets or other places not meant for human habitation (e.g., abandoned buildings, vehicles) on the day of the NSHAPC interview or during the seven days prior to the interview.

[b]This includes clients who reported staying in an emergency shelter, transitional housing program, or voucher program on the day of the NSHAPC interview or during the seven days prior to the interview, or clients who were selected for the study at one of these programs.

[c]This includes clients who reported using a soup kitchen during the seven days prior to the interview, or clients who were found and interviewed for NSHAPC at a soup kitchen.

[d]This includes clients who reported using some other program (food pantry, mobile food, outreach, drop-in center, and/or permanent housing) during the seven days prior to the interview, or clients who were found and interviewed for NSHAPC at one of these programs.

[e]This includes clients who did not report staying in an emergency shelter, transitional shelter, permanent housing, or voucher program over the last seven days but said that they had received food over the last seven days in the shelter where they live.

any other subgroup (either male other clients, or any other subgroup of women).

Major differences in the patterns of service use occurred among men in the different family statuses, and also for the different subgroups of women. Households with children, whether headed by a man or woman, were more likely than other subgroups of men or women to use shelters and/or transitional housing programs. They were less likely to have spent any time in places not meant for habitation. Further, they tended to use shelters only, and not to avail themselves of soup kitchens as much as other groups.

Among women, the subgroup of female other clients stands out as the most different. They were less likely than either of the other two subgroups to use emergency shelter or transitional housing programs. But they were more likely to have slept on the streets, to have been in contact with an outreach program, and to have avoided both shelters and soup kitchens in the past week.

These patterns indicate that if any subgroup is being better served by the system, it is families. On the other hand, single men and female other clients stand out as the two subgroups having the most marginal relationship with the homeless assistance network. Practitioners and policymakers probably need to think more of how to reach and involve these two groups.

Income, Employment, and Income Sources

Regardless of family status, homeless men reported receiving less money (had lower median income) than homeless women in the month before being interviewed for NSHAPC (table 3.5). In a similar vein, regardless of the sex of the head of household, households with children received more money than any of the other four subgroups. These findings have a lot to do with the structure of public benefit programs and their eligibility rules.

The Structure of Public Benefit Programs as It Relates to Risk of Homelessness

At the time of NSHAPC, female-headed households with minor children who were as poor as homeless families would have been eligible to receive Aid to Families with Dependent Children (AFDC),[5] a federal-

Table 3.5 *Income Levels, Income Sources, and Employment of Homeless Clients, by Family Status and Sex* (weighted percentages)

	All Currently Homeless Clients	Clients with Children		Single Clients		Other Clients	
	(UN = 2,938)	Men (UN = 58)	Women (UN = 405)	Men (UN = 1,798)	Women (UN = 444)	Men (UN = 129)	Women (UN = 101)
Mean Income from All Sources (Last 30 Days)[a]	$367	$357	$495	$345	$331	$457	$306
Median Income from All Sources (Last 30 Days)[a]	$300	$400	$437	$200	$288	$255	$300
Income from All Sources over Last 30 Days							
None	13	36	10	14	16	22	29
Less than $100	17			20	20		
$100 to $299	19	8	18	20	14	32	20
$300 to $499	18	47	49	15	21	19	46
$500 to $699	14			13	17		
$700 to $799	4	10	24	5	5	27	5
$800 to $999	5			5	2		
$1,000 to $1,199	3			4	2		
$1,200 or more	4			4	3		
Did Any Paid Work at All in Last 30 Days	44	39	27	51	27	44	48

(Continued)

Table 3.5 *Income Levels, Income Sources, and Employment of Homeless Clients, by Family Status and Sex* (*Continued*)
(weighted percentages)

		Clients with Children		*Single Clients*		*Other Clients*	
	All Currently Homeless Clients (UN = 2,938)	*Men (UN = 58)*	*Women (UN = 405)*	*Men (UN = 1,798)*	*Women (UN = 444)*	*Men (UN = 129)*	*Women (UN = 101)*
Sources of Earned Income in Last 30 Days[b]							
Job lasting 3 or more months	13	5	16	14	10	11	14
Job expected to last 3 or more months	7	2	6	7	6	11	3
Temporary job, farm work	8	*	*	4	1	2	0
Temporary job, non-farm work	3	3	4	8	6	11	26
Day job or pick-up job	14	31	2	19	2	21	4
Peddling	2	0	*	3	*	3	3
Received Money/Benefits from Government Sources in Last 30 Days							
AFDC (among families with children)	52	18	58	NA	NA	NA	NA
General Assistance	9	16	8	10	9	4	5
Supplemental Security Income	11	15	10	10	17	10	2
SSDI	8	2	3	8	13	8	18
Social Security	3	*	1	3	9	*	1
Veteran's disability payments (among veterans)	6	†	†	6	†	†	†
Veteran's pension (among veterans)	2	†	†	2	†	†	†

Food Stamps	37	59	74	30	40	15	38
Received Means-Tested Government Benefits[c]							
Any, including food stamps	45	73	80	38	49	24	43
Any other than food stamps	28	36	67	21	30	13	30
Other Sources of Income over the Last 30 Days							
Parents	9	15	15	7	7	20	3
Friends	12	3	13	11	17	6	20
Asking for money on the street	8	3	1	10	6	8	13

Source: Urban Institute analysis of weighted 1996 NSHAPC client data; *N*s given at top of table are unweighted (designated "UN").

Note: Percentages do not sum to 100 due to rounding. NA = not applicable.

*Denotes values that are less than 0.5 percent but greater than 0. † Denotes insufficient *N*. *Family Status:* "Clients with Children" = client reported that at least one of his/her minor children was living with client; "Single Clients" = client reported that s/he was alone; "Other Clients" = client reported being with one or more persons, none of whom were their minor children.

[a]If a client reported an income range rather than an exact amount, the client was assigned the midpoint of the range for the purpose of calculating the mean and median.

[b]Clients could report receiving income from more than one of these sources.

[c]Includes AFDC, GA, SSI, Food Stamps, and/or housing assistance.

state program available in and throughout every state. Very poor families with children were also a favored group to receive state or local cash assistance under such programs as General Assistance, Public Assistance, Home Relief, General Relief, and so on (hereafter referred to generically as General Assistance). Some states had statewide General Assistance programs at the time of NSHAPC. In states without a statewide program, some cities and counties had their own General Assistance program. Some states had no General Assistance program available anywhere (Uccello, McCallum, and Gallagher 1996). The actual benefit levels of both AFDC and General Assistance varied tremendously from state to state. In some states with General Assistance, its benefit levels did, and still do, vary from community to community within a state.

At the time of NSHAPC, programs available to people without children were fewer and farther between than those available to families, and this differential access has increased since then. Starting in the mid-1990s, some states began to restrict eligibility for General Assistance, often eliminating eligibility for single people or limiting it to a few months in a lifetime, or a few months out of any particular 12-month period. Single homeless people, and some singles who were not homeless, thus lost that resource.

The Food Stamp program, a federal program with nationwide eligibility rules, provides identical benefit levels throughout the country. It was, and is, the country's only universally available resource for poor people. Receipt of AFDC and SSI carried automatic rights to food stamps. Access, however, has often been a problem for homeless people (Burt and Cohen 1988), as well as for people receiving SSI but not AFDC. (The application process for AFDC usually included food stamps, as the TANF [Temporary Assistance for Needy Families] program does now, but the same was and is not true for SSI.) Shortly after the NSHAPC survey, food stamp rules changed for "able-bodied adults without dependents" (that is, single people). The effect was to limit even this resource to a few months, unless the recipient is working or engaged in work-related activity.

Supplemental Security Income (SSI), a federal program, was and is available everywhere. To qualify, however, a person has to be very poor (income below 75 percent of the federal poverty level), as well as seriously disabled and able to prove it, or at least age 65. It also helps to have the assistance of a social worker or case worker, as the application process was, and remains, arduous. At the time of NSHAPC, one could qualify for SSI with a primary diagnosis of a seriously disabling alcohol- or drug-related disorder, which has not been true from 1997 onward. This change has affected SSI eligibility for some homeless people, but was not in effect when the NSHAPC survey was done.

To summarize, getting help as a poor person from public programs was more or less possible, depending on who you were (family or single, disabled or not), where you were, and who you had to help you. To the extent that you were successful, you might have been able to assemble enough resources to avoid homelessness. But the cards were stacked against single people, and especially single men. This is certainly one of the reasons why they formed, and continue to be, such a large proportion of homeless people, especially those homeless a long time. (The general availability of Social Security for those 65 and older, coupled with Medicaid and preference for federal housing subsidies, are primary reasons why very few elderly people are found among homeless people.) The same is true today, but even fewer programs are available for single people, and AFDC has changed to a different program (Temporary Assistance for Needy Families), which is both time-limited and also places new demands on families that receive it.

NSHAPC Findings

The most striking thing about income levels of all homeless subgroups, even the best, is how low they were. Median incomes (the best measure if one is not to be misled by a few outliers with higher incomes) were $200 to $288 a month for singles, $255 to $300 a month for other clients, and only up to $400 to $437 a month for families (table 3.5). Assuming that homeless other clients were in two-person households, female-headed families in three-person households, and male-headed families in four-person households, we can calculate their income as a percent of the 1996 federal poverty level (FPL). Single homeless clients received 29 to 42 percent of the FPL for one-person households; homeless other clients received 29 to 34 percent of the FPL for two-person households. Women with children and men with children received 43 and 30 percent of the FPL for three- and four-person households, respectively. Clearly none of these income levels were sufficient for any of these homeless clients to afford housing on their own.

Forty to 50 percent of each subgroup of men reported doing some work for pay during the month before their NSHAPC interview, but day jobs or pick-up jobs were the most common, and clearly they did not yield much money. Among families, the obvious additional income source that contributed to their higher income levels was AFDC. It was received by 58 percent of women with children, compared to only 18 percent of men with children. Thus *even with* the advantage of eligibility for and receipt of cash assistance, these households remained so poor as to be homeless. In addition, women with children were marginally more likely than comparable men to have worked for pay in the last month at a job that had already lasted at least three months.

Among singles, women's greater receipt of other government benefits, such as SSI and SSDI (Social Security Disability Insurance), contributed to the difference in cash income. Among other clients, women's marginally greater participation in government benefit programs, as well as in paid employment in temporary jobs, probably contributed to the difference. Female other clients were more likely than either women with children or single women to have worked for pay in the past month. There were no differences in work activity among the male subgroups.

Physical Health and Nutrition

Numerous studies have documented the very poor health of homeless people. Some have been able to compare it to the "average" American (Institute of Medicine 1988). We cannot make comparisons to the general public, but we can confirm the high level of certain kinds of health problems among homeless people generally. We also can look at certain health conditions of different groups of homeless people. Please note that NSHAPC did not probe in detail about health conditions. In general, it asked only about conditions that people could probably describe themselves, and for which homeless people are known to be at high risk. For food insecurity and hunger, we *are* able to compare homeless people in NSHAPC to all households in the United States in 1995 with incomes below the federal poverty level. The comparison shows that homeless people in every subgroup are very much more likely to experience hunger and food insecurity.

Women with children were more likely than comparable men to report having acute infectious conditions, such as chest infections, colds, coughs, or bronchitis, but less likely to have chronic conditions related to mobility (problems walking, arthritis, joint problems) (table 3.6).

Table 3.6 *Physical Health and Nutrition Status of Homeless Clients, by Family Status and Sex*
(weighted percentages)

			Clients with Children		*Single Clients*		*Other Clients*	
	All U.S. Households below the FPL (1995)[a]	*All Currently Homeless Clients (UN = 2,938)*	*Men (UN = 58)*	*Women (UN = 405)*	*Men (UN = 1,798)*	*Women (UN = 444)*	*Men (UN = 129)*	*Women (UN = 101)*
Type of Reported Medical Conditions[b]								
Acute infectious conditions (1 or more)	—	26	11	29	25	33	24	27
Acute noninfectious conditions (1 or more)	—	8	13	8	7	8	16	11
Chronic conditions (1 or more)	—	46	51	45	43	57	63	34
Four Most Common Medical Conditions								
Arthritis, rheumatism, joint problems	—	24	28	16	22	29	49	21
Chest infection, cold, cough, bronchitis	—	22	10	28	20	29	22	26
Problem walking, lost limb, other handicap	—	14	24	6	13	25	20	3
High blood pressure	—	15	4	9	16	16	14	14
Needed But Not Able to See Doctor or Nurse in Last Year	—	24	25	27	22	26	27	36

(Continued)

Table 3.6 *Physical Health and Nutrition Status of Homeless Clients, by Family Status and Sex (Continued)*
(weighted percentages)

			Clients with Children		*Single Clients*		*Other Clients*	
	All U.S. Households below the FPL (1995)[a]	*All Currently Homeless Clients (UN = 2,938)*	*Men (UN = 58)*	*Women (UN = 405)*	*Men (UN = 1,798)*	*Women (UN = 444)*	*Men (UN = 129)*	*Women (UN = 101)*
Type of Current Medical Insurance								
Medicaid	—	30	34	67	23	37	15	31
VA Medical Care	—	7	4	*	11	*	7	0
Private insurance	—	4	1	4	4	4	5	5
No insurance	—	55	61	27	60	45	76	62
Other	—	10	1	7	8	23	1	15
Best Description of Food Situation								
Get enough of kinds of food wanted	60[d]	39	53	43	38	40	28	41
Get enough but not always what wanted	29	34	13	37	33	37	47	20
Sometimes not enough to eat	9	18	33	14	18	16	15	28
Often not enough to eat	3	10	1	6	12	6	10	11
In the Last 30 Days, Went a Whole Day without Anything to Eat	3[e]	40	37	40	40	35	61	39
In Last 30 Days, Hungry but Did Not Have Enough Money for Food	5[e]	39	33	22	41	31	61	35

Current Food Problems[c]								
None	—	42	50	45	40	54	20	44
One	—	20	19	24	20	13	21	20
Two	—	17	6	20	16	16	33	12
Three	—	13	25	4	16	11	16	10
Four	—	8	0	6	8	7	10	14

Source: Urban Institute analysis of weighted 1996 NSHAPC client data; *N*s given at top of table are unweighted (designated "UN").

Note: Percentages do not sum to 100 due to rounding.

*Denotes values that are less than 0.5 percent but greater than 0. *Family Status:* "Clients with Children" = client reported that at least one of his/her minor children was living with client; "Single Clients" = client reported that s/he was alone; "Other Clients" = client reported being with one or more persons, none of whom were their minor children.

[a]Data for U.S. households below the federal poverty level taken from the Current Population Survey Food Security Supplement, April 1995, table 1 (Food and Consumer Service 1999).

[b]Conditions asked about include diabetes, anemia, high blood pressure, heart disease/stroke, liver problems, arthritis/rheumatism, chest infection/cold/bronchitis, pneumonia, tuberculosis, skin diseases, lice/scabies, cancer, problems walking/other handicap, STDs (other than AIDS), HIV, AIDS, intravenous drugs, and other.

[c]Each of the following counted as one food problem: sometimes or often not having enough to eat; eating once or less per day; in the last 30 days client was hungry but did not eat because s/he could not afford enough food; and in the last 30 days client went at least one whole day without anything to eat.

[d]*N* associated with these data is 877.

[e]*N* associated with these data is 6,653.

Women with children were much more likely than men with children to report participation in the Medicaid program, and therefore less likely to say they did not have any medical insurance. The high level of these women's participation in Medicaid (and also in the Food Stamp program, as noted in table 3.5) stemmed from their high likelihood of receiving AFDC, and the automatic eligibility it carried in 1996 for both Medicaid and food stamps.

About half of both types of families reported one or more problems getting enough to eat, the only difference being how many problems they reported. Both types of families also were significantly less likely than the poor, housed population to report that they got enough of the kinds of food they wanted. They were very much more likely to report that in the past 30 days they had been hungry but did not have enough money for food (33 and 22 percent for homeless men and women with children, respectively, versus 5 percent for poor, housed people), and had gone at least one day without eating because they did not have the money to obtain food (37 and 40 percent, versus 3 percent of poor, housed people). Thus, even homeless households with the most resources, two-thirds of which had food stamps to help them, suffered significant food problems.

Among singles, women reported more chronic conditions than men, especially problems walking and other physical disabilities. They were more likely than men to have Medicaid (probably stemming from their participation in SSI) or other insurance (probably Medicare stemming from their participation in SSDI), and thus less likely to report having no health insurance at all. Single men reported a unique source of medical insurance (and presumably medical care), the Veterans Administration.

Single women were less likely than single men to report one or more problems getting enough to eat, but 46 percent still had at least one such problem. Single men and single women were equally likely to say they had been hungry or gone a day without eating in the past 30 days because they did not have enough money for food. As with all the subgroups, their responses indicated much greater problems with getting enough food than the nation's poor, housed population.

Among homeless other clients, men rather than women reported more chronic conditions, including arthritis, rheumatism, joint problems, problems walking, and other handicaps. Male other clients were marginally less likely than female other clients to have Medicaid, and much less likely to have other medical insurance. A few (7 percent) did, however, have access to VA medical care, which was not true for any female other clients. They also reported more food problems.

Among the three groups of homeless men, male other clients are the most "different." They had more chronic health problems than single men, in particular arthritis and other joint problems. This is true despite being younger, on average, than single men (21 versus 5 percent are 24 or younger; 40 versus 25 percent are 34 or younger). They were also less likely than single men to have any medical insurance. They were more likely than either other group of men to have one or more food problems. In particular, they had been hungry and had gone at least one day without eating in the past month because they did not have money to buy food.

Among the three groups of women, the patterns are more complex. Single women reported more chronic health conditions than female other clients, despite not being significantly older. Women with children were more likely than those in the other two groups to have Medicaid, and, therefore, less likely to report being without health insurance. There were no important differences in the proportion of women in each subgroup who had food problems.

The levels of health and food problems among homeless people, the finding that at least one-fourth of each subgroup had needed to see a doctor in the past year but could not afford it, the low levels of medical insurance among subgroups without children, and, finally, the difficulties that even homeless households with the most resources had in getting enough to eat, all attest to the severe deprivation of homelessness in at least as telling a way as the absence of housing. It is very likely that these households had been "going without" for some time before they became homeless, and that even the loss of housing and its associated costs did not free sufficient income to meet other needs. Basically, the levels of poverty reported by all subgroups were so high that most necessities of life were out of reach.

Childhood Experiences

A great deal of research has now documented associations between many childhood difficulties and adult homelessness (see chapters 4 and 8). These childhood experiences include school problems, abuse and neglect by a caretaker, being placed in foster care or other settings outside the home, running away from or being forced out of one's home, and being, in fact, homeless. We therefore examine subgroup differences on these factors both here and later in other, descriptive chapters. As will be clear, NSHAPC found the same patterns.

School Problems

Problems in school are a sign of other potential problems among adolescents (Burt, Resnick and Novick 1998), that in turn may become risk factors for a wide variety of adverse conditions of adulthood, ranging from low earning capacity to homelessness. Many homeless clients in NSHAPC reported problems in school, including repeating a grade (25 percent), which may indicate academic problems; being suspended (44 percent) or expelled (18 percent), which may indicate behavior problems; and dropping out (53 percent), which may indicate both academic and behavior problems (table 3.7). No differences appeared in grade repetition or school dropout between men and women *within* any of the family statuses. But male other clients were more likely than single men to have repeated a grade and to have dropped out at some time, and female other clients were more likely than women with children to have repeated a grade.

There were also gender differences within family statuses with respect to being suspended or expelled. More men than women with children reported both experiences, and more single men than single women reported being expelled. In addition, men with children were marginally more likely than single men to report being suspended.

Abuse and Neglect during Childhood

The final panels of table 3.7 describe homeless client reports of abuse and neglect by a childhood caretaker. These include being left without adequate food or shelter (neglect), being beaten or otherwise physically abused, and being forced or pressured to perform sexual acts (sexual abuse). Ample evidence exists that childhood abuse has long-lasting negative consequences (Bassuk et al. 1997; English 1998), including reduced ability to maintain healthy and nonabusive relationships and a higher likelihood of spending time as a child in foster care. Both of these possible consequences have obvious implications for a person's vulnerability to homelessness. We saw earlier that abuse and violence were

Table 3.7 *Adverse Experiences of Homeless Clients, by Family Status and Sex*
(weighted percentages)

	All Currently Homeless Clients (UN = 2,938)	Clients with Children: Men (UN = 58)	Clients with Children: Women (UN = 405)	Single Clients: Men (UN = 1,798)	Single Clients: Women (UN = 444)	Other Clients: Men (UN = 129)	Other Clients: Women (UN = 101)
Adverse Experiences Occurring before Client Reached Age 18							
Received less than high school degree	38	54	53	34	44	29	35
Repeated a grade							
One grade	25	32	17	24	25	51	39
More than one grade	6	6	9	7	5	3	4
Dropped out of school							
Elementary school	2	*	2	2	1	*	*
Junior high/middle school	8	9	11	7	7	8	6
Senior high school	43	56	43	40	46	61	50
Was suspended from school	44	67	32	45	38	55	47
Was expelled from school	18	35	14	21	11	18	13
Someone client lived with							
Left client without adequate food or shelter	12	18	12	12	12	7	25
Physically abused client, to cause physical harm	22	10	24	19	30	29	30
Forced or pressured client to perform sexual acts that client did not want to do	13	5	23	8	27	1	22
Abuse/neglect combinations							
Physical and/or sexual abuse but not neglect	25	10	30	21	37	29	32
One or more abuse/neglect experiences	29	23	31	25	39	32	33

Source: Urban Institute analysis of weighted 1996 NSHAPC client data; *N*s given at top of table are unweighted (designated "UN").
Note: Percentages do not sum to 100 due to rounding.
*Denotes values that are less than 0.5 percent but greater than 0. *Family Status:* "Clients with Children" = client reported that at least one of his/her minor children was living with client; "Single Clients" = client reported that s/he was alone; "Other Clients" = client reported being with one or more persons, none of whom were their minor children.

among homeless women's most important reasons for leaving their most-recent home. Other studies (Koegel, Melamid, and Burnam 1995; Mangine, Royse, and Wiehe 1990; Piliavin, Sosin, and Westerfelt 1993; Shinn et al. 1998; Susser, Struening, and Conover 1987; Susser et al. 1991; Wood et al. 1990) have identified childhood out-of-home placement in foster care as a common experience of homeless people. They also have noted that it occurs among homeless people at a much higher rate than among the population in general, of whom 3.4 percent are estimated to have spent time in foster care as children (Royse and Wiehe 1989). It is important to document these experiences, so we may learn more about these early separations from family, and the ways that lack of any family support after age 18 (when one has to leave foster care), may increase a young person's risk of homelessness. In addition, the familial neglect and abuse that lead to removing a child from its parental home are risk factors in and of themselves.

In NSHAPC, one in four homeless clients reported being physically and/or sexually abused as a child by someone with whom they lived. Many experienced both problems and, with the addition of neglect, a total of 29 percent had been exposed to one or more circumstances of abuse and neglect before age 18. With respect to neglect, gender groups differed only among other clients, with female other clients reporting higher levels than male other clients. For physical abuse, single women reported significantly more than single men, and women with children reported marginally more than men with children, but there were no differences between male and female other clients. Women in all family statuses reported more childhood sexual abuse than men. When the different forms of abuse, or abuse and neglect, are combined, women showed higher rates than men among singles and those with children, but not among other clients. Finally, male other clients reported marginally more physical abuse than men with children. No other within-gender comparisons are significant.

Out-of-Home Experiences in Childhood and Later

With such levels of abuse and neglect, we should not be surprised that many currently homeless people came under the purview of one or more societal institutions, such as child protective services or juvenile justice agencies. Such experiences are also frequently the stimulus for running away from home or being forced to leave before adulthood. In addition, such a variety of difficulties may have made currently homeless people more vulnerable to the criminal justice system as adults.

Overall, 26 percent of homeless clients had ever been removed from their home and placed in a foster home, group home, or institution (table 3.8), compared to 3.4 percent of all American adults (Royse and Wiehe 1989). For 15 percent, this occurred before they were 13 years old; for 20 percent, between the ages of 13 and 17, with about 1 in 10 homeless clients experiencing out-of-home placements during both periods. In addition, 16 percent had spent time in the juvenile justice system before they were 18 (which they may also have reported as an "institution" when asked whether they had ever spent time in foster care, a group home, or an institution, as part of the question about out-of-home placement).

In general, men and women in all three family statuses reported the same levels of out-of-home placement, although there were minor variations in the type of facility where the placement occurred. Among those with children, women were more likely than men to have been removed before they were teenagers. Among other clients, women were more likely than men to experience out-of-home placement as teenagers, and also more likely to report that this placement was in an institution (indicating the possibility of more serious disturbance or illness).

There were no differences among the three subgroups of men in the incidence, nature, or timing of their out-of-home placements. Among the three subgroups of women, female other clients were more likely than either women with children or single women to have been removed from home before age 18. This removal was also more likely to have happened while the women were teenagers, and to have resulted in institutional placement rather than residence in foster care or a group home.

In addition to being placed in various settings through the child welfare system, 16 percent of the homeless clients in NSHAPC had been involved with the juvenile justice system. Single men were more likely than single women to have spent some time in juvenile detention (18 versus 10 percent); the same is true for male other clients in comparison to female other clients (30 versus 11 percent). There were no differences among the three male subgroups, or among the three female subgroups.

The time spent in out-of-home placement may make a big difference for one's ability to maintain ties with family and to "have a place to go home to." Men with children who had any out-of-home placement stand out among all the homeless subgroups, including women with children,

Table 3.8 *Childhood Out-of-Home Experiences of Homeless Clients, by Family Status and Sex*

(weighted percentages)

		Clients with Children		*Single Clients*		*Other Clients*	
	All Currently Homeless Clients (UN = 2,938)	*Men (UN = 58)*	*Women (UN = 405)*	*Men (UN = 1,798)*	*Women (UN = 444)*	*Men (UN = 129)*	*Women (UN = 101)*
Before Age 18, Ever Placed In							
Foster care, group home, or institution	26	28	25	23	28	34	48
Foster care	12	1	13	10	19	7	12
Group home	10	6	12	9	13	13	13
Institution	16	26	14	13	13	30	38
Before Age 13, Ever Placed In							
Foster care, group home, or institution	15	1	13	14	18	20	17
Foster care	9	1	10	9	15	6	3
Group home	6	*	9	5	8	13	10
Institution	6	*	4	6	6	16	8
Between Ages 13 and 17, Ever Placed In							
Foster care, group home, or institution	20	27	21	18	23	18	43
Foster care	8	1	10	7	14	2	9
Group home	8	6	10	7	10	3	13
Institution	13	26	11	11	12	15	35
Juvenile Detention before Age 18	16	14	11	18	10	30	11

Length of Time Lived Away from Home before Age 18[a]							
Less than 1 week	3	0	1	3	*	0	9
1 to 4 weeks	7	61	3	6	7	6	0
1 to 6 months	15	17	12	12	8	3	56
7 to 12 months	12	1	20	8	10	45	1
13 to 24 months	13	0	3	15	15	10	15
More than 2 years	52	22	61	56	60	36	19
Ever Ran Away from Home for More than 24 Hours before Age 18	33	27	37	28	34	50	65
Ever Forced to Leave Home for More than 24 Hours before Age 18	22	13	29	20	23	31	22
First Time Became Homeless Occurred before Age 18	21	21	29	19	22	22	29
History of Incarceration as Adult							
5 or more days in a city or county jail	49	51	15	61	27	74	15
5 or more days in a military jail/lock-up	4	5	0	5	*	4	0
State or federal prison	18	27	1	24	10	20	6
Spent Time Incarcerated (including as juvenile)	54	63	23	66	33	76	21

Source: Urban Institute analysis of weighted 1996 NSHAPC client data; *N*s given at top of table are unweighted (designated "UN").

Note: Percentages do not sum to 100 due to rounding.

*Denotes values that are less than 0.5 percent but greater than 0. *Family Status:* "Clients with Children" = client reported that at least one of his/her minor children was living with client; "Single Clients" = client reported that s/he was alone; "Other Clients" = client reported being with one or more persons, none of whom were their minor children.

[a]Among homeless clients who spent time in foster care, a group home, or an institution before they were 18 years old.

as having the highest proportion reporting very short stays (61 percent had stays of four weeks or less, compared to 4 to 9 percent of the other five subgroups). They were also far less likely than women with children or single men and women to report stays of a year or more. Most women with children and male and female singles who had any out-of-home placement as a child spent at least a year there (indeed, more than half had stays of two years or more).

There is more than one way to be severed from one's home as a child. One in three currently homeless people had run away before their 18th birthday, and 22 percent had been forced to leave. In addition, 21 percent reported that their first period of homelessness, which may have been with their family or on their own, began before they reached age 18. Within family statuses, men and women did not differ from each other on any of these experiences. However, other clients of both sexes were more likely to report running away than the remaining two groups of the same sex.

One would suspect, all other things being equal, that childhood experiences involving alienation or actual separation from parents and family as a result of abuse or neglect would leave a person without many of the social ties that can tide one over in times of great stress. One result could easily be an increased vulnerability to homelessness. As expected, these factors do, indeed, help predict homeless experiences in our analysis in chapter 8.

Incarceration

NSHAPC asked clients about any incarceration experiences, including local jails or lock-ups, military lock-ups, and state and federal prisons. In the case of jails and lock-ups, people were asked only whether they had spent five or more days at a time. The study wanted to be sure it was learning about incarceration from "normal" criminal activity, rather than from status offenses, such as loitering, that are associated with homelessness itself. Status offenses rarely generate jail time longer than a couple of days, so they should not have been reported in response to the NSHAPC questions.

Men reported rates of incarceration that were at least twice as high as women's, in every family status. These results are true for jail time, implying misdemeanors. At least three in five homeless men have spent five or more days at a time in jail. The difference in rates for men and women are even more extreme for incarceration in state or federal prison, which usually does not happen until a person has committed several felony offenses. At least one in five men has spent time in a state or federal prison. The implication is that many homeless men have engaged in significant levels of criminal behavior, regardless of whether they have also spent time in jail for status offenses associated with homelessness.

Concluding Thoughts

This analysis of NSHAPC's homeless sample shows the extreme diversity of people homeless at a particular point in time. In this, NSHAPC results support earlier findings (Rosenheck, Bassuk, and Salomon 1999). For virtually every characteristic, other than extreme poverty, the common denominator of homelessness, it is rare for half, or even one-third, of homeless clients to have the characteristic in common. Even factors thought to be strongly associated with the probability of homelessness, such as childhood abuse or neglect and out-of-home placement, characterize only about one-quarter of homeless people. Clearly this level of diversity, and the widely varying points of vulnerability to homelessness, given extreme poverty, belie the ideas of a "homeless population," or simple solutions to homelessness.

The conditions of homelessness reported by NSHAPC clients appear to be quite dire for all subgroups. Families are the most "cared-for" by the system of homeless assistance programs, yet even they reported far higher levels of hunger and food insecurity than the housed, poor population. In keeping with the philosophical underpinnings of American assistance to poor people (discussed in chapter 11), children may be perceived as the most "blameless" of homeless people, and therefore most deserving of support. Since the children are accompanied by one or both parents, the homeless family as a whole is the unit receiving assistance. In addition to being perceived as "deserving," homeless families also may be perceived as least likely to cause "trouble" for providers. Disproportionate shares of transitional housing resources are devoted to homeless households with children, and emergency shelters geared to serving families often afford the most "home-like," comfortable, and private accommodations.

One may ask whether this investment is reasonable. From the point of view of investment, families present two faces to a homeless service system. First, there is much evidence that many families who become homeless have very short spells of homelessness, but that many very poor families may experience homelessness during the course of a year. Our own analyses in chapter 2 also confirm this pattern. This suggests that some experience of homelessness among extremely poor families may have become so common that it is a fact of life, rather than something to be expected among those with disabilities.

Second, however, because many transitional housing programs have been developed for families, families in such programs prolong their literal homelessness by their attachment to such a program. This may be an important reason why families report spells of homelessness lasting more than a year. Any community with a major investment in transitional housing for homeless families will have a disproportionate share of occupants with long spells. Instead, taking care of the "worst-case" housing needs of the nation as a whole probably would go a long way toward reducing the necessity for many of these families to seek homeless assistance at all (Shinn and Baumohl 1999).

Although male-headed homeless families in the NSHAPC sample were so few that conclusions may be risky, they may actually be worse off than female-headed families. Two-parent homeless families are generally treated in the media as the most "like us," the most "normal," and the least "typically homeless" of all types of homeless households. They are often held up, in the abstract, as examples of "if it could happen to them, it could happen to anyone." This argument is used commonly to generate concern about homelessness and support for homeless services. Yet the NSHAPC picture of men with children is not encouraging, even though they mostly did represent two-parent (or at least two-adult) families. As a subgroup, they had quite low educational attainment, showed other problems with school, had low per-person earnings, worked infrequently, and were very likely to have criminal histories. This is quite different from the image that is sometimes imposed on two-adult homeless families with children.

After families, one might think that women would be the next most cared-for by a homeless service system, if one subscribed to cultural beliefs about men being presumed able, and even obliged, to take care of themselves. We have seen some signs of this orientation, in that single women were more likely to use shelters than single men, and less likely to sleep on the streets. However, the same was not true for female other clients compared to male other clients.

Clients who were homeless with another adult were the least likely to receive services from homeless assistance programs, possibly because shelters are not structured to allow two adults of the opposite sex to stay together, unless they can be treated as a family (i.e., unless they have children with them). Female other clients stood out as the most reclusive among the subgroups of women. They were the most likely to have slept on the streets and to have avoided both shelters and soup kitchens in the week before their interview. Also intriguing is why, among homeless other clients, women who were "with" someone else were so different from men who were "with" someone else. One might have assumed, in contrast, that they would most likely be "with" each other, since the great majority of both subgroups (65 percent of male other clients and 75 percent of female other clients) said they were with a spouse or partner. Spouses and intimate partners usually share quite a few similarities. Yet from simple demographic characteristics, such as race and urban/rural location, to homeless histories, reasons for homelessness, service use, level of hunger, and nature and extent of childhood problems, male and female other clients were significantly different. NSHAPC data cannot really resolve this conundrum, but it is an interesting interpretive question for future research.

The results pertaining to the level and variety of current and childhood problems focus only on people who were actually homeless at the time of the NSHAPC survey. So it may be wondered whether they should be considered "normal" for all poor people, or perhaps indicative of particular issues only with people who have become homeless. Chapter 8 addresses these issues, looking at differences among currently, formerly, and never-homeless clients of homeless assistance programs to sort out factors associated with ever having been homeless and being currently homeless. Suffice it to say, here, that rates of most current and childhood problems discussed in this chapter are significantly higher for people who are or have been homeless than for people who have not, but still are poor enough to need programs such as soup kitchens.

NOTES

1. This was for March 1987, and showed the characteristics of people who were homeless then, just as NSHAPC is for October/November 1996 and reflects the characteristics of the people who were homeless then. Remember that homelessness is a very transient state for many people. There is no static "homeless population," but rather an ever-changing set of people who happen to be homeless when a research study tries to contact them. The characteristics of the "population" at a single point in time will reflect the circumstances of the long-term homeless more than if we could look at all the people who experience homelessness over an extended period such as a year.
2. We reserve the topics of alcohol, drug, and mental health problems and treatment for chapter 4, where we go into the relevant issues more thoroughly.
3. All differences between percentages mentioned in the text without qualification are significant at $p < .05$. Any difference described as "marginal" meets the criterion of $p < .10$. Since the size of several subsamples used in the analysis for this chapter is quite small, seemingly large percentage-point differences still may not be statistically significant.
4. This finding may reflect the movement of homeless people to locations where they hope to find jobs and/or services, as much as it represents any tendency of central cities to *generate* homelessness at substantially greater rates than other parts of the country.
5. NSHAPC was conducted in 1996, when AFDC was still the federal welfare program for families with children.

4

Effects of Alcohol, Drug, and Mental Health Problems on Characteristics and Circumstances of Homeless People

Policymakers and the general public over the years have paid a great deal of attention to the personal problems of alcohol and drug use and mental health problems that routinely surface among samples of homeless people. In addition, since the passage of the Stewart B. McKinney Act in 1987, a great deal of federal and other money has been devoted to developing and maintaining services for homeless people with these difficulties.

As long ago as the 19th century, writers on homelessness were taking pains to differentiate homeless people on the basis of their "worthiness" or "deservingness," as we discuss at greater length in chapter 11. Help, if any was available, would go to those who epitomized American values of hard work and whose reduced circumstances had occurred through no fault of their own. Drinking and drug use were always cited as indicators of "unworthiness," and suspicion attached to any group of homeless people until they could prove themselves members of the "deserving poor." Mental illness was a more anomalous condition, since it could not be attributed to willfulness on the part of those suffering from it. But as homeless people with mental illness behaved often in frightening ways, and often added substance abuse to their mental and emotional problems, they, too, were a difficult group for which to garner sympathy and support.

Perceptions and beliefs about alcohol, drug, and mental health (ADM) problems among homeless people are generally biased upward. They correspond to a general American suspiciousness of homeless people and a tendency to look for conditions of *individuals* on which to lay responsibility for their circumstances, rather than conditions of society, or their interaction. This tendency is reflected in reports of homelessness throughout the 19th and 20th centuries. As Rossi (1989, p. 32) notes, most such reports indicated that only 20 to 30 percent of skid row dwellers or other transient populations were alcoholic. Yet the reports speak of the *population* as alcoholic and focus on alcoholism as the primary reality of the group as a whole. Even homeless people may be at pains to dissociate themselves from the image of the "drunken bum," as Baumohl's (1989) descriptions reveal of everything from the pronouncements of organizers of 19th-century labor actions to opinions of people interviewed on the streets today. The tendency to reify homelessness and ADM problems is exacerbated by most modern reports of homeless people being based on cross-sectional rather than longitudinal data. Further, it reflects the rather strong biases of such data toward the characteristics of the long-term homeless, who tend to have more such problems. Koegel, Burnam, and Baumohl (1996) and Rosenheck, Bassuk, and Salomon (1999) summarize the results of recent studies using reasonably scientific methodologies, but, still, cross-sectional data. They indicate that about half the people homeless at any given time have had problems with alcohol some time in their lives, about one-third have had problems with drugs, and between one-fifth and one-fourth have a diagnosable, major mental illness such as schizophrenia, depression, or bipolar disorder. If the definition of "mental illness" is expanded to include other, less severe, problems, the prevalence rate increases. But, even so, it never encompasses the whole population.

When one considers that not everyone who has had a problem at one time still has it, and that cross-sectional data oversample long-term homeless people (and therefore overestimate serious disabilities), then claims such as those made by Baum and Burnes (1993) or White (1992), that homelessness and ADM problems are virtually synonymous, are seriously exaggerated. On the other hand, while it is likely that only a minority of the people homeless at any given time have had, at some time, the particular problem under consideration, there also is no question that rates of these problems in homeless people are substantially higher than in the general adult population.

The NSHAPC data reported in this chapter reveal the same basic results found in other cross-sectional studies. The NSHAPC rates may actually be a bit higher, because NSHAPC did not use instrumentation, such as the Diagnostic Interview Survey, that is capable of classifying responses into valid diagnostic categories. Thus the NSHAPC designations are based on somewhat looser criteria. This is especially so in the case of mental health problems, where the NSHAPC category includes problems of lesser magnitude than schizophrenia, depression, and bipolar disorder. High rates of ADM problems already have been reported for the NSHAPC survey in the federal report covering basic cross-sectional survey results (Burt et al. 1999). They will be described in more detail here.[1]

There is no point denying serious ADM problems among people who experience homelessness. The real question, from a policy perspective, must be why these problems lead to *homelessness*. Yet that question cannot be answered without also considering both extreme poverty and the absence of sustained and meaningful public programs to ameliorate the combined effects of disability and poverty.

This chapter first examines variations in the existence of ADM problems by the subgroups based on sex and family status used in chapter 3. It also uses data from the 1996 National Household Survey on Drug Abuse (NHSDA) to compare the level of problems among homeless people to the housed, adult population of the United States. Thereafter, it divides the sample of homeless clients into five subgroups based on patterns of ADM problems. Everyone in the sample is in one, and only one, of the five subgroups, making them mutually exclusive and exhaustive. The chapter looks at how these subgroups differ, both from each other and the sample as a whole, on important dimensions of demographics, homeless histories and patterns, employment and income variables, physical health and eating patterns, and other selected variables. No question exists that levels of ADM problems are high among homeless clients in general. But about one in four homeless clients did not report any recent (past year) experience with any of them. Such a level belies the perception that all homeless people suffer from ADM problems. Additional subgroups exist for members recently experiencing only one problem (e.g., only with alcohol, or only mental health problems). As with other perspectives on homeless people, a close look at ADM problems reveals the great diversity of homeless people, and challenges attempts to reduce ADM problems to simple causes or simple solutions.

Defining Alcohol/Drug/Mental Health Status

The NSHAPC survey contained a number of questions pertaining to alcohol and drug use, negative consequences of use, and treatment. It also contained many questions focusing on symptoms of emotional or mental problems and treatment for them. Even with these various questions, however, the NSHAPC instrument did not obtain enough information to confirm any actual diagnoses or conditions in a medical or psychiatric sense. For this reason, we always refer to ADM *problems*, rather than to alcohol*ism*, drug *abuse*, or mental *illness*, which connote formal diagnoses. Nevertheless, the study did gather significant information on clients' experiences with ADM problems, and we use it in this and other chapters to provide insights into homeless histories and current circumstances.

Responses to relevant NSHAPC questions were combined to create three variables each for alcohol, drug, and mental health problems. The three variables reflect different time periods during which a client might have had the problem: within the 30 days of being interviewed for NSHAPC (past month), within the year before the interview (past year), and over the person's lifetime (lifetime). Presence of each problem within the three time periods was defined as follows.

> Clients were classified as having a *past month alcohol use problem* if *any* of the following conditions were met: (1) they scored 0.17 or higher on a modified Addiction Severity Index[2] (ASI) measure, (2) they reported drinking to get drunk three or more times a week within the past month, (3) they reported being treated for alcohol abuse within the past month, or (4) they reported ever having been treated for alcohol abuse *and* drinking three or more times a week within the past month. Clients were classified as having a *past year alcohol use problem* if they met these same criteria within the past year (including the past month), and as having a *lifetime alcohol use problem* if they met these same criteria in their lifetime, or if they reported ever having had three or more of the following eight alcohol-related difficulties at some time: passing out, blackouts,

tremors, convulsions, not being able to stop drinking when they wanted to, problems with close family members due to drinking, arrests because of behavior due to drinking, and attending an Alcoholics Anonymous meeting.

Clients were classified as having a *past month drug use problem* if *any* of the following conditions were met: (1) they scored 0.10 or higher on a modified ASI measure, (2) they reported being treated for drug abuse within the past month, (3) they reported using drugs intravenously (shooting up), or (4) they reported using any of the usual variety of specific illicit drugs three or more times a week within the past month. Clients were classified as having a *past year drug use problem* if they met these same criteria within the past year (including the past month), and as having a *lifetime drug use problem* if they met these same criteria in their lifetime, or if they reported three or more of the following eight drug-related problems at some time in their lives: using more than one drug at a time, blackouts or flashbacks, had friends or relatives know or suspect respondent of using drugs, lost friends because of respondent's drug use, neglected family or missed work because of drug use, had withdrawal symptoms, engaged in illegal activities to get money for drugs, or had medical problems as a result of drug use (e.g., hepatitis, convulsions, bleeding).

Clients were classified as having a *past month mental health problem* if *any* of the following conditions were met: (1) they scored 0.25 or higher on a modified ASI measure, (2) they reported receiving treatment or counseling or being hospitalized for emotional or mental problems within the past month, (3) they reported taking prescribed medications for psychological or emotional problems within the past month, (4) they reported that a mental health condition was the single most important thing keeping them from getting out of homelessness, or (5) they reported receiving treatment or counseling or being hospitalized for emotional or mental problems at some point in their lives *and* having one or more of the ASI's seven emotional or psychological conditions within the past month (serious depression; serious anxiety or tension; hallucinations; trouble understanding, concentrating, or remembering; trouble controlling violent behavior; serious thoughts of suicide; attempted suicide).[3] Clients were classified as having a *past year mental health problem* if they met these same criteria within the past year (including the past month), and as having a *lifetime mental health problem* if they met these same criteria in their lifetime or if they reported ever having stayed in an adult group home, crisis residence, or other housing for the mentally ill.

ADM Problems in the Whole Sample of Homeless Clients

Before looking at differences based on clients' family status and sex, we present a quick overview of ADM problems for the entire group of homeless clients. The relevant information may be found in the first column of table 4.1. This table reports information for three different time periods (past month, past year, and lifetime). For each, it reports the proportion of homeless clients who reported alcohol problems, drug problems, and mental health problems. For the past month, one-fourth of all homeless clients reported a problem with drugs, and close to two in five reported both alcohol and mental health problems. These rates were somewhat higher for the past year, and dramatically higher over the clients' lifetimes. About three in five reported problems in each area during their lifetime.

The proportions of clients reporting each type of problem sum to more than 100 percent, because many clients reported more than one type of problem. There also were clients who did not report any problems. To understand the co-occurrence of problems and also their absence, the entire sample was divided into five groups based on the presence or absence of problems. The five groups, which are mutually exclusive and exhaustive (each client is in one and only one group) are no ADM problems; alcohol use problems only; drug use problems, with or without co-occurring alcohol use problems but *without* co-occurring mental health problems; mental health problems only; and mental health problems *with co-occurring* alcohol and/or drug use problems. This division was done for each time period (table 4.1).

The proportion of clients who had one or more ADM problems was high (66 percent) for the past month (that is, 34 percent did not report any problems), and reached 86 percent for their lifetimes. As the time period increases, the proportion of clients reporting only one problem decreases, and the proportion reporting combinations increases. For lifetime problems, 47 percent reported mental health problems

Table 4.1 *Alcohol, Drug, and Mental Health Problems among Homeless Clients, by Family Status and Sex*

		Clients with Children		*Single Clients*		*Other Clients*	
	All Currently Homeless Clients (UN = 2,938)	*Men* (UN = 58)	*Women* (UN = 405)	*Men* (UN = 1,798)	*Women* (UN = 444)	*Men* (UN = 129)	*Women* (UN = 101)
Problems in Past Month							
Alcohol problems	38	11	19	48	26	31	17
Drug problems	26	13	22	29	19	34	17
Mental health problems	39	35	36	39	51	25	34
Grouped by Co-Occurrence of Problems[a]							
No ADM problems	34	56	50	27	36	40	52
Alcohol problem only	13	9	3	18	5	11	7
Drug problem with or without alcohol problem	14	*	11	16	8	24	8
Mental health problem only	17	20	21	13	33	5	22
Mental health with alcohol and/or drug problems	23	15	15	25	19	21	12
Problems in Past Year							
Alcohol problems	46	41	23	55	31	58	20
Drug problems	38	24	27	42	29	46	29
Mental health problems	45	37	44	45	56	29	40
Grouped by Co-Occurrence of Problems[a]							
No ADM problems	26	34	42	20	32	29	40
Alcohol problem only	12	18	3	16	5	11	7

(Continued)

Table 4.1 *Alcohol, Drug, and Mental Health Problems among Homeless Clients, by Family Status and Sex (Continued)*

	All Currently Homeless Clients (UN = 2,938)	*Clients with Children*		*Single Clients*		*Other Clients*	
		Men (UN = 58)	*Women (UN = 405)*	*Men (UN = 1,798)*	*Women (UN = 444)*	*Men (UN = 129)*	*Women (UN = 101)*
Drug problem with or without alcohol problem	17	11	13	20	7	31	13
Mental health problem only	15	20	22	10	30	5	21
Mental health with alcohol and/or drug problems	31	17	22	36	27	23	19
Problems in Lifetime							
Alcohol problems	62	54	40	73	43	69	35
Drug problems	58	72	46	64	43	71	33
Mental health problems	57	53	54	53	65	65	72
Grouped by Co-Occurrence of Problems[a]							
No ADM problems	14	22	28	10	23	12	8
Alcohol problem only	9	3	3	12	3	6	9
Drug problem with or without alcohol problem	21	22	15	26	10	18	11
Mental health problem only	10	1	18	4	23	3	44
Mental health with alcohol and/or drug problems	47	52	36	50	42	62	28

Source: Urban Institute analysis of weighted 1996 NSHAPC client data; *N*s given at top of table are unweighted (designated "UN").

Note: Percentages may not sum to 100 due to rounding.

*Denotes values that are less than 0.5 percent but greater than 0. *Family Status:* "Clients with Children" = client reported that at least one of his/her minor children was living with the homeless client; "Single Clients" = client reported that s/he was alone; "Other Clients" = client reported being with one or or more persons, none of whom were their own minor children.

[a]These five categories are mutually exclusive and exhaustive, and sum to 100; everyone in the sample appears in one and only one category.

accompanied by either alcohol problems, drug problems, or both. This doubled the rate of 23 percent reporting these problem combinations during the shortest period, the month before being interviewed.

ADM Problems among Men and Women Heads of Families, Singles, and Other Clients

Most of this chapter will focus on the characteristics of subgroups defined by their pattern of ADM problems. But before that, we present the pattern in the basic family status/sex subgroups used in chapter 3. This provides an overview of the types of homeless people who are most likely to experience these problems. We examine differences between men and women within each family status, and then explore differences among men in the three family statuses and women in the three family statuses (table 4.1).[4] This information will be most useful to practitioners designing service structures within particular programs, and to planners making decisions about overall community service needs.

Men and women with children were almost entirely similar with respect to any ADM problem, at any time period. Only for lifetime problems did any distinction occur, with men reporting significantly higher levels than women of problems with drugs. Although men and women with children were equally likely to report lifetime mental health problems, men were much less likely than women to have had *only* mental health problems in their lifetime. Their problems with drugs and alcohol were more likely to place them in a category showing combined problems with mental health and drugs and/or alcohol.

Men and women single clients, in contrast, differed on *every* type of problem and problem combination, during *every* time period. The differences are entirely consistent across time periods: Men reported more problems with alcohol and drugs; women reported more mental health problems. Single men were more likely than single women to report at least one ADM problem for the past year and lifetime periods, but not for the past month. Women were more likely in every time period to report having *only* mental health problems; men were more likely to report all combinations that included alcohol and/or drug problems.

Among male and female other clients, women were always higher in the mental health–only category. For the past month and past year periods, men had higher rates of drug problems with or without accompanying alcohol problems but without mental health problems. However, over their lifetimes, they also added mental health problems, so they had higher rates than women on the lifetime combination of alcohol and/or drugs with mental health problems (62 versus 23 percent).

When we look at the three groups of men, the only differences occur for past month problems. For this period, single men reported more problems with alcohol than either men with children or male other clients, while men in families reported lower rates than either single men or male other clients for drug problems with or without accompanying alcohol problems. However, for the one year and lifetime periods, all differences disappear.

Among women, no differences among the three groups exist for past month and past year problems, but some do appear over their lifetimes. Female other clients stand out, reporting marginally more lifetime mental health problems than the other two groups, and a greater likelihood of having *only* mental health problems. In addition, they also were less likely than either women with children or single women to report no ADM problems.

The picture that emerges, to generalize a bit, is that mental health issues stand out among women, and alcohol and drug problems predominate among men. The major differences appear between men and women within the three family status groups. Far fewer differences are apparent in looking first at men or women and then comparing across the three family status groups. That being said, we are speaking of differences in degree only. When looking at lifetime rates, for example, even the subgroup with the lowest, women with children, still shows 72 percent reporting at least one problem, while those with the highest show 92 percent of female other clients, 88 percent of male other clients, and 90 percent of single men reporting at least one problem.

Comparison with Low-Income Housed Adults

In the preceding discussion, we described ADM problems among homeless clients as "high." But high compared to what? Intuitively, it seems that ADM problems involving half or more a population are high. But it also would be desirable to have a comparison population of housed people who are as similar as possible to NSHAPC's homeless clients. To make such a comparison, we used a subset of the sample from the 1996

National Household Survey on Drug Abuse (NHSDA). We selected respondents whose age corresponded as closely as possible to the NSHAPC sample (18 to 64), and whose incomes were as close to the federal poverty level as could be done within the constraints of the NHSDA public use data file (the appendix to this chapter gives details of how we selected this subsample). We use NHSDA data to compare levels of alcohol and drug use, and treatment for alcohol, drug, and mental health problems, between the homeless clients in NSHAPC and the housed, low-income people in NHSDA.

Alcohol Use

Both NSHAPC and NHSDA collected information about alcohol use during respondents' lifetimes, including their age when they first drank. Seventy-two percent of homeless clients reported drinking alcohol regularly (defined as three or more times a week) at some time in their life. Seventy-nine percent of low-income adults reported ever drinking some type of alcoholic beverage. The NHSDA question, although the only one available for history of drinking, is quite different from the NSHAPC question, and, in general, reports a lower level of consumption. Thus, though they are not really comparable, we present the two statistics as the best we have, and also as telling a dramatic story, for which the NHSDA data form a very conservative comparison.

On issues pertaining to current heavy use of alcohol, questions in NSHAPC and NHSDA match more closely. NSHAPC asked, "When was the most recent time you drank alcohol *to get drunk* three or more times a week?" while NHSDA asked, "During the past 30 days, on how many days did you have five or more drinks on the same occasion?" Seventeen percent of homeless clients reported that during the past month they had been drinking to get drunk three or more times a week. Seven percent of low-income adults said they had had five or more drinks on the same occasion within the past month. By these measures, heavy drinking during the past month was at least twice as common among homeless clients as low-income adults.

Drug Use

The NSHAPC and NHSDA surveys also collected information on the incidence and recentness of drug use. NSHAPC clients were asked,

"During your lifetime, have there been times when you used (Name Drug) regularly?" where "regularly" was defined as three or more times a week. The NHSDA survey inquired, "Have you ever, even once, used (Name Drug)?" People responding yes to either were then asked how recently they had used the drug. Table 4.2 presents the results for those who have used marijuana/hashish, crack/rock, cocaine, heroin, and hallucinogens in the past year and in their lifetime.

Even given the more stringent NSHAPC question, homeless clients were more likely than low-income adults to have used every type of drug over their lifetime. Over the past year, homeless clients were more likely to have used every drug except hallucinogens.

More than half (52 percent) of homeless clients reported using marijuana three or more times a week during their lifetime, compared to

Table 4.2 *Drug Use Patterns Reported by NSHAPC and NHSDA Clients*[a]

	Percentage of Homeless NSHAPC Clients Who Reported Using Drugs Regularly (N = 2,938)	*Percentage of Low-Income Adults, Ages 18 to 64, Who Reported Ever Using Drugs (N = 3,364)*
Use of Specified Drug(s) in Lifetime		
Marijuana/hashish	52	38
Crack/rock	29	6
Powdered cocaine	29	15
Heroin	13	3
Hallucinogens	19	12
Use of Specified Drug(s) in Past Year		
Marijuana/hashish	26	14
Crack/rock	19	2
Powdered cocaine	10	4
Heroin	5	1
Hallucinogens	3	3

Source: For NSHAPC clients, Urban Institute analysis of weighted 1996 NSHAPC client data. For low-income adults, Urban Institute analysis of weighted 1996 NHSDA data.

[a]Low-income adults are included if they ever, even once, used the specified drug during the time period. Homeless clients are included if they reported using the specified drug regularly (defined as three or more times a week) during the time period.

38 percent of low-income adults who had *ever* used it, even once. Homeless clients were also more likely to have used marijuana in both the past year and the past month. Of the 52 percent of homeless clients who ever used marijuana regularly, half (26 percent of all homeless clients) did so in the past year. In comparison, among the 38 percent of low-income adults who reported ever using marijuana, slightly more than one-third (14 percent of all low-income adults) did so in the past year.

Proportions of people using other drugs mirrored the pattern for marijuana. For each of the five drugs in table 4.2, homeless clients were more likely to have used them regularly (three or more times a week) in their lifetime than low-income, housed adults. The differences were greatest for crack and heroin, the drugs considered most debilitating. Twenty-nine percent of homeless clients reported using crack regularly at some point in their lifetime. Nearly two-thirds of these used crack in the past year (19 percent of all homeless clients) and about one-third (9 percent of all homeless clients) reported using crack during the past month. In contrast, the percentage of low-income, housed adults reporting crack use by lifetime, year, and month are 6, 2, and 1 percent, respectively. Similarly, 13 percent of homeless clients used heroin regularly in their lifetime and 5 percent did so in the past year, compared to 3 percent of low-income adults who had ever used heroin and 1 percent who did so in the past year.

Alcohol, Drug, and Mental Health Treatment

Information on treatment history is useful when examining alcohol, drug, and mental health problems, for two reasons. First, it is a strong indicator that the recipient or someone with significant influence over the recipient believed they had a problem. Second, it reveals something about access to treatment among people who have a problem.

The NSHAPC survey asked if clients had ever received inpatient or outpatient treatment for alcohol, drug, or mental health problems. Those responding yes were then asked when their most recent treatment took place. The NHSDA survey asked whether respondents had received treatment at a number of different facilities during the last 12 months. We coded hospitals, rehabilitation facilities, emergency rooms, and prisons as inpatient settings for the purpose of this comparison. Private doctors' offices, self-help groups, and any response that specifically included the word "outpatient" were coded as outpatient settings.

Table 4.3 presents information on inpatient and outpatient treatment, focusing on the past year as the most comparable period in the two surveys.[5] Over the past year, homeless clients were more likely than housed, low-income adults to have received both inpatient and outpatient treatment, and to have received it for alcohol, drug, and mental health problems.[6] Seven percent of homeless NSHAPC clients were treated for alcohol problems at inpatient facilities; 8 percent received outpatient treatment. In contrast, 2 percent of low-income adults received inpatient and another 3 percent outpatient treatment for alcohol problems. The same pattern holds for drug treatment. Seven percent of homeless clients received drug treatment at both inpatient and outpatient facilities in the past year, compared to 2 and 3 percent of low-income, housed adults.

The most significant difference pertains to mental health treatment. In the past year, 8 percent of homeless clients were hospitalized for mental health problems, and 20 percent were treated at outpatient facilities. The percentages of low-income, housed adults receiving mental health

Table 4.3 *Percentage of NSHAPC and NHSDA Clients Reporting Treatment for Alcohol, Drug, and Mental Health Problems*[a]

	Homeless NSHAPC Clients (N = 2,938)	*Low-Income Adults, Ages 18 to 64 (N = 3,364)*
Received Treatment for Alcohol Abuse in the Last Year		
Inpatient	7	2
Outpatient	8	3
Received Treatment for Drug Abuse in the Last Year		
Inpatient	7	2
Outpatient	7	3
Received Treatment for Mental Health Problems in the Last Year		
Hospitalized	8	1
Outpatient	20	7

Source: For NSHAPC clients, Urban Institute analysis of weighted 1996 NSHAPC client data. For low-income adults, Urban Institute analysis of weighted 1996 NHSDA data.

[a]Among all clients/respondents, not just those with reported problems.

treatment at a hospital or outpatient facility in the past year were 1 and 7 percent, respectively.

Implications

The evidence we have suggests that substantial differences exist between homeless clients and housed, low-income adults on most of the available measures. More homeless clients reported significant levels of alcohol consumption and drug use. They also had correspondingly higher levels of both outpatient and inpatient treatment for problems associated with this use. In addition, homeless clients were significantly more likely to report inpatient and outpatient treatment for mental health problems.

These are simple cross-tabulations, and do not control for sex, age, or other characteristics. Thus, any behaviors strongly associated with such characteristics might show quite different percentages, if controlled for, from those reported here. For example, homeless clients as a group are very skewed toward men (68 percent, versus 41 percent among NHSDA's low-income adults). To the extent that some of the reported behaviors are associated more with men than women (e.g., heavy use of alcohol and illicit drugs), then the differences might disappear if the analyses had controlled for sex. On the other hand, men's greater likelihood of being heavy users of alcohol and illicit drugs may well be a reason why we find more men than women among homeless populations. Issues of covariation such as these are very difficult to sort out; we leave the task for the analyses in chapter 8.

Characteristics of Homeless Clients with Various Patterns of ADM Problems

Having seen that homeless clients differ considerably from low-income, housed adults in their ADM problems and treatment, we turn next to homeless people whose ADM problems fall into different patterns. Based on earlier findings, we decided that information about ADM problems during *the year* before the NSHAPC survey would offer the best compromise between what might be the relatively fleeting experiences of the past month and relatively out-of-date experiences of a lifetime. Thus, using past-year information, we created five subgroups:

- No ADM problems during the past year (26 percent of the whole sample);
- Alcohol problems only (12 percent);
- Drug problems, with or without accompanying alcohol problems, but definitely without accompanying mental health problems (17 percent);
- Mental health problems only (15 percent); and
- Mental health problems with accompanying problems with alcohol, drugs, or both (31 percent).

The remaining analyses in this chapter look at demographic, economic, health, homeless history, and other characteristics within and across these groups, comparing members of each group to the entire sample of homeless clients.

Demographic Characteristics

Sex and race/ethnicity were the only demographic characteristics that systematically differentiated the five ADM subgroups (table 4.4). Clients with no ADM problems, or with only mental health problems, were more likely to be women than those in the homeless sample as a whole. Those in the other three groups were more likely to be men. Clients with only mental health problems were more likely to be white and less likely to be black than the sample as a whole; those with only alcohol problems were more likely to be Native American and less likely to be black; and those with drug problems (with or without accompanying alcohol problems) were more likely to be black and less likely to be white. The two remaining subgroups did not differ from the sample as a whole on race/ethnicity. For the most part, the subgroups did not differ from the sample as a whole on issues of age, educational attainment, marital status, or urban/rural location. Families were more prominent among those with no ADM problems, and less prominent among those who only had problems with alcohol.

Patterns of Homelessness

Only minor differences existed among subgroups, or between subgroups and the total homeless sample, on the length of their homelessness during their current spell (table 4.5). One might have thought that ADM

Table 4.4 *Basic Demographic Characteristics of Homeless Clients, by ADM Status*
(weighted percentages)

			ADM Problems in the Past Year				
	U.S. Poor Adult Population (1996)	*All Currently Homeless Clients (UN = 2,938)*	*None (UN = 787)*	*Problems with Alcohol Only (UN = 305)*	*Drug Problems with or without Alcohol Problems; No Mental Health Problems (UN = 561)*	*Problems with Mental Health Only (UN = 424)*	*Mental Health Problems, with Alcohol or Drug Problems or Both (UN = 861)*
Proportion of All Homeless Clients	NA	100	26	12	17	15	31
Sex[a]							
Male	41	68	55	89	81	46	76
Female	59	32	45	11	19	54	25
Race/Ethnicity[a]							
White non-Hispanic	52	41	42	39	22	55	44
Black non-Hispanic	23	40	40	29	62	29	38
Hispanic	20	11	10	7	13	13	10
Native American	2	8	7	26	2	2	8
Other	4	1	1	*	1	1	1
Age[a]							
Under 18	—	1	1	*	1	*	1

(Continued)

Table 4.4 *Basic Demographic Characteristics of Homeless Clients, by ADM Status (Continued)*
(weighted percentages)

			ADM Problems in the Past Year				
	U.S. Poor Adult Population (1996)	*All Currently Homeless Clients (UN = 2,938)*	*None (UN = 787)*	*Problems with Alcohol Only (UN = 305)*	*Drug Problems with or without Alcohol Problems; No Mental Health Problems (UN = 561)*	*Problems with Mental Health Only (UN = 424)*	*Mental Health Problems, with Alcohol or Drug Problems or Both (UN = 861)*
18 to 21 years	12	6	11	1	4	7	5
22 to 24 years	8	5	6	2	4	10	4
25 to 34 years	23	25	25	14	26	24	29
35 to 44 years	20	38	28	53	50	32	36
45 to 54 years	11	17	14	22	11	18	21
55 to 64 years	10	6	10	5	4	8	5
65 or more years	16	2	7	2	*	1	*
Urban/Rural Status[b]							
Central cities	31	71	68	56	74	63	81
Suburban/urban fringe	46	21	23	20	22	29	15
Rural	23	9	9	25	5	8	5
Education/Highest Level of Schooling Completed[a]							
Less than high school	42	38	40	36	36	36	39
High school graduate/G.E.D.	33	34	33	35	55	30	29

More than high school	25	28	27	29	18	34	31
Marital Status[a]							
Married	31	9	14	10	9	13	4
Widowed	12	3	6	4	1	1	4
Divorced	15	24	23	32	17	27	24
Separated	6	15	14	19	18	9	16
Never married	37	48	44	35	55	51	53
In Homeless Family	NA	15	24	6	11	21	9

Source: Urban Institute analysis of weighted 1996 NSHAPC client data; *N*s given at top of table are unweighted (designated "UN").

Note: Percentages do not sum to 100 due to rounding. NA = not applicable.

*Denotes values that are less than 0.5 percent but greater than 0.

[a]Statistics for the poor adult (ages 18 and older) population in the United States calculated from March 1997 Current Population Survey using Unicorn, with poverty status determined for 1996.

[b]Geographic distribution of the poor U.S. population in 1996 taken from Lamison-White (1997), P60-198, table A.

problems would lead to longer spells, or their absence to substantially shorter ones. But, in fact, each group reported only insignificantly different rates of very short (less than one month) or very long (more than two years) spells. With respect to frequency of homeless spells, the major standout is the subgroup without ADM problems. Members of this group were more likely than the sample as a whole to be in their first spell of homelessness, and less likely to have been homeless four or more times.

Type of ADM problem did make a difference for where a client was living the day of the NSHAPC interview, and also for whether the client had been victimized during their spell of homelessness. Clients who had only mental health problems were the most likely to be living in a transitional housing program, and the least likely to be living on the streets or in places not meant for habitation. Those without ADM problems were also less likely than the sample as a whole to be living in places not meant for habitation, while those with mental health problems plus one or more substance use problems were the most likely to be living in such places.

Not surprisingly, reported levels of victimization followed closely on these living situations. Those least likely to be living in risky circumstances (in places not meant for habitation) were clients without ADM problems. They also reported the lowest levels of victimization while homeless in every category except sexual assault. In contrast, clients most likely to be living in risky circumstances reported the highest levels of victimization in every category. As we will see, they also reported the highest levels of physical health conditions and food insecurity. They thus emerge as a large and particularly vulnerable group even within the larger context of vulnerability that is homelessness itself. Considering that they also comprise 3 in 10 of the people who are homeless at any given time, they are a group that seems to need and deserve a lot of attention and support.

Income Levels and Sources

In a chapter on ADM problems, it is important to remember that people who have these problems and also have money are not usually homeless. ADM problems create vulnerabilities; so does poverty. The combination can be devastating. In 1996, the federal poverty level (FPL) for a one-person household was $680 a month. Half of all homeless clients

Table 4.5 *Conditions of Homelessness, by ADM Status*
(weighted percentages)

		ADM Problems in the Past Year				
	All Currently Homeless Clients (UN = 2,938)	*None (UN = 787)*	*Problems with Alcohol Only (UN = 305)*	*Drug Problems with or without Alcohol Problems; No Mental Health Problems (UN = 561)*	*Problems with Mental Health Only (UN = 424)*	*Mental Health Problems, with Alcohol or Drug Problems or Both (UN = 861)*
Length of Current Period of Homelessness						
< 1 week	5	10	4	4	6	3
> = 1 week and < 1 month	8	7	17	9	8	4
1–3 months	15	19	14	14	16	12
4–6 months	11	15	10	10	8	11
7–12 months	15	14	15	13	13	18
13–24 months	16	10	18	22	10	18
25–60 months	10	7	8	11	9	14
5 or more years	20	17	14	18	30	22
Number of Times Homeless or without Regular Housing for 30 Days or More						
1	49	62	48	48	49	41
2	17	16	10	17	23	16
3	12	8	15	10	11	15
4–10	18	9	22	23	14	23

(*Continued*)

Table 4.5 *Conditions of Homelessness, by ADM Status (Continued)*

(weighted percentages)

		ADM Problems in the Past Year				
	All Currently Homeless Clients (UN = 2,938)	*None (UN = 787)*	*Problems with Alcohol Only (UN = 305)*	*Drug Problems with or without Alcohol Problems; No Mental Health Problems (UN = 561)*	*Problems with Mental Health Only (UN = 424)*	*Mental Health Problems, with Alcohol or Drug Problems or Both (UN = 861)*
11 or more	4	4	4	3	4	5
Where Living on Day of Interview						
Emergency shelter/welfare hotel	30	38	23	33	27	27
Transitional shelter/housing	33	26	28	32	47	35
House/apt./room paid for by client	16	22	25	15	15	8
Space not meant for habitation, plus other[a]	21	14	24	20	11	30
While Client Was Homeless						
People stole money or things directly from client while client was there	38	19	36	33	50	49
People stole money or things from client's bags, locker, etc., while client was gone	41	25	40	39	40	55
People physically assaulted client, beat client up	22	9	28	16	22	34
People sexually assaulted client, raped client	7	5	2	2	7	12

Source: Urban Institute analysis of weighted 1996 NSHAPC client data; *N*s given at top of table are unweighted (designated "UN").

Note: Percentages do not sum to 100 due to rounding.

[a]Includes the following types of locations: car or other vehicle, abandoned building, transportation site, place of business, anywhere outside, and other place.

reported income for the 30 days prior to being interviewed for NSHAPC of $300 or less, or 44 percent of the FPL. Fully 30 percent reported receiving less than $100 during that month. Those with only mental health problems and those with no ADM problems had median incomes substantially above the overall median (although still not close to the FPL). The alcohol-only group and those with mental health plus substance use problems had substantially lower median incomes.

Homeless clients reported various sources of income, including work for pay, government cash and near-cash benefits, family and friends, and panhandling. These sources differed considerably by ADM subgroup, and in part may account for the probability that certain subgroups reported considerably lower incomes than others (table 4.6). Clients who had only problems with alcohol, and those with drug problems with or without alcohol problems, were more likely than the sample as a whole to report working for pay during the month before the interview. Very few in either group, however, had "regular" jobs that either had lasted, or could be expected to last, three months or more. Temporary jobs and day labor were much more common sources of paid work.

The subgroups benefiting most from government cash assistance got their incomes from very different sources (table 4.6).[7] Those who had only mental health problems were more likely than any other group to receive income from two federal programs benefiting people with disabilities—Supplemental Security Income and Social Security Disability Insurance (SSI and SSDI). Those with only alcohol problems were least likely to get any of the variety of benefits about which the survey asked. And clients who were in homeless families were particularly likely to receive Aid to Families with Dependent Children (AFDC—as the program still was in 1996), if they had drug problems or a combination of mental health and substance abuse problems. But they were particularly unlikely to get it if they had either only alcohol problems or only mental health problems. This is probably because single men and single women predominate in these groups, and would not have been eligible for AFDC.

Physical Health and Nutrition Problems

As already mentioned, homeless clients suffered from a variety of illnesses and conditions, at rates far higher than the average, housed American. Some of these conditions are a direct result of living as a homeless

Table 4.6 *Income Levels, Income Sources, and Employment of Homeless Clients, by ADM Status*

(weighted percentages)

		ADM Problems in the Past Year				
	All Currently Homeless Clients (UN = 2,938)	*None (UN = 787)*	*Problems with Alcohol Only (UN = 305)*	*Drug Problems with or without Alcohol Problems; No Mental Health Problems (UN = 561)*	*Problems with Mental Health Only (UN = 424)*	*Mental Health Problems, with Alcohol or Drug Problems or Both (UN = 861)*
Mean Income from All Sources (Last 30 Days)[a]	$367	$443	$337	$347	$442	$288
Median Income from All Sources (Last 30 Days)[a]	$300	$400	$182	$300	$480	$175
Income from All Sources over Last 30 Days						
None	13	14	11	10	11	16
Less than $100	17	13	26	14	11	24
$100 to 299	19	13	20	25	14	24
$300 to 499	18	21	16	25	17	14
$500 to 699	14	20	5	12	25	10
$700 to 799	4	4	13	1	8	2
$800 to 999	5	5	2	6	6	4
$1,000 to 1,199	3	4	3	5	3	2
$1,200 or more	4	8	4	2	4	4
Did Any Paid Work in Last 30 Days	44	47	55	54	35	36
Sources of Earned Income in Last 30 Days[b]						
Job lasting 3 or more months	13	17	11	16	14	9
Job expected to last 3 or more months	7	8	6	8	7	5

Temporary job, farm work	8	2	10	3	2	1
Temporary job, non-farm work	3	11	5	10	4	9
Day job or pick-up job	14	9	24	19	8	14
Peddling	2	1	2	5	1	3
Received Money/Benefits from Government Sources in Last 30 Days						
AFDC (among families with children)	52	47	27	81	35	67
General Assistance	9	7	7	8	7	13
Supplemental Security Income	11	12	6	5	21	11
SSDI	8	3	4	3	25	9
Social Security	3	7	4	1	3	2
Veteran's disability payments (among veterans)	6	11	2	*	7	10
Veteran's pension (among veterans)	2	1	5	0	6	2
Food Stamps	37	41	28	34	35	40
Received Means-Tested Government Benefits[c]						
Any, including food stamps	45	48	33	40	49	48
Any other than food stamps	28	34	14	23	36	28
Other Sources of Income over the Last 30 Days						
Parents	9	5	15	13	7	8
Friends	12	8	13	11	9	18
Asking for money on the street	8	3	10	9	5	12

Source: Urban Institute analysis of weighted 1996 NSHAPC client data; *N*s given at top of table are unweighted (designated "UN").

Note: Percentages do not sum to 100 due to rounding.

*Denotes values that are less than 0.5 percent but greater than 0.

[a]If a client reported an income range rather than an exact amount, the client was assigned the midpoint of the range for the purpose of calculating the mean and median.

[b]Client could report receiving income from more than one of these sources.

[c]Includes AFDC, GA, SSI, Food Stamps, and/or housing assistance.

person, and some have been found to have been a factor in precipitating their becoming homeless (Institute of Medicine 1988). NSHAPC did not include a full battery of questions about health and illness, but it did ask about many conditions that seem to be particularly prevalent among homeless populations. Among our five ADM subgroups, those with no ADM problems were less likely than the sample as a whole to report having acute infectious or chronic health conditions (table 4.7). They also had the fewest problems seeing a doctor when they needed one. In contrast, those with mental health problems combined with substance use problems were more likely than the sample as a whole to report acute infectious conditions; acute noninfectious conditions such as lice, scabies, or skin problems; and chronic conditions.

With respect to health insurance, one subgroup, those with only mental health problems, stands out as being particularly well covered. Half this group received Medicaid and 25 percent reported "other" insurance, compared to only 30 and 10 percent, respectively, of the sample as a whole. This Medicaid coverage was undoubtedly linked to their receipt of cash benefits, which would principally have been SSI, but could also have been General Assistance and accompanying state medical assistance, or AFDC. "Other" insurance was probably Medicare linked to their receipt of SSDI. As a consequence, they had the lowest rate of being uninsured of any subgroup. In contrast, those in the alcohol-only subgroup were particularly likely to lack insurance coverage for health care.

Homeless people clearly have more problems getting enough food than the average, nonhomeless American household with income below the FPL. Homeless people in general were more than twice as likely to report sometimes or often not getting enough to eat, and many times more likely to report having gone a whole day without eating in the past month because they could not afford to. These differences were marginally significant even for homeless people who did not have ADM problems, and were dramatically true for the two subgroups whose members had mental health problems with or without substance use problems. Thus even the somewhat elevated (for homeless people) income of the mental health–only subgroup did not appear to ensure adequate access to food.

Adverse Childhood Experiences

Some childhood and youthful behaviors and experiences explored through NSHAPC are generally relevant to a variety of adult difficulties,

Table 4.7 *Physical Health and Nutrition Status of Homeless Clients, by ADM Status*
(weighted percentages)

			ADM Problems in the Past Year				
	All U.S. Households Below the FPL (1995)[a]	*All Currently Homeless Clients (UN = 2,938)*	*None (UN = 787)*	*Problems with Alcohol Only (UN = 305)*	*Drug Problems with or without Alcohol Problems; No Mental Health Problems (UN = 561)*	*Problems with Mental Health Only (UN = 424)*	*Mental Health Problems, with Alcohol or Drug Problems or Both (UN = 861)*
Type of Reported Medical Conditions[b]							
Acute infectious conditions (1 or more)	—	26	14	16	24	33	38
Acute noninfectious conditions (1 or more)	—	8	4	5	7	8	12
Chronic conditions (1 or more)	—	46	32	38	47	54	57
Four Most Common Medical Conditions							
Arthritis, rheumatism, joint problems	—	24	19	20	18	26	32
Chest infection, cold, cough, bronchitis	—	22	13	14	19	27	33
Problem walking, lost limb, other handicap	—	14	15	9	6	17	18
High blood pressure	—	15	8	12	15	15	21

(Continued)

Table 4.7 *Physical Health and Nutrition Status of Homeless Clients, by ADM Status (Continued)*
(weighted percentages)

			ADM Problems in the Past Year				
	All U.S. Households Below the FPL (1995)[a]	*All Currently Homeless Clients (UN = 2,938)*	*None (UN = 787)*	*Problems with Alcohol Only (UN = 305)*	*Drug Problems with or without Alcohol Problems; No Mental Health Problems (UN = 561)*	*Problems with Mental Health Only (UN = 424)*	*Mental Health Problems, with Alcohol or Drug Problems or Both (UN = 861)*
Needed But Not Able to See Doctor or Nurse in Last Year	—	24	14	32	15	30	31
Medicaid	—	30	28	25	21	50	30
VA Medical Care	—	7	3	7	8	5	12
Private insurance	—	4	4	1	6	2	4
No insurance	—	55	59	68	62	37	51
Other	—	10	11	4	5	25	7
Best Description of Food Situation							
Get enough of kinds of food wanted	60[d]	39	51	51	35	35	27
Get enough but not always what wanted	29	34	34	25	41	33	34
Sometimes not enough to eat	9	18	9	16	15	27	22
Often not enough to eat	3	10	5	8	9	5	17
In the Last 30 Days, Went a Whole Day without Anything to Eat	3[e]	40	29	31	42	33	55
In Last 30 Days, Hungry But Did Not Have Enough Money for Food	5[e]	39	24	44	43	38	49

Current Food Problems[c]							
None	—	42	59	39	39	40	32
One	—	20	18	29	22	21	16
Two	—	17	11	16	21	23	17
Three	—	13	7	7	14	12	21
Four	—	8	4	10	5	4	14

Source: Urban Institute analysis of weighted 1996 NSHAPC client data; *N*s given at top of table are unweighted (designated "UN").

Note: Percentages do not sum to 100 due to rounding.

[a]Data for U.S. households below the poverty line taken from the Current Population Survey Food Security Supplement, April 1995, table 1 (Food and Consumer Service 1999).

[b]Conditions asked about include diabetes, anemia, high blood pressure, heart disease/stroke, liver problems, arthritis/rheumatism, chest infection/cold/bronchitis, pneumonia, tuberculosis, skin diseases, lice/scabies, cancer, problems walking/other handicap, STDs (other than AIDS), HIV, AIDS, intravenous drug use, and other.

[c]Each of the following counted as one food problem: client sometimes or often did not have enough to eat; client ate once or less per day; in the last 30 days client was hungry but did not eat because s/he could not afford enough food; and in the last 30 days client went at least one whole day without anything to eat.

[d]*N* associated with these data is 877.

[e]*N* associated with these data is 6,653.

and some have direct relevance to adult patterns of ADM problems. Problems in school, for example, are often general precursors of problems later on. This is so particularly with economic self-sufficiency but also with other high-risk behaviors of youth and young adults as well (Burt, Resnick, and Novick 1998; Office of Juvenile Justice Programs 1995). Likewise, a history of physical or sexual abuse or neglect during childhood has many long-term negative consequences, of which homelessness may be only one. With respect to the ADM problems in this chapter, recent research (Dennis and McGeary 1998) has indicated strong associations between alcohol and/or drug use before age 15 and adult substance abuse problems. We therefore looked at the associations among these behaviors and our five ADM subgroups (table 4.8).

SCHOOL PROBLEMS. We noted earlier that the same proportion of all ADM subgroups had completed less than a high school education. We may also note here that no significant differences appeared among the subgroups in the proportion who had ever repeated one or more grades in school.

Low educational attainment is in itself a barrier to economic self-sufficiency, but other problems associated with school may also reflect children in difficulty or children with barriers to long-term self-sufficiency. Table 4.8 shows the proportion of homeless clients who reported ever being suspended or expelled from school, and also the proportion who reported attending special classes due to a learning or other disability. The first issue is how much more likely than the general population homeless people are to have had these problems. We can make these comparisons for suspensions and expulsions but not for special education. To get the general population figures, we analyzed information from the 1996 National Longitudinal Survey of Youth (NLS-Y), whose 12,686 respondents in 1996 were all between the ages of 31 and 39. Homeless clients were much more likely than this general population sample to report suspension or expulsion from school. Among homeless clients, 44 percent had been suspended and 18 percent expelled at least once from their school, compared to 22 and 4 percent, respectively, of the NLS-Y respondents.

The ADM subgroups also differed considerably among themselves in the proportion who were ever suspended. Three subgroups (those with no ADM problems, those with only alcohol problems, and those with only mental health problems) were similar in their probability of having

Table 4.8 *Adverse Childhood Experiences of Homeless Clients, by ADM Status*
(weighted percentages)

		ADM Problems in the Past Year				
Adverse Childhood Experience	*All Currently Homeless Clients (UN = 2,938)*	*None (UN = 787)*	*Problems with Alcohol Only (UN = 305)*	*Drug Problems with or without Alcohol Problems; No Mental Health Problems (UN = 561)*	*Problems with Mental Health Only (UN = 424)*	*Mental Health Problems, with Alcohol or Drug Problems or Both (UN = 861)*
Ever Suspended from School	44	32	32	59	32	56
Ever Expelled from School	18	14	13	19	13	25
Before Age 18, Someone Client Lived With						
Left client without adequate food or shelter	12	8	5	7	17	20
Physically abused client, to cause physical harm	22	12	10	10	37	34
Forced client or pressured client to perform sexual acts that client did not want to do	13	7	2	4	27	19
Abuse/ Neglect Combinations before Age 18						
Physical and/or sexual abuse but not neglect	25	15	12	11	44	
One or more abuse/neglect experiences	29	19	15	15	45	42
First Started Drinking						
Before age 15	25	6	30	34	14	41
Between age 15 and 17	21	12	21	31	14	25
First Started Drinking to Get Drunk						
Before age 15	13	3	20	17	6	22
Between age 15 and 17	15	4	15	23	9	22
First Started Using Drugs						
Before age 15	19	4	9	27	15	32
Between age 15 and 17	19	9	10	33	14	26
First Started Using Drugs Regularly						
Before age 15	11	3	3	19	12	16
Between age 15 and 17	15	5	10	16	12	25

Source: Urban Institute analysis of weighted 1996 NSHAPC client data; *N*s given at top of table are unweighted (designated "UN").
Note: Percentages do not sum to 100 due to rounding.

been suspended (32 percent of each). They were also considerably lower on this factor than those with drug problems or those with mental health plus substance use problems, 59 and 56 percent of whom, respectively, had been suspended. Only the subgroup mental health plus substance use problems stood out as being more likely than the whole sample to have been expelled.

Fully 20 percent of homeless clients reported having been in special classes because of learning or other disabilities. Clients who reported only alcohol problems were much less likely (8 percent), and clients who reported only mental health problems were much more likely (32 percent) than the sample as a whole to have been in these classes. The remaining subgroups did not differ from each other or from the sample as a whole.

ABUSE AND NEGLECT BY A HOUSEHOLD MEMBER. With respect to childhood abuse and neglect, the two subgroups with mental health problems were far more likely than the other subgroups, and the sample as a whole, to report at least one of these problems. They also were more likely to report both physical and sexual abuse by a household member during childhood. As already noted, such experiences of abuse and neglect are strong risk factors for adult homelessness. It is likely, as present data indicate, that one of the routes to homelessness lies in the effects these experiences have on a person's emotional and mental health.

EARLY INITIATION OF ALCOHOL AND/OR DRUG USE. Since problems with alcohol and drug use were two of the criteria for classifying homeless adults into the ADM subgroups, obvious issues to explore are when these problems began and whether early initiation differentiates the groups with problems as adults from those without. Based on previous research (Dennis and McGeary 1998), we would expect to find that they do, and the data fulfill this expectation (table 4.8). The two groups with no alcohol or drug problems (those with no ADM problems, and those with only mental health problems) were much less likely than groups with these problems to have begun drinking before age 15. The same is true for first drinking to get drunk. Early initiation of drug use likewise differentiates the two subgroups with drug problems as adults from the three other subgroups. *Regular* drug use before age 15 differentiates the two subgroups with drug problems from those with no ADM problems and those with problems with alcohol only, but not from those with only mental health problems.

Out-of-Home Living Experiences before Age 18

FOSTER CARE. Given the abuse and neglect by a household member reported by homeless clients, it is not surprising that they also reported startling levels of out-of-home placement in foster care, a group home, or an institution. For housed adults in the nation as a whole, 3.4 percent have had such a foster care experience in childhood (Royse and Wiehe 1989). The proportion of homeless clients raised in such circumstances—at 26 percent (table 4.9)—is remarkably higher. Among the ADM subsamples, homeless clients with mental health combined with substance use problems were more likely (35 percent) than the sample as a whole to have spent time in foster care. Those with drug problems but no mental health problems were less likely to have done so (15 percent). Homeless clients reporting only alcohol problems were also marginally less likely (18 percent) than the sample as a whole to have spent time in foster care.

RUNNING AWAY AND BEING FORCED TO LEAVE HOME. For the most part, the pattern for foster care also holds with respect to clients running away or being forced to leave home before age 18. Clients who reported problems only with alcohol were less likely, and those who reported mental health combined with substance use problems were more likely, than the homeless sample as a whole to have experienced both. Clients with drug problems were much less likely to have been forced to leave home, but were similar to the homeless sample as a whole on running away.

FIRST TIME HOMELESS. Overall, 21 percent of homeless clients experienced their first period of homelessness while they were still children or adolescents. However, having ADM problems was related to the probability of being homeless this young. Those with no ADM problems were less likely to have experienced childhood homelessness (14 percent), while those with mental health combined with substance use problems were most likely to have done so (32 percent).

TROUBLES WITH THE LAW. Another way of leaving home as a juvenile is to be placed in a juvenile justice facility as a consequence of either

Table 4.9 *Childhood Out-of-Home Experiences of Homeless Clients, by ADM Status* (weighted percentages)

		ADM Problems in the Past Year				
	All Currently Homeless Clients (UN = 2,938)	*None (UN = 787)*	*Problems with Alcohol Only (UN = 305)*	*Drug Problems with or without Alcohol Problems; No Mental Health Problems (UN = 561)*	*Problems with Mental Health Only (UN = 424)*	*Mental Health Problems, with Alcohol or Drug Problems or Both (UN = 861)*
Before Age 18, Ever Placed in						
Foster care, group home, or institution	26	27	18	15	22	35
Foster care	12	13	5	7	13	15
Group home	10	15	3	4	6	15
Institution	16	16	12	9	13	21
Ever Ran Away from Home for More than 24 Hours before Age 18	33	25	15	32	34	45
Ever Forced to Leave Home for More than 24 Hours before Age 18	22	17	14	10	22	37
First Time Became Homeless Occurred before Age 18	21	14	16	16	20	32
Juvenile Detention before Age 18	16	9	17	19	12	21
History of Incarceration as Adult						
5 or more days in a city or county jail	49	28	66	73	27	57
5 or more days in a military jail/lockup	4	1	4	7	1	5
State or federal prison	18	9	17	22	9	30
Spent Time Incarcerated (including as juvenile)	54	31	70	76	34	66

Source: Urban Institute analysis of weighted 1996 NSHAPC client data; *N*s given at top of table are unweighted (designated "UN").
Note: Percentages do not sum to 100 due to rounding.

criminal behavior or behavior that classifies one as a "child/person in need of supervision." The first step down this path is juvenile detention, which may or may not lead to other types of incarceration as a juvenile. It also may or may not be a precursor to incarceration as an adult. The NSHAPC survey inquired about all these experiences. Sixteen percent of the whole homeless sample had spent time in juvenile detention. Clients with no ADM problems were less likely to have done so. The other subsamples revealed no significant differences from each other or the homeless sample as a whole. Clients with no ADM problems were also much less likely to report incarceration as an adult, as was the subsample that reported only mental health problems. In contrast, the subsamples with substance use problems (alcohol, drugs, or both) had higher levels of incarceration in local facilities (city or county jails). Those with mental health combined with substance use problems were more likely to also have spent time in state or federal prison.

Concluding Thoughts

This chapter's information leads inevitably to the conclusion that alcohol, drug, or mental health problems are associated with a whole range of other negative experiences and circumstances. In general, homeless clients with no ADM problems reported the fewest negative experiences and circumstances; those with mental health combined with substance use problems reported the most. But unique patterns also existed for those with only mental health problems and for those with substance use problems, whether or not they also had mental health problems. The mental health–only subgroup stands out as reporting more indicators suggestive of childhood mental health problems (i.e., institutionalization as a child). But it also benefits from cash assistance from public programs for people with disabilities that prevent them from working, and from specially designed transitional housing programs for homeless people with disabilities. The subgroups reporting substance use but not mental health problems were very likely also to have histories of incarceration and early trouble with the law, as well as to have shown signs early in adolescence of being heavy users of alcohol and possibly also of drugs. The subgroup that combines mental health with substance use problems reported the highest levels both of negative experiences and of circumstances that revealed their extreme vulnerability—to hunger, criminal victimization, and health problems associated with living in places not meant for habitation.

It is also clear from comparing the reports of NSHAPC clients to those of housed low-income adults, as reported on NHSDA, that homeless clients have extensive experience with treatment institutions. Given that state and local agencies serving people with ADM problems may see their clients many times, and also supply them with repeated rounds of costly inpatient care, it is alarming how little progress the agencies have made in preventing homelessness among their charges. Evaluations, meantime, have documented model programs that can help clients with ADM problems find and maintain decent, affordable housing. What is lacking clearly are the political will and concomitant resources, not effective strategies.

Appendix: The NHSDA Sample

The National Household Survey on Drug Abuse (NHSDA) provides data on alcohol, tobacco, and illicit drug use in the United States, as well as treatment and other information, that we use to compare homeless adults to housed, low-income adults. Conducted by the federal government since 1971, NHSDA measures the prevalence and correlates of drug use among noninstitutionalized U.S. citizens over age 12. Residents of households and noninstitutionalized housing, such as homeless shelters and dormitories, are included. Persons without a fixed address, as well as those living in institutions such as jails and hospitals, are not.

The 1996 NHSDA used a multistage area probability sample to collect 18,269 interviews from January through December 1996. The five selection stages consisted of

> . . . the selection of primary sampling units (PSUs) (e.g., counties), the selection of subareas (blocks or block groups) within PSUs, the selection of listing units (housing units or individual dwelling units within noninstitutionalized group quarters that are occupied by one or more civilians) with these subareas, the selection of age domains (age groups 12 to 17, 18 to 25, 26 to 34, 35 to 49, and 50 and older) within sampled listing units, and the selection of eligible individuals with the sampled age domains (SAMSHA, 1998).

The survey achieved an overall response rate of 78.6 percent, with similar rates for whites, blacks, and Hispanics (77.1, 79.4, and 80.9 percent, respectively). To assure anonymity and encourage honesty, self-administered answer sheets were distributed to collect sensitive material, such as frequency and recentness of drug use. Interviewers were not privy to respondents' answers, and identifying information was separated from questionnaires (see Office of Applied Studies, SAMSHA, 1997, for a more detailed description of the sample design).

Defining the Appropriate Comparison Group

Before conducting analyses with NHSDA, we had to select that subset of NHSDA respondents that corresponds most closely in age with currently homeless clients in NSHAPC, and who are poor. NHSDA includes people 12 and older, up to people who are more than 100 years in age, whereas NSHAPC includes people 18 and older. In addition, less than 1 percent of currently homeless NSHAPC clients are 65 or older. Finally, our interest in using NHSDA as a comparison group lies in its ability to supply relevant information *for a low-income population,* whereas the total NHSDA sample covers all income groups in the United States. Therefore, we had to select a subsample of NHSDA respondents most similar in age and income to currently homeless NSHAPC clients before we could proceed with comparisons.

Age was the simplest variable on which to limit the sample; only respondents age 18 to 64 were included. Selecting only respondents with household incomes below the federal poverty level (FPL) proved more difficult, and certain compromises had to be made. NHSDA asks for income in income classes, rather than for specific amounts. These income classes are fairly narrowly defined at the low end of the income distribution into $2,000 increments. However, due to concerns about respondent confidentiality, the Substance Abuse and Mental Health Services Administration (SAMSHA) does not release all 28 income categories for personal and family income on its public use data file. The most precise income variable on the public use file provided 13 recoded categories. Therefore, our selection of NHSDA sample members based on income can only approximate the actual FPL. For this reason, we refer to our comparison group as "*low-income*" adults rather than as poor adults. Table 4.10 presents 1996 FPLs by household size, and the closest corresponding maximum annual incomes of NHSDA respondents in our subsample, also by household size.

Table 4.10 *Federal Poverty Thresholds and Corresponding Household Income Categories for Low-Income NHSDA Adults*

Size of Family Unit	*Weighted Average Poverty Thresholds in 1996*	*Maximum Income of Included NHSDA Respondents*
One person (under 65 years)	$8,163	$8,999
Two persons	$10,564	$11,999
Three persons	$12,316	$14,999
Four persons	$16,036	$19,999
Five persons	$18,952	$19,999
Six persons	$21,389	$24,999
Seven persons	$24,268	$24,999
Eight persons	$27,091	$29,999

Source: For federal poverty levels, *1998 Green Book.* For NHSDA respondents, Urban Institute analysis of weighted NHSDA data.

Eighteen percent (*N* = 3,364) of the NHSDA respondents meet the low-income criterion and are included in our final analysis. They represent the general population of low-income households in the United States, and will be referred to hereafter as low-income adults.

NOTES

1. By making a few assumptions, we can make a rough extrapolation to the rate of alcohol/drug and mental health problems among all adults becoming homeless during an entire year's time. We used information about the adults who became homeless within the week before the NSHAPC interview (the same adults we used to project an annual rate of homelessness in chapter 2) and about the remainder of the adults who were homeless at the time of their NSHAPC interview. We assumed that the adults in the NSHAPC sample included in the "homelessness began within the past week" group are typical of weekly entry cohorts throughout the year. We also calculated results using both October/November assumptions and February assumptions. Based on these premises, we estimate that between 50 and 58 percent of adults homeless over the course of a year would have had past-year alcohol and/or drug problems, while between 24 and 38 percent would have had past-year mental health problems.
2. The Addiction Severity Index is an instrument developed by the National Institute on Drug Abuse (Fureman, Parikh, Bragg, and McLellan 1990). Its subscales measure a client's level of problems with alcohol, with drugs, and with mental or emotional problems. Cutoff levels used here are slight modifications of the means reported in Zanis, McLellan, Cnaan, and Randall (1994). For alcohol and drugs, the ASI measures amount and recency of use. For mental health, it measures the eight items reported in the text.

For both, it measures self-reported level of problems with use/disturbance at symptoms, and desire for treatment.

3. The eighth ASI item, "taking prescribed medications for psychological or emotional problems," was a criterion in its own right (criterion 3) for classifying a client as having a mental health problem.

4. All differences mentioned in the text without qualification are significant at $p < .05$. Any difference described as "marginal" meets the criterion of $p < .10$. To account for the sample design and its deviation from simple random sampling, these statistical tests were performed incorporating a design effect of 3. Since the size of several subsamples used in the analysis for this chapter is quite small, seemingly large percentage point differences still may not be statistically significant.

5. The percentages in table 4.3 are for all homeless clients/low-income adults. This is so, rather than reporting proportions only for eligibles (i.e., those with a problem), because we could not identify variables or sets of variables in NHSDA that were comparable to our indicators that someone has a *problem* with alcohol or drug use rather than simply using these substances, or that someone had a mental health *problem*.

6. At these low frequency levels, differences of 5 percentage points are statistically significant at *alpha* = .05.

7. The NSHAPC data collection occurred *before* major changes in these programs that may have affected homeless populations since 1997. Welfare reform, with its changes for the AFDC program in eligibility and shift from an entitlement to a time-limited basis, had just been passed by Congress (in August 1996) and had not yet been implemented in any state. Food stamp changes for able-bodied childless people had not yet gone into effect, nor had changes for immigrants and permanent residents. SSI and SSDI changes in eligibility that eliminated some primary diagnoses that were important for homeless people (especially substance abuse) did not take effect until January 1, 1997.

5

Issues in Child and Youth Homelessness

Of all homeless people, homeless children are the most vulnerable. In a recent review, Rosenheck, Bassuk, and Salomon (1999) summarize a growing number of studies on homeless children. They observe that homeless children have high rates of both acute and chronic health problems, and are more likely than poor, housed children to be hospitalized and to have delayed immunizations (Alperstein, Rappaport, and Flanigan 1988; Parker et al. 1991; Rafferty and Shinn 1991; Weinreb et al. 1998). Homeless children also experience developmental delays and emotional and behavioral difficulties (Bassuk and Rosenberg 1990; Buckner and Bassuk 1997; Molnar and Rath 1990; Zeisemer, Marcoux, and Marwell 1994; Zima, Wells, and Freeman 1994). But studies comparing homeless to housed children find that such difficulties are associated more with their mother's emotional distress than with their homeless condition (Buckner and Bassuk 1997). Homeless children suffer the effects of residential instability and the problems it may entail with respect to family cohesion and changing school environments (Buckner and Bassuk 1997; Simpson and Fowler 1994; Wood et al. 1990, 1993). In addition, homeless compared to poor, housed children are significantly more likely to have lived in households with no parent present, whether with other relatives or in formal foster care (Bassuk et al. 1997).

Further, childhood homelessness and its accompanying vulnerabilities appear to translate into greater risk of homelessness as an adult, and also, most especially, as a young adult. Both longitudinal and other studies have highlighted histories of foster care, other out-of-home placement, physical and sexual abuse (which often precede out-of-home placement), parental alcohol and/or drug use, and childhood residential instability and homelessness with one's family that are much more common among people with experiences of adult homelessness than those without (Bassuk et al. 1997; Caton et al. 1994; Herman et al. 1997; Koegel, Melamid, and Burnam 1995; Mangine, Royse, and Wiehe 1990; Susser, Struening, and Conover 1987; Susser et al. 1991; Weitzman, Knickman, and Shinn 1992; Wood et al. 1990). Chapter 8 presents similar findings from NSHAPC's national sample that corroborate the results of earlier studies, which used samples from single cities or counties.

Ever since Piliavin and his colleagues (Piliavin, Sosin, and Westerfelt 1993) found high rates of foster care and other childhood out-of-home experiences in a study of homelessness in Minneapolis, policymakers and researchers alike have focused on foster care as a risk factor for adult homelessness. There are many reasons for making this association. They all have to do with factors that affect an adult's ability to establish and maintain support networks that might serve as buffers to homelessness. First, the abusive or neglectful treatment by caretakers that precipitates foster care placement affects a child's ability to form healthy and trusting bonds with others. Second, removal from the home, by its very nature, breaks the ties to family that may sustain a person against a crisis that otherwise would precipitate a homeless episode. Third, the foster care system assumes responsibility for a child only until age 18. Most children "aging out" of the system at 18 find themselves abruptly without even the semblance of family they may have had through foster care, and also often without training, skills, or experience to sustain themselves independently. Recent years have seen the development of some transitional programs, but they still are too few for most youth leaving foster care.

Despite the vulnerability of homeless children and the increasingly apparent connections between childhood and adult homelessness, we know relatively little about homeless children compared to homeless adults. Tallies of shelter and other service users usually count children if they are present, but may not separate results for children and adults. Most interview-based studies of homeless people include only adults, plus the occasional youths who are present on their own in facilities serving adults. Some interview studies ask homeless adults whether they have children with them, but only a few have gathered more detailed information about those children. Still fewer have actually examined the situation of children directly.

Even the term "homeless children" is ambiguous. The majority of homeless clients in NSHAPC are parents, yet only 15 percent report that one or more of their own minor children lives with them. This chapter examines the characteristics and circumstances of these children. Homeless parents may also have minor children who do *not* live with them. Some of these children may never have lived with this homeless parent, and should not be thought of as homeless just because a noncustodial parent is. Other children, however, may have lived with the parent until the parent became homeless. There are many reasons why these children may have been separated from their parents. They include emergency shelters not accepting teenage children, parents wanting to minimize disruption in the child's home and school life, and relatives agreeing to care for children until the parent secures stable housing. Such children are obviously affected by a parent's homelessness and, under some definitions, might be considered homeless themselves, at least with regard to eligibility for educational and other support services. This chapter looks at their sex, age, and living situations.

Finally, some homeless people are youth who are homeless on their own, without the company of a homeless parent. Although many studies focus specifically on homeless youth, such youth usually comprise only a very small proportion in studies that find their samples in adult shelters, transitional housing programs, and general street searches (see, for example, Ringwalt et al. 1998; Robertson and Toro 1999). NSHAPC included runaway and homeless youth shelters in its emergency shelters sampling frame, but still was only able to interview a few youth under age 18. If one considers a homeless youth to be someone 17 and younger, then they comprise less than 1 percent of the NSHAPC homeless subsample. However, if one extends the age range of youth up to 24, as do many service programs targeted toward youth, then 12 percent of the NSHAPC homeless sample falls in this age range.

This chapter does two quite different things. First, it examines the situations of children of homeless parents, including those who are homeless with the parent and those living in some arrangement away from the parent. It finds that most homeless adults are parents of minor children, but that homeless women are much more likely than homeless men to be caring for them while homeless. It also highlights the critical importance of children's *mothers.* They, while homeless themselves, are still taking care of their own children, and, when not homeless, are most likely taking care of children they have had with men who now are homeless. Without a mother, children of homeless parents face a much higher probability of foster care.

Second, the chapter looks at the youngest adults in the NSHAPC sample, those 24 and younger, and explores some of the childhood risk factors that may be more prevalent among them. It finds these youth with extremely high levels of vulnerability stemming from their own childhoods. These undoubtedly contribute to their homelessness. Some, in fact, may be the products of family homelessness during the previous decade and a half, a possibility we explore.

Living Situations and Characteristics of the Children of Homeless Clients

Most (63 percent) homeless clients were parents (76 percent of women and 57 percent of men), but only 15 percent had one or more of their own minor children with them. This discrepancy raises the important questions of the whereabouts and living situations of the remaining children. To answer them, we begin by making homeless clients who are parents our unit of analysis, and examining the share of their children under 18 who live with them.

Forty-seven percent of homeless clients had at least one child who was still a minor (table 5.1, upper panel). Of these clients, 17 percent had one, 15 percent had two, and 16 percent had three or more minor children. Homeless men and women were equally likely to have one minor child (17 percent of each), but homeless women were more likely to have two (18 versus 13 percent) and especially three or more (26 versus 11 percent).[1] In addition, 15 percent of homeless clients only had children 18 and older. We know nothing further about these adult children.

Female homeless clients with minor children were much more likely than their male counterparts to live with at least one of them (table 5.1, upper panel, second and third columns). Sixty-five percent of female homeless clients who had minor children lived with one or more of them (39 percent of all homeless women). This compared to only 7 per-

Table 5.1 *Parenting Status of Homeless Clients*

	Percent of All Homeless Clients (N = *2,938*)	*Percent of Homeless Women (32% of homeless clients)* (N = *950*)	*Percent of Homeless Men (68% of homeless clients) (N = 1,985)*
Are Parents	63	76	57
Have only children 18 and older	15	15	15
Have at least 1 minor child	47	60	41
Have 1 minor child	17	17	17
Have 2 minor children	15	18	13
Have 3 or more minor children	16	26	11
Live with at least 1 minor child	15	39	3
Have One Minor Child Who			
Lives with client	26	61	10
Does not live with client	74	39	90
Have 2 Minor Children, And			
Both live with client	28	43	18
1 lives with client	9	23	*
Neither lives with client	63	34	82
Have 3 or More Minor Children, And			
All live with client	30	52	8
2 live with client	7	12	1
1 lives with client	14	12	14
None lives with client	50	25	77

Source: Urban Institute analysis of weighted 1996 NSHAPC client data; *N*s given at top of table are unweighted (designated "UN").

Note: Percentages do not sum to 100 due to rounding.

*Denotes values that are less than 0.5 percent but greater than 0.

cent of male homeless clients with minor children who lived with at least one of them (3 percent of all homeless men).

For the homeless client sample as a whole, it is clear that most of their minor children (72 percent) did not live with them. For clients with one minor child, 74 percent did not live with that child (table 5.1, lower panel, first column). For those with two, 63 percent did not live with either, and another 9 percent lived with only one (thus 68 percent of these children lived away from the homeless client). The majority of children of homeless clients with three or more children did not live with the client. Further, the data for male and female homeless clients make clear that homeless women were much more likely than men to have at least some of their children with them, regardless of how many they had.

Characteristics of Children, by Living Situation

To learn about the living situations and characteristics of minor children of homeless parents, we made the children themselves the unit of analysis. Within the larger categories of living or not living with the homeless parent, we look at the children's sex, age, and, for those not living with the homeless client, where they are living and when they last lived with the client.

Minor children of homeless clients were about equally as likely to be male as female, as was also true for children in the nation as a whole in 1996. Their distribution by sex did not differ for those living with or away from their homeless parent (table 5.2). The majority (62 percent) living with their homeless parent were eight years old or younger, making homeless children, on average, somewhat younger than all American children in 1996 (62 versus 41 percent were eight or younger). Children living with homeless clients were more likely than those living away from them to be very young. Twenty percent were two years old or younger, compared with only 5 percent of those living away from their homeless parent. Considering preschoolers (ages 0 to 5), 42 percent of children living with a homeless parent are this young, compared with only 22 percent of those living away. In contrast, children living away were more likely to be adolescents (35 percent were ages 12 to 17, versus 20 percent for those living with their homeless parent).

These age differences may arise from several causes. They could include restrictions on adolescent children in shelters, the willingness of relatives to take older children, and the desire of parents to give school-age children some continuity in neighborhood and school contexts. Alternatively, they may be an artifact of a parent's length of homelessness, the related difficulties of keeping parents and children together, and the probability that the parent would be less likely to produce new children while homeless (and, therefore, existing children would be older the longer the homeless spell lasted).

Table 5.2 also provides some basic information about the whereabouts of children who did not live with their homeless parent. Most

Table 5.2 *Minor Children[a] of Homeless Clients: Demographic Characteristics and Living Situations*

	Percentage of All Minor Children of Homeless Clients (UN = 3,113)	Child's Living Situation	
		Child Lives with Client (UN = 1,007)	Does Not Live with Client (UN = 2,106)
Percent of All Minor Children of Homeless Parents	100	28	72
Child's Gender			
Male	51	53	51
Female	49	47	49
Child's Age			
0 to 2 years	10	20	5
3 to 5 years	18	22	17
6 to 8 years	18	20	19
9 to 11 years	18	13	21
12 to 14 years	16	11	19
15 to 17 years	15	9	16
Not answered	5	5	4
Where Child Lives			
With client	28	100	0
With other parent	46	0	65
With client's parents or in-laws	6	0	8
With other relatives	9	0	13
In foster care or group home	4	0	6
Other[b]	6	0	8
Time since Child Lived with Client			
0 to 6 months	7	NA	13
7 to 12 months	3	NA	4
1 to 2 years	9	NA	13
3 to 4 years	7	NA	13
More than 4 years	22	NA	36
Child never lived with client	9	NA	15

Source: Urban Institute analysis of weighted 1996 NSHAPC client data; *N*s given at top of table are unweighted (designated "UN").

Note: Percentages do not sum to 100 due to rounding. NA = not applicable.

[a]Refers to children under the age of 18.

[b]To be classified as having one's child living with the client if the client lived in a shelter, the respondent had to say both that the child lived with him/her and that the child was with him/her at the time of the interview. Some parents living in a shelter said one of these but not the other, and were therefore categorized as not having their child(ren) living with them. These people appear as "other," along with children reported to be in jail or another institution, and in other unspecified situations.

(65 percent) were with the other parent; 21 percent were with other relatives in what may or may not be informal foster care; 6 percent were in formal foster care; and 8 percent were in other situations. The majority of children who did not live with the homeless parent had not done so for at least four years (36 percent) or ever (15 percent). In contrast, 13 percent had lived with the homeless parent within the past six months.

The Effect of Parent's Sex on Children's Living Situation

It is already clear from earlier analyses that homeless women who have minor children are much more likely than homeless men to have at least some of their children with them. The living situations of children *not* living with their homeless parent were also greatly affected by the parent's sex (table 5.3, first column, and figure 5.1).[2] Children living apart from their homeless father (93 percent of all children of homeless male clients) were most likely to be with the other parent (i.e., their mother). This was true for 82 percent of these children. Other arrangements included living with other relatives (10 percent) or in foster care or a group home (1 percent). The remaining 7 percent were in some "other" living situation.

The living arrangements of children living apart from their homeless mothers (46 percent of all children of homeless female clients) were quite different. Less than one-quarter (24 percent) lived with the other parent (the father), while close to half (46 percent) were with the children's grandparents or some other relative. Almost one-fifth (19 percent) were in foster care or a group home, and 10 percent were some "other" place.

Carrying this analysis one step further, we asked how recently homeless fathers and mothers lived with the children who were no longer in their care. We anticipated that homeless women would be more likely than homeless men to have lived with their children *recently*, and this, in fact, is the case. One-third (32 percent) of children of homeless mothers who were no longer with them had been living with her within the year before the NSHAPC survey. This compared to only 12 percent of children of homeless fathers who were not with them at the time of the NSHAPC survey. At the other end of the scale, 21 percent of the minor children reported by homeless men had *never* lived with their father, and another 45 percent had not lived with their father for at least four years. This compares to only 4 percent of the minor children of homeless

Table 5.3 *Minor Children of Homeless Clients: Age, Parent's Gender, and Child's Age and Living Situation*

	Percent of All Minor Children of Homeless Clients (UN = 3,113)	*Percent of Minor Children of Homeless Clients Who Do Not Live with the Client (UN = 2,106)*	*Child's Age*				
			0 to 2 Years (%) (UN = 351)	*3 to 5 Years (%) (UN = 548)*	*6 to 11 Years (%) (UN = 1,102)*	*12 to 17 Years (%) (UN = 960)*	*Unknown (%) (UN = 152)*
All Minor Children of Currently Homeless NSHAPC Clients	100	—	9	18	38	31	4
Lives with client	28	—	63	33	29	20	43
Does not live with client	72	—	37	67	71	80	57
Lives with other parent	46	65	55	46	67	73	†
Lives with respondent's parent or in-laws	6	8	10	12	8	5	—
Lives with other relatives	9	13	14	17	12	12	—
Lives in foster care or group home	4	6	8	7	6	7	—
Other[a]	6	8	13	18	7	4	—
All Minor Children of Currently Homeless Female Clients[b]							
Lives with client	54	—	75	52	59	41	75
Does not live with client	46	—	25	48	41	59	25
Lives with other parent	11	24	21	25	21	27	†

(Continued)

Table 5.3 *Minor Children of Homeless Clients: Age, Parent's Gender, and Child's Age and Living Situation* (Continued)

	Percent of All Minor Children of Homeless Clients (UN = 3,113)	*Percent of Minor Children of Homeless Clients Who Do Not Live with the Client* (UN = 2,106)	*Child's Age*				
			0 to 2 Years (%) (UN = 351)	*3 to 5 Years (%)* (UN = 548)	*6 to 11 Years (%)* (UN = 1,102)	*12 to 17 Years (%)* (UN = 960)	*Unknown (%)* (UN = 152)
Lives with respondent's parent or in-laws	9	20		27	23	11	—
Lives with other relatives	12	26	79	32	26	22	—
Lives in foster care or group home	9	19		11	19	29	—
Other[a]	5	10		6	11	10	—
All Minor Children of Currently Homeless Male Clients[c]							
Lives with client	7		37	11	4	5	4
Does not live with client	93		63	89	96	95	96
Lives with other parent	75	82	87	60	85	86	†
Lives with respondent's parent or in-laws	3	3		3	3	4	—
Lives with other relatives	7	7	13	7	6	8	—
Lives in foster care or group home	1	1		4	1	1	—
Other[a]	6	7		26	5	2	—

Source: Urban Institute analysis of weighted 1996 NSHAPC client data; *N*s given at top of table are unweighted (designated "UN").

Note: Percentages do not sum to 100 due to rounding. Shaded cells have been grouped due to small *N*s.

†Indicates insufficient *N*.

[a]To be classified as having client's child living with client if the respondent lived in a shelter, the respondent had to say both that the child lived with him/her and that the child was with him/her at the time of the interview. Some parents living in a shelter said one of these but not the other, and were therefore categorized as not having their child(ren) living with them. These people appear as "other."

[b]$N = 1,401$

[c]$N = 1,712$

Figure 5.1 *Residence of Minor Children Who Do Not Live with a Homeless Parent*

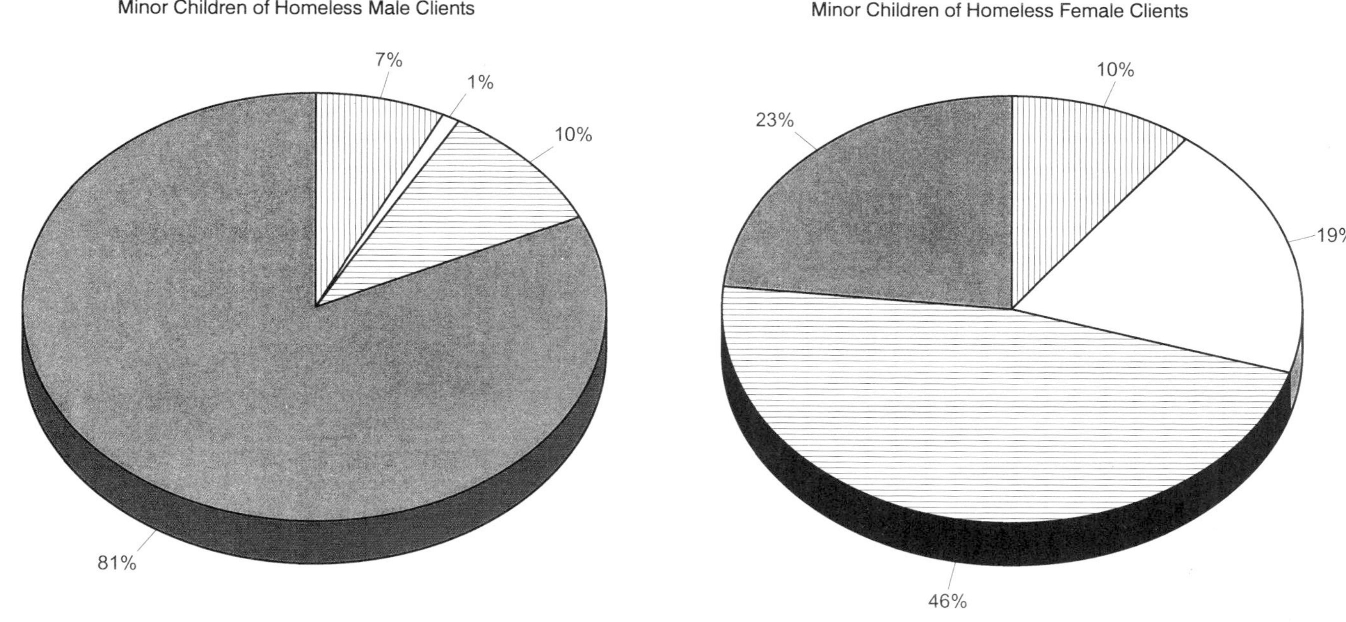

Source: Urban Institute analysis of weighted 1996 NSHAPC client data.
Note: Numbers do not sum to 100 due to rounding.

mothers who had *never* lived with their mother, and 22 percent who had not done so for at least four years. Length of the homeless parent's current spell of homelessness was also associated with the presence of children. Three times as many clients (overwhelmingly women) with homeless spells of a year or less had children with them, compared with clients homeless for more than a year (58 versus 18 percent).

Foster Care and the Children of Homeless Parents

Looking at foster care placement, although only 6 percent of children not living with their homeless parent were living in foster care or a group home, they were more likely to do so if their mother rather than their father was homeless. Conversely, they were much more likely to live with "the other parent," if the homeless parent was a man rather than a woman. In other words, women were doing the caretaking whether homeless or not. If mothers could not do it, then the children were at risk of informal or formal foster care. If the homeless parent was the mother, then her parents, other relatives, or formal foster care or group homes were about equally likely to provide the care. Further, these settings accounted for 75 percent of her children who did not live with her, compared to only 14 percent of homeless men's children not living with them.

Patterns seen in table 5.2 of children's age in relation to living situation are generally maintained for the younger children, as shown in table 5.3, which shows living situations for children of different ages, and by the sex of the homeless parent. As seen earlier, the youngest children (those age 0 to 2) were the most likely to be with the homeless parent, regardless of the parent's sex. However, table 5.3 reveals considerable differentiation by parent's sex for the probability that older children will be in foster care. The age of children who did not live with their homeless father did not affect the probability that they would be in foster care arrangements. However, the older the children of homeless women, the more likely they were to be in formal foster care arrangements. Only 11 percent of 3- to 5-year-olds lived in foster care, compared with 19 percent of 6- to 11-year-olds and 29 percent of 12- to 17-year-olds. Likely, relatives were willing to care for younger children, but either unwilling or unable to care for older children and teenagers.

Implications

We have already mentioned the importance of mothers as a bulwark against family disintegration, as evidenced by the living arrangements of the children of homeless parents. This implies that we should be giving these mothers as much support as possible to keep their children with them, or to reunite with them as early as possible. Alternatively, if it is clear that certain homeless mothers are unlikely ever again to be able to care for their children, then permanent arrangements should be made for their children so they do not remain in uncertain or unstable situations.

Another, very serious, implication has to do with our perceptions of "familyness" among homeless people in general. The data reported here indicate quite strongly that resolving a homeless episode for a "single" homeless woman is quite likely to mean re-creating a family comprised of her and her children. Homeless families are not just those where a child is clearly present; about half of all homeless women with children have at least one minor child living away from them. Therefore, from a policy perspective, one must think of homeless families as those where some, or perhaps all, of the children are *not* immediately present with their homeless mother, and where the most desirable outcome may be to reunite them and help them function again as an intact family. Relatively little public policy, as yet, takes account of this reality, but a few programs are beginning to provide this type of help.

Young Adult Homeless Clients

Given reported childhood homelessness, one must wonder whether such experiences translate into homelessness as an adult. Further, it may be that childhood homelessness affects both the timing of later homelessness as well as its future probability, such that the risk of homelessness in early adulthood increases. NSHAPC allows us to examine some of these relationships.

Since so few NSHAPC clients are youth under 18, we cannot use the survey's data to examine adolescents homeless by themselves. However, the sample does contain enough young-adult clients to let us explore some critical questions. We can explore, for example, who they are, and, most particularly, how their childhood experiences might help explain why they have become homeless so young. To do this, we created two groups of young-adult clients, those under 20 and those age 20 to 24, and compare them to homeless clients 25 and older.

Basic Demographic Characteristics

Young-adult homeless clients in both age groups are more likely to be women than men, in sharp contrast to the gender distribution of older homeless clients (table 5.4). More than half were women (56 and 58 percent, respectively), compared to only 28 percent of older homeless clients. This makes them more similar to the children of homeless parents than to the older group. There were no differences in the racial/ethnic composition of the three groups. However, clients age 20 to 24 were far more likely to be in a homeless family (41 percent) than were either the younger (14 percent) or older homeless clients (12 percent). In addition, 9 percent of 20- to 24-year-olds were pregnant. This rate of pregnancy translates to 16 percent of female clients in this age range. Given the small sample sizes, this rate is only marginally higher than the negligible 2 percent of women younger than 20 who were pregnant, but not significantly different from the 7 percent age 25 and older who were. Most pregnant women in each subsample already had children who lived with them in homeless families.

Neither group of younger clients was as likely as those age 25 and older to have at least a high school diploma (49 versus 64 percent). This may be due to their age and their lower opportunity to have compensated for an incomplete education through G.E.D. or other educational activities, or it may be due to greater problems related to school. The youngest homeless clients were more likely than others to be in central cities, and far less likely to be in the suburbs or urban fringes of MSAs. Studies of shelter and street populations of youth have also noted this concentration, while some other studies using other methods have not (Robertson and Toro 1999).

Finally, younger homeless clients were more likely than older ones to have connections to family and friends. Youth age 20 to 24 were more likely than older homeless clients to have spent time with family or friends in the 30 days before their NSHAPC interview. This may be related to their much higher probability of having children with them, and potentially needing help in relation to the children. Both younger groups were more likely to have received money from family or friends

Table 5.4 *Basic Demographic Characteristics of Young Homeless Clients* (weighted percentages)

	Clients under 20 Years Old (UN = 125)	*Clients Age 20 to 24 (UN = 217)*	*Clients Age 25 and Older (UN = 2,578)*
Percent of All Homeless Clients	5	7	88
Gender			
Male	44	42	72
Female	56	58	28
Race/Ethnicity			
White non-Hispanic	42	45	41
Black non-Hispanic	42	36	40
Hispanic	14	19	10
American Indian	1	1	9
Other	1	*	1
High School graduate or More	49	49	64
In Homeless Family or Pregnant			
Not in a homeless family (not living with own child[ren])	86	59	88
Not pregnant	85	57	87
Pregnant	1	2	1
In a homeless family (living with own child[ren])	14	41	12
Not pregnant	14	34	11
Pregnant	*	7	1
Urban-Rural Status			
Central city	88	66	70
Suburban/balance MSA	7	29	21
Rural	5	5	9
Age First Homeless			
Under 12	1	*	1
12 to 17 years	65	35	17
18 to 19 years	35	23	5
20 to 24 years	0	42	13
25 or older	NA	NA	64
Years since First Homeless Episode			
1 year or less	42	40	21
2 to 9 years	58	52	37
10 years or more	0	9	42
Spent Time with Family/Friends[a]	52	66	51
Received Money from Family/Friends[a]	49	34	18

Source: Urban Institute analysis of weighted 1996 NSHAPC client data; *N*s given at top of table are unweighted (designated "UN").

Note: NA = not applicable

[a]Within the past 30 days.

*Denotes values that are less than 0.5 percent but greater than 0.

in the 30 days before being interviewed, and the youngest subgroup was marginally more likely than the 20- to 24-year-olds to have done so.

Homeless Histories

Simply by token of their age, these young-adult homeless clients began their homeless careers when very young. But how young, and how different are they from older homeless clients, who may also have had an early start in homelessness? It turns out that both groups of young homeless clients were significantly more likely than older homeless clients to have become homeless for the first time as minors (younger than 18); in addition, the two younger groups also differed in age at first homelessness (table 5.4). Fully two-thirds (66 percent) of the youngest group first became homeless as minors, although less than 1 percent were minors at the time of the survey. This compares to 36 percent for the 20- to 24-year-olds, and only 18 percent for older homeless clients. For both younger groups, their early homelessness began in their teens rather than childhood, as very few reported being younger than 12 when they first became homeless. The same was true for older homeless clients. Thus, they may have been older children of homeless parents, left with relatives during a parent's homeless spell. But they are more likely, as described below, to be associated with fractured family relationships that precipitated episodes of running away or being forced to leave home.

Again, by virtue of their young age, one would not expect clients in the two younger groups to report many years of homelessness, in contrast to older homeless clients. This expectation, however, was only partially borne out (table 5.4). It is true that more clients in the two younger groups than in the older one reported a relatively short period (one year or less) since first becoming homeless (42 and 40 percent versus 21 percent). However, more clients in both youth subgroups than in the older group reported experiences of homelessness going back 2 to 9 years, and a remarkable 9 percent of the 20- to 24-year-olds reported that their first experience of homelessness began 10 or more years ago. This would make them no older than 10 to 14 at the time.

Clearly these patterns of early and—in many instances—prolonged homelessness in people so young suggests a high risk for continued homelessness. Chapter 6 explores this matter further, where early onset and multiple episodes of homelessness over a long time period characterize those in the homeless sample classified as "episodically" homeless.

Neglect, Abuse, Out-of-Home Placement, and Running Away

In becoming homeless so young, one might expect that these youth were already showing signs of problems even earlier. The obvious issues to examine are those that differentiate the larger homeless population from those who have never been homeless. These include childhood abuse and neglect, foster care or other out-of-home placement, school problems, problems with alcohol and drugs, and emotional or mental health problems.

The two groups of young homeless clients were alike in each type of abuse or neglect experience—neglect, physical abuse, or sexual abuse by a household member during childhood (table 5.5). When these are combined into physical and/or sexual abuse or these two types of abuse plus neglect, the two youngest groups remain similar. However, both younger groups were considerably more likely than older homeless clients to report at least one such experience, and also more likely to report abuse.

Given the abuse they experienced from household members, one would expect these young homeless clients to also be more likely to experience foster care or other out-of-home placement. In fact, this expectation is supported only for the youngest group, those under 20. These very young clients were more likely than either the 20- to 24-year-olds or those 25 and older to have been in foster care or other placement before reaching age 18 (61 versus 34 and 23 percent, respectively). Placement rates were elevated for both foster care and group homes, but not for institutions. This same pattern holds when looking at out-of-home placement in adolescence (ages 12 to 17). But for childhood (before age 13), only those in the youngest group were more likely than those 25 and older to have experienced this type of placement. There were no differences among the groups in the time spent in out-of-home placement, given that they spent any time in it.

Not everyone who has ever run away from home considers their experiences as experiences of homelessness. However, for the youth in this sample, it is highly likely that such episodes were precursors to their current homelessness, and may also be part of their present homeless spell. We examined reports of running away for 24 hours or more before 18, and also of being forced to leave home for more than 24 hours (table 5.5). The youngest homeless clients reported these experiences at significantly higher rates than either of the other groups. Indeed, *the majority* of homeless clients under 20 reported *each* of these experiences. In

Table 5.5 *Childhood Neglect, Abuse, and Out-of-Home Experiences of Young Homeless Clients*
(weighted percentages)

	Clients under 20 Years Old (UN = 125)	*Clients Age 20 to 24 (UN = 217)*	*Clients Age 25 and Older (UN = 2,578)*
Before Client Reached Age 18, Someone Client Lived With			
Left client without adequate food or shelter	22	14	12
Physically abused client, to cause physical harm	33	33	21
Forced or pressured client to perform sexual acts that client did not want to do	16	21	12
Abuse/Neglect Combinations before Age 18			
Physical and/or sexual abuse but not neglect	42	40	23
One or more abuse/neglect experiences	51	41	27
Before Age 18, Client Was Ever Placed In			
Foster care, group home, or institution	61	34	23
Foster care	40	18	9
Group home	41	21	7
Institution	27	13	15
Before Age 13, Client Was Ever Placed In			
Foster care, group home, or institution	35	21	13
Foster care	20	18	8
Group home	23	13	5
Institution	16	6	6
Between Age 13 and 17, Client Was Ever Placed In			
Foster care, group home, or institution	54	28	18
Foster care	36	10	6
Group home	39	18	5
Institution	24	12	12
Length of Time in Out-of-Home Placement before Age 18[a]			
Less than one week	6	1	2
1 to 4 weeks	3	21	5
1 to 6 months	6	12	16
7 to 12 months	9	6	13

(*Continued*)

Table 5.5 *Childhood Neglect, Abuse, and Out-of-Home Experiences of Young Homeless Clients (Continued)*
(weighted percentages)

	Clients under 20 Years Old (UN = 125)	*Clients Age 20 to 24 (UN = 217)*	*Clients Age 25 and Older (UN = 2,578)*
13 to 24 months	19	9	12
More than 2 years	56	51	51
Client Ever Ran Away from Home for More than 24 Hours before Age 18	51	38	32
Client Was Ever Forced to Leave Home for More Than 24 Hours before Age 18	50	36	20
First Time Client Became Homeless Occurred before Age 18	64	35	18

Source: Urban Institute analysis of weighted 1996 NSHAPC client data; *N*s given at top of table are unweighted (designated "UN").

Note: Percentages do not sum to 100 due to rounding.

[a]Among homeless clients who spent time in foster care, a group home, or an institution before they were 18 years old.

addition, the 20- to 24-year-olds were more likely than older homeless clients to have been forced to leave home at least once before 18. There are also likely to be strong connections between abuse/neglect experiences and running away or being pushed out of the house, as reported in much of the literature on homeless youth (Robertson and Toro 1999).

In the NSHAPC data, abuse and neglect appear to play a substantial role in other experiences of youth that disrupt family life. Among the entire sample of homeless clients, 46 percent of those in out-of-home placement as a child also reported abuse and/or neglect, as did 53 percent of those who had run away from home and 52 percent of those who had been forced to leave before 18. The youngest group stands out as the most likely to report the associations of abuse/neglect with out-of-home placement. More than three-quarters (77 percent) of the youngest group who had been in out-of-home placement reported abuse and/or neglect in their childhood home, compared to 53 percent of 20- to 24-year-olds and 42 percent of clients 25 and older. They were also more likely than those 25 and older to reveal an association between running away and abuse/neglect. Sixty-nine percent of those who had run away said they also experienced abuse and/or neglect in childhood, compared to 51 percent of clients 25 and older.

Early Signs of Difficulties

When youth are in trouble, it often comes in more than one form (Basen-Engquist, Edmundson, and Parcel 1996; Burt, Resnick, and Novick 1998; Lindberg, Boggess, and Williams 2000; Resnick, Harris, and Blum 1993; Zweig, Lindberg, and Alexander 2000). NSHAPC gathered information about the age at which clients experienced a variety of difficulties. We can use it to see whether the youngest groups among the homeless are differentially likely to report these difficulties in childhood or adolescence. We examine problems with alcohol and drugs, school problems, and, for recent years, mental health problems (table 5.6).

The youngest group was more likely than either of the others to have begun drinking before age 15 (32 versus 15 and 26 percent), and also to have begun using drugs before 15 (31 versus 12 and 19 percent). However, the differences apparent in table 5.6 with respect to drinking to get drunk and using drugs regularly are not statistically significant.

These early experiences with alcohol and drugs translated into high levels of reported problems with alcohol, and, especially, drugs in the year before the NSHAPC interview and in their lifetimes. However, for past-year and lifetime alcohol problems, these levels were significantly lower than those reported by older homeless clients. For lifetime drug problems, older homeless clients reported higher rates than those 20 to 24, but similar to those younger than 20. Past-year and lifetime mental health problems did not differ among the groups. While seemingly unremarkable at first, as no group stands out, it means remarkably that each group of homeless youth was already quite troubled by mental health problems, as young as they were.

Earlier we saw that the two younger groups had completed fewer years of education than older homeless clients, and speculated this might be due to their youth and that their education was not yet complete. Data in table 5.6 indicate that with respect to repeating one or more grades or dropping out, the two younger groups and the remaining homeless clients did not differ. However, homeless youth under 20 were significantly more likely than either of the other groups to have been suspended or expelled. This probably contributed to their failure to complete a high school education or G.E.D. They do not appear to have been in more trouble with the law, however, as reports of juvenile detention did not differ among the groups.

Table 5.6 *History of Alcohol, Drug, and Mental Health Problems among Young Homeless Clients*
(weighted percentages)

	Clients under 20 Years Old (UN = 125)	*Clients Age 20 to 24 (UN = 217)*	*Clients Age 25 and Older (UN = 2,578)*
Adverse Experiences before Age 18			
First started drinking			
Before age 15	32	15	26
Between age 15 and 17	9	17	22
First started drinking to get drunk			
Before age 15	23	11	13
Between age 15 and 17	12	14	15
First started using drugs			
Before age 15	31	12	19
Between age 15 and 17	17	15	20
First started using drugs regularly			
Before age 15	20	9	11
Between age 15 and 17	23	13	15
Problems in Past Year			
Alcohol problems	26	27	49
Drug problems	43	29	38
Mental health problems	46	46	45
Problems in Lifetime			
Alcohol problems	37	40	65
Drug problems	48	38	60
Mental health problems	50	56	57
Less than High School Degree	51	51	37
Ever Repeated a Grade			
One grade	33	33	24
More than one grade	10	7	6
Ever Dropped Out of School			
Elementary school	1	1	2
Junior high/middle school	8	16	7
Senior high school	48	51	42
Ever Suspended from School	72	41	43
Ever Expelled from School	32	17	18
Juvenile Detention before Age 18	23	23	15

Source: Urban Institute analysis of weighted 1996 NSHAPC client data; *N*s given at top of table are unweighted (designated "UN").

Concluding Thoughts

The different circumstances of children of male and female homeless clients is striking. Children of homeless males were overwhelmingly with their other parent, their nonhomeless mother, and were not likely to have lived with their father for a very long time, or ever. Very few were in foster care. Nonhomeless mothers, obviously, were assuming responsibility for their children. The importance of this maternal caretaking is made particularly apparent when one considers the circumstances of children whose mothers are homeless. These children are caught between two very undesirable alternatives—either they share their mother's homelessness, or they run a high risk of being placed in foster care. Each is well known to have serious negative consequences. It is clear that mothers are their children's last line of defense. When mothers are in trouble, their children are in trouble.

It is also clear that the two younger groups of clients differ from older clients—and also from each other—in important ways. The two younger subgroups differ from older homeless clients in that they were in more trouble, earlier in their lives, and that many already had prolonged histories of homelessness even though the oldest was only 24. Differences between the two younger subgroups are also important. The 20- to 24-year-olds were more likely to be in homeless families (to have children with them) than any subgroup in this book that is not itself based on family status. Forty-three percent were in homeless families and/or were pregnant. In fact, they comprised 27 percent of all women with children in the homeless sample, as seen in chapter 3. These young homeless clients do not appear to have experienced quite as many varieties of trouble early in life as those under 20, but neither do they appear headed for self-sufficiency and stable housing.

The youngest group of adult homeless clients, those under 20, reported an array of problems and experiences that greatly resemble those (we will see in chapter 6) describing clients with an episodic pattern of homelessness. In particular, three in five were products of the foster care system. We will defer discussion of these connections to chapter 6. There we will draw together more of the threads that weave a pattern of intermittent but prolonged exposure to homelessness. If one thing is clear already, however, it is the failure of many institutions to intervene effectively in children's lives with sufficient resources and environments to prevent homelessness.

NOTES

1. All differences between percentages mentioned in the text without qualification are significant at $p < .05$. Any difference described as "marginal" meets the criterion of $p < .10$. To account for the sample design and its deviation from simple random sampling, these statistical tests were performed incorporating a design effect of 3. Since the size of several subsamples in this chapter is quite small, seemingly large percentage point differences still may not be statistically significant.
2. Some cells of table 5.3 have been combined to provide cell sizes large enough to analyze.

6

Patterns of Homelessness

People's experiences of homelessness vary considerably. Some are homeless only once in their life and, often, for only a short time. Others experience several short or medium-length spells before finally securing stable housing. Yet others live on the streets or in other places not intended for human habitation for many years, or keep going into and out of homelessness without being able to establish permanent housing. Understanding these patterns is important for both policy-making and service system design and delivery. Addressing and even preventing first-time or crisis homelessness is likely to involve more-focused and relatively inexpensive interventions, such as assistance with rent, mortgage, and utility payments; tenant-landlord mediation; or job-search assistance. Individuals who are episodically or chronically homeless may require more long-term and intensive services. These may include basic treatment for addictions or mental disorders, basic life skills, and follow-up supportive services, in addition to secure housing. Understanding the characteristics of people with different patterns of homelessness can help policymakers and program staff both design more effective services and also use limited resources more wisely.

Unfortunately, determining how long and how many times people have been homeless proves to be less simple than might be expected. A number of early studies attempting to collect such information simply asked homeless people, *When was the last time you had a home or other* *permanent place to stay?* (e.g., Burt and Cohen 1989). The answer was compared to the date of the interview to calculate how long the person had been homeless. However, when a 1991 study of the Washington, D.C., metropolitan area (DC*MADS; Bray, Dennis, and Lambert 1993) asked this question and then compared answers to details of the same person's housing history, an important discovery was made. While it may have been many years since those interviewed considered themselves as having a home, they nevertheless had stayed places during their homeless spell where they would not be considered literally homeless. These included the homes of family or friends, the military, inpatient treatment programs, detoxification facilities, and correctional facilities.

In the process of trying to identify factors that promote permanent exits from homelessness and understand its dynamics, other studies also document significant movement of homeless people into and out of literal homelessness for shorter and longer, and stable and unstable, periods. Some have used shelter tracking databases to do this (e.g., Culhane and Kuhn 1998; Wong, Culhane, and Kuhn 1998). Others have used prospective longitudinal approaches (e.g., Piliavin, Wright, Mare, and Westerfelt 1996; Wong and Piliavin 1997; Zlotnick, Robertson, and Lahiff 1999). Still others have used retrospective housing histories similar to the DC*MADS approach (e.g., Hopper, Jost, Hay, Welber, and Haugland 1997).

As we present NSHAPC information on patterns of homelessness, it is important to remember that the analyses are strongly affected by the type of data being analyzed. Studies of homeless people identified at a single point in time, such as NSHAPC, overrepresent those with long and/or continuous histories of homelessness and underrepresent those whose homelessness is more recent. This is true simply because point-in-time snapshots cannot adequately represent the large numbers of people who are homeless only for short periods.

A 1987 national study by the Urban Institute, for example, found that 41 percent of its homeless sample had been homeless for more than two years, and only 21 percent had been homeless for less than three months (Burt and Cohen 1989). Similarly, the DC*MADS Homeless and Transient Population Study found 78 percent of the homeless people in its sample were intermittently or chronically homeless, and only 23 percent were newly homeless (Dennis et al. 1999). Some variation exists in the proportion of people in a one-time homeless study who will be long-term based on geography and other factors. For instance, studies in rural areas tend to find higher proportions of homeless people with short spells than in urban areas (Burt 1999; First et al. 1994; Kentucky Housing Corporation 1993). Nevertheless, *any* one-time study of homelessness exaggerates the proportion of those who have been homeless for a long time.

Point-in-time findings on the distribution of short- and long-term homelessness are strikingly different from those from databases that record all people using shelters over time in particular communities. These databases are able to eliminate double counting, and thus can develop a count of how many *different* people have used homeless shelters over long periods. Data from these shelter tracking databases in New York and Philadelphia, for example, suggest that only 10 percent of the shelter-using homeless population should be considered long-term or chronically homeless (Kuhn and Culhane 1998). By contrast, people experiencing first-time/crisis or transitional homelessness comprise the vast majority of shelter stayers over periods as short as a year (78 percent in New York and 81 percent in Philadelphia). On this single point, the distribution of short- and long-term homelessness, cross-sectional studies should not produce results much different from prospective longitudinal studies, which also identify their initial sample within a relatively short time period and then reinterview them several times. Prospective longitudinal studies, however, have much more detail about homeless careers from the day of sample selection forward.

Despite these limitations, there still are important reasons for examining patterns of homelessness with the type of point-in-time data available from NSHAPC. First, there is no single *best* data source. All have their biases, all miss certain important parts of either populations or life histories, and all should be used with appropriate cautions. Once we see what NSHAPC offers, we end this chapter with a discussion of the relative merits of different types of data in understanding patterns of homelessness.

Second, as most studies of homeless people have collected data at a single point in time, NSHAPC data offer a useful comparison with similar studies that may have occurred earlier or had a more limited geographical scope. Using respondents' self-reported housing histories can also compensate for some of the limitations of point-in-time data. Analyses that rely on data from shelter systems are always limited to the homeless people who use them, and usually are limited to the community with the data system. In contrast, point-in-time studies may cover more than one community, and may also be structured to include homeless people who do not use shelters (as we shall see, some significant proportion of homeless clients with the longest spells are in this group). NSHAPC, in particular, covered the entire nation, and sampled homeless people from many non-shelter types of homeless assistance programs. NSHAPC, therefore, reflects a much larger and qualitatively different segment of the homeless population than shelter-based data systems.

This chapter first explores patterns of homelessness, using information about length of current spell and number of times the client reported being homeless to identify subgroups with episodic, chronic, and other patterns of homelessness. We use two different approaches, and look at the effects of pattern definitions on the characteristics of people classified into each category. We then consider the meaning of a "spell," focusing especially on issues related to breaks in spells. We examine length of homeless spells as reported by clients, and then inquire into their living situations *during their homeless spell* that *would not qualify* a person as literally homeless. Using this information, we then calculate a "net spell length" that reflects the proportion of time the client was in a literally homeless condition. We conclude with a discussion that is partly philosophical (what *is* a spell, and who should be the arbiter of its definition?) and partly pragmatic (how can we take advantage of movements in and out of homelessness to help keep people stably housed?).

Patterns or Typologies of Homelessness

Many researchers have used information on the number and length of homeless spells to develop typologies that are thought to distinguish among qualitatively different groups of homeless people and experiences of homelessness (Dennis et al. 1999; Humphreys and Rosenheck 1995; Kuhn and Culhane 1998; Piliavin et al. 1996; Wong and Piliavin 1997). A nomenclature dating from at least 1984 (Arce and Vergare 1984) classifies homeless people into three not-always completely distinct groups—first-time/crisis/transitional, episodic, and chronic. The hope is that doing so will lead to insights into understanding and helping them, as well as helping the public understand that not all homeless people are alike. The first group is expected to include individuals or families who are homeless only once or twice, and usually for a relatively short time (e.g., less than 6 or 12 months). The assumption is that these are people who were precariously housed. They encountered an unexpected crisis, such as unemployment, divorce/separation, or eviction, and found themselves homeless. Usually, they will secure some type of housing relatively quickly, and often not become homeless again.

In contrast, the concept of episodic homelessness reflects a tendency to cycle into and out of homelessness repeatedly, and for varying lengths of time. Time in various institutions, such as inpatient treatment centers, detoxification programs, and jail, may be part of these cycles (Hopper et al. 1997). The category of chronic homelessness is reserved for people who have relied on shelters or lived on the streets for many months or years, and usually have multiple barriers to securing stable employment and housing. They may have only a few distinct spells of homelessness, but each lasts a very long time.

In our effort to parallel previous typologies, we used two approaches to grouping clients into meaningful patterns of homelessness. The first relied on simple cross-tabulation of information about spell length and number of homeless episodes. The second was more methodologically sophisticated. It used cluster analysis with the same two variables, following the analytic approach reported by Culhane and Kuhn (1998), using quite different data (and producing quite different results). Both methods produce groupings that can fit the three-way classification, but the size of the subgroups and characteristics of their members differ is some important ways.[1]

Cross-Tabulation Analysis

The cross-tabulation we used is simple, based on the two key variables in much previous research: length of current homeless spell and number of spells in the client's lifetime. Homeless clients who reported being homeless only once and for a year or less were classified as *crisis;* those with multiple spells but whose current one had not exceeded a year were classified as *episodic;* those whose current spell was already longer than a year were classified as *chronic*, regardless of whether the spell was their first.[2] These criteria produced a distribution in which 20 percent of currently homeless clients were in the crisis group, 24 percent in the episodic group, and 56 percent in the chronic group (table 6.1).

Table 6.1 *Classification of Homeless Clients by Length of and Number of Homeless Spells*
(weighted percentages)

	Number of Times Homeless			
	1	*2*	*3*	*4 or more*
Spell Length				
1/2 month or less	6.9[a]	1.7[b]	1.3[b]	1.2[b]
More than 1/2 through 1 month	2.8[a]	2.0[b]	0.3[b]	2.0[b]
More than 1 through 3 months	4.0[a]	2.5[b]	0.9[b]	2.8[b]
More than 3 through 6 months	4.0[a]	2.7[b]	1.5[b]	1.7[b]
More than 6 through 12 months	2.7[a]	1.1[b]	0.5[b]	1.5[b]
More than 12 through 24 months[c]	6.1	1.0	2.9	2.7
More than 24 through 48 months[c]	9.9	2.6	2.3	6.0
More than 48 months[c]	12.8	3.1	2.1	4.7

Source: Urban Institute analysis of weighted 1996 NSHAPC client data.

[a]Clients in this group are homeless for the first time and/or experiencing a crisis, and represent 20 percent of respondents.

[b]Homelessness for this group is defined as being episodic, and affects 24 percent of respondents.

[c]Homelessness for this group is defined as being chronic, and affects 56 percent of respondents.

Cluster Analysis

Another common way to classify a set of observations into groups based on specific characteristics is to use a method known as cluster analysis. In homeless research, Culhane and Kuhn (1998) applied cluster analysis to data from Philadelphia and New York City shelter tracking databases (which are quite different from the data available from NSHAPC). In our analysis, we used the same two variables as Culhane and Kuhn, although they were defined within the NSHAPC framework, rather than from shelter tracking information. Homeless clients were clustered into three groups, based on the same two variables used for the cross-tabulations: the number of times clients reported ever having been homeless (including "this time"), and the length of their current homeless spell.[3]

An initial clustering of all homeless clients revealed that the model did a very good job of clustering clients with many spells (an episodically homeless group) or very long spells (a chronically homeless group). But the vast majority of the unweighted sample (over 90 percent) remained in a third group, which was much too heterogeneous to be characterized as anything in particular. To resolve this, another round of three-level clustering was done on the largest cluster. Clients appearing in the episodically and chronically homeless clusters from this second round were combined with those from the first. The second clustering reduced the size of the largest cluster to just under 80 percent of the unweighted sample. A third round of clustering was again done on the still-largest cluster, yielding a final three-level classification.

The largest cluster consists of 1,729 clients (or 62 percent of the *unweighted* homeless sample). Members of this cluster had an average current homeless spell of 9.1 months and had been homeless on average 1.9 times, including the current spell. We designated this group "crisis/residual." The second cluster consists of 459 clients (16 percent of the unweighted sample) whose mean homeless spell was slightly longer than those in the first group (11.3 months), but who reported having been homeless an average of 7.4 times. The third cluster includes 624 individuals (22 percent of the unweighted sample) who had unusually long homeless spells of more than four years (50.2 months) on average, but who reported relatively few homeless spells in their lifetime, for an average of only 1.6 spells.

Having developed two different classification schemes for crisis, episodic, and chronic patterns of homelessness, we turn to two important questions: First, how the three groups differ on characteristics other than the two used in creating the classifications, and, second, how the characteristics of groups based on each method (cross-tabulation or cluster analysis) differ from each other. We address them simultaneously.

Table 6.2 shows the distributions of the three groups, for each classification method, as a proportion of the *weighted* currently homeless sample, and the mean number of spells and current spell length for each group. These statistics make clear that the two methods created groups of very different sizes. The cross-tabulation method put more than half of homeless clients in the chronic group, and the cluster method put more than half in the crisis (or residual) group. Yet the mean number of episodes and the mean length of current spells also make it clear that both methods produced three groups with reasonable claims to their labels. The crisis groups reported relatively short (3 or 9 months, on average) and relatively few spells (1 or 2, on average). The episodic groups reported significantly more episodes (5.2 or 7.4, on average), but not necessarily longer *current* spells (3.2 or 11.3 months, on average). And the chronic groups reported by far the longest current spells

Table 6.2 *Characteristics of Crisis, Episodic, and Chronically Homeless Clients, Using Two Methods of Deriving Categories* (weighted percentages)

	By Cross-Tabulation[a]			*By Cluster Analysis*[b]		
	Crisis Homeless (UN = 363)	*Episodically Homeless (UN = 422)*	*Chronically Homeless (UN = 1,003)*	*Crisis Homeless (UN = 1,729)*	*Episodically Homeless (UN = 459)*	*Chronically Homeless (UN = 624)*
Percent of All Homeless Clients	20	24	56	56	17	27
Number of Times Homeless (Mean)	1.0	5.2	2.8	1.9	7.4	1.6
Months Homeless (Mean)	2.8	3.2	56.2	9.1	11.3	50.2
Male	61	62	77	65	72	71
Race						
White non-Hispanic	38	48	37	40	56	33
Black non-Hispanic	38	34	49	41	27	52
Hispanic	15	11	9	12	10	10
Other	9	6	6	7	8	5
Urban/Rural Status						
Central city	72	73	75	75	64	76
Suburban/balance MSA	16	20	21	18	28	19
	12	6	4	7	7	5
High School Graduate	66	65	60	67	67	54
Current Age						
Under 25	21	15	6	13	10	13
25 to 44 years	61	67	59	65	65	57
45 years or older	18	18	35	22	26	30

Age First without Regular Housing or a Place to Stay						
Under 18	16	40	25	18	36	20
18 to 34 years	45	43	45	46	53	49
35 years or older	39	18	30	36	11	31
Years since First without Regular Housing or a Regular Place to Stay						
1 year or less	72	24	18	35	2	12
2 to 9 years	15	42	36	37	31	47
10 years or more	13	33	46	27	68	42
Member of Homeless Family	25	20	7	22	10	6
Foster Care, Etc., as Child	23	30	22	21	45	23
Past-Year Alcohol/Drug Problem	49	30	67	63	64	56
Lifetime Alcohol/Drug Problem	65	63	83	78	79	77
Past-Year Mental Health Problem	32	51	53	42	54	57
Lifetime Mental Health Problem	49	60	62	54	71	65

Source: Urban Institute analysis of weighted 1996 NSHAPC client data.

[a]Crisis = first spell, one year or less; episodic = 2+ spells, current spell is one year or less; chronic = current spell more than one year.

[b]Groups generated by cluster analysis.

MSA = metropolitan statistical area.

(56.2 or 50.2 months, on average) and relatively few total spells (2.8 or 1.6, on average).

The big difference seems to be that cross-tabulation, by identifying everyone whose current spell had already lasted more than 12 months as chronic, put a considerable number of people in that group whom the cluster analysis placed in either the crisis or the episodic groups (as attested by the considerably higher mean number of months in the current spell for these two groups, as defined by clustering rather than cross-tabulation). Further, by restricting the crisis group to those with only one spell, the cross-tabulation analysis forced more people into the episodic group than the cluster analysis. Cluster analysis paid more attention to *very* long spells for the chronic group, and very *many* spells for the episodic group, leaving everyone else in the crisis/residual category.

Comparing Results to Those of Other Studies

Given that, even using the same data set, two different classification methods produce such strikingly different results, it should not be surprising that other studies are so inconsistent in calculating and reporting patterns of homelessness that we cannot do much with putting our results into historical context. In the DC*MADS study, Bray, Lambert, and Dennis (1993) classified 29 percent of their currently homeless clients as chronic, 22 percent as first-time, and 49 percent as intermittent. The 1987 Urban Institute study (Burt and Cohen 1989) found that 47 percent of its central city sample had homeless spells lasting a year or more, which would put them in the "chronic" category, based on our present cross-tabulation method. In Los Angeles, the Course of Homelessness study found that 45 percent of its homeless sample had current homeless spells lasting more than a year, and that 67 percent had been homeless more than once. The proportions in Los Angeles and in the 1987 Urban Institute study who would be classified as "chronic," using the definition of "more than one year," are roughly similar to the results produced by the present cross-classification method (45, 47, and 56 percent, respectively). The DC*MADS result, on the other hand, more closely resembles the proportion chronic derived from our cluster analysis (29 and 27 percent, respectively). There is much less convergence on the definitions, and hence the distributions, of clients considered episodic and crisis/first-time.

Using shelter tracking data, Culhane et al. (1994) produce startlingly different results for patterns of shelter stay in New York City and Philadelphia (78/81 percent transitional, 12/9 percent episodic, and 10/10 percent chronic, with chronic defined as using more than 180 days of shelter a year). The differences, we believe, stem from reliance on shelter information rather than on patterns of homelessness that take into consideration when people do not use shelters, or use them only intermittently. In the NSHAPC sample, only 32 percent of homeless clients used shelters all or most of the time they were homeless during their current spell. Families were significantly more likely than other homeless clients to use shelters this intensively (45 versus 29 percent). At the other extreme, 40 percent of homeless clients reported not using shelters at all, or using them very rarely during their current spell. Other homeless clients were more likely than families to avoid shelters this much, but the pattern was still true for almost one in three families (42 versus 30 percent). With this high a proportion of homeless clients avoiding shelter systems altogether or using them only sparingly, it is not surprising that analyses based on data coming only from shelters show very different patterns than data coming from a broader sample. Neither database and set of results is more right than the other; the major issue is to recognize the limitations of the data that went into them.

Does the Grouping Method Make a Difference?

The next questions are how different the characteristics of clients in the three groups are, and whether the different classification methods produce such different demographic and other characteristics for groups with the same name that we might draw different conclusions about crisis, episodic, and chronic homelessness depending on which method we employed. As might be expected, the three groups differ fairly dramatically on some variables but not others. Also, for some characteristics, the grouping method makes little or no difference, but for others, it makes a considerable difference.

Characteristics for Which It Makes Little Difference

RACE/ETHNICITY. Racial/ethnic characteristics varied substantially among the three groups, but the method used to create the groups did not affect the pattern of variation. By either method, the episodic groups included a higher proportion of white non-Hispanic clients than the chronic groups, and a marginally higher proportion of white non-Hispanic clients than the crisis groups.[4] Both chronic groups included more black non-Hispanic clients than their comparable crisis and episodic groups. In addition, the crisis/residual group created by cluster analysis also had significantly more black non-Hispanics than the cluster-created episodic group.

URBAN/RURAL STATUS. Each method shows that in every group, the large majority of people were found in central cities, and the fewest in rural areas. Minor variations reach statistical significance (more of the crisis homeless were in rural areas in the cross-tabulation groupings; in the cluster groupings, clients in the episodic group were less likely to be in central cities and more likely to be in suburban areas), but they do not alter the basic patterns.

BEING A HIGH SCHOOL GRADUATE. By either method, groups hovered around 60 percent high school graduates. The chronically homeless groups contained somewhat lower proportions of high school graduates, significantly so for the cluster-derived groups and non-significantly so for the cross-tabulation-derived groups.

AGE AT WHICH CLIENTS WERE FIRST WITHOUT REGULAR HOUSING/PLACE TO STAY. Regardless of method, the episodic group had the highest proportion of clients whose homelessness began before they reached age 18, and the fewest who were at least 35 years old when they first became homeless.

PAST-YEAR AND LIFETIME MENTAL HEALTH PROBLEMS. By either method, those in the crisis homeless groups were less likely than episodic or chronic group members to report either past-year or lifetime mental health problems. The difference between the crisis and episodic groups created by cross-tabulation was marginal; all others were significant.

Characteristics for Which It Makes an Important Difference

GENDER. Among the three groups created by cross-tabulation, the chronically homeless one stood out as including significantly more males than the other two. When the groups were created by cluster analysis, the crisis/residual group was the different one, having marginally fewer males than the episodic group.

CURRENT AGE. The chronic group produced by the cross-tabulation method included significantly more clients 45 and older, and significantly fewer under 25, than either of the other cross-tabulation groups. In contrast, the three groups produced by the cluster method did not differ in age structure.

BEING IN A HOMELESS FAMILY. Using the cross-tabulation method, the chronically homeless group included a significantly lower proportion of homeless families than either the crisis or episodic groups, which did not differ from each other. However, the clustering method produced a different pattern: The crisis homeless group had the most families, while the episodic and chronic groups did not differ from each other.[5]

Because the issue of homeless families is so important from a policy perspective, we also examined group membership to answer the question, "What pattern of homelessness is most typical for homeless families?" The cross-tabulation method placed 36 percent of homeless families in the crisis group, 35 percent in the episodic group, and 28 percent in the chronic group. In contrast, the cluster method placed 88 percent of families in the crisis/residual group, 12 percent in the episodic group, and 11 percent in the chronic group.

Remembering that NSHAPC, as a point-in-time survey, captures relatively more clients with more, and longer, spells, we still can note that half of all homeless families in its sample were in their first spell, and half had had at least one prior spell. In addition, one-fourth of all homeless families were in a spell lasting more than 12 months.

If, on the one hand, we believe that the vast majority of homeless families should be considered crisis cases, with crisis being defined to allow for more than one spell, then the cluster method produces groupings that best reflect this attitude. On the other hand, if we believe that crisis should really mean first time and short, then the cross-tabulation method produces a better reflection. But we then also have to come to terms with a reality that includes a significant proportion of families in the more unstable and/or longer-term patterns of the episodic and chronic groups. In either case, some families do not leave homelessness quickly. They may not be in crisis, however. For example, 48 percent of homeless families in NSHAPC were in transitional housing at the time of their interview. Thus, their very receipt of appropriate services may have the effect of prolonging their spell of official homelessness (NSHAPC, and many policies, define someone in a transitional program for homeless people as still homeless).

PAST-YEAR AND LIFETIME ALCOHOL AND/OR DRUG PROBLEMS. The chronic group produced by cross-tabulation had a significantly higher proportion of clients with past-year and lifetime problems with alcohol and/or drugs, compared to the crisis and episodic groups produced by the same method. In addition, the crisis group was more likely than the episodic group to report these problems. However, the three groups produced by cluster analysis did not differ from each other on either past-year or lifetime alcohol/drug problems. Thus, regardless of the pattern of homelessness to which clients might be assigned, it appears that a criterion of having been homeless for more than a year is a good one in identifying the most homeless people with significant alcohol and/or drug problems.

EXPERIENCING FOSTER CARE/OUT-OF-HOME PLACEMENT BEFORE AGE 18. The three groups produced by cross-tabulation did not differ from each other in the proportion who had experienced foster care or other out-of-home placement in their youth or childhood. In contrast, the episodic group produced by cluster analysis included significantly more clients with a history of foster care than was true for the cluster-analysis crisis or chronic groups.

YEARS SINCE CLIENT FIRST FOUND HIM/HERSELF WITHOUT REGULAR HOUSING OR A REGULAR PLACE TO STAY. This is where grouping method makes the most dramatic differences, and the groups affected most are the episodic groups. By both methods, the crisis group had the highest proportion of people whose earliest experience of homelessness (or, to be literal, lack of a regular place to stay for at least 30 days, which is how the question was phrased) began less than a year ago, although the pattern was significantly more extreme for the cross-tabulation crisis group.[6] The two crisis groups also had the fewest members whose experience of housing instability and homelessness extended back 10 years or more, while the two chronic groups had the highest proportion of members with homeless experiences lasting this long. These patterns are as might be expected, and are consistent regardless of grouping method.

In the episodic groups, however, the cluster-analysis group had more than twice the proportion of clients whose experience of homelessness/being without regular housing began at least 10 years ago as the cross-tabulation group (68 versus 33 percent). It also had vastly fewer who reported beginning their homelessness/being without regular housing less than a year earlier (2 versus 24 percent). In this case, the combination of findings for the groups defined by cluster analysis makes the most sense to the authors. People in the cluster-defined episodic groups report significantly younger ages at first homelessness, significantly longer periods since they were first homeless, much higher foster care/out-of-home placement rates before age 18, and a general pattern suggesting long and repeated struggles with homelessness, beginning at an early age. This pattern is not nearly as clear in the cross-tabulation group.

Base and Net Spell Length, Or, What Is a Spell?

The foregoing analysis assumed that the meaning of a homeless spell, and, by implication, homelessness itself, was clear to both the people who might experience it and to researchers. However, the NSHAPC data contain sufficient evidence of confusion to raise serious questions. Suppose, for example, someone who lived with parents until reaching adulthood, then married and lived with a spouse, left the spouse on several occasions for varying periods and lived with friends or relatives, slept in the car a few days occasionally during these transitions, and eventually entered a homeless shelter. This person might date their homelessness from when they entered the shelter, or first left the marital household, or ceased to feel "at home" in the marital house. Or, to take quite a different example, consider someone who lived with parents until late adolescence, then slept and kept personal possessions in the home of one girlfriend after another, for varying periods, without paying rent or establishing any "rights" of residence, and periodically slept outdoors, in vehicles, in shelters, or on the couches of friends or relatives, for varying periods. This person might believe he never had been homeless, had had many short homeless spells, or had not had a home of his own since leaving his parents. As we will see, even the meaning a person assigns to "a spell" may be quite different, depending on the person and their experiences. Breaks in literal homelessness, as when a person can afford to pay for a room for a week or two or stays in a hospital for a month, may cause one person to say their spell ended and a new one began, and another to see a single period of homelessness despite occasional interruptions.

Base Length of Homeless Spell

We start with a description of base spells, and then ask how much of the base spell might have been spent in nonhomeless situations. We use this information to calculate net spell length. The NSHAPC survey asked all homeless clients: *When was the last time you had a place of your own such as a house, apartment, room, or other housing for 30 days or more in the same place?* We used the responses to establish the base length of their current homeless spell (table 6.3 and figure 6.1). The first four spell-length categories (half a month or less, more than half a month, up to one month, two to three months, and four to six months) each capture about the same share of clients (8 to 11 percent).[7] Fifteen and 16 percent, respectively, reported base spell lengths of 7 to 12 months and 13 to 24 months.

Table 6.3 *Base and Net Spell Lengths, and Number of Times Homeless*

	Base Spell Length (Percent of Clients)	*Net Spell Length (Percent of Clients)*	*Mean Number of Times Homeless, by Base Spell Length*
Spell Length			
1/2 month or less	11	16	1.9
More than 1/2 through 1 month	8	5	3.6
More than 1 through 3 months	9	12	4.3
More than 3 through 6 months	11	9	2.9
More than 6 through 12 months	15	10	3.7
More than 12 through 24 months	16	13	2.9
More than 24 through 48 months	7	14	2.8
More than 48 months	24	22	2.6
All Homeless Clients	100	100	3.0

Source: Urban Institute analysis of weighted 1996 NSHAPC client data.

Note: Data are drawn from question 2.23, which asks, "How many times in your life have you been without regular housing? That is, not living in a house, apartment, or other housing for 30 days or more in the same place?" The number of times includes "this time."

Figure 6.1 *Base and Net Spell Lengths of Currently Homeless Clients*

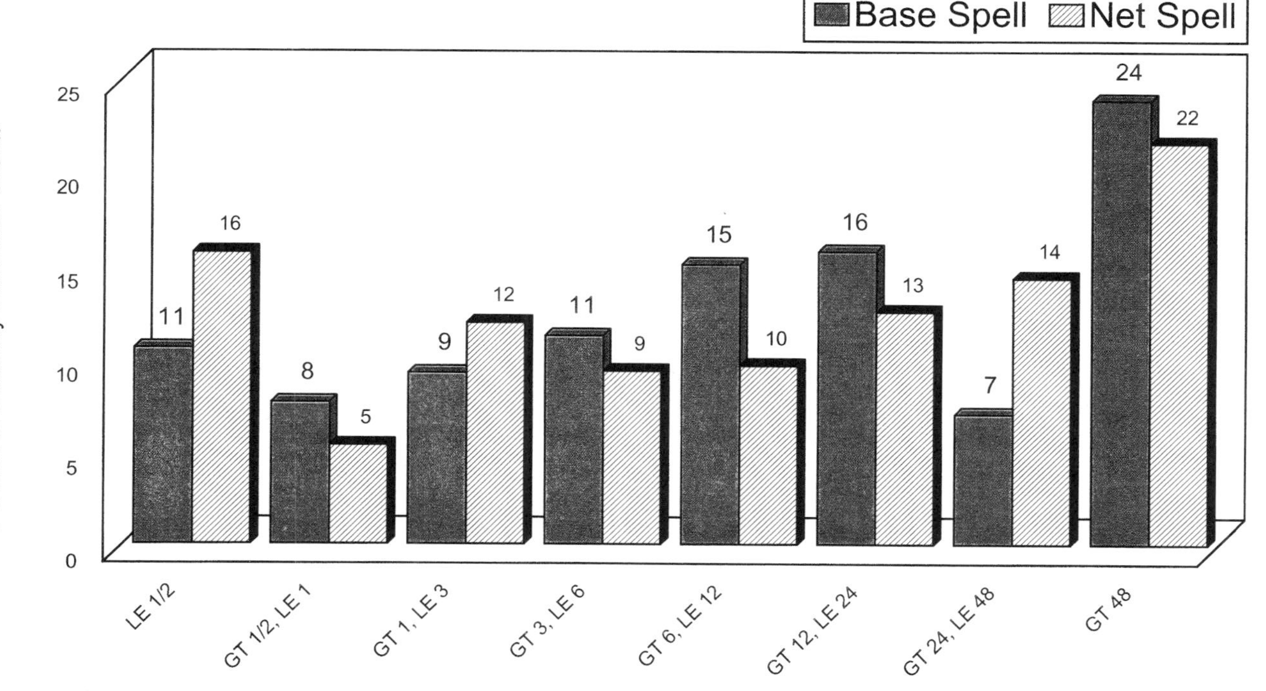

Source: Urban Institute analysis of weighted 1996 NSHAPC client data.
Note: Numbers do not sum to 100 due to rounding.

Thirty-one percent reported a spell lasting more than two years, of whom the large majority, 24 percent, had been homeless for more than four years. In addition to how long they were homeless, clients also reported how many times they had been homeless, including the present one. Homeless clients averaged 3.0 spells, including their current one (table 6.3). When examined separately by base spell length, the range was 1.9 to 4.3 times, with most categories clustering pretty close to the average.

Time Spent in Housed Situations while Homeless

The most important insights we can gain from NSHAPC pertain to the meaning of "spell length" as it typically has been measured. Is this a period of consistent homelessness from beginning to end, or were there periods during the base spell when the client was not literally homeless? If so, what proportion of the base spell was spent in situations of literal homelessness and what in other situations? We can answer these two questions, but, ultimately, we cannot answer how clients themselves define a "spell."

All homeless clients were asked if they had spent time in a variety of housed situations since leaving their "last regular place." These situations included 15 specific places, such as the homes of friends or relatives, inpatient treatment programs, penal institutions, or the military. Table 6.4 shows the percentage of homeless clients who reported spending time in each place while homeless, and the mean length of time they spent in each.

Almost a quarter (23 percent) of homeless clients did not spend any time in any place asked about. Thus all the time in their base spell was "homeless" time, spent in places where we would count them as being literally homeless. Close to 60 percent, however, spent an average of four months in a temporary home they paid for themselves or in someone else's home (36 percent in the homes of friends, 22 percent in a temporary place they paid for themselves, 19 percent in the homes of relatives other than parents, and 15 percent with their parents). Over a quarter spent some time (three months on average) in some type of hospital or nursing or recovery home. The most common venues were residential recovery programs, where 11 percent stayed during their current homeless spell. Nineteen percent spent time in jail, prison, or a halfway house for people on probation or parole. The average length of time in such places was six months. Finally, less than 2 percent stayed in a foster home since their current homeless spell began, but the average length of stay was very long, over two years.

Table 6.4 *Types of Places Where Homeless Clients Spent Time during Their Current Homeless Spell*

	Percent Spending Any Time	*Mean Length of Time*
Any of the Places Listed Below	77	5
Temporary place of client's own, paid for by client	22	3
Parent's home	15	6
Home of other relatives	19	5
Home of friends	36	2
Any of the Above Four Places	*59*	*4*
Foster home	1	25
Mental hospital or psychiatric ward	8	5
Veterans Affairs hospital	7	1
Other hospital	8	2
Nursing home	1	2
Residential recovery program	11	4
Adult group home/crisis residence or other housing for mentally ill	2	2
Any of the Above Six Places	*27*	*3*
Migrant workers' camp	1	1
Military	1	0
Jail or prison	19	6
Halfway house/probation or parole	3	0
Either of the Above Two Places	*19*	*6*

Source: Urban Institute analysis of weighted 1996 NSHAPC client data.

Number of Housed Situations while Homeless

Table 6.5 reports the different types of "nonhomeless" places clients stayed during their current homeless spell, and relates these to the length of the spell. These numbers are quite low, suggesting that people did not stay in many different types of places while they were homeless. On average, homeless clients spent time in 1.7 different types. Of course, they could have stayed in several different venues within a single type, such as several different SRO hotels, several different friends' or relatives' homes, or even several different mental hospitals, and the NSHAPC question

Table 6.5 *Mean Number of Places Clients Have Spent Time during Their Current Homeless Spell, by Base Spell Length*

	Mean Number of Places (Max = 15)
All Clients	1.7
By Base Spell Length	
1/2 month or less	0.8
More than 1/2 through 1 month	1.2
More than 1 through 3 months	1.4
More than 3 through 6 months	1.4
More than 6 through 12 months	1.8
More than 12 through 24 months	1.6
More than 24 through 48 months	2.0
More than 48 months	2.2

Source: Urban Institute analysis of weighted 1996 NSHAPC client data.
Note: The maximum number of places a client could have reported was 15.

would not detect the movements. When we analyze these figures by base spell length, we note that people with very short spells (a month or less) had stayed in the fewest types of places, while those with very long spells (more than two years) had stayed in the most, but even they had stayed in only two different types of places, on average.

Net Spell Length

A key finding is how much clients' base spell length is reduced when time spent in places that would not qualify them as literally homeless is subtracted. We report this in terms of how homeless clients are distributed by *net* spell length (table 6.3 and figure 6.1). A quick perusal of figure 6.1 indicates that the entire distribution of spell lengths has shifted toward the shorter end when reported as *net* rather than *base* lengths.

We also report both the mean *net* spell length in months and the percentage reduction in base spell length for each subgroup of homeless clients defined in terms of base spell length (table 6.6). Netting out time spent in housed situations reduces the length of homeless spells by almost one-fifth, resulting in a mean net spell length of 28.2 months compared to the mean base length of 32.7 months.[8]

Table 6.6 *Net Spell Length: Base Spell Length, Less Time Spent in Other Places*

	Mean Base Spell Length (in Months)	*Mean Net Spell Length (in Months)*	*Mean Percent Reduction*
Currently Homeless Clients	32.7	28.2	19.0
Base Spell Length			
1/2 month or less	0.2	0.1	46.0
More than 1/2 through 1 month	0.9	0.7	27.4
More than 1 through 3 months	2.4	2.0	16.7
More than 3 through 6 months	5.0	3.7	27.6
More than 6 through 12 months	8.8	7.3	17.3
More than 12 through 24 months	13.3	10.7	20.0
More than 24 through 48 months	28.5	25.2	12.0
More than 48 months	101.4	95.2	7.1

Source: Urban Institute analysis of weighted 1996 NSHAPC client data.

Note: Findings include 50 homeless clients who reported staying in housed situations for a total amount of time that exceeded their base spell length. In these cases, the percent reduction was set to 100 and the net spell length to 0. Had these cases been excluded from the calculations, the mean percent reduction and net spell length would have been 17 percent and 31 months.

Reductions are greatest among clients with the shortest base spell lengths. The spells of clients homeless for half a month or less are reduced by just under half when one accounts for nonhomeless situations. Reductions among clients with other base spell lengths are not as high, but still are important (12 to 28 percent for all but spells lasting more than four years). Even those homeless for very long periods (four years or more) have spell lengths 7 percent lower when all nonhomeless situations are accounted for.

Concluding Thoughts

We have seen that people's experiences of homelessness can vary greatly: Some are homeless only once or twice and for a relatively short time; others appear to cycle into and out of homelessness repeatedly over many years; still others seem to have a single episode of homelessness that lasts very many years. Understanding such patterns is critical for improving program design and service delivery, in part because the types of intervention may depend on people's pattern of homelessness.

People homeless for the first time, and other short-term homeless people, may need only a simple form of emergency assistance that tides them through whatever crisis triggered their fall into literal homelessness. These crises might include losing a job or transportation to and from a job, losing income due to the death of a spouse, failed child care arrangements, eviction, and so on. Given the extremes to which housing costs have risen and the persistence of extreme poverty among a sizable portion of the population, the probability that the average very poor family or person will experience such a crisis at some time appears extremely high (as we saw in chapter 2, just for a single year).

In contrast, those with periodic spells of homelessness over a number of years may need assistance in finding more-affordable housing, developing a support network, managing limited finances, or continuing treatment for alcoholism or other drug use. There probably also is a role for subsidized housing, with or without supportive services, for those who have little hope of ever being able to achieve housing stability on their own. Finally, chronically homeless people may need basic life-skills training, longer-term mental health treatment (including medications), remedial education and basic job training, and, above all, subsidized housing with supportive services. Rather than providing all sorts of emergency and supportive services to all homeless people (or even *requiring* certain unneeded services), selected services can be designed that are better suited to the particular needs of individual homeless people and families.

Also, from this chapter's analyses, it should be obvious that people attach very different meanings to the concept of "home," and, therefore, "homelessness." When asked when they last had "a home," "a place of your own," or even "a permanent place to stay," some people may go back to when they actually felt "at home." As a consequence, researchers will classify them as having very long homeless spells. Other people may consider a wide variety of temporary places to be "their own place," thus reporting shorter periods since they last had one, and being classified, therefore, as having shorter homeless spells. Many people may also consider that time in institutions or community-based programs is time away from homelessness, while others will not. The definition of "a spell" is further complicated by government policy, which defines certain conditions as "literal homelessness" and other conditions as "not homeless," regardless of how people feel about the nature and stability of their circumstances.

In our analyses of net spell length, we examined the consequences of imposing on people's lives the definition of "literal homelessness" commonly used in complying with regulations on federal funding under the McKinney Homeless Assistance Act. The results suggest that researchers may draw inconsistent conclusions in trying to differentiate one homeless "spell" from another, calculate how long a person has been homeless, or learn about other aspects of homeless histories, depending on how much additional information they have collected and how they use it in interpreting survey responses. The results also suggest that an overly strict application of the definition of literal homelessness may not be particularly useful for policy purposes.

Further, the patterns we have seen, plus the different experiences reported by people in the different groups, suggest several approaches to preventing initial and ongoing homelessness.

Obviously, societal institutions intended to protect vulnerable children are failing in some fundamental ways when the rates of childhood abuse, neglect, and out-of-home placement among homeless people are 7 to 13 times higher than the 3.4 percent rate thought to reflect foster care and other childhood out-of-home placement among all American adults (Royse and Wiehe 1989). Long stays in foster care, especially those from which youths are discharged at 18 without significant family connections, appear to result in substantial vulnerability to adult homelessness, coupled as it is with almost certain poverty and unpreparedness for adult responsibilities. To prevent such homelessness, as well as avert myriad other ills besetting abused and neglected children in foster care, the foster care system needs substantially more resources. They should be applied both early and late in the careers of abused and neglected children, and they should include substantial investment in aiding youth aging out of foster care to transition to adulthood with a reasonable chance at self-sufficiency.

In similar fashion, many homeless people have had extensive contacts as adults with a variety of public systems of care, from mental health, to physical health, to substance abuse treatment, to criminal justice. None of these systems have seriously taken on the task of ensuring that those in their care are not discharged into situations where they immediately, or at least very quickly, will fall into homelessness. Instead, these systems need to devote more resources to helping their clients sustain community tenure. They also need to form partnerships with housing authorities to secure adequate permanent housing for those who clearly cannot maintain themselves on their own.

NOTES

1. A few (4 percent) of homeless clients said they had never had a place of their own, or housing for 30 days or more in the same place. They were not included in any of the analyses of homelessness patterns, because we could not calculate a spell length for them without having a starting point.
2. These cut-offs have been used frequently in homeless research. Readers interested in seeing the consequences of using different cut-off points can do so by examining the data presented in table 6.1.
3. The procedure used for this analysis, PROC FASTCLUS from the Statistical Application System (SAS), uses nearest centroid sorting to group observations into a prespecified number of clusters. This is the same procedure used by Kuhn and Culhane (1998). Solutions with more than three prespecified clusters simply divided the already small chronic group into smaller subgroups, but did not substantially alter the episodic and crisis groups.
4. All differences in percentages mentioned in the text without qualification are significant at $p < .05$. Any difference described as "marginal" meets the criterion of $p < .10$. To account for the sample design and its deviation from simple random sampling, these statistical tests were performed incorporating a design effect of 3.
5. Some analyses (e.g., Culhane and Kuhn 1998) performed separate cluster analyses for families and other homeless people. While we fully expected that families and other homeless people would have different patterns of homelessness, on average, we preferred the approach of first identifying patterns of homelessness for everyone. Once the patterns were identified, then we could examine which patterns were most common among families and among other homeless clients.
6. The results of calculating the length of time since first homelessness and cross-tabulating it with patterns of homelessness reveal the perils of questionnaire wording. The question, "How old were you when you FIRST found yourself without regular housing or a regular place to stay?" was intended to determine the age at which the client first experienced homelessness. It did not use the word "homeless" because the survey was trying not to force the self-definition of homelessness on people who chose not to describe their situation that way, even though *we* classified them as homeless, based on our own criteria for literal homelessness. However, it is clear that some people responded to this question with information about housing instability that occurred earlier than the beginning of their current spell and was somehow different from it. This can be seen in the responses of the crisis homeless group defined by cross-classification. These are supposed to be people in a first homeless spell that had not yet lasted one year (based on their answers to two other questions). Yet 28 percent said that it was more than a year ago when they first found themselves without regular housing or a regular place to stay. If they were talking about literal homelessness, then either their current spell, if their first,

should have been reported as longer than a year, or they have actually had more than one spell. Unfortunately, we have no way to determine whether the situations to which they refer were ones of literal homelessness or not. We, nevertheless, refer to the variable as "time since first homelessness" as a convenient shorthand.

7. Clients could have reported a length of time expressed in days, weeks, or months. All answers were first converted into days and then into months (assuming that all months have 30 days).

8. "Mean percent reduction" was calculated as follows. First we calculated "percent reduction" for each client by subtracting that client's net from base spell length and dividing by his/her base spell length. We then calculated the mean of this new variable to get "mean percent reduction." We also calculated mean percent reduction within each subgroup defined by base spell length. The results differ from the results one would get by comparing the mean net spell length to the mean base spell length (that is, by comparing column 1 to column 2 in table 6.6), due to an uneven distribution of spell lengths within each subgroup and for the sample as a whole.

7

Comparing Homeless Subgroups within Community Types

Previous chapters have focused exclusively on homeless clients. They have presented estimates of the size of the homeless population at a given point in time and as projections over a year's time, looked at the characteristics of different subgroups, and examined patterns of homelessness. They have not, however, taken advantage of two of the most important and unique aspects of the NSHAPC design—its national coverage, and its inclusion of formerly and never homeless people who use homeless assistance programs.

Different Types of Community

NSHAPC was designed to generate valid and reliable information about homelessness not just in central cities, which have been the primary focus of homeless research, but also in suburban and urban fringe areas, which make up the balance of metropolitan statistical areas (MSAs), and even outside MSAs, where almost one-quarter of Americans live.[1] Many have argued that homelessness outside central cities is different from central-city homelessness, and that funders should acknowledge these differences and support correspondingly different programs and services (Burt 1995 summarizes issues relating to rural homelessness). However, only a handful of studies (First et al. 1993; Kentucky Housing Corporation 1993) have actually collected data from people homeless in rural areas, and only in two states (Ohio and Kentucky). Lack of information to support sound policy has hampered developing programs and services in rural areas. Suburban and urban fringe areas have received even less research and policy attention. NSHAPC is the only study that can supply information characterizing suburban and rural homelessness for the nation as a whole.

That being said, it is also important to acknowledge NSHAPC's limitations. Because NSHAPC used a service-based sampling strategy, it could only find people to sample if a community contained the types of homeless assistance programs included in the sampling design (chapter 1 describes them). If no soup kitchens or outreach programs existed in a community, then NSHAPC could not sample people from them. Likewise, if a community did not have *any* homeless assistance programs, as happened in two rural NSHAPC sampling areas, then the study could not interview anyone in that community, whether or not some happened to be homeless. In every type of community, NSHAPC undoubtedly missed homeless people who did not use homeless assistance programs. But the probability of missing them increased in communities with only a few services, and rose to complete certainty in communities with none. As suburban and rural communities tend to have fewer, and smaller, homeless assistance programs, the probability that NSHAPC missed homeless people in those communities may be higher than in central cities, which tend to be well supplied with such services. However, when services are calculated in relation to the total, or poor, population of a community (as we show in chapter 10), many suburban and rural communities turn out to be less service-poor than is commonly believed. All this is by way of caution to treat a bit more tentatively NSHAPC-based characteristics of homeless people in suburban and rural areas, to the extent that they also prove to be less service-rich.

Formerly and Never Homeless Clients

Designing policies and programs to alleviate or prevent homelessness has also been hampered by the relative paucity of studies that support comparisons of homeless and housed populations, examining factors that predict who is most likely to experience it. One of the biggest problems is selecting an appropriate comparison group of housed persons. For some factors, census data or other general population surveys can be used. But many researchers and advocates feel that such a comparison is unfair. They say that a better comparison would be to a group of people who were equally (or almost equally) poor, but not homeless. However, it is much harder to find data for such a group, especially for people homeless by themselves as opposed to being in homeless families. Researchers studying family homelessness have selected comparison families from welfare caseloads and public housing rolls, but no reasonable equivalents exist for single homeless people.

The NSHAPC sample provides an option for appropriate comparisons through its reliance on homeless assistance programs as its point of sampling for both homeless and other people. Many programs that focus on serving homeless people also serve those who are not homeless. These include soup kitchens, mobile food programs, outreach programs, food pantries, drop-in centers, and some others. The people who use these programs are almost universally poor, and sufficiently in need to come to the programs for help in making ends meet. If researchers could detect important differences between homeless and other people using these programs, where poverty and, to some extent, household structure are held fairly constant, then the factors creating these differences could be inferred as probably important predictors of homelessness. Thus NSHAPC's second advantage over many other studies is its inclusion of both those who have been homeless in the past but were not homeless at the time of the study, and those who have never been homeless.[2]

This chapter and chapter 8 take advantage of NSHAPC's unique aspects of national coverage and inclusion of formerly and never homeless clients. Some descriptive information on community type for currently homeless clients has been presented in other publications (Burt et al. 1999, summary report, chapter 2; technical report, chapter 13). Likewise, some information about differences among currently, formerly, and never homeless clients has been presented elsewhere (Burt et al. 1999, summary report, chapter 3; technical report, chapters 3 through 11). This chapter does not repeat these descriptions. Rather, it first divides the sample into subgroups of clients in central cities, suburban/urban fringe areas, and rural areas. Then, within these geographically defined subgroups, the chapter focuses on differences among currently, formerly, and never homeless clients. Our hope is to separate factors associated with geographic location from those associated with homeless status. Once this has been done through the cross-tabular analyses in this chapter, then chapter 8 uses the most promising factors in regression analyses to control for many factors at once, while examining the effects of others.

Demographic Characteristics

Looking first at basic demographic characteristics across homeless status subgroups within community types, age provides the most outstanding pattern. Within all three community types, never homeless clients were consistently older (more likely to be at least 55) than either formerly or currently homeless clients (table 7.1).[3] Conversely, in both central cities and suburban/urban fringe areas, currently homeless clients were more likely than formerly or never homeless clients to be 34 or younger.

Looking next at race/ethnicity, no differences exist among the homeless status subgroups within either central cities or suburban/urban fringe areas. This would be true for rural areas also, but for a significant proportion of Native Americans among the currently homeless population, which appears to be an anomaly of the NSHAPC sampling and weighting strategy.[4] This homogeneity suggests that even in communities of different types, the people who are poor and needy enough to use homeless assistance programs share common racial/ethnic characteristics, rather than homeless persons presenting a distinct set.

Likewise, no statistically significant differences appear in the proportion of clients who were in families (defined as living with one's own minor children) across homeless statuses within the different types of community. In central cities, 13 to 16 percent of households in each homeless status contained a parent and at least one minor child. Corresponding figures for suburban/urban fringe areas were 11 to 20 percent, and for rural areas, 18 to 30 percent. As a rough validity check on NSHAPC's methods applied to rural areas, we can compare NSHAPC's 18 percent of families among currently homeless households in rural areas to the proportions in the Ohio and Kentucky studies (First et al. 1994; Kentucky Housing Corporation 1993, cited in Burt 1999), which used quite different methods. Each of them reported that 20 percent of homeless households were homeless families—a proportion not significantly different from the NSHAPC result.

Sex and marital status, however, *did* differ significantly among homeless status subgroups in both central cities and rural areas. In communities of these types, currently homeless clients were significantly more likely to be male than formerly or never homeless clients, while both currently and formerly homeless clients were more likely than never homeless clients never to have married (and, therefore, less likely to be married or widowed). The lack of family connection through marriage

Table 7.1 *Basic Demographic Characteristics of Homeless Clients, by Homeless Status within Community Type*
(weighted percentages)

	Central City Residents			*Suburban/Urban Fringe Residents*			*Rural Residents*		
	Currently Homeless (UN = 2,295)	*Formerly Homeless (UN = 483)*	*Never Homeless (UN = 223)*	*Currently Homeless (UN = 410)*	*Formerly Homeless (UN = 90)*	*Never Homeless (UN = 90)*	*Currently Homeless (UN = 233)*	*Formerly Homeless (UN = 104)*	*Never Homeless (UN = 205)*
Sex									
Male	71	63	51	55	52	43	77	28	26
Female	29	38	49	45	48	57	23	72	75
Race/Ethnicity									
White non-Hispanic	37	33	33	54	58	60	42	74	72
Black non-Hispanic	46	53	54	33	37	26	9	5	14
Hispanic	11	7	10	11	5	10	7	19	13
Native American	5	3	*	1	1	4	41	2	1
Other	1	4	2	1	0	1	*	0	0
Age									
Under 18	1	*	2	*			*		1
18 to 21 years	7	2	4	5	3	5	3	7	4
22 to 24 years	5	2	2	7			3		7
25 to 34 years	25	13	7	27	15	10	17	29	17
35 to 44 years	34	42	22	40	29	23	64	20	12
45 to 54 years	21	25	25	9	33	11	8	27	11
55 to 64 years	7	10	12	6			4		24
65 or more years	1	7	26	6	20	51	2	17	24

(*Continued*)

Table 7.1 *Basic Demographic Characteristics of Homeless Clients, by Homeless Status within Community Type (Continued)*
(weighted percentages)

	Central City Residents			*Suburban/Urban Fringe Residents*			*Rural Residents*		
	Currently Homeless (UN = 2,295)	*Formerly Homeless (UN = 483)*	*Never Homeless (UN = 223)*	*Currently Homeless (UN = 410)*	*Formerly Homeless (UN = 90)*	*Never Homeless (UN = 90)*	*Currently Homeless (UN = 233)*	*Formerly Homeless (UN = 104)*	*Never Homeless (UN = 205)*
Education/Highest Level of Completed Schooling									
Less than high school	36	43	51	35	34	40	64	43	51
High school graduate/ G.E.D.	34	32	26	40	40	38	13	37	35
More than high school	30	25	22	25	26	22	23	21	15
Marital Status									
Married	7	6	16	16	8	15	11	21	33
Widowed	2	5	20	8	4	40	3	14	21
Divorced	25	21	16	17	40	5	25	27	19
Separated	14	13	15	14	10	11	25	21	5
Never married	51	56	33	45	38	29	36	17	22
Living in a Family (i.e., with Own Minor Child[ren])	14	13	16	16	20	11	18	30	29

Source: Urban Institute analysis of weighted 1996 NSHAPC client data; *N*s given at top of table are unweighted (designated "UN").
Note: Percentages do not sum to 100 due to rounding.
*Denotes values that are less than 0.5 percent but greater than 0. Shaded cells have been combined to accommodate small subsample size.

thus typifies central city and rural clients who had experienced homelessness, while it was not so common among those who had never been homeless. In suburban areas, in contrast, the three homeless status subgroups did not differ in proportion male and female, while the extremely high proportion of elderly people among never homeless clients in suburban areas (51 percent were 65 or older) contributed to the marital status of "widowed" predominating in that subgroup.

Homeless Histories and Use of Homeless Assistance Programs

Homeless Histories

Formerly homeless clients in the different types of community did not differ in the number of homeless spells they reported in their past. Eighteen to 20 percent reported four or more spells, and 40 to 47 percent reported only one (table 7.2). However, among currently homeless clients, those in rural areas stand out as being significantly more likely than those in suburban areas, and marginally more likely than those in central cities, to have been in their first homeless spell (60 versus 50 and 41 percent, respectively). In contrast, currently homeless clients in suburban areas were more likely than those in either central cities or rural areas to report that their current spell was at least their fourth (31 versus 21 and 17 percent, respectively).

Currently homeless rural clients also reported spells of significantly shorter duration than their central city or suburban counterparts. Fifty-five percent indicated a current spell of three months or less, compared to 27 percent of central city and 22 percent of suburban homeless clients who reported current spells this short. These differences were reversed for very long spells (longer than two years). Central city homeless clients were significantly more likely, and suburban homeless clients marginally more likely, than rural homeless clients to have reported spells this long (32 and 30, versus 20 percent, respectively).

Combining duration of current spell with number of spells, rural homeless clients were clearly the most likely to have been in a first spell lasting six months or less, compared to central city or suburban homeless clients (44 versus 16 and 15 percent, respectively). Suburban homeless clients were the most likely to have been in a current spell lasting more than six months that was not their first (43 versus 28 and 20 percent, respectively). While these findings are clear, they may reflect the relative

Table 7.2 *Homeless Histories and Use of Homeless Assistance Programs, by Homeless Status within Community Type*

(weighted percentages)

	Central City Residents			*Suburban/Urban Fringe Residents*			*Rural Residents*		
	Currently Homeless (UN = 2,295)	*Formerly Homeless (UN = 483)*	*Never Homeless (UN = 223)*	*Currently Homeless (UN = 410)*	*Formerly Homeless (UN = 90)*	*Never Homeless (UN = 90)*	*Currently Homeless (UN = 233)*	*Formerly Homeless (UN = 104)*	*Never Homeless (UN = 205)*
Number of Times Homeless or without Regular Housing for 30 Days or More									
1	50	40	†	41	47	†	60	40	†
2 or 3	29	40	†	28	35	†	24	40	†
4 or more	21	20	†	31	18	†	17	20	†
Spell History and Current Spell Length									
First time homeless									
6 months or less	16	†	†	15	†	†	44	†	†
More than 6 months	34	†	†	25	†	†	18	†	†
Not first time homeless									
Current spell 6 months or less	22	†	†	17	†	†	18	†	†
Current spell more than 6 months	28	†	†	43	†	†	20	†	†
Where Slept or Ate within Last Seven Days or on Day of Interview									
Street[a]	36	0	0	23	0	0	16	0	0
Shelter[b]	71	0	2	76	2	0	84	5	3

Soup kitchen[c]	45	52	65	27	53	72	29	23	10
Other[d]	29	69	51	21	61	38	27	73	87
Other Programs Clients Reported Using within the Seven Days before Being Interviewed									
Food pantry	6	12	10	3	7	*	3	5	5
Mobile food program	6	6	19	5	9	0	*	1	2
Outreach	6	5	*	10	*	2	5	1	0
Drop-in center	11	13	10	4	5	2	4	1	1
Programs Ever Used									
Emergency shelter	67	76	0	57	52	0	61	40	0
Transitional housing	41	28	0	40	14	0	29	13	0
Permanent housing	11	24	0	11	19	0	3	3	0
Shelter vouchers	14	15	0	23	22	0	12	28	0
Soup kitchen	68	83	45	50	78	47	45	40	12
Food pantry	39	53	49	44	58	21	31	81	67
Mobile food program	24	21	28	17	27	11	9	2	9
Outreach	116	18	9	17	11	18	22	3	4
Drop-in center	30	31	17	18	19	3	14	20	9

Source: Urban Institute analysis of weighted 1996 NSHAPC client data; *N*s given at top of table are unweighted (designated "UN").

Note: Percentages do not sum to 100 due to rounding.

*Denotes values that are less than 0.5 percentage points but greater than 0.

†Indicates insufficient *N*.

[a]Includes clients who reported staying in the streets or other places not meant for human habitation (e.g., abandoned buildings, vehicles) on the day of the NSHAPC interview or during the seven days prior to the interview.

[b]Includes clients who reported staying in an emergency shelter, transitional housing program, or voucher program on the day of the NSHAPC interview or during the seven days prior to the interview; clients who were selected for the study at one of these programs; or those who said they got food at the shelter where they live.

[c]Includes clients who reported using a soup kitchen during the seven days prior to the interview, or clients who were found and interviewed for NSHAPC at a soup kitchen.

[d]Includes clients who reported using another program (food pantry, mobile food, outreach, drop-in center, and/or permanent housing) during the seven days prior to the interview, or clients who were found and interviewed for NSHAPC at one of these programs.

inability of NSHAPC's methods to find and interview homeless people in rural areas who are not already in shelters. We turn to this issue next.

Use of Homeless Assistance Programs

Since homeless assistance programs were the avenue through which people were selected into the NSHAPC sample, it is important to understand how the different subgroups used them. Different patterns of service use were certainly related to homeless status, because they were among the criteria for defining homeless status (for instance, only currently homeless people should have used emergency or transitional shelters during the week before being interviewed, and never homeless people should never have used any type of shelter).

Before looking at the within-community differences across homeless status groups, it is important to corroborate the effects of community type. We expected them to be related to patterns of service use, if only because certain types of community are more likely than others to have particular programs. Among currently homeless subgroups, for example, those in central cities were much more likely to have used a soup kitchen on the day of the NSHAPC interview or during the preceding week than those in suburban or rural areas. This difference is almost certainly attributable to the sheer availability of soup kitchens in central cities compared to elsewhere. Another difference was sleeping location. Those in central cities were significantly more likely to report sleeping in places not meant for human habitation than suburban or rural clients. Currently homeless people in rural areas were, by contrast, more likely than their central city counterparts to report shelter stays during the index period. The findings about soup kitchen use and "street" sleeping are interrelated. In communities where soup kitchens were available as venues for finding and interviewing homeless clients, NSHAPC was more able to include homeless people who did not use shelters. The paucity of soup kitchens in suburban and rural areas undoubtedly affected the NSHAPC finding about "street" sleeping among rural homeless clients. Thus the finding contains an unknown mix of "reality" plus methodological bias.

We next examine program use among the three homeless status subgroups within each type of community.

In central cities, all three homeless status subgroups were equally likely to have used soup kitchens either on the day they were interviewed or in the seven previous days (table 7.2). In addition, currently homeless clients were the least likely to have used homeless assistance programs other than soup kitchens and shelters, while formerly homeless clients were the most likely.[5] With respect to other types of homeless assistance programs, never homeless, in contrast to currently and formerly homeless, central city clients were more likely to report recent use of mobile food programs, while currently and formerly homeless clients were more likely than never homeless clients to have been in touch with an outreach program.[6]

In the suburbs, currently homeless clients were less likely than either of the other two homeless status subgroups to have used a soup kitchen in the previous seven days or been found in one the day of the interview. Formerly homeless clients were more likely than the other homeless status subgroups to have used or been found in an "other" type of homeless assistance program. Except for outreach programs, with which currently homeless clients reported more contact, no differences were reported in use of "other" programs within the seven days before being interviewed for NSHAPC.

In rural areas, far fewer currently than formerly or never homeless clients used programs other than soup kitchens and shelters, while more currently than never homeless clients used soup kitchens. No differences of importance were evident among the three rural homeless status subgroups in their use of a variety of other homeless assistance programs. This lack of difference persists, even after taking account of the significantly higher ages of never homeless clients.

The last panel of table 7.2, revealing *lifetime* use of homeless assistance programs, shows that the majority of clients in every homeless status occasionally made use of these programs. By definition, never homeless clients did not report shelter use. But it is interesting to note that 11 percent of currently homeless people in both central cities and suburban/urban fringe areas reported living at some time in their life in permanent housing programs for formerly homeless people. That they no longer do so, but again are actively homeless, indicates that these programs may not permanently resolve homelessness for all people. The lower use of permanent housing programs in rural areas probably denotes their relative absence, rather than people's reluctance to use them were they there.

Food programs were the most commonly used of all homeless assistance programs, by all homeless status subgroups in all types of community. This is not so surprising, given the level of hunger and food insecurity in all subgroups that we report below (see discussion pertaining to table 7.4), and that food needs are constant and recurring (satisfying them on one day does not solve the problem of satisfying them on the next). Almost half of never homeless clients in both central city and suburban communities reported lifetime use of soup kitchens; formerly homeless clients in these community types were the most likely to report lifetime soup kitchen use, followed by currently homeless clients. In central cities, all three homeless status subgroups were about equally likely to report lifetime use of other food programs (food pantries and mobile food programs). In suburban/urban fringe areas, never homeless clients reported the lowest levels of lifetime use of food pantries, while formerly homeless clients reported the highest. This pattern differed from lifetime food pantry use in rural areas, where formerly and never homeless clients were significantly more likely than currently homeless clients to report it.[7]

Income Levels and Sources

Some consistencies exist in the pattern of income sources among the three homeless status subgroups across communities, but some striking differences appear in income levels (table 7.3). Not surprisingly, having less income was strongly associated with being currently homeless.

In suburban and rural communities, currently homeless clients were more likely than either formerly or never homeless clients to have done any work for pay in the 30 days preceding their NSHAPC interview, probably because they had fewer other sources of income. No differences existed among the three subgroups in central cities in the likelihood that they had worked for pay in the last 30 days. Among those who did, however, currently homeless clients were more likely than formerly or never homeless clients to have done day labor or pick-up jobs. This held for all three types of community.

In all three types of community, never homeless clients were significantly more likely than currently or formerly homeless clients to report receiving Social Security. Of course, since one-fourth to one-half of the never homeless subsamples were 65 or older, it is not surprising that they received Social Security. Indeed, 87 percent of never homeless clients aged 65 and older reported Social Security income. This was their most dramatic difference from younger clients, whether homeless or not. However, it is also important to note that the availability of Social Security to older citizens is one of the reasons that so few among currently homeless populations are 65 or older. In both central cities and rural areas, formerly and never homeless clients were more likely than currently homeless clients to get Supplemental Security Income, but in

Table 7.3 *Income Levels, Income Sources, and Employment of Homeless Clients, by Homeless Status within Community Type*

(weighted percentages)

	Central City Residents			*Suburban/Urban Fringe Residents*			*Rural Residents*		
	Currently Homeless (UN = 2,295)	*Formerly Homeless (UN = 483)*	*Never Homeless (UN = 223)*	*Currently Homeless (UN = 410)*	*Formerly Homeless (UN = 90)*	*Never Homeless (UN = 90)*	*Currently Homeless (UN = 233)*	*Formerly Homeless (UN = 104)*	*Never Homeless (UN = 205)*
Mean Income from All Sources (Last 30 Days)[a]	$341	$465	$584	$422	$502	$729	$449	$459	$489
Median Income from All Sources (Last 30 Days)[a]	$250	$458	$480	$395	$462	$688	$475	$470	$490
Income from All Sources Over Last 30 Days									
None	16	4	5	8	7	4	6	8	6
Less than $100	18	11	2	15	6	9	22	8	9
$100 to $299	21	21	14	21	6	2	7	8	12
$300 to $499	19	24	33	18	42	7	16	44	28
$500 to $699	11	22	16	21	20	31	22	13	23
$700 to $799	3	6	8	3	6	7	17	5	7
$800 to $999	5	6	4	5	3	16	4	9	6
$1,000 to $1,199	4	2	4	4	2	4	1	1	3
$1,200 or more	4	5	15	6	8	21	5	3	6

(Continued)

Table 7.3 *Income Levels, Income Sources, and Employment of Homeless Clients, by Homeless Status within Community Type (Continued)*
(weighted percentages)

	Central City Residents			*Suburban/Urban Fringe Residents*			*Rural Residents*		
	Currently Homeless (UN = 2,295)	*Formerly Homeless (UN = 483)*	*Never Homeless (UN = 223)*	*Currently Homeless (UN = 410)*	*Formerly Homeless (UN = 90)*	*Never Homeless (UN = 90)*	*Currently Homeless (UN = 233)*	*Formerly Homeless (UN = 104)*	*Never Homeless (UN = 205)*
Did Any Paid Work in Last 30 Days	40	36	33	49	30	17	65	31	29
Sources of Earned Income in Last 30 Days[b]									
Job lasting 3 or more months	13	14	19	17	11	7	9	19	17
Job expected to last 3 or more months	7	9	4	6	3	1	3	4	5
Temporary job, farm work	2	*	3	1	*	0	12	*	0
Temporary job, non-farm work	7	5	1	12	11	5	11	5	3
Day job or pick-up job	12	6	4	16	4	3	23	3	6
Peddling	2	2	*	3	3	*	2	*	*
Received Money/Benefits from Government Sources in Last 30 Days									
AFDC (among families with children)	57	44	53	44	39	25	32	50	45

General Assistance	11	16	6	5	29	19	2	6	2
Supplemental Security Income	12	30	30	11	26	19	5	29	27
SSDI	6	15	12	17	17	5	4	20	10
Social Security	2	7	32	7	7	35	4	5	33
Veteran's disability payments (among veterans)	7	17	17	1	2	2	15	12	12
Veteran's pension (among veterans)	2	2	2	*	0	0	14	2	2
Food Stamps	38	44	39	38	51	14	31	60	48
Received Means-Tested Government Benefits[c]									
Any, including food stamps	46	70	58	45	74	48	35	69	59
Any other than food stamps	29	56	49	27	68	44	23	52	46
Other Sources of Income in Last 30 Days									
Parents	8	5	5	6	4	3	20	3	8
Friends	11	6	6	14	6	4	16	21	5
Asking for money on the street	9	5	*	6	1	*	5	1	0

Source: Urban Institute analysis of weighted 1996 NSHAPC client data; *N*s given at top of table are unweighted (designated "UN").

Note: Percentages do not sum to 100 due to rounding.

*Denotes values that are less than 0.5 percent but greater than 0.

[a]If a client reported an income range rather than an exact amount, the client was assigned the mid-point of the range for the purpose of calculating the mean and median.

[b]Client could report receiving income from more than one of these sources.

[c]Includes AFDC, GA, SSI, Food Stamps, and/or housing assistance.

suburban areas only formerly homeless clients exceeded currently homeless clients in receipt of SSI.

Summarizing all income sources, in both central cities and rural areas, formerly and never homeless clients were more likely than currently homeless clients to receive at least one type of government benefit. This contributed to both their higher income levels and their nonhomeless status. Further, it was true whether or not food stamps were included in the calculation. Excluding food stamps, the proportion of each subgroup that received any other government benefit was lower, but the relationship among the subgroups still held. In suburban areas, in contrast, formerly homeless clients were more likely than either currently or never homeless clients to receive one or more government benefits. Never homeless clients did not differ from currently homeless clients in this regard. One is left wondering whether being poor in suburban and urban fringe areas leaves people with less access to programs, services, and assistance in getting benefits than in central cities or rural areas, where higher proportions of the population are poor. The low level of food stamps among never homeless suburban clients raises this issue.

Lack of paid employment and relatively low receipt of government benefits accounted for the extremely low incomes of most users of homeless assistance programs, as noted in earlier chapters. However, relative incomes of the three homeless status subgroups were not the same across the three community types. In central cities and suburban areas, currently homeless people definitely reported the lowest incomes of the three subgroups, as measured by either mean or median income. But in central cities, the median incomes of formerly and never homeless clients did not differ, whereas in the suburbs, both mean and median incomes of never homeless clients exceeded those of formerly homeless clients. Now we can see that never homeless suburban clients had the highest mean and median income of any subgroup in any community type. So, perhaps their failure to receive government benefits stemmed from being ineligible rather than lacking access.

Physical Health and Food Insecurity

On matters of physical health and food insecurity, community type appears to make little difference, whereas homeless status matters a great deal. Much the same pattern of findings among homeless status subgroups appeared in all three types of community for many aspects of health and hunger (table 7.4). Consistently, more formerly and never homeless clients than currently homeless clients reported at least one chronic condition. This probably was because they were older (for never homeless clients) or sufficiently disabled to qualify for supported housing, SSI, or other benefits (for formerly homeless clients). Also, they were more likely to have some type of health insurance (that is, currently homeless clients were least likely to have it).

On hunger, currently and formerly homeless clients were consistently more likely than never homeless clients to experience one or more problems related to hunger and inability to get enough food. This included being hungry or going a whole day without eating because they lacked money to buy food. In central cities, the differences between formerly and never homeless clients were marginal. However, the differences between currently and formerly homeless clients were significant, with currently homeless clients experiencing more food problems. Formerly homeless clients in both suburban and rural communities reported the same level of hunger and food insecurity as currently homeless clients, while in central cities, their level was lower than for currently homeless clients, but still substantial (about half experienced one or more problems in the month before NSHAPC). Clearly, people able to leave homelessness and remain in regular housing were still considerably disadvantaged in 1996 in meeting such a basic need as regularly getting adequate food.

The only health circumstance for which community type did appear to make a difference was in homeless clients' ability to see a doctor. In central cities, clients in all three homeless statuses were equally able, or unable, to see a doctor when they needed one. In contrast, currently and formerly homeless clients in suburban/urban fringe and rural areas were less able than never homeless clients to see one when necessary. In these types of communities, the observed differences probably stemmed from access problems rather than lack of insurance, as formerly and never homeless clients had equivalent insurance coverage, but still were not equally able to obtain medical care when needed.

Alcohol, Drug, and Mental Health Problems

As with physical health and food insecurity problems, the dominant patterns of reported alcohol, drug, and mental health (ADM) problems

Table 7.4 *Physical Health and Nutrition Status of Homeless Clients, by Homeless Status within Community Type*

(weighted percentages)

	Central City Residents			*Suburban/Urban Fringe Residents*			*Rural Residents*		
	Currently Homeless (UN = 2,295)	*Formerly Homeless* (UN = 483)	*Never Homeless* (UN = 223)	*Currently Homeless* (UN = 410)	*Formerly Homeless* (UN = 90)	*Never Homeless* (UN = 90)	*Currently Homeless* (UN = 233)	*Formerly Homeless* (UN = 104)	*Never Homeless* (UN = 205)
Type of Reported Medical Conditions[a]									
Acute infectious conditions (1 or more)	24	27	30	35	28	31	25	31	27
Acute noninfectious conditions (1 or more)	7	6	5	10	1	1	11	10	3
Chronic conditions (1 or more)	49	62	70	43	55	60	33	74	68
Needed But Not Able to See Doctor or Nurse in Last Year	22	21	15	22	27	10	47	41	11
Type of Current Medical Insurance									
Medicaid	31	49	49	31	68	26	25	51	47
VA Medical Care	8	6	3	6	6	8	6	5	1
Private insurance	4	6	12	5	1	19	1	3	10
No insurance	55	34	33	52	25	23	63	35	34
Other	7	10	26	22	12	39	8	12	25

In the Last 30 Days, Went a Whole Day without Anything to Eat	43	33	22	32	28	8	32	38	16
In Last 30 Days, Hungry But Did Not Have Enough Money for Food	41	23	14	36	32	4	29	31	11
Current Food Problems[b]									
None	40	51	63	46	46	76	48	38	64
One	18	23	22	20	21	20	33	22	20
Two	20	15	10	11	18	3	11	27	9
Three	14	6	5	17	14	1	4	9	5
Four	9	6	*	6	2	0	4	6	2

Source: Urban Institute analysis of weighted 1996 NSHAPC client data; *N*s given at top of table are unweighted (designated "UN").

Note: Percentages do not sum to 100 due to rounding.

*Denotes values that are less than 0.5 percent but greater than 0.

[a]Conditions asked about include diabetes, anemia, high blood pressure, heart disease/stroke, liver problems, arthritis/rheumatism, chest infection/cold/bronchitis, pneumonia, tuberculosis, skin diseases, lice/scabies, cancer, problems walking/other handicap, STDs (other than AIDS), HIV, AIDS, intravenous drugs, and other.

[b]Each of the following counted as one food problem: client sometimes or often did not have enough to eat; client ate once or less per day; in the last 30 days client was hungry but did not eat because s/he could not afford enough food; and in the last 30 days client went at least one whole day without anything to eat.

relate most strongly to homeless status. The same differences appear in communities of all types. The most consistent pattern is that never homeless clients were more likely than either currently or formerly homeless people to be problem-free in all three domains, regardless of whether the past month, past year, or client's lifetime is examined (table 7.5). Further, currently and formerly homeless clients did not differ in the proportion who were entirely free from ADM problems (by their own report), again regardless of community type or time frame. In addition, more currently than never homeless clients reported drug problems, in every type of community and for every time frame. These consistencies are strong and striking.

Beyond these findings, we can make a few generalizations about patterns that pertain *within* a particular type of community that do not appear to be shared so strongly in other types. Within central cities, for instance, the basic finding for every combination of ADM problems where significant differences exist is that currently and formerly homeless clients resemble each other, and differ from never homeless clients, compared to whom they reported more ADM problems. This pattern is not so strong in suburban/urban fringe areas, where the major anomaly is that currently homeless clients were more likely than never homeless clients to report *only* mental health problems. Formerly homeless clients did not differ significantly from either group, but more closely resembled never homeless clients for past-month and past-year problems.

In rural areas, we note a couple of quite different patterns. First, *formerly* homeless clients showed higher levels of mental health problems in every time frame than either currently or never homeless clients. This also contributed to their being the standouts in reporting *only* mental health problems. Second, *currently* homeless clients stood out in the proportion who reported *only* alcohol problems, again in each time frame, with *formerly* homeless clients more closely resembling never than currently homeless clients.

Adverse Experiences and Out-of-Home Placement

The patterns emerging on adverse childhood experiences and incarceration are essentially similar across community types. The same relations among the three homeless status subgroups appear in each type of community (table 7.6). The main findings are that currently and formerly

Table 7.5 *Alcohol, Drug, and Mental Health Problems among Homeless NSHAPC Clients, by Homeless Status within Community Type*

(weighted percentages)

	Central City Residents			*Suburban/Urban Fringe Residents*			*Rural Residents*		
	Currently Homeless (UN = 2,295)	*Formerly Homeless (UN = 483)*	*Never Homeless (UN = 223)*	*Currently Homeless (UN = 410)*	*Formerly Homeless (UN = 90)*	*Never Homeless (UN = 90)*	*Currently Homeless (UN = 233)*	*Formerly Homeless (UN = 104)*	*Never Homeless (UN = 205)*
Problems in Past Month									
Alcohol problems	39	31	22	30	35	20	48	20	8
Drug problems	28	23	5	24	8	8	15	6	1
Mental health problems	41	40	17	37	35	14	26	50	17
Specific combinations									
No ADM problems	33	40	62	36	50	66	33	36	77
Alcohol problem only	12	10	16	10	9	18	33	13	6
Drug problem with or without alcohol problem	13	10	5	18	7	1	7	2	1
Mental health problem only	15	19	13	23	10	6	16	41	15
Mental health with alcohol and/or drug problems	26	21	4	15	25	9	11	9	2
Problems in Past Year									
Alcohol problems	48	35	23	36	38	21	55	25	9

(Continued)

Table 7.5 *Alcohol, Drug, and Mental Health Problems among Homeless NSHAPC Clients, by Homeless Status within Community Type (Continued)*

(weighted percentages)

	Central City Residents			*Suburban/Urban Fringe Residents*			*Rural Residents*		
	Currently Homeless (UN = 2,295)	*Formerly Homeless (UN = 483)*	*Never Homeless (UN = 223)*	*Currently Homeless (UN = 410)*	*Formerly Homeless (UN = 90)*	*Never Homeless (UN = 90)*	*Currently Homeless (UN = 233)*	*Formerly Homeless (UN = 104)*	*Never Homeless (UN = 205)*
Drug problems	41	31	10	35	24	10	21	8	4
Mental health problems	48	46	20	43	37	16	30	56	24
Specific combinations									
No ADM problems	25	33	59	28	42	65	28	31	68
Alcohol problem only	9	11	16	11	8	18	33	11	6
Drug problem with or without alcohol problem	18	10	6	19	13	2	9	2	2
Mental health problem only	13	18	15	21	11	6	13	40	22
Mental health with alcohol and/or drug problems	35	28	5	22	26	9	17	16	2
Problems in Lifetime									
Alcohol problems	65	61	49	51	50	31	66	43	26
Drug problems	63	53	24	53	51	21	30	34	11
Mental health problems	60	59	27	54	52	18	36	71	34

Specific combinations									
No ADM problems	13	13	34	18	13	50	18	17	51
Alcohol problem only	6	9	28	6	11	22	36	3	9
Drug problem with or without alcohol problem	21	19	12	23	25	11	10	9	7
Mental health problem only	8	14	13	17	15	5	10	30	21
Mental health with alcohol and/or drug problems	52	46	14	37	36	13	26	42	12

Source: Urban Institute analysis of weighted 1996 NSHAPC client data.
Note: Percentages do not sum to 100 due to rounding.
*Denotes values that are less than 0.5 percent but greater than 0.

Table 7.6 *Adverse Experiences of Homeless Clients, by Homeless Status within Community Type*

(weighted percentages)

	Central City Residents			*Suburban/Urban Fringe Residents*			*Rural Residents*		
Adverse Experience Occurred before Age 18	*Currently Homeless (UN = 2,295)*	*Formerly Homeless (UN = 483)*	*Never Homeless (UN = 223)*	*Currently Homeless (UN = 410)*	*Formerly Homeless (UN = 90)*	*Never Homeless (UN = 90)*	*Currently Homeless (UN = 233)*	*Formerly Homeless (UN = 104)*	*Never Homeless (UN = 205)*
First Started Drinking									
Before age 15	25	21	6	28	15	6	22	16	5
Between age 15 and 17	23	19	20	17	30	15	9	9	10
First Started Drinking to Get Drunk									
Before age 15	13	8	*	15	4	2	15	8	4
Between age 15 and 17	17	13	5	12	16	5	8	6	2
First Started Using Drugs									
Before age 15	18	15	4	22	17	2	14	4	5
Between age 15 and 17	21	11	2	17	4	9	8	13	2
First Started Using Drugs Regularly									
Before age 15	11	8	*	11	4	1	13	3	3
Between age 15 and 17	16	10	6	13	5	9	7	1	3
Ever Suspended from School	46	37	21	43	22	24	23	19	14
Ever Expelled from School	19	19	13	13	12	5	24	20	4
Before Age 18, Someone Client Lived with									
Left client without adequate food or shelter	13	8	5	13	9	1	6	14	4

Physically abused client, to cause physical harm	21	18	6	29	14	3	10	23	6
Forced or pressured client to perform sexual acts that client did not want to do	12	11	2	17	11	*	4	25	4
Abuse/Neglect Combinations before Age 18									
Physical and/or sexual abuse but not neglect	25	20	6	33	19	3	12	31	8
One or more abuse/neglect experiences	29	21	7	34	20	4	13	32	11
Juvenile Detention before Age 18	16	11	6	12	9	4	24	3	2
History of Incarceration as Adult									
5 or more days in a city or county jail	49	48	18	41	43	7	65	25	11
5 or more days in a military jail/lock-up	4	4	3	2	1	1	7	0	3
State or federal prison	21	11	4	12	8	8	12	5	2
Spent Time Incarcerated (including as juvenile)	55	51	18	44	45	13	68	25	12

Source: Urban Institute analysis of weighted 1996 NSHAPC client data; *N*s given at top of table are unweighted (designated "UN").
Note: Percentages do not sum to 100 due to rounding.
*Denotes values that are less than 0.5 percent but greater than 0.

homeless clients, compared to never homeless clients, reported more drinking and use of drugs before age 15 (to go along with the higher levels just described for related problems as adults), more school problems, more physical and sexual abuse as children, and a higher likelihood of ever having been incarcerated. Differences between currently and formerly homeless clients generally were not significant, although in some cases currently homeless clients reported marginally higher levels than formerly homeless clients. Only in rural areas did formerly homeless clients stand out as reporting *higher* levels of physical and sexual abuse than either currently or never homeless clients.

Out-of-home experiences as children were only ascertained for currently and formerly homeless clients, so these are the only comparisons we can make (table 7.7). However, we do know that only about 3.4 percent of American adults spent any time in foster care as children (Royse and Wiehe 1989). Therefore, we can assume that had NSHAPC obtained this information from never homeless clients, differences between them and the other two homeless status subgroups would have been highly significant.

As with other issues in this chapter, no significant differences exist in the probability of out-of-home placement (in foster care, a group home, or institution) attributable either to community type or homeless status. Differences do exist, however, for clients in central cities and suburban areas, with respect to running away from or being forced to leave home before age 18, or being homeless for the first time before 18. In central cities, currently homeless clients were more likely than formerly homeless clients to have been homeless for the first time before 18; the same difference was marginally significant in suburban areas. Also in suburban areas, currently homeless clients were twice as likely as formerly homeless clients to have run away from home before 18.

Concluding Thoughts

This chapter helps to fill some of the gaps in knowledge about homelessness in suburban and rural areas. It is not easy to distill meaningful generalizations from the mass of numbers, but we will try. The focus is on identifying factors for which community type does and does not affect the associations among the three homeless status subgroups.

First, we note that for race/ethnicity and family status, no important differences existed among the three homeless status groups within each

Table 7.7 *Childhood Out-of-Home Experiences of Homeless Clients, by Homeless Status within Community Type*
(weighted percentages)

	Central City Residents		*Suburban/Urban Fringe Residents*		*Rural Residents*	
	Currently Homeless (UN = 2,295)	*Formerly Homeless (UN = 483)*	*Currently Homeless (UN = 410)*	*Formerly Homeless (UN = 90)*	*Currently Homeless (UN = 233)*	*Formerly Homeless (UN = 104)*
Before Age 18, Ever Placed In						
Foster care, group home, or institution	26	18	26	28	23	13
Foster care	12	10	10	7	12	6
Group home	10	7	9	11	9	8
Institution	16	11	15	17	16	9
Before Age 13, Ever Placed In						
Foster care, group home, or institution	16	13	11	11	14	4
Foster care	10	9	7	5	10	3
Group home	7	4	4	2	5	1
Institution	7	3	3	4	8	2
Between Ages 13 and 17, Ever Placed In						
Foster care, group home, or institution	20	15	23	27	15	12
Foster care	8	6	7	4	4	4
Group home	8	6	7	9	5	8
Institution	12	10	15	14	11	8

(*Continued*)

Table 7.7 *Childhood Out-of-Home Experiences of Homeless Clients, by Homeless Status within Community Type (Continued)*

(weighted percentages)

	Central City Residents		*Suburban/Urban Fringe Residents*		*Rural Residents*	
	Currently Homeless (UN = 2,295)	*Formerly Homeless (UN = 483)*	*Currently Homeless (UN = 410)*	*Formerly Homeless (UN = 90)*	*Currently Homeless (UN = 233)*	*Formerly Homeless (UN = 104)*
Length of Time Lived Away from Home before Age 18[a]						
Less than 1 week	3	2	1	0	1	0
1 to 4 weeks	3	20	19	0	5	48
1 to 6 months	12	2	27	10	9	9
7 to 12 months	14	6	1	1	22	15
13 to 24 months	12	10	15	13	15	4
More than 2 years	56	60	37	76	49	23
Ever Ran Away from Home for More than 24 Hours before Age 18	32	27	37	18	32	36
Ever Forced to Leave Home for More than 24 Hours before Age 18	23	21	22	14	11	19
First Episode of Homelessness Occurred before Age 18	20	9	24	11	26	20

Source: Urban Institute analysis of weighted 1996 NSHAPC client data; *N*s given at top of table are unweighted (designated "UN").

Note: Percentages do not sum to 100 due to rounding.

*Denotes values that are less than 0.5 percent but greater than 0.

[a]Among homeless clients who spent time in foster care, a group home, or an institution before they were 18 years old.

community type, for any community type. Since some discussion of suburban and rural homelessness stresses the higher proportion of families in these venues, the lack of differences in the NSHAPC data is important, and so also is the similarity of NSHAPC information on family status among rural homeless households to other studies of rural areas. This similarity suggests that NSHAPC's use of soup kitchens, food pantries, and other homeless assistance programs in rural areas produced results that approximately paralleled those of other "homeless-finding" approaches. This suggests that people poor and needy enough to use homeless assistance programs within particular communities share racial/ethnic and family-structure characteristics, whether or not they are or ever have been homeless.

Second, a goodly number of factors showed differences among homeless status subgroups that followed the same pattern regardless of the type of community from which clients were selected into NSHAPC. They include age, chronic health conditions, lack of medical insurance, level of food insecurity, absence of ADM problems, and most adverse childhood experiences, including out-of-home placement.

Finally, some factors produced very different patterns among the three homeless status subgroups, depending on the type of community from which clients came. They included being male (central city and rural areas were similar, but showed a different pattern from suburban areas) and marital status (the relationships among currently, formerly, and never homeless clients were different in each of the three community types). For ADM problems and physical and sexual abuse as a child, relationships among currently, formerly, and never homeless clients resembled each other in central cities and suburban areas. But in rural areas, formerly homeless clients showed higher levels of childhood physical and sexual abuse from a household member, and of mental health problems in every time frame (the two may be related).

Income and its sources was the domain for which community type made the greatest difference in the pattern among the three homeless status subgroups. In central cities, currently homeless people had significantly lower incomes, with no difference reported between formerly and never homeless clients. In the suburbs and urban fringe areas, never homeless clients had the highest income of any subgroup in any type of community, and even formerly homeless clients reported significantly higher incomes during the previous 30 days than currently homeless clients. In rural areas, all three groups reported equivalent income levels.

The probability of working and access to means-tested and non-means-tested government benefits help to explain some of these differences, with access probably varying by community type.

In interpreting these results and using them to characterize homeless populations in suburban and rural areas, remember the caveat that NSHAPC depended on programs and services to obtain its sample. In areas with lots of services, this strategy captures the vast majority of homeless people, including those who are relatively rare service users. The only ones missed are people who *never* use services, *never* are contacted by a street outreach program, and *never* get food, blankets, coffee, or company from a mobile food van or midnight blanket run. However, as the availability of programs declines, the coverage afforded by a service-based enumeration is similarly reduced.

If significant numbers of homeless people in suburban and rural areas live in their vehicles and never go to soup kitchens or avail themselves of any other services from homeless assistance programs, then they will not be captured by a service-based methodology. To the extent that their characteristics differ from those of people who *do* use programs, or who live in suburban or rural communities that have programs to use, the descriptions in this chapter will be inaccurate.

Even with this important caveat, however, the scope of NSHAPC offers a unique opportunity to probe the differences in homelessness across community types, and in the realities of very poor people within particular communities who may or may not have experienced literal homelessness. Perhaps the most remarkable findings are the extent to which (1) major characteristics of homeless populations differ consistently from those of nonhomeless comparison groups across community type, and (2) *within* community type, certain population characteristics often associated with homelessness, such as race/ethnicity, do *not* differ *across* the different homeless status subgroups.

Holding poverty or need relatively constant, by focusing on people poor enough to need and use homeless assistance programs, this chapter has identified some factors associated with homelessness itself. They include being younger, having more adverse childhood experiences, having no medical insurance, being hungrier, and having more problems with alcohol, drugs, and/or mental health. It has also identified other factors associated with community characteristics, rather than homeless status, such as race/ethnicity and family status. Finally, it has identified income levels and income sources as factors subject to important interactions between community type and homeless status. These interactions suggest not only that the availability of and access to services and benefits differ from one community type to another, but also that specific homeless status subgroups within a given community type have unique problems getting and/or maintaining benefits and services.

Future research in specific communities should probe further to understand the unique contributions of community type, service structure, and population group, alone and in combination, to providing appropriate and needed services for very poor people.

NOTES

1. Throughout this book, the following definitions are used for community types: central city = cities within MSAs designated as central cities by the U.S. Bureau of the Census; suburban/urban fringe = the remaining geographic area and population within MSAs, after subtracting the central cities; rural = all geographic areas and people outside of MSAs (including small cities and towns whose population size does not qualify them for MSA status).

2. In looking at results presented in this chapter, readers should remember that NSHAPC used homeless assistance programs as locations from which to obtain a sample, because it was trying to find and interview as much of the currently homeless population as possible. NSHAPC took advantage of the fact that some people who are not currently homeless also use these programs to interview others who, by their presence at homeless assistance programs, may be at high risk of becoming homeless. Formerly and never homeless clients in the NSHAPC sample are thus a random and representative sample of formerly and never homeless *users of NSHAPC homeless assistance programs,* but are *not* a representative sample of all formerly and never homeless people in the United States. Obtaining such a sample would require a completely different data collection strategy, involving a random sample of the *housed* population of the United States, such as those conducted by Link and his colleagues (Link et al. 1994, 1995). However, any differences between NSHAPC's currently homeless clients and those who are formerly or never homeless are likely to be *smaller* than any differences if data were available for the entire formerly and never homeless population. So, the findings reported here have a conservative bias.

3. All differences between percentages mentioned in the text without qualification are significant at $p < .05$. Any difference described as "marginal" meets the criterion of $p < .10$. To account for the sample design and its deviation from simple random sampling, these statistical tests were performed incorporating a design effect of 3. Since the size of several subsamples used in the analysis for this chapter is quite small, seemingly large percentage point differences still may not be statistically significant.

4. The high share of Native Americans among currently homeless clients in rural areas is due to the weights attached to each sample observation to make them nationally representative. The *unweighted* data indicate that the share of Native Americans in central

city, suburban, and rural areas are 82, 6, and 12 percent, respectively. When the data are weighted, however, these percentages change to 50, 3, and 47 percent. The difference is due to the very high weights attached to three Native American men interviewed in an emergency shelter in a rural area.

5. The reader may note that in table 7.2, a few formerly and never homeless clients are shown as using "shelter" on the day of the interview or in the previous seven days. These people are included in the "shelter" category by reason of the sampling frame in which they were found, although they never reported having used such facilities during that period. They were sampled in the context of vouchering programs rather than emergency or transitional shelters, and the Census Bureau could not be sure that these vouchering activities actually focused on homeless people and offered temporary accommodation, rather than being permanent housing vouchers or certificates offered by public housing authorities. When no other indicators of past-week shelter use were found in a client's actual responses to survey questions, we left these few people classified as formerly or never homeless rather than moving them into the currently homeless category.

6. The differences in the proportion of clients reported as using other programs in the first panel of table 7.2 and the statistics in the second panel, which are much lower, arise because many people using "other" programs were found in them the day they were interviewed. Many "other" programs either restrict access to once a month (e.g., many food pantries), or are structured to contact clients less than once a week (e.g., outreach programs). Thus, having found a client in one of these programs on the day they were interviewed, one would not expect them to report having been in contact with the program again in a period as short as a week.

7. However, estimated use of food pantries in rural areas is probably affected by the NSHAPC sampling structure, which, *in rural areas only*, included food pantries as sites for identifying and interviewing clients for the study. This was necessary to compensate for the relative absence of other feeding programs in rural areas, but obviously also affected results with respect to program-use information.

8

Factors Associated with Homeless Status

How to understand the causes of homelessness? Over the past two decades, when homelessness has been an important issue on the American political scene, both structural and individual explanations have been proposed and defended. They were discussed in chapter 1. Most people now understand that both types of factors, in fact, play a role. However, any given study of homelessness can usually look at only one set or another. NSHAPC is no exception. Although individual users of homeless assistance programs are the unit of analysis for the client aspect of NSHAPC, the study's database does not lend itself well to analyzing structural predictors of homelessness that vary across communities.[1] Therefore, the analyses in this chapter necessarily focus on characteristics of individuals. The danger is that their conclusions may be taken as meaning the causes of homelessness all lie within individuals. Since no reader should come away from this chapter with such an impression, its concluding section provides some structural context and interpretation for the reported findings.

Factors Identified by Previous Research

To identify characteristics of high-risk individuals, past studies have employed several methods of analysis. They have included descriptive techniques, such as frequencies and cross-tabulations, and multivariate techniques, such as regression and cluster analysis. The results indicate that several large categories of factors differentiate homeless from non-homeless populations. These include demographic, childhood, mental health, criminal, and substance abuse characteristics. Remember that these characteristics are usually identified within a context of people who already are extremely poor. Further, some of these characteristics are themselves associated with a greater probability of being poor (e.g., some racial/ethnic groups), and some may help explain why particular people are or have become poor (e.g., mental illness, which makes it hard to hold a job or earn enough to be self-sufficient).

Most studies have found that some demographic characteristics, such as race, education, and marital status, are associated significantly with increased risk of homelessness. For example, studies of homeless female-headed families (Bassuk et al. 1997; Shinn et al. 1998; Wood et al. 1990), in comparing homeless families to poor, housed families, found that African-American families had a greater risk of homelessness than white families, but the same was not true for Hispanic female-headed families. Studies of single adults (Bray, Lambert, and Dennis 1993; Burt and Cohen 1989; Culhane et al. 1994; Koegel, Melamid, and Burnam 1995) also found higher rates of African Americans than in the general population, and far higher rates of men. (These comparisons were to the *general*, not the *poor*, population, and the differences observed combine differences between poor and nonpoor people with those between homeless and nonhomeless poor people.) In addition, lack of a high school degree has been found in association with homelessness, whether of homeless families or singles (Bassuk et al. 1997; Burt et al. 1999; Koegel, Melamid, and Burnam 1995). Homeless families generally appear not to differ in age from their poor, housed counterparts. But very young and very old people are underrepresented in most samples of single homeless adults, when compared to the general public.

Beyond demographic characteristics, previous studies also have found that several adult characteristics are associated with increased vulnerability to homelessness, when examined one at a time. These characteristics include physical and mental illnesses, alcohol and drug problems, and criminal behavior serious enough to result in incarceration as an adult. More-complex analyses, which are able to account for several factors at once, using regression techniques, only sometimes sustain these simple relationships.[2]

In addition to these adult characteristics, regression analyses from several different studies confirm that several childhood experiences increase the risk of adult homelessness. For instance, Herman and colleagues (1997) reported that, in a national sample of currently housed adults, those who reported sexual or physical abuse as children were much more likely to report at least one period of literal homelessness in their lifetime. Foster care or other out-of-home placement in childhood also differentiated homeless families (Bassuk et al. 1997; Shinn et al. 1998) from their poor, housed counterparts, and homeless singles from the general public (Koegel, Melamid, and Burnam 1995).

Many of the factors explored in NSHAPC were included to examine the association with homelessness found in earlier studies comparing homeless and housed populations. Several of this book's chapters have created different subgroups within the homeless population, and then *described* the subgroups with respect to a range of factors. Decisions about which subgroups to examine reflect the interests of policymakers and service providers who focus on particular subgroups. Thus, chapter 3 examined subgroups defined by family status and sex. This was because many shelters and other services cater to some but not all of these subgroups, and also because past research has indicated that the subgroups differ dramatically in their patterns of homelessness, personal resources and problems, and needs for assistance. Chapter 4 examined subgroups defined by alcohol, drug, and mental health problems. This was because some funding agencies and service programs define their missions by people with one or more of these problems, because people with these problems pose difficult decisions of inclusion or exclusion for service providers, and because the common, if inaccurate, perception of homeless people is that they *all* have one or more of these problems. Chapter 6 identified three patterns of homelessness among NSHAPC clients, and then looked at some characteristics that distinguished people with different patterns.

Finally, as a precursor to this chapter's analyses, chapter 7 focused on clients in different homeless statuses (currently, formerly, or never homeless clients), and then looked at differences across these subgroups for clients in urban, suburban, and rural areas. Chapter 7 went about as far as cross-tabulations can go in assessing how different factors affect each other in differentiating people who have ever experienced homelessness from those who have not. We had two reasons for examining how people in each homeless status resemble or differ from each other, depending on the type of community in which they live. First, the central city/suburban/rural analyses came as close as NSHAPC can to characterizing some structural factors that may be important contexts generating homelessness. Second, since many people do not associate suburban and rural areas with homelessness, we thought it important to give policymakers and service providers information about it.

However, the results reported in previous chapters can take us only part of the way toward increasing our understanding of homeless people and their experiences, because any finding that one factor varies across subgroups does not simultaneously control for other important factors. Considerable uncertainty persists as to which factors are most important in predicting who will be homeless and how community type affects these predictions. Race, sex, or age can look like a really important difference among subgroups, but, in fact, be merely a proxy for other factors that better reflect what "really" is going on. For instance, factors associated with homelessness in studies comparing homeless people to the *general* population may simply be associated with poverty itself, and thus may *not* appear different among the generally poor NSHAPC subsamples.

This chapter tries to "pull it all together." It uses logistical regression analyses to sort out factors really associated with homeless status among very poor people from those that only seem to be. NSHAPC offers a unique opportunity to conduct this examination. It uses data collected through similar sampling procedures, uses the same survey instruments within the same study, and does so with subgroups that are all sufficiently poor to need the services of homeless assistance programs. Examining these relationships using regression analysis with the NSHAPC data will provide an important test of how strongly specific variables are associated with ever having been homeless, and being currently rather than formerly homeless. NSHAPC's national scope, large sample size, and use of identical venues and methods to collect data from both homeless and non-homeless people all lend significance to any emerging results. This will be useful information for policy workers, even though the data represent people homeless at a single point in time rather than over time.

Approach

The analyses that follow use the entire NSHAPC sample of 4,133 people who used homeless assistance programs in the study's primary sampling areas. They represent all users of such services in the United States in fall 1996. Many of the programs designated by NSHAPC as homeless assistance programs, such as soup kitchens, mobile food programs, drop-in centers, and outreach programs, served both homeless and nonhomeless people. Homeless people comprised 54 percent of those served. Among those who were not homeless at the time of the study, we classified some as having been homeless at some time in their life (formerly homeless, 22 percent), and the remainder (24 percent) as never having been homeless.[3] Chapter 1 described how we used the type of program in which the client was found plus information from each client's interview to define the groups in this analysis: currently, formerly, and never homeless clients. In the remainder of this chapter, when analyses concentrate on risk of homelessness, both currently and formerly homeless clients are combined into a larger group called "ever homeless clients." When analyses, in contrast, focus on factors differentiating currently from formerly homeless clients, the two subgroups are kept separate.

Several caveats before proceeding: Remember that while NSHAPC was designed to produce as close to a nationally representative sample of *currently homeless clients* as possible, that is not the case for *formerly* and *never homeless* people. Any research strategy seeking a representative sample of these two groups would have to sample from the housed population, as did Link and his colleagues (Herman et al. 1997; Link et al. 1994, 1995). Instead, NSHAPC provides a representative sample of formerly and never homeless adults *who used homeless assistance programs* in fall 1996. Including them in the sample provides an opportunity to compare the currently homeless population with nonhomeless individuals who were poor or needy enough to approach these programs, and whose risk of future homelessness was undoubtedly much higher than the general public's (who either have never been homeless or had been once but not when the NSHAPC data were collected). Making comparisons among these three groups thus provides an important opportunity to identify characteristics that significantly distinguish among them, *given* fairly extreme poverty as a shared experience (albeit currently homeless people clearly are the poorest).

Preliminary Analyses

As a first step toward performing the regression analyses, we selected variables in the NSHAPC data that represent previous research findings of the most important known or suspected risk factors for homelessness. We then calculated descriptive statistics for each of these variables for each of the homeless status subgroups. For demographic characteristics (table 8.1), the results are similar to those presented elsewhere in this book and will not be described here in detail. However, we note the preponderance of clients who were nonwhite, male, never married, and living in a central city among the currently and formerly homeless subgroups, in sharp contrast to never homeless clients. Even among NSHAPC's never homeless clients, in keeping with their poverty, it is important to note that African Americans were still overrepresented compared to the general public, as were women, and, especially, old women.[4] We tested the joint effects of these characteristics on homeless status as the first step in the regression analysis, but then went on to also assess the degree to which they remained important as more behavioral and experiential variables were added.

Variables representing homeless history; adverse childhood experiences; health problems; current and longer-term alcohol, drug, and mental health problems and treatment; incarceration; and employment, income level, and income sources were calculated for the three homeless status subgroups (table 8.2). Some were slightly redefined from how they appeared in previous chapters to reflect configurations that proved more useful in the regressions. We also included several variables that were expected to differentiate between currently and formerly homeless clients (such as age at first homeless spell), as well as those expected to differentiate between ever and never homeless clients. Because the data set often included several different variables that could reasonably be expected to represent a particular factor, we examined all the possibilities and include many in the descriptive data in table 8.2.

As expected from the literature, adverse childhood experiences differed dramatically between ever and never homeless clients,[5] as did reported rates of suspension or expulsion from school, and drug use and problem drinking before age 18.[6] Adult experiences with mental health, alcohol and drug problems, treatment for substance use, and incarceration as both a juvenile and an adult also differentiated ever from never homeless clients.

In addition to distinguishing ever from never homeless clients, several factors differentiated currently from formerly homeless clients at the descriptive level. Compared to formerly homeless clients, currently homeless clients were twice as likely to report their first homeless spell

Table 8.1 *Demographic Characteristics of Currently, Formerly, and Never Homeless Clients*

	Homeless Status		
Characteristic	*Currently Homeless Clients (UN = 2,938)*	*Formerly Homeless Clients (UN = 677)*	*Never Homeless Clients (UN = 518)*
Location			
Central city	71	64	39
Suburb/urban fringe	21	17	21
Rural	9	19	40
Race/Ethnicity			
White non-Hispanic	41	45	55
Black non-Hispanic	40	41	32
Hispanic	11	9	11
Other	8	5	2
Age			
Age 18 to 24	12	4	9
Age 25 to 54	79	77	45
Age 55 and over	8	17	45
Education			
Less than high school degree	38	42	49
Marital Status			
Married	9	9	22
Never married	48	45	28
Divorced, separated, widowed	42	45	50
Sex			
Male	68	54	39
Female	32	46	61
Family Status			
In family (lives with at least one minor child)	18	17	20

Source: Urban Institute analysis of weighted 1996 NSHAPC client data; *N*s given at top of table are unweighted (designated "UN").

Note: Percentages do not sum to 100 due to rounding.

Table 8.2 *Risk Factors among Currently, Formerly, and Never Homeless Clients*

	Homeless Status		
Characteristic	*Currently Homeless Clients (UN = 2,938)*	*Formerly Homeless Clients (UN = 677)*	*Never Homeless Clients (UN = 518)*
Age at First Homeless Spell			
Age 0 to 18	22	10	NA
Age 19 to 30	30	19	NA
Age 31 or older	35	38	NA
Adverse Childhood Experiences			
Victimization			
Physical abuse, sexual abuse, and/or neglect by household member	29	23	8
Alcohol and Drug Use			
First time drank to get drunk was before age 18	32	26	10
First time used drugs was before age 18	41	27	8
Out-of-Home Experiences			
Foster care before age 13	9	7	Not Asked
Group home before age 13	6	3	Not Asked
Any other institutional placement before age 13	6	3	Not Asked
Ever forced to leave home before age 18	30	19	Not Asked
Ever ran away from home before age 18	20	13	Not Asked
Ever in juvenile detention center	16	9	4
School Problems			
Suspended, expelled, or repeated a grade	63	58	44
One or More Chronic Physical Health Problems	46	63	67
Mental Health Problems			
In past month	39	41	16
In past year	45	46	21
In lifetime	57	60	28
Alcohol and/or Drug Problems			
In past month	49	37	19
In past year	59	45	20
In lifetime	76	70	41

Table 8.2 *Risk Factors among Currently, Formerly, and Never Homeless Clients (Continued)*

	Homeless Status		
Characteristic	*Currently Homeless Clients (UN = 2,938)*	*Formerly Homeless Clients (UN = 677)*	*Never Homeless Clients (UN = 518)*
Alcohol and/or Drug Treatment			
Received alcohol or drug treatment in past 30 days	11	6	2
Received alcohol or drug treatment during lifetime	33	32	10
Adult Victimization: Robbed or Assaulted while Homeless	47	33	NA
Ever Incarcerated as an Adult	51	43	14
Employment			
Performed no paid work in past 30 days	56	66	72
No full-time employment in the 2 years before NSHAPC	72	79	83
Income Level and Sources in 30 Days before NSHAPC			
Income less than 50% of poverty level	61	40	33
Received Aid to Families with Dependent Children (AFDC)	22	24	24
Received General Assistance	27	38	18
Received Social Security	7	13	33
Received Supplemental Security Income	14	32	26
Received Social Security Disability Insurance	9	17	10
Received housing voucher or other housing subsidy	20	29	17
Received Food Stamps	72	83	62
Rent Source Just before This/Most Recent Homeless Episode			
Client paid at least part of rent him/herself	69	37	NA
Moves while Homeless			
Became homeless this/most recent time in a state other than where interviewed	18	6	NA

Source: Urban Institute analysis of weighted 1996 NSHAPC client data; *N*s given at top of table are unweighted (designated "UN").

Note: Percentages do not sum to 100 due to rounding. NA = not applicable.

occurring before age 18, and to report higher rates of childhood out-of-home placement. Youthful drug use was more prevalent among currently than formerly homeless clients, as was time in juvenile detention. Currently homeless clients received significantly less cash income than formerly homeless clients during the 30 days before being interviewed for NSHAPC. They were thus more likely to report incomes less than half the federal poverty level. Their low incomes derived in large part from their lower likelihood of receiving many forms of government cash assistance (General Assistance, Social Security, SSI, and SSDI). In addition, they were less likely to receive the other important government benefits of food stamps or a housing voucher or subsidy. Few people in any of the three subgroups derived significant income from steady employment. Currently homeless clients had also been more dependent on their own resources than formerly homeless clients, as indicated by being more likely to have paid all or part of their own housing costs during the period just before their current or most recent homeless episode. They were also more mobile, being three times as likely to be in a different state now than where they became homeless for their current or most recent spell. This combination of dependence on their own resources and high mobility may reflect a somewhat lower level of attachment to people and place among currently, as opposed to formerly, homeless people. Considering that these factors were coupled with a lower likelihood of receiving important government benefits, which can be the difference between housing and no housing, currently homeless clients appear to have had very few resources that could help them leave homelessness.

Regression Analyses

The next step was to use the same variables in logistical regression analyses to help sort out which differences are "real" and which are derivative of other, underlying factors. In the regression analyses presented below, we show only the final models that incorporate the combination of variables that helped us explain the most variance without canceling each other out.[7]

We conducted two regression analyses, and present two models for each.[8] The first analysis examined factors that differentiate ever from never homeless clients; the second examined factors differentiating between currently and formerly homeless clients. Within each analysis, we first present a model that includes only the basic demographic variables of age, race, education, gender, marital status, and urban/rural location. This is followed by a model that also incorporates variables related to childhood experiences, employment, incarceration, physical and mental health, and substance use and treatment.

Factors Associated with Homelessness

Table 8.3 presents the odds ratios derived from logistic regression for each of the characteristics associated with increased risk of having ever had a homeless episode.[9] As illustrated in the first regression, the demographic characteristics of sex, age, marital status, and geographic location showed significant associations with homelessness, even when each was examined while controlling for the presence of the others. The six demographic variables included in regression 1 account for 21.9 percent of the variance between the ever and never homeless groups. Even in this simple model, however, race/ethnicity notably does not attain significance, especially since the differences among the groups being compared are quite dramatic on the proportion who were white (which is the group to which the others in the model are being compared).

The explanatory contribution of the demographic variables diminished considerably once additional characteristics such as physical health, childhood experiences, and variables relating to alcohol and drug use were added, as shown in regression 2. Only geographic location and age remained strongly associated with homelessness. Clients located in central cities or suburban/urban fringe areas were much more likely to have ever been homeless than clients found in rural areas. Similarly, clients age 25 to 54 had a higher risk of experiencing homelessness at some time in their lives than clients age 55 and older. Contrary to the implication of the simple descriptive statistics seen in table 8.2, being African American or Native American was not significantly associated with homeless experiences (although of course such racial/ethnic group membership *is* associated with poverty). In addition, failing to finish high school and never having married did not significantly predict a person's status as ever homeless. Being male would have remained significant, but the main effect of sex was reduced to insignificance, because we included in regression 2 an interaction effect of being male and also having been incarcerated as an adult, and this proved to be significant when compared to being either a woman or a man who had never been incarcerated.

Table 8.3 *Characteristics Associated with Ever Being Homeless: Results from Logistic Regressions*

Characteristic	*Regression 1* *Odds Ratio* *(UN = 4,087)*	*Regression 2* *Odds Ratio* *(UN = 4,087)*
Geographic Location		
Central city	4.769*	4.986*
	(1.526)	(1.721)
Suburb/urban fringe	3.355*	3.805*
	(1.366)	(1.667)
Race/Ethnicity		
Black non-Hispanic	0.831	0.952
	(0.276)	(0.323)
Hispanic	0.966	1.022
	(0.436)	(0.499)
Native American or other ethnic group	2.417	2.507
	(1.384)	(1.577)
Education		
Less than a high school degree	0.918	0.907
	(0.249)	(0.247)
Age		
Age 18 to 24	4.255*	1.729
	(2.028)	(0.960)
Age 25 to 54	5.808*	2.486*
	(1.904)	(0.858)
Marital Status		
Never married	2.403*	1.864
	(0.960)	(0.757)
Divorced, widowed, separated	1.871+	1.688
	(0.696)	(0.610)
Male	2.140*	1.108
	(0.617)	(0.383)
At Least One Chronic Health Problem		0.633+
		(0.182)
Mental Health Problem during Lifetime		2.215*
		(0.676)
Alcohol and/or Drug Problem during Past Year		1.701[a]
		(0.636)
Adverse Childhood Experiences		
Physical and/or sexual abuse by household member		3.204*
		(1.483)

Table 8.3 *Characteristics Associated with Ever Being Homeless: Results from Logistic Regressions (Continued)*

Characteristic	*Regression 1 Odds Ratio (UN = 4,087)*	*Regression 2 Odds Ratio (UN = 4,087)*
First time drank to get drunk was before age 18		1.585[a]
		(0.589)
Incarceration		
Male incarcerated as an adult		3.471*
		(1.576)
Income Last 30 Days Less than 50% of Poverty		2.079*
		(0.604)
Pseudo R^2	0.219	0.318

Source: Urban Institute analysis of weighted 1996 NSHAPC client data.

Note: + indicates $p < .10$, *indicates $p < .05$. The standard errors used to calculate these significance levels (in parentheses below the odds ratios) incorporate a design effect equal to 2.

[a]Both past-year alcohol and/or drug problems and drinking to get drunk before age 18 are significant at $p < .05$ when each is included separately in the model. Tests for joint significance indicate joint statistical significance at $p < .05$.

Characteristics including physical and mental health and alcohol or drug use were also significantly associated with the probability that a client would ever have been homeless. Clients with chronic physical health problems were less likely to have experienced a homeless spell than those without them. This was true even in a model that controlled for client age, because older clients reported more chronic health problems. In contrast, having had mental health problems during one's lifetime or a problem with alcohol and/or drug use during the past year increased the likelihood that a client would ever have been homeless.

Incarceration as an adult was also related to clients' homeless status, as already noted. Drastic poverty, even among people who were already very poor, also increased the likelihood of homelessness. Clients with incomes during the last month that were lower than 50 percent of the federal poverty level had a higher likelihood of experiencing homelessness than those with incomes above it.

Along with these adult characteristics, childhood experiences also influenced clients' likelihood of having had a homeless spell. Adults who reported that as children they had been physically or sexually abused or neglected (left without food and shelter) by a household member were more vulnerable to becoming homeless. Likewise, the probability of experiencing homelessness was higher among clients who drank and who first drank to get drunk before they were 18.

Taken together, the variables included in regression 2 account for 31.8 percent of the variance between ever and never homeless clients. The analysis supports the effects of childhood experiences of abuse and neglect (and, by proxy, of out-of-home placement), and of early initiation of alcohol abuse reported in previous studies. Mental health problems of long standing also played a significant role in differentiating the ever from the never homeless clients, again as reported in numerous other studies. Thus the picture drawn by our ever/never regression analysis is that people with many personal vulnerabilities, some of childhood origin, were more likely than those without them to experience a homeless spell. However, the role of money and other resources cannot be ignored. As the next regressions show, income, and its sources in government cash and noncash benefits, plays an important role in helping ever homeless clients avoid being *currently* homeless, even when personal vulnerabilities persist.

Similar Effects for Families and Singles, Men and Women

Much previous research on factors predicting homelessness has used samples that were homogeneous with respect to family status; samples were either all homeless families, or not. We tested the possibility that different factors would be important in predicting family homelessness and the homelessness of single people. We ran separate logistical regressions for ever and never homeless families and ever and never homeless adults who were not in homeless families.[10] We found that the same factors differentiated ever from never homeless families as differentiated ever from never homeless people who were not in homeless families. The size of coefficients for the same predictor variables in each analysis did not differ significantly from each other. We therefore returned to treating clients with children and those without in the same analyses, and do not include a variable for family status, because it did not prove to be significant. Splitting the sample into subgroups of men and women produced the same results, with one exception. Both being male and having been incarcerated were strong predictors of ever having been homeless when each was included by itself in the analysis, but not when included together. Male clients were much more likely than female clients to report having been incarcerated, so we created an interaction term, which we included in regression 2 of table 8.3. When it was included, it was quite significant, but reduced the otherwise fairly powerful effect of being male to insignificance.

Differentiating Currently from Formerly Homeless Clients

Having examined the factors that differentiate ever from never homeless people who use homeless assistance programs, we next turned to identifying factors that could help explain why some people had been able to leave homelessness while others had not. In addition to predicting a higher likelihood of experiencing a homeless episode at all, several demographic and adult characteristics also differentiated currently from formerly homeless clients (table 8.4). Of course, for clients who go into and out of homelessness with some regularity, part of their homeless status would depend simply on which status they were in when interviewed for NSHAPC. We might expect, therefore, that even with all the explanatory variables at our disposal, we still will be less able to predict homeless status between currently and formerly homeless people, because the status itself is not stable. This is, indeed, what we found.

Looking first at regression 3 in table 8.4, which includes only demographic variables, currently homeless clients were significantly more likely than their formerly homeless counterparts to be younger than 55, and to have been located for NSHAPC within MSAs, either in central cities or in their suburban/urban fringe areas.[11] They were also more likely to be male. Other demographic characteristics, including race/ethnicity, education, and marital status, did not significantly differentiate currently from formerly homeless clients.

Most of the demographic characteristics that were significant in regression 3 remained so when information was added about client circumstances and behavior (regression 4), but the age variables diminished considerably in importance, to only marginal or no significance. The most powerful variables in regression 4 were those related to dependence on one's own resources, mobility, and youthfulness at the time of one's first homeless spell. The direction of these differences, coupled with the depth of poverty of currently compared to formerly homeless clients, strongly suggests that broken ties to community, friends, family, or even government programs, or lack of any available ties either at

Table 8.4 *Characteristics Differentiating Currently from Formerly Homeless Clients: Results from Logistic Regressions*

Characteristic	*Regression 3 Odds Ratio (UN = 3,589)*	*Regression 4 Odds Ratio (UN = 3,589)*
Geographic Location		
Central city	2.991*	2.897*
	(1.040)	(1.187)
Suburb/urban fringe	3.835*	4.153*
	(1.721)	(2.148)
Race/Ethnicity		
Black non-Hispanic	0.905	1.018
	(0.241)	(0.295)
Hispanic	1.295	1.248
	(0.487)	(0.596)
Native American or other ethnic group	2.870	3.519
	(1.986)	(2.796)
Education		
Less than high school degree	0.964	1.069
	(0.244)	(0.291)
Age		
Age 18 to 24	8.259*	3.264+
	(4.477)	(2.084)
Age 25 to 54	2.234*	1.003
	(0.776)	(0.403)
Marital Status		
Never married	0.785	0.884
	(0.323)	(0.405)
Divorced, widowed, separated	0.961	1.148
	(0.393)	(0.525)
Male	2.008*	1.726*
	(0.524)	(0.474)
At Least One Chronic Health Problem		0.570*
		(0.149)
Income in Last 30 Days Less than 50% of Poverty		2.050*
		(0.517)
Moved to a Different State after Becoming Homeless		3.065*
		(1.099)
Respondent Paid for All or Portion of Rent		7.233*
		(3.287)
Employment		
Did not perform any type of paid work in past 30 days		0.609+
		(0.176)
No full-time employment in last two years and paid a portion of the rent		0.384*
		(0.185)

Table 8.4 *Characteristics Differentiating Currently from Formerly Homeless Clients: Results from Logistic Regressions (Continued)*

Characteristic	*Regression 3 Odds Ratio (UN = 3,589)*	*Regression 4 Odds Ratio (UN = 3,589)*
Age at First Homeless Spell		
Age 0 to 18		2.859*
		(1.166)
Age 19 to 30		1.699*
		(0.475)
Alcohol and/or Drug Treatment		
Received alcohol or drug treatment in past 30 days		1.943+
		(0.794)
Pseudo R^2	0.074	0.218

Source: Urban Institute analysis of weighted 1996 NSHAPC client data.

Note: + indicates $p < .10$, * indicates $p < .05$. The standard errors used to calculate these significance levels (in parentheses below the odds ratios) incorporate a design effect equal to 2.

present or from the past, pose significant barriers to leaving homelessness. Currently, as opposed to formerly, homeless clients were more likely to have begun their homeless careers before age 18, to have changed communities while homeless to the extent of moving out of state, to have had no one else help pay the rent just before their current/most recent homeless spell, and to have incomes below half the federal poverty level (with corresponding lack of participation in cash assistance and other public safety net programs). They were also more likely to have an active substance abuse problem, as indicated by their participation in alcohol or drug treatment as recently as the month preceding their NSHAPC interview.

Despite a higher likelihood of chronic health problems and a lower likelihood of working, formerly homeless clients could maintain themselves in housing, while currently homeless clients could not. The descriptive statistics of table 8.2 strongly suggested that formerly homeless clients' chronic health problems and inability to work were actually responsible for their receipt of government disability benefits (both SSI and SSDI), and might also have been responsible for their greater receipt of General Assistance and housing subsidies. These, in turn, would have accounted for their higher income and greater ability to maintain themselves in housing. The obvious implication for reducing the rolls of currently homeless individuals is to increase their access to some of the same benefits.

Concluding Thoughts

Before doing the regression analyses reported here, we knew that major differences existed by homeless status in both demographic characteristics and many of the childhood and adult circumstances and conditions that previous research had found to be predictive of homeless status. But, because we were not controlling for some important differences while examining others, we could not be confident that the differences we observed were really important. We found the usual racial and gender disparities, as well as geographic differences that other studies had not had the data to examine. Our question was whether the demographic differences were really *predictive,* or just shorthand ways of representing life circumstances that would be difficult for anyone to handle. We also found the expected differences in childhood circumstances, but wanted to examine whether some were contingent on others, and which were most important.

Regression analyses have supplied the answers to some of these questions within NSHAPC's national sample. Many correspond to answers in studies that were more local in scope. The demographic variables of race/ethnicity, education, and marital status were significantly associated with ever having been homeless, when included in an equation *that contained only other demographic variables.* However, when more proximate risk factors for homelessness were included (e.g., low or no income, mental health and substance abuse problems, adverse childhood experiences), these demographic variables lost their association with homelessness. Even gender stayed significant only in interaction with incarceration. Factors differentiating currently from formerly homeless clients were also more proximate than demographic, and indicate both greater poverty and broken or never-existing ties to networks that might protect against homelessness.

Thus, importantly, we have been able to confirm with this national sample the findings of previous research in single cities with smaller samples. The results support common understandings of the factors that help determine risk for homelessness—that is, *who* will become homeless—given structural conditions of sufficient stress to ensure that *some* among the very poorest will become homeless at a particular time in a particular place.

It is important, also, to remember that American society is structured to aid some types of households (in particular, families with children) and not others (single people, and especially single males), in keeping with our ideas of who should be held responsible for taking care of themselves and who should be held blameless. We have seen that particular forms of societal aid, such as cash assistance, health, food, and housing benefits, increase incomes or income-equivalent goods to the point where they differentiate those who can afford housing from those who cannot. Finally, in the effects of mental health, alcohol, and drug problems on the likelihood of homelessness, we see the broad failure of formal care systems to adequately treat their clients and to develop effective support mechanisms that will prevent their descent into homelessness.

NOTES

1. The NSHAPC sample comes from 74 sampling areas, ranging from the nation's largest cities and their surrounding areas to rural counties with very sparse populations. One might think that information about structural conditions in these 74 sampling areas could be attached to individual records to permit assessment of both personal and structural factors in the same data set. However, we believe that problems with both the NSHAPC sample and the complexity of the sampling areas make such an analysis unadvisable. First, NSHAPC was designed to create a client sample that would be statistically defensible for generalizing to three geographic sectors of the United States: central cities, the balance of the MSAs containing those central cities, and all areas outside of MSAs (which for simplicity we refer to in this book as rural areas). It was never intended to, nor can it, support analyses of information about *clients* (as opposed to programs, which we do in chapter 10) within individual sampling areas. NSHAPC included only approximately 50 people for each sampling area, not all of whom were homeless. When the sampling area contained both central cities and suburban/urban fringe areas, NSHAPC took half those people from central cities and half from the rest of the MSA. This means that cities with millions of inhabitants are represented in NSHAPC by 25 people, with another 25 representing the additional millions who dwell in all their surrounding suburbs and more-distant areas that are part of the counties making up the MSA. These subsample sizes are too small to support any interpretation that they represent homelessness "in their community." Second, even if one were to ignore the inadequacies of sample size, one is left with the problem of selecting structural factors to include in an analysis. Would one want to characterize whole MSAs with single levels of a structural factor? For instance, would one want to apply the unemployment rate (poverty rate/cost of housing/etc.) for the whole MSA to each person sampled from the MSA, when the unemployment rate (poverty rate/cost of housing/etc.) varies dramatically between central cities and suburbs, and also between different central cities or suburbs within the same MSA? If yes, many intra-MSA differences important for understanding homelessness will be missed. If no, which should be picked? We concluded that the difficulties of

conducting this analysis were so overwhelming, and the validity of any conclusions one might draw sufficiently questionable, that we abandoned the exercise.

2. Regression techniques, of which there are a whole family, are statistical techniques that allow a researcher to isolate the effects of any particular variable by holding constant the effects of others. Because so many factors are *associated* with homelessness, but are also strongly associated *with each other,* analyses of the causes or antecedents of homelessness must use techniques such as regression to sort out which factors are really important and which are not. Throughout the rest of this chapter we use, and discuss results from, these techniques. This makes it sound the most "researchy." We have tried to keep statistical jargon to an absolute minimum, but some is necessary to describe the analyses we performed, as well as those conducted by other researchers.

3. *Unweighted N*s for these three groups are 2,938 currently homeless adults, 677 formerly homeless adults, and 518 never homeless adults. Percentages reported in this chapter and elsewhere in the book are based on analyses of data *weighted* to represent all users of homeless assistance programs in the United States during the time frame of NSHAPC.

4. People living in rural areas made up a disproportionate share of never homeless clients, because the programs sampled for NSHAPC in rural areas included more "generic" programs (e.g., community action agencies, welfare offices, public housing authorities) used mostly by nonhomeless people. In addition, to compensate in part for the relative lack of homeless-specific programs in rural areas, in those areas only, NSHAPC added food pantries to the types of program from which it drew clients. These too were used very heavily by nonhomeless people, including very high proportions of single-parent families and older women. The result was that 40 percent of never homeless clients were found in rural areas (compared to 13 percent of all NSHAPC clients), and 40 percent of clients found in rural areas were never homeless (compared to 24 percent of all NSHAPC clients).

5. Through an inadvertent skip pattern in the NSHAPC interview protocol, never homeless clients were not asked some critical questions about out-of-home experiences such as foster care, running away, or being forced to leave home before the age of 18. We cannot, therefore, use these variables in models focusing on the differences between ever and never homeless clients. We can, however, speculate with some confidence about the effects of foster care, since we know that 3.4 percent of American adults had any foster care experience before the age of 18 (Royse and Wiehe 1989). It is not clear whether this statistic refers specifically to *foster care* (i.e., placement with a foster family), or to any type of out-of-home placement arranged through child protective services, which many refer to by the generic designation of "foster care." In any event, the experience of American adults is significantly lower than the 12 percent of currently and 8 percent of formerly homeless clients who reported foster care *specifically*, and than the 26 percent of currently and 19 percent of formerly homeless clients who reported any type of out-of-home placement before reaching age 18.

6. All differences mentioned in the text without qualification are significant at $p < .05$. Any difference described as "marginal" meets the criterion of $p < .10$. To account for the sample design and its deviation from simple random sampling, these statistical tests were performed incorporating a design effect of 3.

7. It should be noted that most of the variables associated with a particular factor that we left out of the final models also yielded significant coefficients when included in a model as the only representative of their factor. However, their effects were slightly less powerful than those of the variable ultimately chosen to represent their factor in the final models. For example, we examined the separate and joint effects of the following (often interconnected) variables representing abuse, neglect and out-of-home experiences as a child or youth: (1) physical and/or sexual abuse and/or neglect, (2) foster care before age 13 and/or before age 18, (3) other types of out-of-home placement at different ages, (4) any type of out-of-home placement at different ages, and (5) running away from home. Each of them significantly differentiated between clients who had ever been homeless (currently and formerly homeless clients) and those who had never been homeless. But when two or more of them were included in the same model, both became insignificant. The one finally chosen, physical and/or sexual abuse by a household member, was the strongest single variable, and also was stronger than any combination of variables entered as a group.

8. We used STATA to run logistic regression models with NSHAPC data weighted using sampling/probability weights. The standard errors used to calculate statistical significance incorporate an estimated design effect equal to 2, to account for sampling design characteristics that differed from simple random sampling due to clustering.

9. An "odds ratio" gives the odds, or probability, that a given characteristic is associated with homelessness, compared to another characteristic which is left out of the model. An odds ratio greater than 1.0 means the included characteristic is *more* likely than the excluded characteristic to be associated with homelessness, whereas an odds ratio less than 1.0 (e.g., 0.63) means that the included characteristic is *less* likely than the excluded characteristic to be associated with homelessness. Thus, for geographic location, "rural" location is left out (only central city and suburban/urban fringe appear in table 8.3). The odds ratio of 4.769 for "central city" means that clients in the NSHAPC sample who were found in central cities are 4.769 times as likely to have experienced homelessness at some time in their lives as people living in rural areas. An odds ratio of, for example, 0.75 would have meant the opposite.

10. For this purpose, clients whom we have classified as "single" and as "other" in chapter 3 were all treated as "single"—that is, as nonfamilies as we have defined them (no children present).

11. Earlier in this chapter, we alluded to the possibility that some formerly homeless and some currently homeless clients with episodic patterns of homelessness might be similar, differing only in the chance of when NSHAPC found them and interviewed them. Analyses conducted to assess this possibility found that only about 5 percent of formerly homeless clients reported patterns of homelessness (many episodes, recent end to the latest episode) making them likely to fit this description.

9

Homeless Assistance Programs in 1996, with Comparisons to the Late 1980s

The recession of 1981–1982 provoked a significant increase in demand for emergency shelter and meal services. The nation's poverty rate soared. For the first time, women with children and two-parent families added substantial numbers to the more-expected single men among the ranks of homeless and hungry people. The sheer volume of demand, coupled with the shifting nature of the population, caused the country to focus for the first time since the Great Depression on homelessness as a serious national issue. In 1983, Congress took the first step to involve federal resources in providing services to homeless and hungry people through the Emergency Food and Shelter Program, under the auspices of the Federal Emergency Management Agency. In addition, HUD made the first federal attempt to describe the scope of the shelter system nationwide and estimate the size of the homeless population using systematic sampling techniques (HUD 1984). That study estimated that about 100,000 shelter beds existed nationwide in 1984, in approximately 1,900 shelters.

By the late 1980s, several additional estimates of the country's growing shelter capacity had been developed. HUD's second national survey of shelter supply, conducted in summer 1988, indicated that the availability of shelter beds had grown by then to an estimated 275,000 in 5,400 shelters (HUD 1989). This was almost three times the number estimated for 1984. Funding sources also had shifted dramatically in four years. HUD found that about two-thirds of 1988 shelter funding (about $1.5 billion in total) came from government sources, compared to only one-third of about $300,000 in total funding four years earlier (HUD 1989, pp. 17–18). HUD also found that approximately 40 percent of shelter occupancy was accounted for by women and children in family groups—up from 21 percent in the 1984 survey, both of which were a profound shift from earlier decades. In a few cities (New York, Philadelphia, and Washington, D.C.), right-to-shelter laws added significantly to these numbers. Virtually all the shelter accommodations available at this time were emergency shelters (including hotel/motel accommodation) with few or no attendant services.

Two additional studies that produced estimates of shelter capacity focused exclusively on the nation's largest cities (those with 100,000 or more population). The Urban Institute's 1987 study, conducted for the USDA's Food and Nutrition Service, estimated the number of shelter beds in these cities in March 1987 at about 120,000. At the same time, the study estimated the number of urban homeless men, women, and children who used homeless services at about 230,000 (Burt and Cohen 1989).

Burt (1992) also was able to track the growth of shelter capacity from 1981 through 1989 in the cities she studied. She found that about one-third of the growth occurred in the last three years of the period, 1987 to 1989. This growth spurt coincided with the first availability of significant federal funding for shelter programs, through the Stewart B. McKinney Homeless Assistance Act of 1987. McKinney Act funding made available, for the first time, a source of support for new types of shelter for which service providers and advocates were identifying a need. These included transitional housing to help homeless families and single persons with disabilities acquire the skills to maintain themselves in conventional housing, and permanent housing for homeless persons with handicapping conditions serious enough to preclude their achieving and/or maintaining independent and secure housing. The McKinney Act also included support for other elements of what would come to be known as a continuum of care, including outreach to street homeless persons and some prevention efforts through the Emergency Food and Shelter Program (see Foscarinis 1998 for a thorough discussion of the act's provisions through a period very close to the date of NSHAPC). By 1996, a considerable number of such programs had developed nationwide. During the same period, and stimulated by the availability of federal support through the McKinney Act and its requirements for planning and for matching funds, state and local governments increased their activities and spending related to homeless services (Watson 1996).

Service Growth by 1996

NSHAPC offers the first opportunity in many years to update our knowledge about homeless assistance programs from the national perspective. We look first at changes in the capacity of shelter/housing programs, because they are the programs for which we have the best historical series. We then examine changes in the capacity of soup kitchens between 1987 and 1996, focusing only on central cities due to limitations in the information from 1987.

Shelter/Housing Capacity

Estimates based on NSHAPC data indicate that the nation's shelter/housing capacity within the homeless assistance system grew by 220 percent between 1988 and 1996, from the 275,000 beds estimated by HUD for 1988 to almost 608,000 beds in 1996 (the 1996 figure has a 90 percent confidence interval of ± 6 percent). This growth came on top of the 275 percent increase in shelter capacity between 1984 and 1988, from 100,000 to 275,000 beds. Table 9.1 summarizes the growth of capacity in emergency shelter, transitional housing, and other programs within the homeless assistance system.

One of the most striking things about the growth of shelter/housing capacity is the extent to which the system has gone beyond emergency shelter to include large numbers of transitional housing units and permanent housing units for disabled people who were once homeless. In fact, relatively little growth occurred specifically in emergency shelter programs or beds between 1988 and 1996. HUD estimated 5,400 shelter programs in 1988, with a capacity of 275,000 beds. Virtually all these programs and beds supplied emergency accommodation, either through emergency shelters or through voucher arrangements with hotels and motels. In 1996, NSHAPC data indicate that the number of beds available through emergency shelter plus voucher programs had grown to only 333,500, a mere 21 percent over the level in 1988.

Table 9.1 *Changes in Shelter and Soup Kitchen Capacity in the United States, as Registered by Five Studies*

	National		*Big/Central City Only*[a]	
Program Type	*Programs*	*Capacity (Beds/Meals)*	*Programs*	*Capacity (Beds/Meals)*
Shelter/Housing Programs				
1984 (HUD 1984)	1,900	100,000	—	—
1987 (Burt and Cohen 1989)	—	—	1,700	120,000
1988 (HUD 1989)	5,400	275,000	2,600	113,000
1996 (NSHAPC)				
Total	15,900	607,700	8,000	397,700
Emergency shelters	5,700	239,600	2,900	156,100
Transitional housing	4,400	160,200	2,900	120,600
Permanent housing	1,900	114,000	1,000	80,900
Voucher distribution	3,100	67,000	800	25,500
Voucher acceptance	800	26,900	400	14,600
1981 (Burt 1992)	—	—	550	31,000
1983 (Burt 1992)	—	—	700	43,000
1986 (Burt 1992)	—	—	1,100	88,000
1989 (Burt 1992)	—	—	1,500	117,000
Soup Kitchens/Mobile Food Programs				
1987 (Burt and Cohen 1989)	—	—	1,200	97,000
1996 (NSHAPC)				
Total	4,000	569,100	2,600	382,100
Soup kitchens	3,500	522,300	2,300	352,600
Mobile food programs	500	46,800	300	29,500

Sources: NSHAPC data—Urban Institute analysis of weighted NSHAPC program data representing estimates of program activities on an average day in February 1996; other sources as noted.

[a]For HUD (1989), "big/central city" equals "cities or counties with 250,000 or more population"; for Burt and Cohen (1989) and Burt (1992), it equals "cities with populations of 100,000 or more"; for NSHAPC, it equals central cities of Metropolitan Statistical Areas, of whatever size.

In contrast, the number of transitional and permanent housing units exploded, going from basically none in 1988 to 274,200 by 1996. Thus, this entirely new capacity to help people with housing needs beyond emergency shelter was essentially equal, in 1996, to what the entire homeless shelter system had been in 1988. This remarkable growth coincides with the initial availability and eventual expansion of funding for new types of shelter/housing stimulated by the McKinney Act.

The nation's largest cities showed more-vigorous growth in emergency shelter and voucher accommodation than other parts of the nation. Capacity increased 74 percent, from 113,000 in 1988 (HUD 1989) to 196,200 in 1996. This growth in emergency capacity was coupled with the development of an equal number (201,500) of transitional and permanent housing units. Communities sought to meet emergency needs and also to develop more complete arrays of housing and related services for homeless people who would not be able to leave homelessness without extended help.

Soup Kitchen/Meal Capacity

There is no national picture of prepared-meal distribution programs for 1987 equivalent to HUD's 1988 survey of shelter capacity.[1] However, the 1987 Urban Institute study does provide a roughly equivalent look at soup kitchen and mobile food program capacity in cities over 100,000, which we can contrast to NSHAPC's estimates for central cities in 1996. The bottom panel of table 9.1 shows the relevant figures. They indicate that big-city, prepared-meal capacity increased almost four-fold between 1987 and 1996, from 97,000 to 382,100 meals a day. Nationally, NSHAPC data produce estimates that soup kitchens and mobile food programs expected to serve almost 570,000 meals a day in February 1996, of which one-third were served in suburban/urban fringe or rural areas.

Unlike most shelter/housing programs, users of which are presumed to be literally homeless, soup kitchens and mobile food programs commonly serve many nonhomeless people (although some may be formerly homeless). In addition, people may eat more than one meal a day at these programs. For both reasons, the meal-service capacity reported in table 9.1 cannot be interpreted as a level of homelessness, although it certainly reflects a level of need. Also, unlike the situation with shelter/housing programs, there has not been anywhere near the same federal incentive over the past decade to increase the availability of soup kitchen and other prepared meals. In some ways, this makes the growth of capacity in the emergency food arena between 1987 and 1996 even more remarkable. It attests to the responsiveness of many communities' emergency capacity, as well as to the ongoing problem of hunger even in a decade when most Americans enjoyed remarkable prosperity.

Other Homeless Assistance Programs in 1996

Just as shelters and soup kitchens multiplied and expanded their services in the 1990s, the homeless assistance network experienced an explosion of other types of programs as well. These new programs, including those addressing health needs and needs for connection through outreach and drop-in centers, helped fill the gaps in services needed by many homeless people but that were previously extremely difficult to access.

NSHAPC collected data about many types of homeless assistance programs, as long as they met the definition of such programs adopted by the study. A homeless assistance program was defined as *a set of services offered to the same group of people at a single location* that had a focus on serving homeless people (although they did not have to serve homeless people exclusively). They also had to offer direct service, and be within the geographical boundaries of an NSHAPC sampling area. Sixteen types of homeless assistance programs were included in NSHAPC, as noted in the accompanying box. The appendix gives full definitions.

Figure 9.1 and the first column of table 9.2 show the distribution of NSHAPC programs, and how we grouped them into four more-general program types of housing, food, health, and other. Note that financial/housing programs (e.g., FEMA/EFSP, welfare, public housing programs) were not an original NSHAPC category. But they were mentioned so frequently as "other programs" to warrant presentation as a separate category. On the other hand, migrant housing used to accom-

NSHAPC Program Types

- Emergency shelters
- Transitional housing
- Permanent housing
- Voucher distribution for emergency housing
- Accept vouchers in exchange for housing
- Food pantries
- Mobile food programs
- Soup kitchens/meal distribution programs
- Physical health care programs
- Mental health programs
- Alcohol and/or drug programs
- HIV/AIDS programs
- Outreach programs
- Drop-in centers

Figure 9.1 *Number of Homeless Assistance Programs in the United States, 1996*

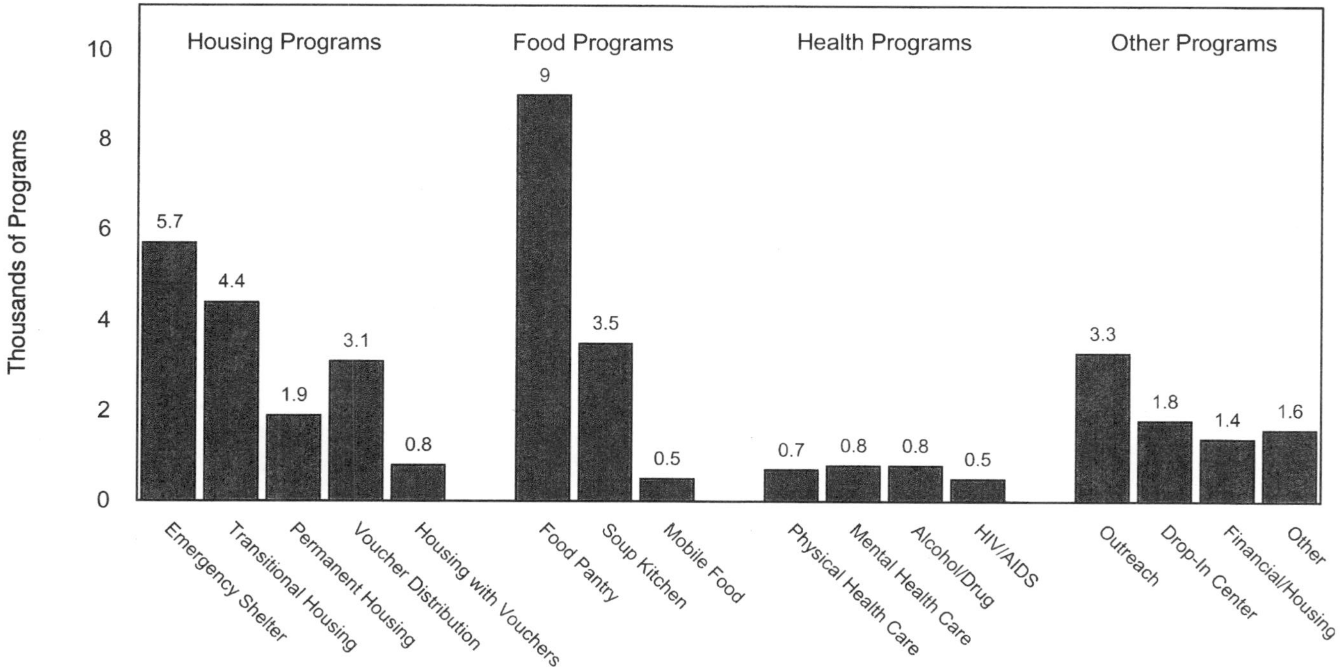

Source: Weighted NSHAPC data representing programs operating during "an average week in February 1996."

Note: Financial (usually welfare) and housing assistance services were mentioned often enough under "Other" to warrant a category of their own, and migrant housing was combined with "Other" because there were so few programs.

Table 9.2 *Distribution of NSHAPC Programs, by Urban/Rural Location*

Program	*Estimated Number of Programs*	*Central Cities*	*Suburb/Urban Fringe*	*Rural*
Total	39,670	49	19	32
Housing	15,890	50	20	30
Emergency shelter	5,690	50	21	29
Transitional housing	4,400	65	21	15
Permanent housing	1,920	53	18	29
Voucher distribution	3,080	25	19	56
Housing with vouchers	800	54	26	20
Food	13,000	46	23	31
Food pantry	9,030	39	25	36
Soup kitchen/meal dist.	3,480	65	20	15
Mobile food	490	52	15	32
Health	2,740	50	9	41
Physical health care	710	47	9	44
Mental health	800	50	10	41
Alcohol or drug	780	49	7	44
HIV/AIDS	450	59	13	28
Other	8,050	51	15	34
Outreach	3,310	59	16	25
Drop-in center	1,790	58	17	25
Financial/housing assist.	1,380	12	8	80
Other	1,570	59	17	24

Source: Urban Institute analysis of weighted NSHAPC program data. Data represent reports of program activities on "an average day in February 1996."

modate homeless people in the off-season was so uncommon it was regrouped into "other."

Food pantries were the most numerous type of program, with an estimate of about 9,000 nationwide that served homeless people.[2] Emergency shelters were next with almost 5,700 programs, followed closely by transitional housing (4,400), soup kitchens and other distributors of prepared meals (3,500), outreach programs (3,300), and voucher distribution programs (3,100). As a group, homeless assistance programs with a health focus were the least numerous.

About half (49 percent) of all homeless assistance programs were found in central cities. Rural communities offered the next-largest share (32 percent), and suburban/urban fringe communities, the smallest (19 percent) (table 9.2). However, this generalization hides considerable variation in location for programs of different types. Among shelter/housing programs, for example, voucher distribution programs were much more common in rural areas than central cities (56 versus 25 percent), reflecting the relative inefficiency of creating permanent structures for housing assistance in areas where the volume of need may not warrant them.[3] Conversely, central cities had more, and rural areas less, than their share of transitional housing programs.

Other dramatic differences include the distribution of soup kitchens, health programs, and financial/housing assistance programs across community types. Soup kitchens were disproportionately found in central cities, where ease of transportation and the possibility of walk-ins make them viable. They were underrepresented in rural areas, where the opposite conditions prevail. In rural areas but not in other types of communities, homeless assistance was available at mainstream financial and housing programs. Much the same pattern may have been operating with most of the health program types included in NSHAPC. All but the HIV/AIDS programs were underrepresented in suburban areas and other parts of metropolitan statistical areas outside central cities, and overrepresented in rural areas.

The Difference between Programs and Program Contacts

Because programs can vary considerably in the number of people they serve, it is not enough to look only at the distribution of programs. The level and distribution of "program contacts" must also be examined. A "program contact" is a service provider's report of someone who is expected to use the program on a given day. We used estimates of program contacts, for example, not whole programs, when we looked earlier at changes in shelter/housing services and soup kitchen/mobile food program services between 1984 and 1996 (table 9.1). Now we need to say more about the idea of a program contact, so it is clear what is being reported and how a *program* differs from a *program contact.*

Since people may use more than one type of service during an average day, all of which were reported by NSHAPC programs, these reports necessarily contain an unknown and unknowable amount of duplication. Such estimates by service providers cannot simply be added together to determine the total number of people using services on an average day, even though such addition is often done at the local level. For this reason, we do not speak of "people served." Further, many of the people using programs included in NSHAPC were not homeless. So, care must be taken to understand that *program contacts* are simple estimates of program use by people who may need a variety of services, and get some at programs that assist homeless persons among others. Estimates of program contacts are very important in understanding the level of service needed, or used, in a given community on a given day. In fact, they may be even more valuable to service providers than an unduplicated count of homeless people. However, they are not the same as the number of homeless people using the services. The difference in estimates will be discussed further below.

Armed with this understanding of *program contacts,* we now can examine their reported level for the country as a whole, by program type (figure 9.2). We can also look at their distribution, again within program type, across types of community—central cities, suburban/urban fringe areas, and rural areas (table 9.3).

Total Number of Expected Program Contacts

For each type of NSHAPC program, figure 9.2 shows how many program contacts the programs expected on an average day in February 1996. Taken together, homeless assistance programs expected over three million such contacts a day. Food pantries as a group clearly expected the most (over 1 million), followed by soup kitchens (at 522,000).

Figure 9.2 *Number of Program Contacts Expected at Programs of Different Types on an Average Day in February 1996*

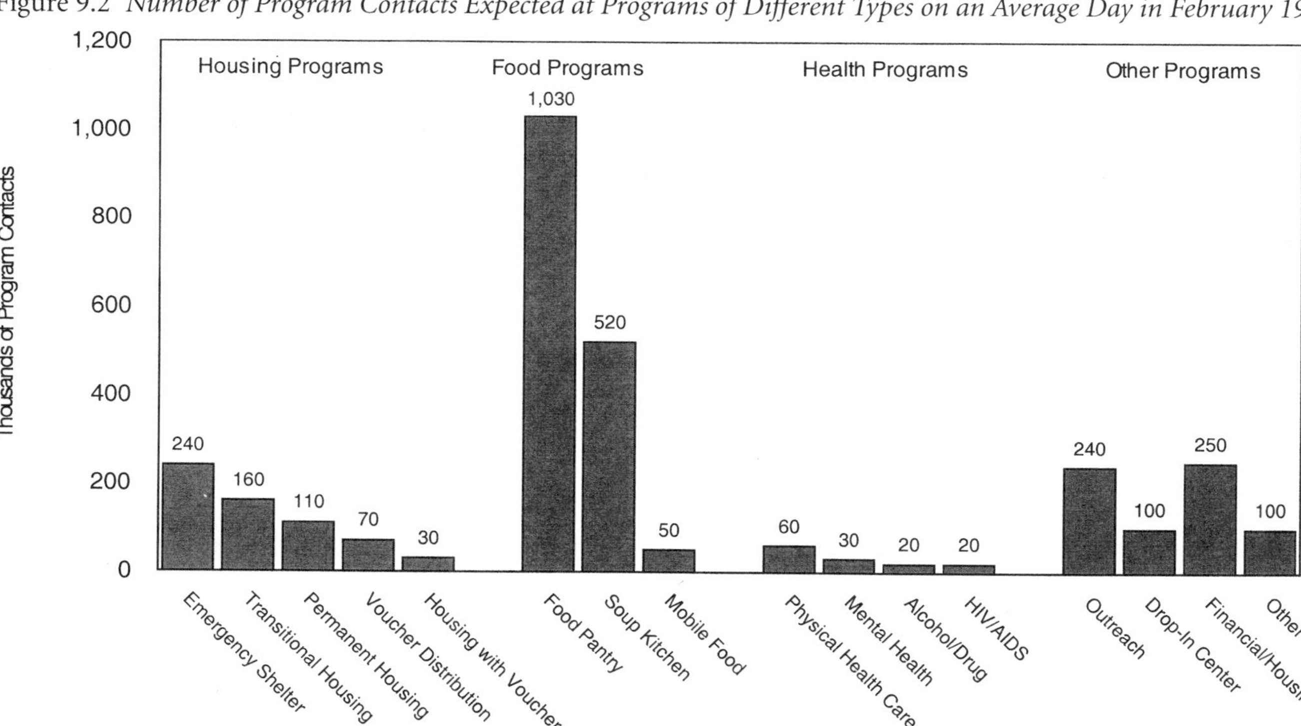

Source: Weighted NSHAPC data representing programs operating during "an average week in February 1996."

Note: These are estimates from NSHAPC program representatives of how many contacts their program expected on an average day in February 1996. They contain duplication and cannot be added together to get the total number of *people* served on an average day.

Table 9.3 *Distribution of Estimated Program Contacts, by Urban/Rural Status*

Program Type	*Estimated Number of Program Contacts*	*Urban/Rural Status (%)*			
		Total	*Central City*	*Suburban/ Urban Fringe*	*Rural*
All Programs	3,058,700	100	57	20	23
Housing	607,600	100	65	21	13
Emergency shelter	239,500	100	65	20	15
Transitional housing	160,200	100	75	19	6
Permanent housing	113,900	100	71	16	13
Distribute vouchers	67,100	100	38	36	26
Accept vouchers	26,900	100	54	38	7
Food	1,603,600	100	61	25	13
Soup kitchen/meal dist.	522,300	100	68	26	6
Food pantry	1,034,500	100	58	25	17
Mobile food	46,800	100	63	26	10
Health	141,000	100	52	11	37
Physical health	64,000	100	38	10	53
Mental health	30,300	100	49	13	39
Alcohol or drug	23,900	100	69	8	23
HIV/AIDS	22,800	100	78	14	8
Other	706,500	100	40	10	50
Outreach	244,800	100	55	12	32
Drop-in center	104,000	100	68	15	17
Financial/housing assist.	252,800	100	3	2	96
Other	104,900	100	69	17	14

Source: Urban Institute analysis of weighted NSHAPC program data representing estimates of program activities on an average day in February 1996.
Note: Numbers have been rounded to the nearest 100.

Programs offering financial and/or housing assistance, outreach programs, and emergency shelters each expected between 240,000 and 253,000 program contacts a day. In contrast, the estimate of program contacts for all four types of health programs with a focus on serving homeless people, taken together, is only about 141,000, and this estimate is accurate only if each person used one and only one type of health service on an average day.

These figures probably are high for average daily service use, in part because February is a peak month for many homeless assistance services. In addition, a universal reality of NSHAPC's type of program survey is that program respondents tend to recall peak periods rather than average days, even though asked for the average. Further, homeless people may comprise a relatively small proportion of the clients of some program types. So, not only should one refrain from interpreting these estimates of service contacts as estimates of people served, but most especially they should not be interpreted as estimates of *homeless* people served. Data from the NSHAPC client survey indicate that only 27 percent of those who reported using food programs were currently homeless, as were 44 percent of those using "other" programs.

Distribution by Community Type

Program contacts were not distributed evenly around the country. In fact, for most program types, they were even more concentrated in central cities than the programs themselves. Figure 9.3 shows that shelter/housing program contacts and food program contacts were disproportionately higher in central cities and lower in rural areas than might be expected from the distribution of programs. Program contacts expected at voucher distribution programs were still the anomaly among shelter/housing programs (table 9.3). Fewer occurred in central cities, and more occurred in both suburban and rural areas, than for other types of shelter/housing. On the face of it, this pattern for voucher arrangements makes eminent sense for communities where the demand for emergency shelter is believed to be too low to justify a fixed or permanent shelter facility. However, "believed to be" is the critical phrase. Many rural communities that *have* created a permanent shelter capacity, either in apartments or a full-scale facility, have found that their facilities are in constant demand. Moreover, neighboring communities without a shelter capacity routinely find they need to send people to these scarce

Figure 9.3 *Distribution of Programs and Program Contacts across Community Types, by Program Type*

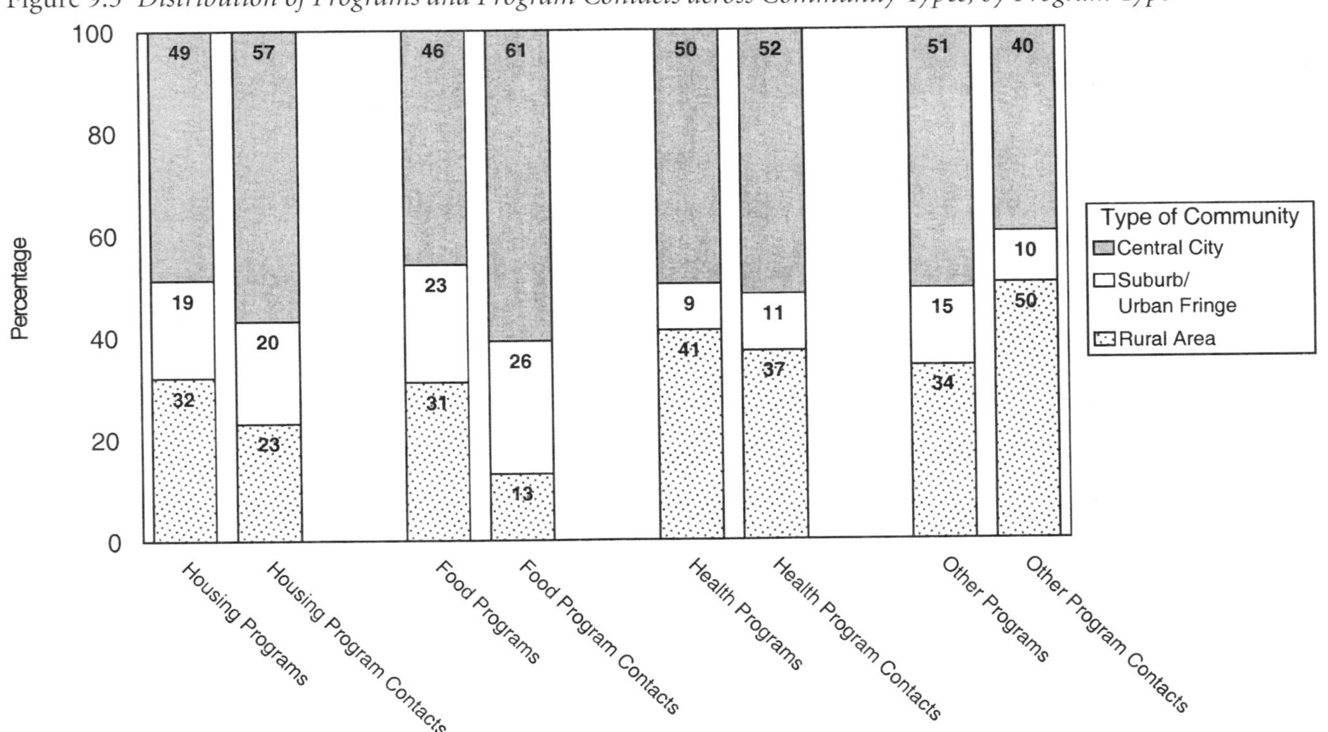

Source: Weighted NSHAPC data representing programs operating during "an average week in February 1996." Housing programs include emergency, transitional, permanent housing and voucher programs; food programs include pantries, soup kitchens, and mobile food programs; health programs include general health, mental health, substance abuse, and HIV/AIDS programs; other programs include outreach, drop-in centers, financial/housing assistance, and other.

resources (Burt 1995). The odds are that if the facilities existed in more small communities, they would be used.

In contrast, "other" programs showed a pattern of disproportionately more contacts in rural areas and fewer in central cities than implied from the distribution of the programs themselves. Expected contacts at financial/housing assistance programs showed this pattern to an extreme degree, and expected outreach program contacts to a lesser one. As noted, these patterns probably reflect approaches to serving homeless people that were believed reasonable and feasible in communities of different types. Rural areas tended to rely more on generic services and less on homeless-specific ones, because they felt they had lower levels of or greater variability in demand (Burt 1995).

Variability in Program Size

One reason the distribution of programs and program contacts was so different across community types is that homeless assistance programs varied greatly in size, defined as the number of people respondents estimated would be served on an average day in February 1996. Figure 9.4 shows how programs of different types are distributed by size. The figure makes clear that food programs were most likely to be quite large (26 percent expected to serve 101 to 299 people daily, and 11 percent, more than 300 people daily). In contrast, shelter and housing programs were most likely to be small (28 percent expected to serve 1 to 10 people a day, and 31 percent, 11 to 25 people a day). Only 2 percent expected to serve more than 300 people daily. Health and other homeless assistance programs were the most evenly distributed across a range of sizes, with about 40 percent of each expecting 25 or fewer people daily and between 44 and 45 percent of each expecting between 26 and 100 people daily.

One may ask whether small programs as a group, because there were many more of them, together actually served the same number of people as the few large programs. The answer is "no." The biggest programs, though few, accounted for very large proportions of the people being served on an average day (see figure 9.5). This was the case regardless of which type of program one examined, though it was most true for shelter/housing programs. The 80 percent of shelter/housing programs serving 50 people or less daily served only 32 percent of the people expected to use the programs on an average day (in February 1996). On the other hand, the 8 percent of shelter/housing programs serving more than 100 people daily served 51

Figure 9.4 *Size of Homeless Assistance Programs*

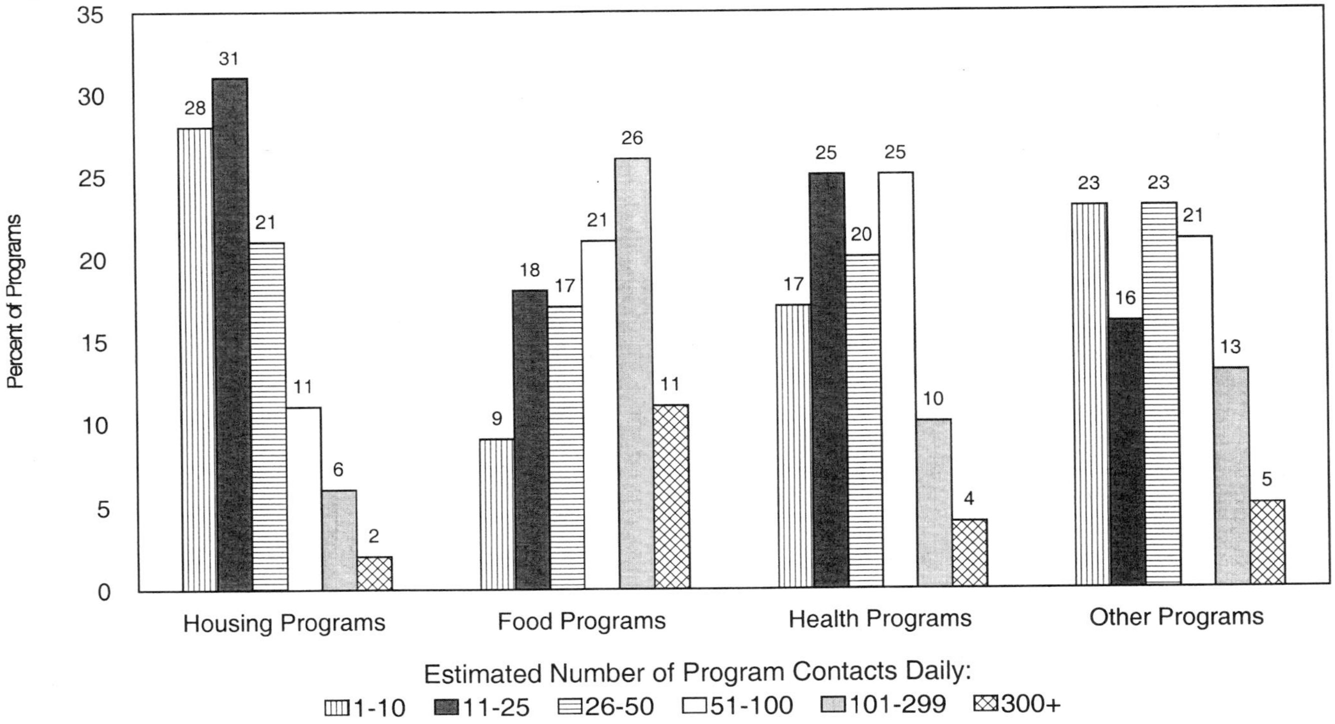

Source: Weighted NSHAPC data representing programs operating during "an average week in February 1996."

Note: These are program staff estimates of how many program contacts their own program expected on an average day in February 1996. They contain duplication and cannot be added together to get the total number of *people* served on an average day. Housing programs include emergency, transitional, permanent housing and voucher programs; food programs include pantries, soup kitchens, and mobile food programs; health programs include general health, mental health, alcohol/drug, and HIV/AIDS programs; other programs include outreach, drop-in centers, financial/housing assistance, and other.

Figure 9.5 *Proportion of Daily Program Contacts Provided by Larger Programs*[a]

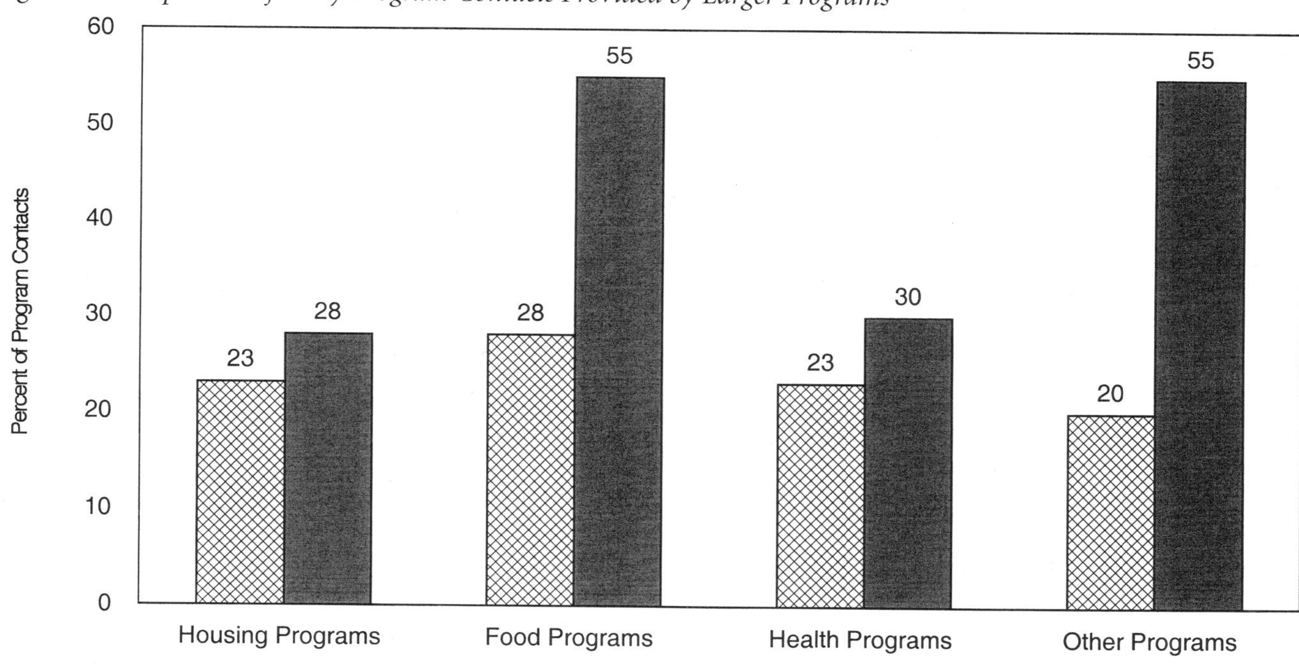

Source: Weighted NSHAPC data representing programs operating during "an average week in February 1996."

Note: These are program staff estimates of how many program contacts their own program expected on an average day in February 1996. They contain duplication and cannot be added together to get the total number of *people* served on an average day. Housing programs include emergency, transitional, permanent housing and voucher programs; food programs include pantries, soup kitchens, and mobile food programs; health programs include general health, mental health, alcohol/drug, and HIV/AIDS programs; other programs include outreach, drop-in centers, financial/housing assistance, and other.

[a]Larger programs are defined as those serving more than 100 clients per day.

percent of the people using shelter/housing programs. Indeed, the 2 percent serving more than 300 people daily served 28 percent of all shelter/housing users on an average day. Further, most of the very large programs were in central cities, helping explain the pattern examined earlier.

Focusing on this extreme skew in the number served by very large shelter/housing programs, one may ask further whether the nature of services differed in any significant ways from very large programs to those of more reasonable size. The most obvious expectation is that emergency shelters may be very large and impersonal, but that transitional and permanent housing programs, being smaller, ought to offer more personal attention and supportive services to residents. In fact, the opposite was true. Forty percent of permanent housing programs served 300 or more people every day, and another 29 percent served between 101 and 299 people (thus, 69 percent of all program contacts for permanent housing programs were in facilities serving at least 100 people daily). Comparable figures for transitional housing and emergency shelter were still high, but not as much. Forty-seven percent of emergency shelter contacts occurred at facilities serving at least 100 people a day (26 percent at those serving 300 or more a day, and 21 percent with 101 to 299 clients a day). And 43 percent of transitional housing contacts occurred at facilities of this size (21 percent at those with 300 or more contacts, and 22 percent at those serving 101 to 299 people a day). One could also make the argument that emergency shelters should be smaller, so that personal attention could help people leave homelessness quickly. Regardless of which direction the argument goes, the reality is that half of all homeless people using homeless assistance shelter/housing programs are being served in very large and possibly significantly "institutionalized" settings. If this is the case, then in its development toward a permanent "industry," the homeless service network has simply become the new location of residential services that once were offered by other service systems (e.g., mental hospitals). Whether this is a positive accomplishment, data alone cannot answer. But policymakers and service providers should certainly ask themselves the question.

The story of "bigness" was the same with food and other homeless assistance programs. But for them, bigness may not be as significant a problem as it is likely to be for housing programs. Only 11 percent of food programs and 5 percent of other programs served more than 300 people daily, but on an average day they accommodated, respectively, 55 percent of everyone getting food from food programs and

55 percent of everyone getting help from other programs. Service delivery in health programs for homeless clients was less skewed toward the very large programs (over 300 contacts daily) and away from the very small programs (25 or fewer daily). But even here, the 42 percent of programs that are very small served only 7 percent of those who use health programs on an average day, while the very large programs served 30 percent.

Operating Agencies

Homeless assistance programs may be operated by nonprofit agencies, for-profit organizations, and government agencies. In turn, nonprofit agencies may be secular or affiliated with religious organizations or congregations. Over the years, these agencies have responded to community needs by developing homeless assistance programs, and a considerable degree of specialization has resulted. Nonprofit agencies, for example, offered the vast majority (85 percent) of homeless assistance programs. Figure 9.6 shows which types of agencies were most likely to offer housing, food, health, and other programs.

Figure 9.6 makes obvious that the different types of programs were operated by quite different types of agencies. Secular nonprofit agencies dominated the housing category, offering 60 percent of all programs, while religious nonprofits dominated the food category, offering 55 percent of the programs. Health programs were about evenly split between government and nongovernment agencies, with secular nonprofits dominating among the nongovernment agencies.

With respect to homeless assistance, government agencies were least likely to operate food programs (5 percent of those programs), and most likely to offer health programs (51 percent of health programs). Secular nonprofits were most prominent among other programs offering homeless assistance, which included outreach programs, drop-in centers, housing and financial assistance programs, and other programs. For-profit organizations played almost no role in operating homeless assistance programs.

Funding Sources

Given the different types of agencies, it should not be surprising that considerable differences also existed across program types in the extent

Figure 9.6 *Types of Agencies Operating Housing, Food, Health, and Other Programs*

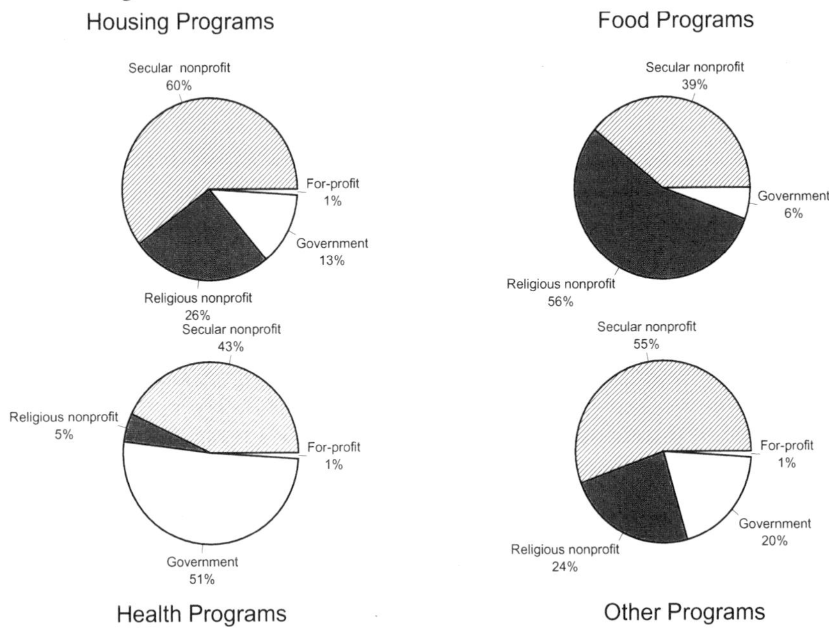

Source: Weighted NSHAPC data representing programs operating during "an average week in February 1996."

Note: Numbers do not sum to 100 due to rounding. Housing programs include emergency, transitional, permanent housing and voucher programs; food programs include pantries, soup kitchens, and mobile food programs; health programs include general health, mental health, substance abuse, and HIV/AIDS programs; other programs include outreach, drop-in centers, financial/housing assistance, and other.

to which they relied on private or government sources (federal, state, or local) to support their operations. Figure 9.7 shows these differences as the proportion of program budgets that came from government funding; private funding made up the balance of each program's budget.

Food programs were the most likely to rely solely on private funding and to report that they used no government funds (true for 51 percent). They were also the least likely to be fully supported by government funds (6 percent). Given this reliance on private means, the growth in food programs is even more remarkable. Conversely, health programs were least likely to rely solely on private funding (only 12 percent operated entirely without government funding), and most likely to have been fully supported from government sources (55 percent). In between were housing and other types of homeless assistance programs. Housing programs were the most evenly split across the different levels of reliance on public support, indicating a fairly highly differentiated market that has succeeded in drawing in a considerable amount of nongovernmental funding. Other homeless assistance programs were split quite evenly. One-third relied entirely on private funding; 34 percent were completely supported by government (usually they *were* government, in the form of welfare or public housing agencies); and one-third fell somewhere in between.[4]

These funding patterns reflect a certain historical reality, as well as a quite remarkable change. In the early 1980s and before, most of the formal services serving homeless persons—missions, soup kitchens, and various other skid row facilities—were run without public funds, or with relatively small amounts, and then for specific purposes such as helping chronic alcoholics. Both religious and secular nonprofits operated these programs, with very rare exceptions. There were, of course, local jails that provided shelter on many a freezing night to many an inebriated homeless person, and they were supported with public monies. Some cities also ran, or helped support, hostels and work programs for street alcoholics, for which some federal funding also was available through the National Institute on Alcohol Abuse and Alcoholism, once it was established in 1972. In addition, federal legislation in the 1970s provided funding to develop and operate centers for runaway and homeless youth. But the scale was much smaller (far fewer people were involved), and so was the funding.

By the mid-1990s, not only had the number and variety of programs grown tremendously, but also government had become a much larger contributor. Food programs remained the last hold-out for completely private charity, although even half of them took some public money. Programs of other types had become fairly eclectic in accepting funds from a variety of sources. This reflected both greater availability of public monies, and also greater demand pressing providers to take any support they could find. The net effect is a veritable homeless "service industry" that developed during a period when the *only* area of growth in public spending was for homeless programs. NSHAPC data cannot answer whether the continued existence of such a permanent service structure is the best way to help people who experience homelessness. But the question is worth asking, and deserves some significant focus in public debate.

Figure 9.7 *Program Reliance on Government Funding*

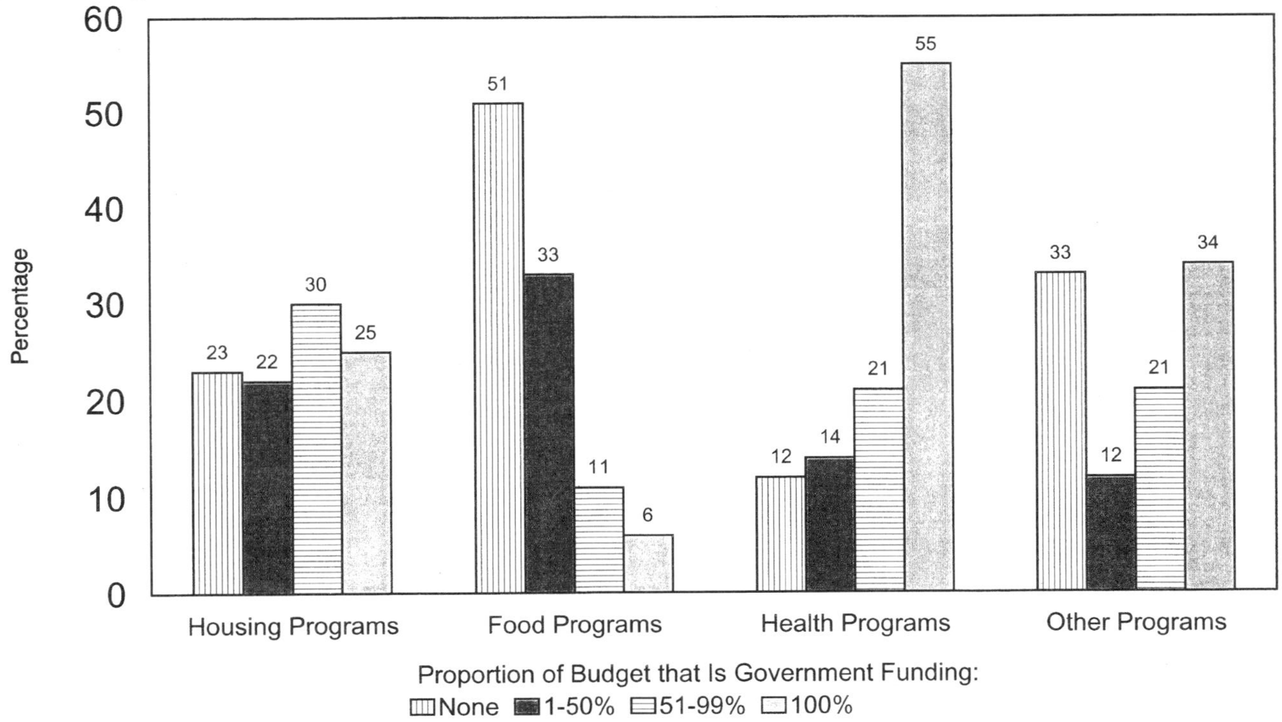

Source: Weighted NSHAPC data representing programs operating during "an average week in February 1996."

Note: Numbers do not sum to 100 due to rounding. Housing programs include emergency, transitional, permanent housing and voucher programs; food programs include pantries, soup kitchens, and mobile food programs; health programs include general health, mental health, substance abuse, and HIV/AIDS programs; other programs include outreach, drop-in centers, financial/housing assistance, and other.

Concluding Thoughts

The 1990s saw a vast expansion of homeless assistance programs, both in the volume and variety of services offered. At the national level, it appears that we are coming closer to including in the homeless assistance network many services and programs beyond emergency shelter, designed to fill the gaps in communities' abilities to meet the diverse needs of homeless people. It is also clear that, except for shelter/housing programs, homeless people share the use of most programs in the homeless assistance network with others, including formerly homeless people and many who have never been homeless. It is also important to note that programs included in NSHAPC as homeless assistance programs are not the only sources of assistance to homeless persons, although they do serve homeless people as a target population group. Many programs similar to NSHAPC programs also may exist in a community, and homeless people also may use them, including mainstream welfare, health, housing, food pantry, and social services programs. However, they were not included in the NSHAPC sample because they do not focus on serving homeless people.

The growth of the homeless assistance network can be considered a success story from the point of view of people experiencing a period of homelessness. The network makes it more likely that they will receive services, and receive them from people who are dedicated to working with homeless people and treating them with respect. However, there is reason to ask whether this amelioration of the homeless condition is what we as a society should be trying to do, and how much of the resources available to address homelessness should be directed toward these activities. The problem is that only resources devoted to permanent housing programs directly address the issue of *ending* homelessness.

There is no question that the expanded services of the network provide more, and more appropriate, assistance to people who are actually homeless. And there can be little question that this assistance is needed, is humane, and actually ameliorates, at least for a time, hunger, health problems, exposure to the elements, and so on. But by itself, it does not, and probably cannot, end homelessness.

In the concluding chapter, we pursue further a discussion of the most reasonable directions for future policy related to homelessness. Here, we want to lay some more groundwork for that discussion by pointing out some of the complexities of making such policy recommendations or setting such future policy.

Most importantly, keep in mind that our society still produces, and maintains, enough people living in extreme poverty to keep the services of an emergency/homeless assistance network busy, even at double its present scope. Nothing we say ever should be taken to deny the existence of a basic level of *unmet need*, or to deny society's responsibility for meeting it. However, that being said, an argument also can be easily made that an expanded homeless assistance network lets mainstream programs "off the hook" of responsibility for helping all people in need, and also may contribute to the continued isolation of homeless people.

We have, in the past decade, built a homeless assistance "industry." But, ironically, its very growth, especially in emergency shelter and transitional housing, provides more opportunities for people to enter the ranks of the "literally" homeless, and, in the case of transitional programs, to stay there for quite a while (see also Culhane 1992).

Becoming homeless, defined in many cases by entering a formal homeless assistance program, may be a sign of desperation, and some have argued that in the absence of sufficient resources, it is as good a sign as any that these are the people whom the system should help (McAllister and Berlin 1994). Yet there also are indications that people come to homeless assistance programs or intake centers because they are the only visible help around, even though what the clients really may need, and want, is mental health or substance abuse services, child care, or even a place to stay a few days in a new city when they cannot afford a motel. Mainstream programs should be available to meet these needs, but for most of the 1990s mainstream programs were being cut, and had neither the resources nor the inclination to serve these "hardest-to-serve" potential clients. Programming for homeless populations was the only "new" money, the only potential "growth industry," around. That it grew is not surprising. Whether it should continue growing in its present configuration, or whether it is time for a little rethinking, are other questions entirely.

NOTES

1. "Prepared meals" are cooked or assembled meals such as those served by soup kitchens or distributed as bag lunches by mobile food programs, in contrast to the bags or boxes of uncooked food distributed by food pantries for preparing at home.

2. Many programs similar to NSHAPC programs may exist in a community but were not included because they do not target their services toward homeless people (food pantries and health programs are examples). For example, the 9,000+ food pantries in the NSHAPC sample (which include food pantries in metropolitan as well as rural areas) are only 27 percent of the 34,000+ food pantries, and the NSHAPC's approximately 3,500 soup kitchens are only 45 percent of the 7,700+ soup kitchens identified by Second Harvest in its 1997 survey (Second Harvest 1997).

3. All differences between percentages discussed in the text are statistically significant at $p < .05$, all numbers (e.g., the number of soup kitchens) have a 95 percent confidence interval of no more than 2 percent of their value (e.g., if the number is 10,000, the C.I. is $\pm$ 200), and all percentages presented by themselves have a 95 percent confidence interval no larger than $\pm$ 4 percentage points. A confidence interval of $\pm$ 4 percentage points means that if the reported percent is 60, 60 is the estimate of the value and the probability is 95 percent that the value falls between 56 and 64 percent.

4. The value of in-kind contributions from private sources is not included in these figures. For many programs, these contributions can be of considerable value, and include food, rent-free buildings, equipment, and volunteer time to perform critical program functions.

10

Program Structures and Continuums of Care

Organized *systems* of programs serving homeless people have been a long time coming in the United States, but they made significant progress during the 1990s. During the early 1980s and before, homeless assistance services were provided primarily by missions and soup kitchens, operating with a religious or charitable motivation. Most operated essentially on their own. They raised their own money, served whom they wished, and made no major effort to coordinate with other programs. Located almost exclusively in old "skid row" areas of the nation's cities, relatively few received government funding. They offered the bare minimum of meals or overnight shelter. They did not form a coherent system of care, nor assess local need for service and try to fill gaps. They focused primarily on serving a single-male, homeless and near-homeless clientele. They were often supplemented by the police (who of course *were* publicly funded), serving an "outreach" function of last resort for public inebriates (as chronic drunks were often designated in government programs). They also offered the shelter of the "drunk tank" on freezing nights, until laws changed to decriminalize public drunkenness and remove this resource from the homeless service pantheon. There were few or no programs such as today's transitional and permanent housing programs. Few facilities allowed people to stay past 7 or 8 o'clock in the morning, and few programs offered counseling, health care, or help with overcoming alcohol, drug, or mental health problems.

The Need for Continuums of Care

Just as there was no plan or "structure" to the array of homeless assistance services before the mid-1980s, initial McKinney Act funds, while increasing capacity, were not structured to "complete" a service system, or ensure that homeless people received all the care they needed, even if it was available elsewhere in the community. Emergency shelter grants were awarded on a formula basis to government agencies in most communities eligible for Community Development Block Grants. Funding for specialized services, such as transitional and permanent housing, was awarded through national competitions once a year. The availability of funds spurred a dramatic growth in shelters appropriate for families, and in transitional and permanent housing programs for people attempting to leave homelessness. Further, local governments and private sources increased their financial support, in part, because a local match was required to access federal dollars.

Applicants for McKinney Act support to create transitional and permanent housing programs could be, and usually were, individual shelter or housing programs with grant-writing capacity. Their applications had to justify that a need existed for the services proposed, but they did not have to show where the services fit into the entirety of services available in the community, or that theirs was the *best* use of the next homeless assistance dollar.

It was the norm during this period that government agencies had a hard time keeping track of which services were available, which were being applied for, and which were on the drawing boards. They had formal sign-off authority, meaning they could block an application, but since they could not require funds to be redirected to activities that were needed more, they rarely did. Indeed, they often had little way to determine what the greatest needs were, as few had established any methodical approach to collecting data about service or demand levels. In some jurisdictions, the responsible government agency chafed at these constraints. But in many other communities, government agencies wanted little to do with homeless services, and signed off with little attempt at oversight. Nor did federal program managers have information to assess whether the proposals they received represented the best, or most-needed, use of federal dollars. Neither could they fund something that might have been needed more, in the absence of relevant proposals.

First Efforts toward Continuums of Care

During the late 1980s and early 1990s, some communities responded to the relative disorganization of homeless assistance services by trying to introduce some control and planning. Columbus, Ohio, and Boston, Massachusetts, were among the earliest. Columbus instituted a shelter tracking database to document need and help make resource allocations, and Boston inaugurated regular surveys (first in 1983, and then annually from 1986 on) to assess needs. Both communities placed responsibility for planning and resource allocation in a single shelter board, which also strove to control all public funds going into their homeless shelter and housing programs. In New York City, where a right-to-shelter law made control of the overall system of care difficult, the New York City Commission on the Homeless (1992) devoted considerable thought to what an excellent system of care might look like, and produced one of the first articulations of a continuum of care.

To make continuums of care the norm rather than the exception, a strong incentive was essential. Relatively soon after the Clinton administration assumed office in 1993, it included the idea of a continuum of care in its plan to address homelessness (Interagency Council on the Homeless 1994). HUD provided the financial incentive through reorganizing how it distributed McKinney funds. Starting with the FY 1994 funding cycle, HUD dropped the old approach of individual programs competing nationally in many categories. Instead, it focused on whole jurisdictions and disallowed applications from individual programs, with rare exceptions. It also developed a formula for estimating the funds a jurisdiction could expect if it wrote a good proposal, and published these preliminary estimates in the *Federal Register.* Thus people could see what a jurisdiction stood to lose if it did not submit an application.

An essential element of these applications was (and still is) a requirement for jurisdiction-wide cooperation among providers. Providers that wanted federal homeless assistance dollars from a McKinney program run by HUD had to work together to develop a coherent plan and file a joint application. In addition, the application had to document existing stocks of different kinds of shelter and housing for homeless and formerly homeless people, and the level of need, as indicated by homeless population size and characteristics. Further, it had to use this information to identify gaps in services, and to request funding to fill the gaps, following a ranking of projects against greatest need.

Over the years, the incentive of federal funding has brought more and more jurisdictions toward a continuum of care. The HUD approach appears to have changed the name of the game, and also how it is played. When some jurisdictions get more money and others get none, based on the quality of their continuum plans, people pay attention.

To date, there has been no opportunity to summarize progress toward developing comprehensive homeless service systems at the national level. NSHAPC, however, provides information that supports such an examination, looking at some aspects of homeless service systems' "completeness" (adequate supplies of all relevant services). Because NSHAPC collected data in 1996, its findings reflect only the first years of effort to develop continuums of care. Nevertheless, NSHAPC can provide (1) a comprehensive national snapshot of homeless service systems in its 76 primary sampling areas; (2) provider views about the availability within their community of services they feel their clients need; and (3) detailed information about the way programs are configured into individual service locations. Because HUD's funding strategy for homeless services has remained the same, we can assume that the process of developing continuums of care has continued through to the present. This chapter, therefore, can serve as a baseline against which to assess evolving homeless service systems.

Capacity and Variety in Local Homeless Service Systems

Chapter 1 described the basic design for the NSHAPC study, including its use of 76 sampling areas and 16 types of homeless assistance programs. Chapter 9 focused on describing homeless assistance programs at the national level. Here we use the providers' estimates of program contacts *within* each of the 76 areas, and attribute them directly to those areas. The result is a sense of the scope and nature of different local service structures.[1]

All else being equal, one might expect the sampling areas with the most population to provide the most homeless assistance program contacts. The top panel of figure 10.1 provides the information to check on this expectation. In figure 10.1a, each of this study's 76 sampling areas is

Figure 10.1 *Program Contacts in Primary Sampling Areas, by Overall Population, per 10,000 Population, and per 10,000 Living in Poverty*

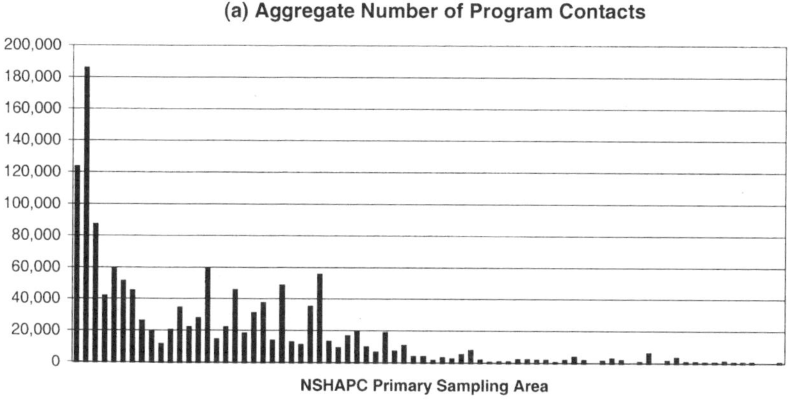

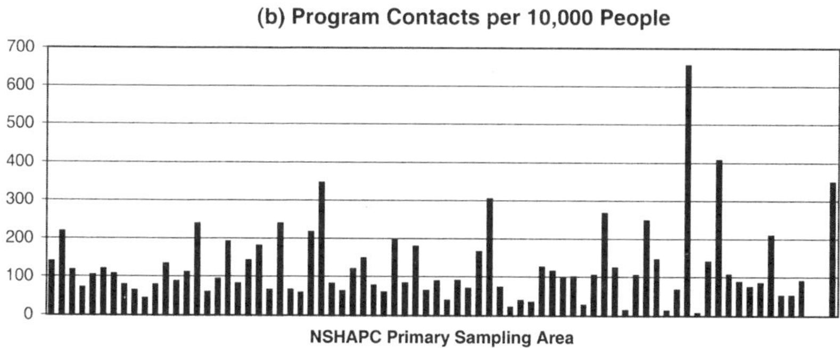

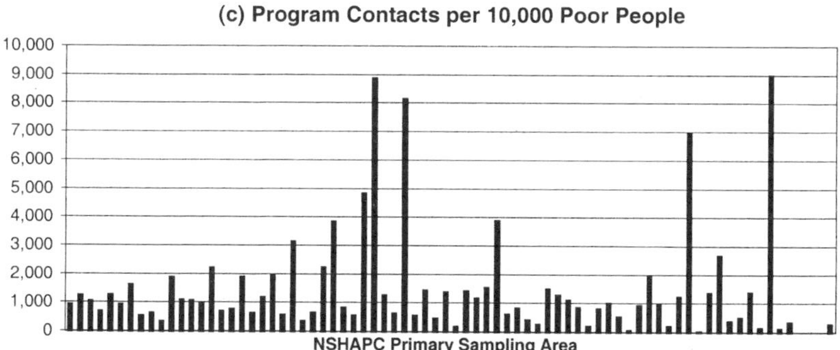

Source: Urban Institute analysis of weighted NSHAPC telephone survey of program representatives.

Note: Primary sampling areas are listed in order of population size from largest on the left to the smallest on the right. Data may be found in appendix table 10.A1.

arrayed from largest (on the left) to smallest (on the right).[2] Each bar shows the total number of program contacts that providers said they expected on an average day in February 1996.[3] These program contacts could be made by anyone, whether currently, formerly, or never homeless. Thus, they do not indicate a level of service use by homeless people, but, rather, the availability of services that homeless people *could* use.

The bars of figure 10.1 combine program contacts of all types. It is clear from the figure that the expectation of more program contacts on the left (in the largest sampling areas) and fewer on the right (in the smaller sampling areas) was correct. The average estimated number of program contacts per sampling area was about 17,600 on an average day in February 1996 (table 10.1). But the estimated number of program contacts ranged from a high of about 186,000 to a low of nothing (for two sampling areas that had no programs of any kind). And variation existed even at the highest end. For example, providers in the largest sampling area (the Los Angeles–Long Beach primary metropolitan statistical area) estimated only about two-thirds the number of program contacts (about 123,000) as did providers in the next largest sampling area (about 186,000 for New York City).

A critical question is how communities compare on the *level* of service they offer in relation to their population size. The usual way to make this comparison is to construct a *rate* that will equalize what is happening in communities of different sizes. To get an idea of how much population size alone can account for the differences among sampling areas in figure 10.1a, we used the estimated number of program contacts and the sampling area's population to create a *rate of program contacts per 10,000 people.*

Figure 10.1b shows this rate for each of the 76 sampling areas, arrayed in the same order as in figure 10.1a. The average estimated *rate of program contacts per 10,000 people* in a sampling area was 122, ranging from about 660 down to 0 (table 10.1). Obviously, creating a rate, rather than looking at raw numbers, eliminates the extreme highs and lows that arise simply because of differences in the size of jurisdictions. Now one can see that some of the sampling areas with less population, in the middle and toward the right of figure 10.1, provided more units of homeless assistance services per capita than some of the largest.

Yet another way to look at these data is to examine whether the variability in service levels can be accounted for by the size of an area's *population in poverty.* There is reason to expect that services should be

Table 10.1 *Statistics for Program Contacts in Primary Sampling Areas*

	Average	*High*	*Low*	*Standard Deviation*
Total number of program contacts (figure 10.1a)	17,600	186,000	0	29,600
Program contacts/10,000 population (figure 10.1b)	120	660	0	104
Program contacts/10,000 poor people (figure 10.1c)	1,437	9,000	0	1,858
Percentage of all contacts that are shelter/housing contacts (figure 10.2a)	24%	100%	0%	17%
Percentage of all contacts that are food program contacts (figure 10.2b)	49%	90%	0%	23%
Percentage of all contacts that are health program contacts (figure 10.2c)	5%	59%	0%	9%
Percentage of all contacts that are other program contacts (figure 10.2d)	19%	92%	0%	18%
Shelter/housing program contacts/10,000 poor people (figure 10.3a)	195	860	0	153
Emergency shelter contacts/10,000 poor people (figure 10.3b)	81	405	0	66
Transitional housing program contacts/10,000 poor people (figure 10.3c)	49	238	0	52
Permanent housing program contacts/10,000 poor people (figure 10.3d)	40	453	0	72
Voucher program contacts/10,000 poor people (figure 10.3e)	26	445	0	39

related to need, and the number of poor people in an area is the best measure of need we can get consistently for all 76 sampling areas. Some areas could have a lot of people but not very many poor people, while some smaller areas might actually have more poor people than some larger areas. Therefore, a second rate was constructed for each sampling area—its *rate of program contacts per 10,000 poor people.* Figure 10.1c shows the results.

The average estimated *rate of program contacts per 10,000 poor people* in a sampling area was 1,437, with a high of about 9,000 and a low of 0 (table 10.1). The rate of contacts per 10,000 poor people smoothes out the level of service provision considerably among the largest sampling areas at the left. The variability in the middle (medium- and small-sized metropolitan areas) appears to have increased compared to figure 10.1b. The mostly rural areas to the right appear to have the greatest variability, whichever rate is used.

Distribution of Services within Sampling Areas by Program Type

We next look at how the total estimated number of program contacts within each sampling area is distributed among the four major program types of shelter/housing, food, health, and other programs. The results, shown in figure 10.2, reveal great variation in the proportion of service contacts among shelter/housing, food, health, and other program types.

Figure 10.2 shows four panels, one each for shelter/housing, food, health, and other program contacts. The average proportion of program contacts devoted to shelter/housing programs was 24 percent (range = 100 percent down to 0). For food programs, the average proportion was 49 percent, and ranged from 90 percent to 0. For health programs the average proportion was 5 percent (range = 59 percent to 0), and for other programs the average proportion was 19 percent, and ranged from 92 percent to 0.

Looking at all four panels together, one can see the predominance of food program contacts and the relative paucity of health program contacts. Food program contacts comprised at least 40 percent of all program contacts in most sampling areas (only 17 of the 74 areas with any services had less than 40 percent of their program contacts at food programs, and one-third had more than 60 percent of program contacts at food programs). In contrast, only five sampling areas had as much as 20 percent of program contacts occurring at health programs, and most had less than 10 percent in the health area.

The greatest variability occurred in smaller metropolitan and rural areas, which were the most likely to have either *much more* of a concentration in a particular type of service than was true nationally, or *much less.* Some of these sampling areas had all or virtually all of their program contacts in housing programs; others had all or almost all their contacts in "other" programs (such as outreach, drop-in, or housing/financial assistance programs); a few had a significant share in health programs.

Summarizing, we conclude that once a jurisdiction reaches a certain size, it probably has enough demand, and enough people interested in

Figure 10.2 *Program Contacts in Primary Sampling Areas, by Program Type*

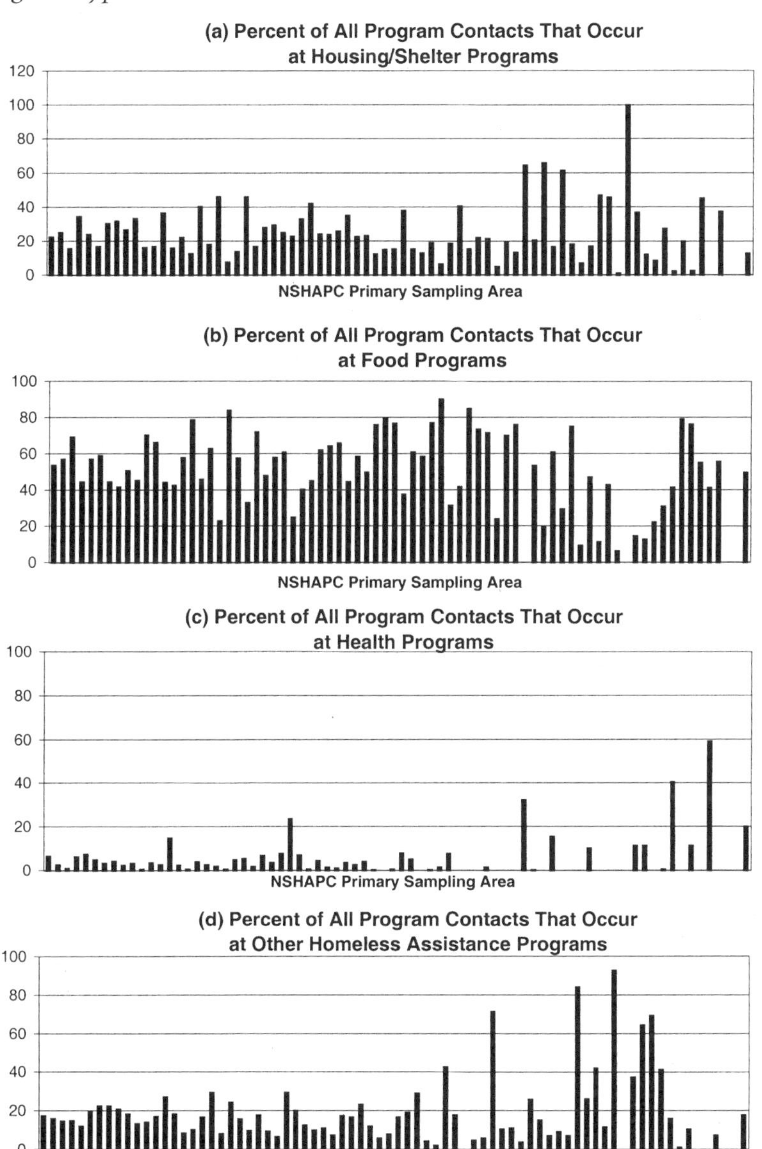

Source: Urban Institute analysis of weighted NSHAPC telephone survey of program representatives.

Note: Primary sampling areas are listed in order of population size from largest on the left to the smallest on the right. Data may be found in appendix table 10.A2.

and able to meet it, to provide at least minimum levels of a wide variety of homeless assistance programs and services. Decisions may need to be made about which program types require expansion, but the odds are that these communities will cover the basics. Smaller communities, however, may not have a level of demand that justifies developing certain specialty services. They may rely more on generic services, or be more dependent on the commitment and determination of a particular provider or funding source (and what it knows how to do or is willing to support). In a later section of this chapter we will explore these possibilities further.

Distribution within Sampling Areas of Contacts with Different Types of Shelter/Housing Programs

A final way to view the service offerings in NSHAPC's sampling areas is to apply a *rate per 10,000 poor people.* Shelter/housing program distributions in sampling areas reflect very different decisions about where to invest homeless housing resources. Figure 10.3 provides information, first for all shelter/housing program types (figure 10.3a), and then, separately, for each type (emergency shelter—figure 10.3b; transitional housing—figure 10.3c; permanent housing for the formerly homeless—figure 10.3d; and vouchers for temporary shelter—figure 10.3e).

For the nation as a whole, the rate of availability was an average of 178 shelter/housing program contacts per 10,000 people in poverty. Shelter/housing program rates ranged from a high of 860 contacts/10,000 poor people to a low of 0/10,000 poor people. Of NSHAPC's 76 sampling areas, 34 exceeded this national average and 42 fell below it. In addition to the two sampling areas with no programs of any kind, one additional area had no shelter/housing program contacts at all.

Emergency shelter contacts per 10,000 poor people ranged from a high of 810/10,000 poor people down to nothing, with a national average of 74/10,000. Six sampling areas offered 300 or more shelter/housing contacts per 10,000 poor people, while eight areas offered 20 or fewer emergency shelter contacts per 10,000, including four that did not offer any. Variability was even greater among primary sampling areas for rates of transitional housing, permanent housing, and voucher distribution:

- Transitional housing contacts within sampling areas ranged from a high of 868/10,000 down to nothing. The national mean was

Figure 10.3 *Rate of Shelter/Housing Program Contacts per 10,000 Poor People, by Type of Housing Program*

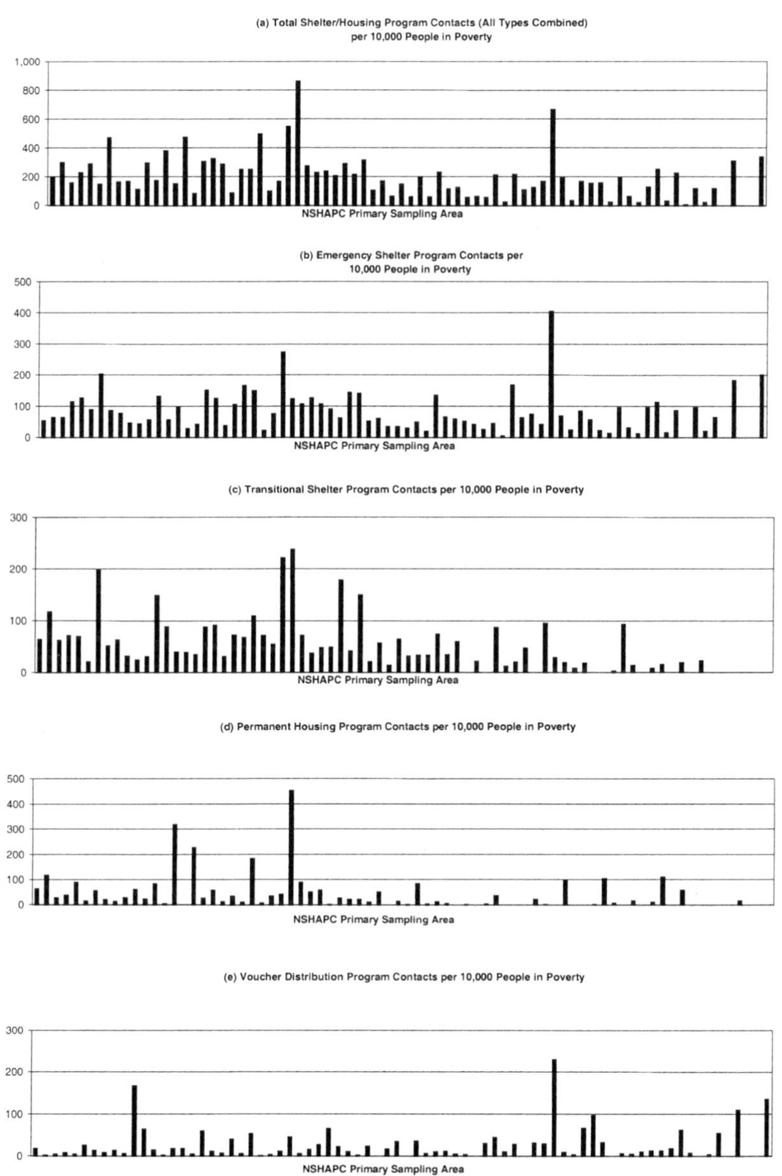

Source: Urban Institute analysis of weighted NSHAPC telephone survey of program representatives.
Note: Primary sampling areas are listed in order of population size from largest on the left to the smallest on the right. Data may be found in appendix table 10.A3.

49/10,000 poor people, with 12 areas offering more than 100 transitional housing contacts per 10,000 poor people and 23 offering 20 or fewer, including 13 that offered none.

- Permanent housing contacts within sampling areas ranged from a high of 453/10,000 down to nothing. The national mean was 35/10,000 poor people, with 9 areas offering more than 100 permanent housing contacts per 10,000 poor people and 38 offering 20 or fewer, including 20 that offered none.
- Voucher distribution contacts within sampling areas ranged from a high of 445/10,000 down to nothing. The national mean was 21/10,000 poor people, with 4 areas offering more than 100 voucher distribution contacts per 10,000 poor people and 46 offering 20 or fewer, including 9 that offered none.

Implications of Service Patterns

Figure 10.1 showed that the sheer size of a sampling area is no indication of how extensive its homeless assistance services were in 1996, in relation to its total population or its poor population. On average, though, the larger areas clearly had more services than the smaller ones, in an absolute sense. The figure also made clear the critical importance of considering service levels as *rates*—that is, in the context of and in relation to the total population that may need the services. It also made clear that either the total population or the poor population was equally useful in producing these rates. Each was able to show how well available services might "cover" the population in need.

Figure 10.2 showed that sampling areas varied greatly in the proportion of their services represented by the four major service groups (shelter/housing, food, health, and other). In addition, figure 10.3 showed that this variability also occurred even within the single service group of shelter/housing programs. Some sampling areas made their major investment in emergency shelter accommodations; others favored transitional and permanent housing facilities for homeless and formerly homeless people; many smaller areas relied on vouchers for emergency accommodation rather than invest in permanent structures (on the theory that permanent structures might operate at low levels of occupancy for extended periods). However, the experience in rural areas when a shelter actually is developed or built is that it is constantly occupied. Actual occupancy levels call the "voucher theory" into serious question.

Once shelters exist in rural areas, surrounding counties without a program constantly refer homeless people to them. The facilities, not surprisingly, thus come to function as frequently overloaded regional resources, turning away many people for lack of space (Burt 1995). Even this experience, it seems, does not inspire surrounding communities to open facilities of their own.

Within the shelter/housing arena, emergency shelter beds still dominated in many areas. But many others appeared to offer at least as many spaces in transitional housing programs, and a few had made major investments in permanent housing programs for formerly homeless people. These investments were not limited to the largest MSAs, although most of them certainly had both types of housing. Medium- and small-sized MSAs had also developed facilities of these types, as had an occasional rural area outside MSAs. These developments indicate that many communities were filling in their continuums of care to offer needed housing services, beyond emergency shelter, that did not exist in the 1980s.

In NSHAPC's rural areas, half the available program contacts were at "other" programs, which was quite different than the 16 and 11 percent of program contacts at "other" programs in central cities and suburban/urban fringe areas. Conversely, only 11 percent of the available program contacts in rural areas were at shelter/housing programs of different types, compared to 23 and 21 percent in central cities and suburban/urban fringe areas.[4] Although not accounting for a large proportion of program contacts, contacts at health programs were also twice as high in rural areas as in the other two types of communities.

This distribution of program contacts, with peaks in rural areas for other programs and health programs, suggests that many mainstream programs were included in rural areas because they were the only available sources of help for homeless people. Public health departments, community action agencies, and even welfare and public housing agencies were sources of assistance for homeless people in rural areas. (Remember that these provider estimates of program contacts cover *everyone* expected to use that provider/agency on an average day in February 1996, *not just homeless people.*) Many of these health and other program contacts in rural areas were undoubtedly not made by homeless people, although certainly the people using the programs were needy. It is interesting and important to recognize the ability of many rural areas to help homeless people through mainstream agencies, because this is a goal most urban areas do not achieve. Development of separate homeless assistance networks is testimony to the *inability* or *unwillingness* of mainstream programs in major population centers to serve the needs of homeless people.

Soup Kitchen Meals Relative to Population in Poverty

In addition to shelter and housing, NSHAPC also lets us examine the ability of primary sampling areas to provide prepared meals to people in need through soup kitchens and other programs. "Prepared meals" usually means breakfast, lunch, or dinner as served in a soup kitchen or mobile food program. But it can mean anything from bag lunches consisting of a sandwich, salad, and fruit distributed at a church doorstep to restaurant-style service in some innovative instances. It does not, however, include the typical offerings of a food pantry, such as canned, raw, or bulk food that would usually need cooking or preparation to eat.

In this section, we examine what representatives of soup kitchens said in response to NSHAPC's telephone survey about how many contacts their program would be likely to have on an average day in February 1996. Issues in the way answers were given prompted us to present low, average, and high estimates.[5]

On an average *weekday* in February 1996, soup kitchens throughout the country expected to serve an average of 173 meals per 10,000 people in poverty (midpoint estimate). This midpoint estimate for the country as a whole was bracketed by a low estimate of 129 and a high estimate of 217 soup kitchen meals per 10,000 poor people. However, rates varied tremendously among the different sampling areas. For example, the average rate per 10,000 poor people of soup kitchen meals ranged from 0 in 12 sampling areas up to over 600 in 4.

Figure 10.4 shows results separately for each NSHAPC sampling area, with each line representing an area. The lines are arrayed in the same order as for figures 10.1, 10.2, and 10.3—that is, in descending order of population. Figure 10.4 shows *weekday* soup kitchen contacts.[6] The bottom point of each line represents the low estimate; the top point, the high estimate; and the small black dot, the midpoint. If the figure shows only a dot and no line, then all three measures were identical (i.e., all soup kitchens in the area served only one meal a day—breakfast, lunch, or dinner).

Figure 10.4 *Soup Kitchen Weekday Service Units and Meals Served per 10,000 Poor People: Low, High, and Average Estimates*

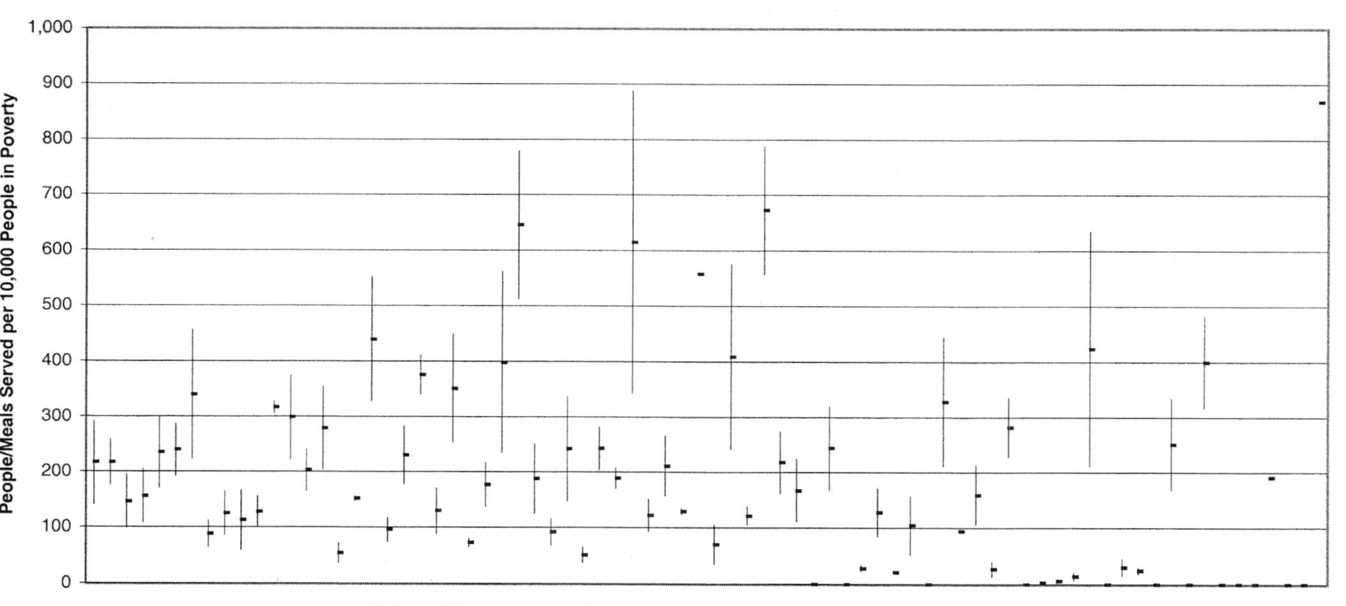

Source: Urban Institute analysis of weighted NSHAPC telephone survey (CATI) data from program representatives.

Note: The bottom point of each vertical line is the number of program contacts at soup kitchens on an average weekday in February 1996. This bottom point is also the minimum number of soup kitchen meals on an average weekday, assuming that each person comes to only one meal. The top point of each vertical line estimates the maximum number of soup kitchen meals on an average weekday, if every person at soup kitchens that offer more than one meal (i.e., breakfast and lunch) comes to every meal. The small black boxes are the midpoint of the low and high estimates, representing the average number of weekday program contacts in a primary sampling area. Data may be found in appendix table 10.A4.

The overwhelming impression is that the size of a sampling area had very little to do with the availability of soup kitchen meals. It is true that all but one of the 12 sampling areas that reported *no* soup kitchen meals were rural (i.e., located outside MSAs). But of the four sampling areas with more than 600 meals per 10,000 poor people, one was among the largest 28 MSAs in the country, two were medium-sized MSAs, and one was the smallest rural area of all. In fact, at 868 per 10,000 poor people, it had the highest *rate* of soup kitchen meals of any area. These rates indicate that not all service of prepared meals is concentrated in large cities.

At the other extreme, two of the nation's largest MSAs had *high* estimates below 100 weekday meals per 10,000 poor people, which was lower than all but three of the high estimates for small and medium-sized MSAs. Thirty sampling areas—17 of the 28 largest MSAs in the country, 13 of the smaller MSAs in the sample, and 4 of the rural areas in the sample—had higher midpoint rates of meal availability per 10,000 people in poverty than the national average.

Figure 10.4 also provides a sense of whether programs in a sampling area provided more than one meal a day. The length of the line for each sampling area shows the difference between the estimated minimum and maximum number of soup kitchen meals per 10,000 people in poverty. In most cases, the high estimate is 150 to 200 percent above the low estimate, and the line for many areas is quite long, indicating that a substantial number of soup kitchens in those areas offered more than one meal a day. However, in other sampling areas the low and high estimates were quite close or identical. Thus their line in figure 10.4 is quite short or is only the black dot, indicating that most or all soup kitchens in that area offered only one meal a day.

Implications for the Development of Continuums of Care

Information on soup kitchen meal availability, together with information on shelter/housing availability and the distribution of service contacts over programs of different types, adds to our understanding of homeless assistance networks in communities of many types. These data make clear that some of our largest communities did not necessarily have larger or more varied networks *in proportion to the probable level of need among their citizenry* than medium-sized or small communities. Yet, the basic image of homelessness is urban. Because of their sheer size and volume of services, our largest MSAs, many people assume, must be helping homeless people the most. The data show this is not necessarily the case. Responsive service systems, even relatively complete continuums of care, may exist in communities of any size.

Other NSHAPC data let us look at provider perceptions of service need and availability in their communities, and how programs are configured at places where they are offered. The remainder of this chapter focuses on these issues.

Program Reports of Service Availability

One component of NSHAPC's design was a survey mailed to homeless assistance programs identified through telephone interviewing. This mail survey asked program staff for their perceptions of whether services to meet client needs were available in their community, and if so, where they were located. While program staff seldom know the whole scope of services available in an entire jurisdiction, they certainly know whether their own program offers a service, and usually have a reasonable idea whether they have been able to help their own clients obtain other services their program does not offer. We can use these perceptions to paint a more detailed picture of services in community service systems. In addition, this information offers another way to understand the structure of the homeless service system.[7]

One way to meet the needs of a program's homeless clients is to offer the needed services in the program itself. The first column of table 10.2 shows the proportion of programs that offered particular services at their site. The service may have been offered through the program itself, or by another provider that regularly came to the program site to allow clients ready access. In either case, the client did not have to leave the program site to get the service. The remaining columns of table 10.2 show service availability at other locations, and/or indicate that no program known to program staff offered the service. A service would only appear in the second column, labeled "Services Are Only Offered Off-Site," if the reporting program *did not itself* offer it. Quite possibly, many services are offered by the reporting programs and also elsewhere in the community; the NSHAPC mail survey data cannot tell us *in how many places* a service is offered.

Food, clothing, and all case management services were most likely to be offered at a respondent's program. At the other extreme, no more

Table 10.2 *Provider Perceptions of Service Availability*

Service	*Services Are Offered at Program Site, by Respondent's Program or Other Program at Same Site*	*Services Are Only Offered Off-Site*	*Services Are Not Available in Community*
Basic Needs			
Food (prepared meals or food supplies)	84	15	1
Clothing	69	28	1
Life Skills Services			
Money management or budgeting	58	30	11
Household skills—cooking, cleaning, maintenance	51	32	16
Personal relations counseling—conflict resolution	63	32	4
Parenting training	44	50	5
Case Management Services			
Needs assessment	72	23	3
Development of individual goals and service plans	69	23	8
Referral or assistance with entitlements	73	25	1
Follow-up after client leaves	69	21	9
Housing Services			
Locating housing	62	32	5
Applying for subsidized housing	44	53	3
Financial assistance with rent and/or utilities	53	43	4
Assistance with landlord/tenant relations	56	33	10
Education Services			
Helping children enroll in school	59	35	5
Head Start	36	62	1
Other early childhood education	31	65	3
Tutoring for school children	38	53	8
English as a Second Language courses	17	77	5
GED courses	22	75	3
Family literacy services	17	73	9
Basic literacy training	20	72	7
Basic skills training/adult education courses	22	73	4
Employment Services			
Assessment of job skills	37	58	5
Job finding/retention skills	38	56	5
Job referral or placement	41	54	4
Training for specific jobs	17	76	7
Vocational rehabilitation	13	82	4
Placement in volunteer jobs	49	46	3

Table 10.2 *Provider Perceptions of Service Availability (Continued)*

Service	*Services Are Offered at Program Site, by Respondent's Program or Other Program at Same Site*	*Services Are Only Offered Off-Site*	*Services Are Not Available in Community*
General Health Care			
Health care assessment/health history	34	60	5
Primary care—physical exam, etc.	21	72	7
Acute care	14	79	6
Prenatal care	13	82	3
Immunizations	20	78	1
TB testing	30	67	2
TB treatment	17	79	4
Dental care	10	73	16
Hospice care	10	82	7
General health education	40	50	8
Substance Abuse Services			
Alcohol/drug testing	24	69	7
Clinical assessment for alcohol or other drugs	25	70	4
Detoxification	10	86	3
Outpatient treatment	17	81	2
Residential treatment	17	79	3
Alcoholics/Cocaine/Narcotics Anonymous	26	72	1
Substance abuse education	46	50	4
Mental Health Services			
Mental health assessment	31	66	2
Medication administration/monitoring	48	55	7
Crisis intervention	54	43	2
Outpatient therapy/counseling	20	68	2
Inpatient and/or residential treatment	17	78	4
Peer group/self-help (other than AA/CA/NA)	41	54	5
Mental health education	37	57	6
HIV/AIDS Services			
HIV/AIDS treatment services	23	75	1
HIV/AIDS prevention and/or education	53	42	3
Other Services			
Child care	26	65	8
Domestic violence counseling	40	58	2
Legal assistance	20	72	7
Veteran's special services	17	80	3

Source: Urban Institute analysis of weighted responses from the NSHAPC mail survey to homeless assistance programs.

than 25 percent of programs reported that any of the adult education services, vocational rehabilitation or training for specific jobs, many of the health services, any of the specialized substance abuse services, inpatient or outpatient mental health treatment, HIV/AIDS treatment, child care, legal assistance, or special services for veterans were available at their program site.

Variations by Program and Community Type

Housing programs as a group were consistently above these overall levels for almost all service groups. Voucher distribution programs were the most prominent exceptions, and permanent housing programs also were low on some services, such as domestic violence counseling and educational services, that are less relevant to their usual clientele. Food programs were above the mean on food service, at the mean on clothing distribution, and below it for everything else. Health programs were above the mean for all four health services and for special services for veterans, at the mean for domestic violence counseling and for the life skills and case management service groups, and below it on everything else.

Looking at program offerings by community type and, within that, by major program group, and summing across programs of different types, we found some differences among offerings by programs located in central cities, suburban/urban fringe areas, and rural areas. In general, for each service group, programs in central cities were more likely than elsewhere to report offering each service. This translates into the likelihood that any given program offering services to homeless people in a central city would have had a more diverse array of services to offer within its own walls than programs elsewhere. Only food, educational services, and assistance with finding housing were equally likely to be offered, regardless of the program's urban/rural status.

Services Available Only Off-Site, or Not Available

Thirty-nine individual services were most likely to be available only at off-site locations, using a difference of 10 percentage points or more in availability as the criterion for "most likely." These were all of the education services except helping children enroll in school, four of the five employment services, all ten general health care services, six of seven substance abuse services, five of seven mental health services, HIV/AIDS treatment, and all four other services. In addition, 10 percent or more of program staff said that four individual services were not available anywhere in their community for homeless people: help with money management and budgeting, training in household skills, assistance with landlord/tenant relations, and dental care.

Implications

These reports give a clearer picture of service availability within communities, albeit not of the adequacy of service levels or, lacking evaluation data, of the most useful or effective way to arrange services. Nevertheless, the picture of availability is remarkably consistent.

Specialized services were available primarily off-site. On the other hand, basic needs, such as the need for food, were met on-site, as were fundamental assistance services such as life-skills training and case management. This pattern, of course, reflects that most NSHAPC programs were food or shelter/housing programs. The relatively few offering specialized services at their program site for the most part actually *were* the mainstream or specialized programs (e.g., health, child care, mental health, employment). Those most likely to report service availability only off-site were the shelter/housing and, especially, food programs. The last section of this chapter examines the specific offerings of these shelter/housing programs and of soup kitchens, the NSHAPC food program serving the most homeless people.[8]

We next ask the degree to which the on-site availability of a service helped program staff feel that their clients' need for that service was being met. In answer, we looked at the association between staff perceptions that a service need was always or usually met and the ability of clients to get that service on-site. The resulting correlation is $r = .600$. Thus, 36 percent of the variation in the likelihood that program staff perceived client needs being met is attributable to having the service on-site. That, of course, leaves a lot of room for other factors, such as excellent coordination and transportation services to off-site service locations. It also suggests that enriched service sites, those that offer many services, may be a strong option for meeting client needs.

Organization of Programs into Service Locations

NSHAPC defined a *service location* as the single physical site at which one or more programs operated. We estimate there were about 21,000 service locations nationwide in 1996 that operated at least one homeless assistance program meeting NSHAPC definitions. Unfortunately, NSHAPC did not collect information that would allow us to understand the connections from one service location to another. This might include, for instance, when such a location was one site among many run by a larger organization, or when representatives of different service locations or programs worked together on area-wide planning and coordination. But even without this information, we still can use the information we do have to learn a great deal about service interconnections and ease of access to services for clients.

As the array of programs serving homeless people has grown in the past decade, agencies that once had only an emergency shelter or a soup kitchen might have added one or more additional programs at their same *service locations* by 1996. For instance, some soup kitchens and shelters added mobile food vans to their activities to serve homeless people who would not come to their other programs. Some shelters specializing in services to mentally ill or substance-abusing homeless people added an outreach program to find people living on the streets and offer them services. Some emergency shelters added a transitional shelter program for people who need more help before they are ready to go back into regular housing. These program expansions could have happened independently as providers responded to needs among their homeless clients or to the availability of funds to develop new programs. Or they could have happened as part of a planned expansion of services, as the larger homeless services community tried to develop a comprehensive and coordinated system.

Geographic and Other Characteristics of Service Locations

Table 10.3 presents the distribution of service locations and programs across regions and across central cities, suburbs and urban fringe, and rural areas. The distribution mirrors the geographic distribution of homeless assistance programs, with virtually identical proportions of service locations and programs in each region of the country. Slightly fewer than half of all service locations were found in central cities, one-third were in rural areas, and one-fifth were in suburban and urban

Table 10.3 *Geographic Distribution of NSHAPC Service Locations*

	Percent Distribution of	
	Programs	*Service Locations*
Total		
Number	39,700	21,400
Percent	100	100
Census Region		
Northeast	18	18
South	28	29
Midwest	30	29
West	24	23
Urban/Rural Location		
Central Cities	49	47
Suburbs/Urban Fringe	19	19
Rural Areas	32	34
Number of Homeless Assistance Programs		
1	Not Applicable	52
2		27
3		12
4		5
5 or more		4

Source: Urban Institute analysis of weighted NSHAPC program data representing program activities on "an average day in February 1996."

Note: Estimated numbers are rounded to the nearest 100.

fringe communities. The same was true for homeless assistance programs.

Service locations varied considerably with respect to the number of homeless assistance programs offered on their premises (table 10.3). Slightly over half (52 percent) offered only one homeless assistance program, another 27 percent offered two, and only 21 percent offered three or more.

Organization of Programs within Service Locations

The 52 percent of service locations that operated only one program (or only one serving homeless people), we refer to as "stand-alone" programs. They may have provided their clients with a wide array of health or social services as part of their basic program, but they were not co-located with another program meeting an NSHAPC program definition. In addition, they might have housed other programs serving different groups of people, but not focusing on homeless people. The question then becomes what types of homeless assistance programs were most likely to be "stand-alone."

Stand-Alone Programs

The estimated 10,900 service locations nationwide that offer only one program meeting NSHAPC's definition of programs serving homeless people are presented in table 10.4, by major program group and individual program. One way to examine stand-alone programs is to ask what proportion within each program type was stand-alone (first column of table 10.4). Food programs were most likely to be stand-alone (33 percent were so), followed by housing programs (27 percent), and other programs (21 percent). Health programs as a group were least likely to stand alone (17 percent).

This information about major program groups masks considerable variation by individual program type, however. *Within* individual program types, two types of "other" programs were most likely to be the only NSHAPC homeless assistance program at their service location. These were housing/financial assistance programs (48 percent were stand-alone) and other programs (39 percent were stand-alone, including child care, social services, education and training, and clothing programs). Other individual program types with a high likelihood of having stand-alone programs were food pantries (37 percent were stand-alone), transitional housing programs (33 percent), and emergency shelters (32 percent). At the other extreme, drop-in centers and outreach programs were least likely (7 and 8 percent, respectively) to operate from a location that did not run any other homeless assistance programs.

Another way to look at stand-alone programs is to ask what proportion of all service locations each type of stand-alone program represented (second column of table 10.4). Stand-alone food programs comprised 21 percent of all NSHAPC service locations. Roughly three-fourths were food pantries, comprising the single largest category of stand-alone programs. Stand-alone housing programs comprised

Table 10.4 *Stand-Alone Programs*

	Percent of Each Program Type That Are Stand-Alone Programs	*Stand-Alone Programs, by Type of Program, as Percent of All Service Locations*
Totals		Service Locations = 100%
Housing	**27**	**21**
Emergency shelter	32	9
Transitional housing	33	7
Permanent housing	26	2
Voucher distribution	15	2
Housing with vouchers	15	1
Food	**33**	**21**
Food pantry	37	16
Soup kitchen/meal dist.	25	4
Mobile food	16	0
Health	**17**	**2**
Physical health care	30	1
Mental health	10	0
Alcohol or drug	15	1
HIV/AIDS	16	0
Other	**21**	**8**
Outreach	8	1
Drop-in center	7	1
Financial/housing assist.	48	3
Other	39	3

Source: Urban Institute analysis of weighted NSHAPC program data. Data represent reports of program activities on "an average day in February 1996."

another 21 percent of all service locations, with emergency shelters and transitional housing programs being the most numerous among them.

Service Location Specialization

Before looking at how homeless assistance programs clustered within service locations, we examine their specialization or population focus. For example, some service locations focused on homeless youth, while others offered generic services for any homeless individual or family, regardless of characteristics. We then use information on program specialization to take a more sophisticated look at program and service co-location.

The first step was to examine specialization among programs.[9] This was done by looking at each program's report of its agency's primary mission and any specific population that was the program's primary focus.

The most important finding is that most programs did not specialize.[10] As many as 84 percent of soup kitchens did not specialize with respect to particular populations or health-related service needs. Lack of specialization also characterized 65 percent of permanent housing programs and 43 percent of both transitional housing and emergency shelter programs.

Programs for battered women were the largest specialty group among emergency shelters (29 percent), with an additional 6 percent reporting families as a specialization. Thus, more than one-third of all emergency shelters appear to have had one or another type of family focus. Programs focused on people with alcohol and/or other drug disorders, or on youth, were the next most common, each with 8 percent of emergency shelters.

Programs for battered women and families continued to be a large component of transitional housing, at 14 and 7 percent respectively. But specialty programs for people with alcohol and/or other drug disorders (14 percent of transitional shelters), people with mental illness (9 percent), or both (5 percent) were equally prominent. HIV/AIDS was rarely a focus for emergency shelters (1 percent), but increased in prominence in the categories of transitional shelter and permanent housing (3 and 9 percent, respectively). Among housing programs, those offering permanent housing were least likely to name one population as a specialty.[11] When they did, people with mental disorders topped those with alcohol and/or other drug disorders as the main focus, reversing the situation for transitional shelters.

Program Clustering and Service Offerings, by Program Type and Specialization

The final question is how program clustering and service offerings varied among service locations with different types of programs and different specialties. This analysis will give us the most complete picture possible from NSHAPC of what was actually available to the people who went to service locations offering one or more of NSHAPC's main shelter/housing and soup kitchen programs.

Tables 10.5 through 10.8 give this information. Table 10.5 shows program and service configurations for all service locations offering an emergency shelter; tables 10.6, 10.7, and 10.8 do the same for service locations offering transitional housing, permanent housing, and soup kitchen programs, respectively.[12] To give a full picture of what programs and services accompany each type of program, tables 10.5 through 10.8 necessarily contain some redundancy. A service location offering both emergency shelter and transitional housing, for example, will appear in both table 10.5 and 10.6; one offering all four programs will appear in all four tables.

EMERGENCY SHELTERS—PROGRAM CO-LOCATION AND AVAILABLE SERVICES. Looking first at table 10.5, the first row shows the total estimated number of service locations with an emergency shelter (approximately 5,690) and estimates for how many emergency shelters specialized in serving different subgroups of homeless people. The second row shows the percent of all emergency shelters reporting each specialty.

Looking at the first column in table 10.5, one can see how many emergency shelters were co-located with nine other NSHAPC program types, and how many offered at least some services from 11 service clusters. For example, 33 percent of service locations with an emergency shelter also offered a transitional housing program, 20 percent offered an outreach program, and so on. In addition, 83 percent served meals or otherwise assisted their clients to obtain food, 77 percent helped clients get housing, 64 percent offered mental health services of some variety, and 20 percent offered child care.

Looking *across* the columns, one can see that these percentages for all service locations offering an emergency shelter program sometimes varied considerably, depending on what population or special needs group the program focused on. For example, looking first at the panel of other types of NSHAPC programs, 20 percent of all service locations with an emergency shelter also had an outreach program. However, this percentage more than doubles when looking at emergency shelters with a mental health focus (to 46 percent), and goes down to almost nothing among emergency shelters with a family focus (4 percent). Clearly, core

Table 10.5 *Programs and Services Attached to Emergency Shelters*

		Emergency Shelters with							
	Total	*No Specialization*	*DV Focus*	*Family Focus*	*Youth Focus*	*CD Focus*	*MH Focus*	*MH/CD Focus*	*HIV/AIDS Focus*
Total (number)	5,690	2,420	1,630	340	480	460	200	80	80
Percent of all emergency shelters	100	43	29	6	8	8	4	1	1
Percent Located with									
Transitional housing	33	37	27	16	12	55	47	56	54
Permanent housing	11	16	3	5	1	13	22	19	44
Soup kitchen	22	30	7	11	11	47	32	48	44
Food pantry	34	39	26	52	9	33	42	35	80
Mobile food	2	2	1	1	2	4	1	4	13
Outreach	20	22	13	4	21	29	46	18	12
Drop-in center	14	13	9	2	14	32	35	22	45
Voucher distribution	12	12	9	36	2	6	9	8	41
Housing with vouchers	8	12	3	4	—	7	7	9	11

Services Provided On-Site: *									
Food	83	80	85	88	87	83	83	87	76
Clothing	70	65	84	56	86	73	76	82	76
Life skills	65	59	77	49	90	67	70	75	87
Housing	77	70	85	88	59	68	85	83	97
Employment	55	54	46	73	45	65	45	78	53
General health care	49	48	43	30	64	64	53	52	91
Substance abuse treatment	47	49	40	28	64	75	48	71	36
Mental health care	64	51	84	54	95	64	81	85	82
Child care	20	11	36	38	12	13	3	8	3
Domestic violence counseling	43	30	89	44	39	29	12	31	1
HIV/AIDS treatment	40	36	42	20	66	51	37	49	93

Source: Urban Institute analysis of weighted NSHAPC program data. Data represent reports of program activities on "an average day in February 1996."

* Selected services only. DV = domestic violence. CD = chemical dependency. MH = mental health.

programs were expanding their offerings in relation to needs in their primary clientele. Also, the availability of specialized federal funding opportunities obviously made a difference in the case of mental health programming. Voucher distribution programs were most likely to be co-located with emergency shelters that had a family or an HIV/AIDS focus, but were not very common in service locations with other, or no, specializations.

Service locations with an emergency shelter focusing on families, unaccompanied youth, or battered women were least likely to have many program components. The biggest exceptions are that half of emergency shelters for families had an attached food pantry, over one-third distributed vouchers for housing, and one in five emergency youth shelters had an outreach component. No-specialty emergency shelters and shelters with a health specialization (mental health, substance abuse, both, or HIV/AIDS) were most likely to be co-located with a soup kitchen.

Service availability on-site shows a good deal less variation related to emergency shelter specialization than co-location with other NSHAPC programs. Help in obtaining food was available in 83 percent of all service locations with an emergency shelter. Most of the remaining columns in table 10.5, reporting on emergency shelters with specializations, do not differ from that average in any significant way. Youth-focused service locations were least likely to offer help finding housing or employment, as might be expected from their clients' ages, but were higher than average on all health-related services. Emergency shelters with a domestic violence focus were at least twice as likely to offer domestic violence counseling as emergency shelters with any other focus, even when compared to programs with a family or youth focus, which were also quite high in comparison to all other program focuses.

TRANSITIONAL HOUSING PROGRAMS—PROGRAM CO-LOCATION AND AVAILABLE SERVICES. For transitional shelter/housing programs, table 10.6 gives statistics that parallel those for emergency shelters. Of the estimated 4,390 service locations reporting a transitional shelter program, 40 percent were co-located with an emergency shelter program. One-fifth of service locations with a transitional housing program also had a permanent housing program, 23 percent had an outreach program, and 26 percent had a food pantry. Transitional housing programs with a mental health or HIV/AIDS emphasis were most likely to be co-located with a permanent housing program, whereas transitional programs for battered women and families were most likely to have a food pantry. Many programs of these types expect clients to cook for themselves, and many offer a starter food package when the client leaves the shelter. Food pantries help these programs fulfill these functions. Also, non-specialized transitional shelters were quite likely to have a food pantry (30 percent), outreach (27 percent), and permanent housing program (23 percent) operating in their same location. Availability of particular services for clients in service locations with a transitional housing program show variations by program specialization that are very similar to those for emergency shelter programs.

PERMANENT HOUSING PROGRAMS—PROGRAM CO-LOCATION AND SERVICE AVAILABILITY. Table 10.7 shows permanent housing programs' specializations, programs co-located with them, and services available through them. This table does not include columns for domestic violence, families, or youth because permanent housing programs for formerly homeless people do not, as a rule, have these specializations. Table 10.7 indicates that an estimated 1,920 service locations included a permanent housing program. Thirty percent were co-located with an emergency shelter, 44 percent with a transitional shelter, 35 percent with an outreach program, and 30 percent with a food pantry. There were only a few points of variation in program co-location due to specialization (looking across the columns), largely because these permanent housing programs either had no specialization or had a health-related one. Food pantries were most likely to be present in service locations with no specialization or those that specialized in serving persons with HIV/AIDS. Drop-in centers were most likely to be found together with permanent housing programs having a focus on persons with both mental health and alcohol and/or other drug abuse disorders. Voucher distribution most commonly happened in service locations with no specialization. At least one-third of all service locations with permanent housing also reported an outreach program.

SOUP KITCHENS—PROGRAM CO-LOCATION AND SERVICE AVAILABILITY. Finally, table 10.8 examines program co-location and service availability among locations offering a soup kitchen (an estimated 3,480 service locations). About half (51 percent) were co-located with a food

Table 10.6 *Programs and Services Attached to Transitional Housing Programs*

		Transitional Housing Programs with							
	Total	*No Specialization*	*DV Focus*	*Family Focus*	*Youth Focus*	*CD Focus*	*MH Focus*	*MH/CD Focus*	*HIV/AIDS Focus*
Total (number)	4,390	1,900	620	310	190	620	400	220	130
Percent of all transitional housing programs	100	43	14	7	4	14	9	5	3
Percent Located with									
Emergency shelter	40	42	70	33	32	36	24	11	30
Permanent housing	20	23	12	24	7	11	30	17	41
Soup kitchen	16	19	6	14	16	20	8	9	29
Food pantry	26	30	36	48	15	11	11	10	30
Mobile food	2	3	2	*	9	2	1	*	7
Outreach	23	27	19	14	22	15	35	23	15
Drop-in center	14	17	12	3	8	10	12	10	31
Voucher distribution	11	14	5	27	8	5	7	3	24
Housing with vouchers	9	13	4	5	2	5	12	8	2
Services Provided On-Site:*									
Food	76	72	85	79	80	81	74	74	78
Clothing	69	67	83	79	72	67	61	64	75
Life skills	73	69	88	76	81	70	68	65	85
Housing	81	80	92	87	77	60	88	68	94
Employment	63	62	65	71	82	68	52	74	54
General health care	55	48	52	58	78	61	61	63	91
Substance abuse treatment	56	52	53	47	65	78	55	67	45
Mental health care	67	58	80	51	80	67	85	80	81
Child care	21	19	49	33	12	16	1	5	6
Domestic violence counseling	38	30	82	46	52	35	23	46	6
HIV/AIDS treatment	49	43	52	38	69	49	53	61	93

Source: Urban Institute analysis of weighted NSHAPC program data. Data represent reports of program activities on "an average day in February 1996."
* Selected services only. DV = domestic violence. CD = chemical dependency. MH = mental health.

Table 10.7 *Programs and Services Attached to Permanent Housing Programs*

		Permanent Housing with				
	Total	*No Specialization*	*CD Focus*	*MH Focus*	*MH/CD Focus*	*HIV/AIDS Focus*
Total (number)	1,920	1,250	90	300	100	170
Percent of all permanent housing programs	100	65	5	16	5	9
Percent Located with						
Emergency shelter	30	35	23	16	12	25
Permanent housing	44	44	49	44	55	36
Soup kitchen	14	14	13	19	8	4
Food pantry	30	39	10	10	11	24
Mobile food	2	2	4	*	8	*
Outreach	35	35	41	42	27	25
Drop-in center	13	14	9	14	24	1
Voucher distribution	18	24	4	5	7	11
Housing with vouchers	13	13	19	14	12	11
Services Provided On-Site:†						
Food	61	52	73	65	58	63
Clothing	52	49	74	54	45	48
Life skills	65	58	84	66	57	84
Housing	84	85	70	83	72	88
Employment	59	60	88	47	53	54
General health care	47	39	72	52	43	84
Substance abuse treatment	50	49	78	60	54	50
Mental health care	66	54	82	86	78	69
Child care	15	16	17	1	1	13
Domestic violence counseling	28	34	40	15	31	11
HIV/AIDS treatment	47	46	50	52	41	86

Source: Urban Institute analysis of weighted NSHAPC program data. Data represent reports of program activities on an average day in February 1996.

* Indicates insufficient *N*.

† Selected services only.

pantry, 35 percent with an emergency shelter, and 19 to 21 percent with a transitional housing program or a drop-in center. As noted earlier, the great majority of soup kitchens (84 percent) had no specialization, so the distribution of co-located programs in the second column looks almost identical to the distribution for all soup kitchens. Among the few

Table 10.8 *Programs and Services Attached to Soup Kitchens*

		Soup Kitchens with				
	Total	*No Specialization*	*CD Focus*	*MH Focus*	*MH/CD Focus*	*HIV/AIDS Focus*
Total	3,480	2,920	230	200	90	50
Percentage of all soup kitchens	100	84	6	6	3	1
Percent Located with						
Emergency shelter	35	33	69	27	32	52
Permanent housing	19	16	44	15	30	58
Soup kitchen	7	6	5	26	13	16
Food pantry	51	51	58	52	49	72
Mobile food	6	5	8	3	17	8
Outreach	17	17	22	13	19	14
Drop-in center	21	16	51	34	36	62
Voucher distribution	11	11	7	7	14	46
Housing with vouchers	5	5	4	1	2	—
Services Provided On-Site:†						
Food	88	88	87	81	87	99
Clothing	69	67	74	64	80	94
Life skills	52	47	66	68	63	80
Housing	58	54	63	58	71	93
Employment	47	45	59	42	57	49
General health care	42	41	57	33	42	94
Substance abuse treatment	37	35	77	28	66	36
Mental health care	45	38	64	59	76	93
Child care	10	8	12	2	5	1
Domestic violence counseling	20	17	34	8	30	4
HIV/AIDS treatment	33	28	60	34	41	95

Source: Urban Institute analysis of weighted NSHAPC program data. Data represent reports of program activities on "an average day in February 1996."

† Selected services only.

with a specialization, the health concerns of substance abuse and mental illness prevailed, but services to meet basic needs of food, clothing, and life skills were also available from about two-thirds or more of these service locations.

Concluding Thoughts

In this chapter, we have followed the logic of continuums of care to the extent that NSHAPC data allow us to do so. We have examined the variety and level of different types of homeless assistance programs within sampling areas; we have reviewed provider perceptions of service availability in their communities; and we have looked at different program and service configurations within service locations. What we have seen is that if one were in a shelter/housing program, one would quite likely also have access to food and many other services. Through co-location with other programs, two-thirds of emergency shelters and transitional housing programs were able to connect clients to other needed programs. In addition, many housing programs offered a wide variety of services through their own auspices.

Did programs in 1996 offer a wider variety of services than in years past? Data limitations make this a hard question to answer. But we can compare NSHAPC's emergency shelters to those in the Urban Institute's 1987 study (Burt and Cohen 1989, pp. 83 and 89) for the services the studies asked about in roughly similar ways.[13] The five services for which a comparison is possible are food, clothing, physical health care, help finding housing, and job-related services. There appears to have been no change in the proportion offering food (83 percent in 1996 versus 80 percent in 1987), and there may have been a decrease in the proportion that made clothing available (70 percent in 1996, down from 85 percent in 1987). In contrast, significant increases occurred in the proportion offering physical health care on-site (49 percent in 1996 compared to 31 percent in 1987), and offering help in finding housing (77 percent in 1996 compared to 17 percent in 1987). The proportion offering job-related services also did not change significantly (61 and 55 percent in 1996 and 1987, respectively).

These comparisons obviously only scratch the surface of what we would like to know. We cannot tell, for example, whether there were more meals, better food, more variety, and so on in NSHAPC's emergency shelters compared to those of 1987, or whether the job-related services in 1996 were more extensive, more appropriate, or more effective. We can, however, be reasonably sure that the services reached more people, based on the large expansions in program capacity we observed in chapter 9.

It is also hard to be *certain* that programs were more organized into a continuum of care in 1996 than in 1987. But it does seem as if most programs in 1996 were operating with connections, rather than as isolates. They were often co-located with complementary programs and services. They also appear to have been linked by outreach programs and drop-in centers that tried to connect with people and either bring them into services or bring services to them. Such efforts were virtually nonexistent in 1987. Programs with a mental health specialty appeared most likely to do this in 1996, probably because the McKinney Act includes special funds to support such efforts. By the same token, health care availability in emergency shelter locations owes much of its increase to the stimulus of the Health Care for the Homeless Program of McKinney.

Thus, the NSHAPC findings suggest that the availability of federal support since 1988 through McKinney, and the insistence of HUD since 1994 that communities create and follow detailed plans for developing their homeless assistance network, were already paying off. The proof is more-extensive and more-differentiated service networks in many communities throughout the nation.

Appendix: Supporting Tables

Appendix Table 10.A1 *Total Service Units per Day*

*NSHAPC Primary Sampling Area**	*Total Population*	*Total Units*	*Service Contacts per 10,000 People*	*Service Contacts per 10,000 People in Poverty*
United States	248,718,291	1,335,325	—	—
Los Angeles-Long Beach, CA	8,863,052	123,466	139	923
New York, NY	8,546,846	185,778	217	1,242
Chicago, IL	7,410,858	87,008	117	1,039
Philadelphia, PA	5,893,019	41,890	71	684
Boston, MA	5,685,763	58,737	103	1,260
Detroit, MI	4,266,654	51,324	120	918
Washington, DC-MD-VA-WV	4,222,830	45,144	107	1,620
Houston, TX	3,321,926	26,231	79	523
Atlanta, GA	2,959,500	18,975	64	635
Dallas, TX	2,676,248	11,358	42	345
Nassau-Suffolk, NY	2,609,212	20,513	79	1,872
Riverside-San Bernardino, CA	2,588,793	34,387	133	1,089
Minneapolis-St. Paul, MN	2,538,776	22,055	87	1,073
San Diego, CA	2,498,016	27,660	111	980
St. Louis, MO-IL	2,492,348	59,327	238	2,204
Orange County, CA	2,410,668	14,338	59	700
Pittsburgh, PA	2,394,811	22,209	93	766
Baltimore, MD	2,382,172	45,609	191	1,896
Phoenix, AZ	2,238,498	18,130	81	628
Cleveland-Lorain-Elyria, OH	2,202,069	31,270	142	1,183
Oakland, CA	2,080,434	37,476	180	1,937
Tampa-St. Petersburg-Clearwater, FL	2,067,959	13,556	66	575
Seattle-Bellevue-Everett, WA	2,033,128	48,364	238	3,130
Miami, FL	1,937,194	12,652	65	365
Newark, NJ	1,915,694	11,121	58	660
Denver, CO	1,622,980	34,994	216	2,223
San Francisco, CA	1,603,678	55,515	346	3,846
Kansas City, MO-KS	1,582,874	12,971	82	836

(*Continued*)

Appendix Table 10.A1 *Total Service Units per Day (Continued)*

*NSHAPC Primary Sampling Area**	*Total Population*	*Total Units*	*Service Contacts per 10,000 People*	*Service Contacts per 10,000 People in Poverty*
Norfolk-Virginia Beach-Newport News, VA-NC	1,444,710	9,040	63	549
Indianapolis, IN	1,380,491	16,569	120	4,824
Sacramento, CA	1,340,010	19,803	148	8,866
Bergen-Passaic, NJ	1,278,682	9,807	77	1,257
Salt Lake City-Ogden, UT	1,072,227	6,317	59	627
Oklahoma City, OK	958,839	18,794	196	8,149
Birmingham, AL	839,942	6,979	83	550
Springfield, MA	602,878	10,814	179	1,435
Youngstown-Warren, OH	600,895	3,823	64	448
Melbourne-Titusville-Palm Bay, FL	398,978	3,525	88	1,386
Shreveport, Bossier City, LA	376,330	1,447	38	172
York, PA	339,574	3,044	90	1,423
Utica-Rome, NY	316,645	2,192	69	1,157
Boise City, ID	295,851	4,890	165	1,545
Savannah, GA	257,899	7,857	305	3,879
Lincoln, NE	213,641	1,536	72	604
6-county area in western South Carolina	199,918	424	21	828
Bremerton, WA	189,731	744	39	417
5-county area in south-central Pennsylvania	172,742	594	34	266
7-county area in central Illinois	168,394	2,114	126	1,499
9-county area in north-central Florida	162,933	1,879	115	1,273
4-county area in northwestern Ohio	152,720	1,522	100	1,108
Jackson, MI	149,756	1,507	101	839
Redding, CA	147,036	394	27	196
Bangor, ME	146,601	1,551	106	814
Las Cruces, NM	135,510	3,628	268	1,010
Kenosha, WI	128,181	1,588	124	530
2-county area in southeastern New Mexico	113,614	148	13	58

Appendix Table 10.A1 *Total Service Units per Day (Continued)*

*NSHAPC Primary Sampling Area**	*Total Population*	*Total Units*	*Service Contacts per 10,000 People*	*Service Contacts per 10,000 People in Poverty*
Dover, DE	110,993	1,174	106	936
8-county area in northwestern Iowa	106,933	2,660	249	1,936
6-county area in northwestern Wisconsin	106,664	1,558	146	950
4-county area in southeastern Oklahoma	105,124	130	12	187
Douglas County, OR	94,649	631	67	1,223
Iredell County, NC	92,935	6,096	656	6,978
8-county area in west-central Georgia	92,343	54	6	21
2-county area in northwestern New Mexico	84,480	1,190	141	1,362
9-county area in northwestern Missouri	78,855	3,204	406	2,670
5-county area in northeastern Kentucky	66,346	708	107	374
3-county area in southeastern Nebraska	65,836	573	87	495
4-county area in southeastern Texas	60,559	445	74	1,373
Enid, OK	56,735	475	84	138
2-county area in eastern Virginia	44,764	933	208	8,996
2-county area in northeastern California	37,276	196	52	119
3-county area in northwestern Tennessee	32,310	167	52	337
2-county area in north-central Wyoming	29,707	270	91	0
5 towns in south-central Connecticut	21,106	0	0	0
Union Parish, LA	20,796	0	0	0
2-county area in southwestern Nevada	7,819	273	349	282

Source: Urban Institute analysis of weighted NSHAPC telephone survey of program representatives.
*Arrayed in descending order by population size.

Appendix Table 10.A2 *Percent of Program Contacts in a Primary Sampling Area That Are Allocated to Different Types of Services*

*NSHAPC Primary Sampling Area**	*Housing*	*Food*	*Health*	*Other*	*Total*
United States	23	55	5	17	100
Los Angeles-Long Beach, CA	22	54	6	18	100
New York, NY	25	57	3	16	100
Chicago, IL	15	69	1	15	100
Philadelphia, PA	34	44	6	15	100
Boston, MA	24	57	7	12	100
Detroit, MI	17	59	5	20	100
Washington, DC-MD-VA-WV	30	44	3	22	100
Houston, TX	32	42	4	22	100
Atlanta, GA	26	51	2	21	100
Dallas, TX	33	45	3	18	100
Nassau-Suffolk, NY	16	70	0	13	100
Riverside-San Bernardino, CA	16	66	4	14	100
Minneapolis-St. Paul, MN	36	44	3	17	100
San Diego, CA	16	42	15	27	100
St. Louis, MO-IL	22	58	2	18	100
Orange County, CA	13	79	1	8	100
Pittsburgh, PA	40	46	4	10	100
Baltimore, MD	18	63	2	17	100
Phoenix, AZ	46	23	2	29	100
Cleveland-Lorain-Elyria, OH	8	84	0	8	100
Oakland, CA	14	57	5	24	100
Tampa-St. Petersburg-Clearwater, FL	46	33	5	16	100
Seattle-Bellevue-Everett, WA	17	72	2	10	100
Miami, FL	28	48	7	18	100
Newark, NJ	29	58	4	9	100
Denver, CO	25	61	8	7	100
San Francisco, CA	22	25	24	29	100
Kansas City, MO-KS	33	40	7	20	100
Norfolk-Virginia Beach-Newport News, VA-NC	42	45	0	12	100
Indianapolis, IN	24	62	4	10	100
Sacramento, CA	24	64	1	11	100
Bergen-Passaic, NJ	26	66	1	7	100
Salt Lake City-Ogden, UT	35	44	3	17	100
Oklahoma City, OK	22	58	3	17	100
Birmingham, AL	23	50	4	23	100
Springfield, MA	12	76	0	12	100
Youngstown-Warren, OH	15	80	0	6	100
Melbourne-Titusville-Palm Bay, FL	15	77	0	8	100

Appendix Table 10.A2 *Percent of Program Contacts in a Primary Sampling Area That Are Allocated to Different Types of Services (Continued)*

*NSHAPC Primary Sampling Area**	*Housing*	*Food*	*Health*	*Other*	*Total*
Shreveport, Bossier City, LA	38	37	8	17	100
York, PA	15	61	5	19	100
Utica-Rome, NY	13	58	0	29	100
Boise City, ID	19	77	0	4	100
Savannah, GA	6	90	1	2	100
Lincoln, NE	18	31	8	43	100
6-county area in western South Carolina	41	42	0	18	100
Bremerton, WA	15	85	0	0	100
5-county area in south-central Pennsylvania	22	73	0	5	100
7-county area in central Illinois	21	71	1	6	100
9-county area in north-central Florida	5	24	0	71	100
4-county area in northwestern Ohio	19	70	0	11	100
Jackson, MI	13	76	0	11	100
Redding, CA	64	0	32	4	100
Bangor, ME	21	53	0	26	100
Las Cruces, NM	66	19	0	15	100
Kenosha, WI	17	61	15	7	100
2-county area in southeastern New Mexico	61	29	0	9	100
Dover, DE	18	75	0	7	100
8-county area in northwestern Iowa	7	9	0	84	100
6-county area in northwestern Wisconsin	17	47	10	26	100
4 county area in southeastern Oklahoma	47	11	0	42	100
Douglas County, OR	46	43	0	11	100
Iredell County, NC	1	6	0	93	100
8-county area in west-central Georgia	100	0	0	0	100
2-county area in northwestern New Mexico	37	14	11	37	100
9-county area in northwestern Missouri	12	13	11	64	100
5-county area in northeastern Kentucky	8	22	0	69	100
3-county area in southeastern Nebraska	27	31	1	42	100
4-county area in southeastern Texas	2	41	41	16	100
Enid, OK	20	79	0	1	100
2-county area in eastern Virginia	2	76	11	10	100
2-county area in northeastern California	45	55	0	0	100
3-county area in northwestern Tennessee	0	41	59	0	100
2-county area in north-central Wyoming	37	55	0	7	100
5 towns in south-central Connecticut	0	0	0	0	100
Union Parish, LA	0	0	0	0	100
2-county area in southwestern Nevada	13	49	20	18	100

Source: Urban Institute analysis of weighted NSHAPC telephone survey of program representatives.
*Arrayed in descending order of population size.

Appendix Table 10.A3 *Housing/Shelter Program Contacts by Primary Sampling Area*

		Total Available Housing/Shelter Program Contacts		*Emergency Shelter Program Contacts*		*Transitional Shelter Program Contacts*		*Permanent Housing Program Contacts*		*Voucher Distribution Program Contacts*	
*NSHAPC Primary Sampling Area**	*Total Population*	*Total Number Reported by Providers*	*Program Contacts per 10,000 People in Poverty*	*Total Number Reported by Providers*	*Program Contacts per 10,000 People in Poverty*	*Total Number Reported by Providers*	*Program Contacts per 10,000 People in Poverty*	*Total Number Reported by Providers*	*Program Contacts per 10,000 People in Poverty*	*Total Number Reported by Providers*	*Program Contacts per 10,000 People in Poverty*
United States	**248,718,291**	**290,463**	**220**	**103,254**	**85**	**90,555**	**65**	**77,336**	**50**	**19,318**	**20**
Los Angeles–Long Beach, CA	8,863,052	26,554	198	7,168	54	8,517	64	8,491	63	2,378	18
New York, NY	8,546,846	44,794	299	9,450	63	17,594	118	17,495	117	256	2
Chicago, IL	7,410,858	13,307	159	5,363	64	5,209	62	2,322	28	414	5
Philadelphia, PA	5,893,019	14,123	230	7,003	114	4,338	71	2,336	38	447	7
Boston, MA	5,685,763	13,483	289	5,853	126	3,237	69	4,208	90	184	4
Detroit, MI	4,266,654	8,358	150	4,944	88	1,176	21	786	14	1,452	26
Washington, DC–MD–VA–WV	4,222,830	13,166	472	5,675	204	5,509	198	1,605	58	377	14
Houston, TX	3,321,926	8,296	165	4,306	86	2,576	51	1,035	21	378	8
Atlanta, GA	2,959,500	4,981	167	2,317	78	1,871	63	397	13	395	13
Dallas, TX	2,676,248	3,692	112	1,515	46	1,047	32	939	29	191	6
Nassau–Suffolk, NY	2,609,212	3,258	297	478	44	269	25	674	62	1,838	168
Riverside–San Bernardino, CA	2,588,793	5,509	174	1,772	56	978	31	727	23	2,032	64
Minneapolis–St. Paul, MN	2,538,776	7,815	380	2,716	132	3,070	149	1,723	84	306	15

San Diego, CA	2,498,016	4,246	150	1,573	56	2,491	88	113	4	69	2
St Louis, MO–IL	2,492,348	12,794	475	2,638	98	1,064	40	8,602	320	491	18
Orange County, CA	2,410,668	1,738	85	581	28	800	39	4	0	352	17
Pittsburgh, PA	2,394,811	8,882	307	1,192	41	996	34	6,573	227	121	4
Baltimore, MD	2,382,172	7,860	327	3,641	151	2,112	88	661	27	1,446	60
Phoenix, AZ	2,238,498	8,266	286	3,597	125	2,642	92	1,695	59	332	12
Cleveland–Lorain–Elyria, OH	2,202,069	2,306	87	987	37	801	30	353	13	165	6
Oakland, CA	2,080,434	4,877	252	2,050	106	1,393	72	667	34	768	40
Tampa–St. Petersburg–Clearwater, FL	2,067,959	5,920	251	3,932	167	1,587	67	258	11	143	6
Seattle–Bellevue–Everett, WA	2,033,128	7,673	497	2,327	151	1,692	110	2,832	183	822	53
Miami, FL	1,937,194	3,476	100	749	22	2,459	71	236	7	32	1
Newark, NJ	1,915,694	2,826	168	1,278	76	901	53	601	36	47	3
Denver, CO	1,622,980	8,635	548	4,312	274	3,496	222	651	41	176	11
San Francisco, CA	1,603,678	12,410	860	1,782	123	3,432	238	6,541	453	656	45
Kansas City, MO–KS	1,582,874	4,256	274	1,666	107	1,102	71	1,405	91	82	5
Norfolk–Virginia Beach–Newport News, VA–NC	1,444,710	3,782	230	2,075	126	604	37	846	51	257	16
Indianapolis, IN	1,380,491	3,272	239	1,459	107	648	47	806	59	360	26
Sacramento, CA	1,340,010	3,125	206	1,365	90	735	49	31	2	994	66
Bergen-Passaic, NJ	1,278,682	2,272	291	487	62	1,395	179	216	28	174	22
Salt Lake City–Ogden, UT	1,072,227	2,191	217	1,458	145	415	41	218	22	101	10
Oklahoma City, OK	958,839	4,196	315	1,869	140	2,001	150	291	22	35	3
Birmingham, AL	839,942	1,354	107	653	51	265	21	142	11	293	23
Springfield, MA	602,878	1,278	170	458	61	429	57	391	52	0	0
Youngstown–Warren, OH	600,895	563	66	293	34	117	14	6	1	146	17
Melbourne–Titusville–Palm Bay, FL	398,978	535	147	123	34	236	65	53	15	123	34

(Continued)

Appendix Table 10.A3 *Housing/Shelter Program Contacts by Primary Sampling Area (Continued)*

		Total Available Housing/Shelter Program Contacts		*Emergency Shelter Program Contacts*		*Transitional Shelter Program Contacts*		*Permanent Housing Program Contacts*		*Voucher Distribution Program Contacts*	
*NSHAPC Primary Sampling Area**	*Total Population*	*Total Number Reported by Providers*	*Program Contacts per 10,000 People in Poverty*	*Total Number Reported by Providers*	*Program Contacts per 10,000 People in Poverty*	*Total Number Reported by Providers*	*Program Contacts per 10,000 People in Poverty*	*Total Number Reported by Providers*	*Program Contacts per 10,000 People in Poverty*	*Total Number Reported by Providers*	*Program Contacts per 10,000 People in Poverty*
Shreveport, Bossier City, LA	376,330	530	63	253	30	267	32	11	1	0	0
York, PA	339,574	431	201	105	49	71	33	180	84	75	35
Utica–Rome, NY	316,645	240	62	75	19	128	33	16	4	21	5
Boise City, ID	295,851	733	232	426	135	237	75	39	12	31	10
Savannah, GA	257,899	500	118	280	66	144	34	27	6	49	12
Lincoln, NE	213,641	280	125	134	60	136	60	0	0	10	5
6-county area in western South Carolina	199,918	172	57	154	51	1	0	7	2	10	3
Bremerton, WA	189,731	113	63	74	41	39	22	0	0	0	0
5-county area in south-central Pennsylvania	172,742	129	58	55	25	0	0	8	4	66	30
7-county area in central Illinois	168,394	431	213	89	44	177	87	75	37	90	45
9-county area in north-central Florida	162,933	89	26	15	4	40	12	0	0	34	10
4-county area in northwestern Ohio	152,720	295	215	230	167	27	20	0	0	38	28
Jackson, MI	149,756	197	110	112	62	85	47	0	0	0	0
Redding, CA	147,036	254	126	148	74	0	0	43	22	62	31

Bangor, ME	146,601	319	168	80	42	181	95	4	2	54	28
Las Cruces, NM	135,510	2,386	664	1,454	405	104	29	0	0	828	230
Kenosha, WI	128,181	254	194	89	68	25	19	129	99	11	8
2-county area in southeastern New Mexico	113,614	91	36	61	24	20	8	0	0	10	4
Dover, DE	110,993	212	169	107	85	23	18	0	0	83	66
8-county area in northwestern Iowa	106,933	179	155	66	57	0	0	2	2	111	96
6-county area in northwestern Wisconsin	106,664	261	159	36	22	0	0	172	105	53	32
4-county area in southeastern Oklahoma	105,124	58	25	32	14	7	3	19	8	0	0
Douglas County, OR	94,649	275	195	134	95	132	94	0	0	9	6
Iredell County, NC	92,935	57	65	27	31	12	14	14	16	4	5
8-county area in west-central Georgia	92,343	54	21	28	11	0	0	0	0	25	10
2-county area in northwestern New Mexico	84,480	439	128	328	95	29	8	39	11	43	12
9-county area in northwestern Missouri	78,855	370	251	167	113	23	15	162	110	18	12
5-county area in northeastern Kentucky	66,346	60	31	27	14	0	0	0	0	33	17
3-county area in southeastern Nebraska	65,836	156	225	60	87	13	19	40	58	43	62
4-county area in southeastern Texas	60,559	10	6	0	0	0	0	0	0	10	6
Enid, OK	56,735	94	118	76	95	19	23	0	0	0	0
2-county area in eastern Virginia	44,764	21	22	18	19	0	0	0	0	3	3
2-county area in northeastern California	37,276	61	118	33	64	0	0	0	0	28	54
3-county area in northwestern Tennessee	32,310	0	0	0	0	0	0	0	0	0	0
2-county area in north-central Wyoming	29,707	101	310	60	184	0	0	5	16	36	110
5 towns in south-central Connecticut	21,106	0	0	0	0	0	0	0	0	0	0
Union Parish, LA	20,796	0	0	0	0	0	0	0	0	0	0
2-county area in southwestern Nevada	7,819	35	337	21	202	0	0	0	0	14	135

Source: Urban Institute analysis of weighted NSHAPC telephone survey of program representatives.
*Arrayed in descending order by population size.

Appendix Table 10.A4 *Soup Kitchen Weekday/Weekend Program Contacts per 10,000 Poor People: Low, High, and Average Estimates*

	Weekday per 10,000 People in Poverty			*Weekend per 10,000 People in Poverty*		
*NSHAPC Primary Sampling Area**	*Minimum Number of Meals*	*Average Number of Meals*	*Maximum Number of Meals*	*Minimum Number of Meals*	*Average Number of Meals*	*Maximum Number of Meals*
United States	**129**	**173**	**217**	**75**	**110**	**145**
Los Angeles-Long Beach, CA	141	217	292	87	133	178
New York, NY	176	217	259	75	98	121
Chicago, IL	98	146	195	51	78	105
Philadelphia, PA	108	156	205	54	81	108
Boston, MA	170	235	299	116	178	240
Detroit, MI	192	240	287	80	115	150
Washington, DC-MD-VA-WV	223	340	457	135	222	309
Houston, TX	64	88	113	56	75	94
Atlanta, GA	86	125	165	62	95	128
Dallas, TX	59	113	167	35	70	104
Nassau-Suffolk, NY	101	128	156	6	7	8
Riverside-San Bernardino, CA	306	317	328	169	177	185
Minneapolis-St. Paul, MN	222	299	375	132	205	278
San Diego, CA	165	203	241	135	161	186
St. Louis, MO-IL	204	279	354	155	223	291
Orange County, CA	36	54	72	36	58	80
Pittsburgh, PA	156	152	147	55	72	89
Baltimore, MD	328	440	552	191	273	354

Phoenix, AZ	74	96	117	40	61	81
Cleveland-Lorain-Elyria, OH	178	230	283	77	97	117
Oakland, CA	340	376	412	124	146	169
Tampa-St. Petersburg-Clearwater, FL	88	130	171	72	113	155
Seattle-Bellevue-Everett, WA	253	351	450	142	208	274
Miami, FL	65	73	80	42	52	62
Newark, NJ	137	177	217	85	102	118
Denver, CO	235	398	562	169	315	461
San Francisco, CA	512	646	780	336	467	599
Kansas City, MO-KS	125	188	251	88	151	214
Norfolk-Virginia Beach-Newport News, VA-NC	68	92	116	54	82	109
Indianapolis, IN	147	242	337	79	137	196
Sacramento, CA	37	51	65	41	55	69
Bergen-Passaic, NJ	204	243	282	114	133	151
Salt Lake City-Ogden, UT	170	189	208	170	189	208
Oklahoma City, OK	343	615	887	302	538	774
Birmingham, AL	93	122	151	87	116	145
Springfield, MA	157	211	266	51	59	66
Youngstown-Warren, OH	134	129	124	65	114	164
Melbourne-Titusville-Palm Bay, FL	558	558	558	534	534	534
Shreveport, Bossier City, LA	35	70	105	35	70	105
York, PA	241	409	576	94	188	282
Utica-Rome, NY	105	121	138	34	50	67
Boise City, ID	558	673	788	153	266	379
Savannah, GA	162	218	275	56	113	169

(Continued)

Appendix Table 10.A4 *Soup Kitchen Weekday/Weekend Program Contacts per 10,000 Poor People: Low, High, and Average Estimates (Continued)*

	Weekday per 10,000 People in Poverty			*Weekend per 10,000 People in Poverty*		
*NSHAPC Primary Sampling Area**	*Minimum Number of Meals*	*Average Number of Meals*	*Maximum Number of Meals*	*Minimum Number of Meals*	*Average Number of Meals*	*Maximum Number of Meals*
Lincoln, NE	111	167	224	60	100	141
6-county area in western South Carolina	0	0	0	0	0	0
Bremerton, WA	168	244	320	0	0	0
5-county area in south-central Pennsylvania	0	0	0	0	0	0
7-county area in central Illinois	23	28	34	0	0	0
9-county area in north-central Florida	85	128	171	78	117	156
4-county area in northwestern Ohio	21	21	21	0	0	0
Jackson, MI	52	105	157	52	105	157
Redding, CA	0	0	0	0	0	0
Bangor, ME	211	328	445	133	211	288
Las Cruces, NM	94	94	94	0	0	0
Kenosha, WI	106	159	213	106	159	213
2-county area in southeastern New Mexico	13	27	40	13	27	40
Dover, DE	228	282	336	120	120	120
8-county area in northwestern Iowa	0	0	0	0	0	0
6-county area in northwestern Wisconsin	3	3	3	0	0	0
4-county area in southeastern Oklahoma	3	6	9	3	6	9
Douglas County, OR	7	14	20	0	0	0

Iredell County, NC	212	424	635	212	424	635
8-county area in west-central Georgia	0	0	0	0	0	0
2-county area in northwestern New Mexico	15	30	45	15	30	45
9-county area in northwestern Missouri	18	24	29	6	11	17
5-county area in northeastern Kentucky	0	0	0	0	0	0
3-county area in southeastern Nebraska	168	251	335	0	0	0
4-county area in southeastern Texas	0	0	0	0	0	0
Enid, OK	317	400	483	83	166	249
2-county area in eastern Virginia	0	0	0	0	0	0
2-county area in northeastern California	0	0	0	0	0	0
3-county area in northwestern Tennessee	0	0	0	0	0	0
2-county area in north-central Wyoming	191	191	191	0	0	0
5 towns in south-central Connecticut	0	0	0	0	0	0
Union Parish, LA	0	0	0	0	0	0
2-county area in southwestern Nevada	868	868	868	0	0	0

Source: Urban Institute analysis of weighted NSHAPC telephone survey of program representatives.

*Arrayed in descending order by population size.

NOTES

1. In two rural sampling areas, NSHAPC telephone interviews could not discover any homeless assistance programs at all. Results for these two areas are shown in the following figures as zeros.
2. The appendix to this chapter provides the data for figures 10.1, 10.2, and 10.3, including the names of each sampling area. Each bar in these figures represents one sampling area; they are ordered by the population size of the sampling area, from largest to smallest. The 28 largest MSAs are the 28 leftmost bars. However, 5 rural areas have more population than 5 of the medium- and small-sized MSAs, so the remaining bars do not divide cleanly into the 24 medium- and small-sized MSAs and the rural sampling areas.
3. The reader is not expected to follow each sampling area through each of the panels in figures 10.1, 10.2, and 10.3. Rather, these figures provide an overall visual impression of the large variation across sampling areas in the level of program contacts of all types (figure 10.1), the share of all programs falling within a given program type (figure 10.2), and the share of housing/shelter programs falling within emergency, transitional, permanent, and voucher programs (figure 10.3). For specific information on each sampling area, see the tables in the appendix to this chapter.
4. All differences between percentages discussed in the text are statistically significant at $p < .05$, all numbers (e.g., the number of soup kitchens) have a 95 percent confidence interval of no more than 2 percent of their value (e.g., if the number is 10,000, the C.I. is $\pm$ 200), and all percentages presented by themselves have a 95 percent confidence interval no larger than $\pm$ 4 percentage points. A confidence interval of $\pm$ 4 percentage points means that if the reported percent is 60, 60 is the estimate of the value and the probability is 95 percent that the value falls between 56 and 64 percent.
5. These responses were used to estimate the rate of soup kitchen meals per 10,000 poor people within each primary sampling area. Estimating the rate of soup kitchen meals was not as straightforward as estimating the rate for shelter/housing program contacts, for a number of reasons. First, some soup kitchens offered only one meal a day (e.g., only breakfast, or only dinner), but others offered two or even three meals a day. Second, some soup kitchens were open seven days a week, but others only on weekdays. Some were open for only one or two days a week, and some at different times, depending on the week of the month (e.g., they were open only on the last two Mondays of each month). Third, the survey asked each soup kitchen representative how many *people* would be served on an average day in February 1996, but did not obtain separate estimates for each meal offered (i.e., breakfast, lunch, and/or dinner). If the service location offered its meals on fewer than seven days a week, it gave its answer as "the average number of people served *on the days we are open* in February." If the service location offered more than one meal in a day, it gave its answer as "the average number of people we serve *in a day.*" Other questions ascertained the days on which the program was open, and whether the service location offered breakfast, lunch, and/or dinner.

The nature of the information available for soup kitchens thus required several adjustments to produce a rate of available meals, including adjusting for the number of days a week the program was open and that, for a service location that offered more than one meal (e.g., both breakfast and lunch), some of the people reported as being served on an average day might have eaten one, two, or three meals. Because there is no way to know the extent of this duplication, we present a range of estimates.

For the *low* estimate, when a service location offered more than one meal a day we assumed that *each person contacted the program only once* (i.e., for one meal). For example, if a service location reported that it fed 75 people on an average day, and offered both breakfast and lunch, we assumed for the low estimate that 75 different people contacted the program, for one meal each, either breakfast or lunch, and that nobody came for both meals, so the total number of program contacts was 75. For the *high* estimate, when a service location offered more than one meal in a day, we applied the average number of people reported *to each meal offered*. Thus, for the example just given, the high estimate would be 150 program contacts (75 people at each of two meals). There is no way to distinguish where the truth lies, but, on average, it probably lies somewhere in between, so we also calculated the midpoint between the high and low estimates.

6. Estimates for soup kitchen meals on *weekend* days ranged from a low of 75 per 10,000 to a high of 145 per 10,000, with an average of 110 per 10,000 poor people. Average weekend soup kitchen meals were 57 percent of the average number of meals served on weekdays, ranging from 47 to 64 percent of weekday levels. Rural areas reported substantially lower number of meals available on weekends than other sampling areas. Exact statistics may be found in table 10.A4 in the appendix for this chapter.

7. Other results from the mail survey may be found in Burt et al. 1999, *Homelessness—Programs and the People They Serve: Technical Report*, chapter 16.

8. Food pantries served more people overall, but most of those people were not homeless. Many food pantries actually require the household to have an address with a kitchen before they will provide food bags or boxes. Soup kitchens are far more likely to have homeless people as a high proportion of their clientele, so we focused on this type of program.

9. A program's specialization, or lack of it, was determined using responses to questions about its primary population focus and the service location's primary mission. If *either or both* of these answers indicated a specialization, the program was classified according to that specialization. Decision rules included the following: Any combination that included domestic violence was classified as having a domestic violence specialization; any combination that included HIV/AIDS was classified as having a HIV/AIDS specialization; and any combination that included youth was classified as having a youth specialization.

10. Percentages of emergency shelter, transitional and housing programs, and soup kitchen programs naming a specialization are given in the second rows of tables 10.5 through 10.8, respectively.

11. If these programs were funded with McKinney Act grants, they were supposed to focus on one or another disabled population. The absence of reported specialization among many of these programs is, therefore, a point of some interest. It may be that these programs did not focus on a *single* population, although the people they served were people for whom the funding is intended. Among permanent housing programs, 33 percent named persons with mental illness as a population focus, 17 percent named persons with substance abuse problems, 27 percent named those with dual diagnosis, 23 percent named persons with HIV/AIDS, 15 percent named veterans, 16 percent

named victims of domestic violence, and 19 percent said they focus on some other (unspecified) population. If a significant proportion of these programs refused to choose a *single* population as their primary focus, it is not hard to see how so many might end up being described as having no specialization.

12. Information about program co-location comes from the telephone survey of providers; information about service offerings comes from the mail survey to program directors (as described in chapter 1).

13. Too few transitional and permanent housing programs existed in 1987 to make over-time comparisons possible for these program types.

11
Conclusions

Chapter 1 posed the question, "What will it take to end homelessness?" This, after a decade and a half of concerted action to develop homeless services, has not reduced in any way the probability that far too many Americans will experience a homeless episode.

Now, it is time to summarize what the preceding chapters have shown and attempt to answer that question. In making this effort, we operate on the assumption that ending homelessness is the correct goal. Instead, what we have been doing in recent years, with a good deal of money, is making the homeless condition a little less onerous for people who find themselves in it, while doing relatively little to help them leave it by supplying the one essential—housing.

Several things resonate throughout the detailed information presented in this book. They are of paramount importance. Four have to do with the sheer numbers of people who are likely to experience homelessness. First, homelessness has not gone away, as anyone could have reported without help from this book. Second, people who fit official government definitions of literal homelessness seem to have increased.

Third, NSHAPC estimates of homelessness, when projected over a year, confirm results from other studies that a large pool of people living in desperate circumstances exists in many communities, some of whom will need and use homeless assistance services at some time during a year. Producing the same findings with three very different methods

(NSHAPC, household telephone surveys, and shelter databases) gives them considerable weight. They should greatly influence the direction of our thinking and the structure of our future actions. Fourth, high levels of homelessness, it is important to acknowledge, continue to exist in tandem with, and perhaps in part because of, the booming economy of the last half of the 1990s.

Several additional findings on individual-level risk factors for homelessness also appear consistently in our analyses. First, extreme poverty (less than half the federal poverty level) is a universal reality for homeless people. It is the platform upon which all other individual characteristics play out, toward the potential of homelessness.

Second, at least half the adults homeless at any given point have one or more problems with alcohol, drugs, or mental health, no matter how we divide NSHAPC's homeless sample or the time frames we examine. As the time frame increases, so, too, do the proportions with ADM problems, resulting in about four out of five people identified as homeless at any given point reporting one or more such problems some time in their life. Third, certain adverse experiences during childhood and adolescence are strongly associated with the probability that a person will experience a spell of homelessness, experience it early, and experience it often or for a long duration. Finally, many of these same experiences also are associated with the likelihood of having one or more ADM problems as an adult.

In chapter 1, we presented a model of homelessness that centered on an association between household income and housing cost. If they were out of balance, a household could not afford housing. We have seen that the incomes of homeless service users are extremely low. They contribute a negative on the household-income (left) side of the inequality symbolizing housing affordability in figure 1.1. Since NSHAPC interviewed individuals, the data we have can tell us only about the risk factors for homelessness that lie within individuals, and cannot contribute information about the housing-cost (right) side.

Personal factors contributing to a household's difficulty in obtaining enough income to keep itself in housing were also amply documented, and confirm findings from many previous studies. They include being single (that is, having only one potential wage earner); having low levels of educational attainment and indifferent attachment to the labor force; being disconnected from family, friends, and other sources of social and financial support; having physical health problems; and having significant present and historical levels of alcohol, drug, and/or mental health problems. Another factor, being relatively unlikely to receive public cash and other benefits in lieu of earned income, also certainly characterizes homeless people. But it is not a personal factor. Rather, it reflects the weakness of the American safety net and its failure altogether to address the needs of many segments of the population. This failure puts such people at increased risk of homelessness.

Not only were these factors evident in descriptions of NSHAPC's homeless clients, but they also figured prominently in regression analyses. These showed that income levels, chronic health problems, mental health problems, and alcohol and/or drug problems were significantly related to the probability that one would have ever experienced a homeless episode.

NSHAPC itself cannot supply data on the structural aspects of housing markets that form the housing-cost (right) side of figure 1.1. However, other sources amply document the persistence and worsening of the housing crunch for low-income people throughout the 1990s.[1] A recent HUD report (Department of Housing and Urban Development 1999) documents an increase of 3 percent in the number of struggling renter households, reaching the level of one in four renter households nationally; increases in rents that were double the overall rate of inflation, as measured by the Consumer Price Index; a reduction of 5 percent between 1991 and 1997 in the housing stock affordable to struggling families; and a mismatch between family incomes and rents such that for every 100 struggling renter households, only 36 units were both available and affordable. A second report (HUD 2000) shows that more renter households than ever before, more than 5.4 million, face "worst-case" housing needs. That means paying more than 50 percent of their income for rent, and also possibly living in dangerously dilapidated housing. What these reports do not mention is that government housing subsidies for poor people were shrinking during the same period, leaving more poor households on their own to face an ever-tightening market.

Moreover, the structural situation, and therefore housing affordability, has not gotten better in the years since NSHAPC. In fact, the booming economy has given many people the resources to bid up the price of housing, while leaving behind those who still earn at or near minimum wage. Dolbeare (1999) has shown that a full-time, minimum-wage worker in 1999 could not afford the fair market rent for a one-bedroom apartment in a single local jurisdiction in the United States. Indeed, in many communities, a minimum-wage worker would have had to work two and a half full-time jobs to afford a one-bedroom unit.

Thus, the key to persistent widespread homelessness in the United States appears to be the persistent and worsening mismatch of housing cost to available household resources. With this mismatch as the structural backdrop, personal vulnerabilities combine and interact to increase the risk that a given person will be extremely poor, and also become homeless. But remember that all the vulnerabilities we could amass to explain the probability of homelessness, plus extreme poverty, could account for only 32 percent of the variance in whether a person had or had not ever been homeless. Without the poverty and the affordable housing crisis, the same vulnerabilities would not produce homelessness. *With* them, it is to some degree a random process that determines which individuals and households will experience the one crisis too many that will push them into homelessness.

In the days when we still calculated the homeless population at a single point in time, failed to appreciate its dynamism, and estimated that only 0.2 percent of all Americans were homeless, it did not seem reasonable to hold a general housing crunch responsible for pushing a relatively small number of people, many with admitted disabilities, into homelessness. However, with the recognition that we should be considering only the poor population as the denominator (the rest of us, however disabled, can afford housing), and the far-larger number of people who experience homelessness some time over a year as the numerator, we arrive at the conclusion that 1 out of every 10 poor households is living such a precarious existence that a spell of homelessness is a strong possibility. Given that an ever-increasing proportion of extremely poor people cannot afford the available housing, it is not so surprising that one or two additional personal vulnerabilities translate into spells of actual homelessness.

When we began to write this book, we went back and reread the introductory chapter to *America's Homeless*, written 10 years earlier (Burt and Cohen 1989). We were struck forcefully by the uncanny pertinence of the 10-year-old issues to today's search for solutions. Policy questions are still formulated, for example, in the hope that information about population size and characteristics, and knowledge about service systems, will somehow point us in the direction of helping people who currently are homeless and preventing others from becoming homeless. In the past decade, we have learned a good deal about what works to help people leave homelessness. This knowledge was usefully summarized in *Practical Lessons* (Fosburg and Dennis 1999), a recent conference and publication sponsored by the Departments of Health and Human Services and Housing and Urban Development. While we appreciate that we still do not know many things about which services to offer and how best to deliver them, one conclusion is inescapable: Every available study indicates that giving homeless people housing, through shelter plus care, vouchers, group homes, or any other mechanism, helps ensure that they will not be homeless any more. On the other hand, giving them a vast array of different services, absent housing or the income to obtain it, does not (Shinn and Baumohl 1999).

Thus, we come full circle, back to the calls of advocates in the early 1980s: Housing affordability is a major part of the problem, and providing housing or the financial resources to acquire it must be a major part of the solution. Paradoxically, doing more for homeless people by way of services, but falling short of providing housing, may actually draw more people into the official category of "homeless," while not affecting the homeless "problem." We have built a homeless service industry, and it now has its own entrenched interests and expectations for continued funding. This homeless establishment, in the absence of new resources, actually reduces the likelihood that new or creative approaches to *ending* rather than *ameliorating* homelessness will be developed or implemented.

We have built more and different types of homeless assistance services, and managed to organize them in relatively helpful ways, but we have not seen reductions in either the one-day or one-week count or the annual flow of homeless people. In part *because* we now have more programs and services, we have better ways to *contact and identify* people who are homeless. Also in part, we *define* people as homeless when they use certain types of homeless assistance programs, such as emergency shelters and transitional housing programs. The availability of more such programs, coupled with the level of need that pushes more people to use them, means more people get counted as being homeless. The implication is *not* that we should have fewer programs so we then would count fewer homeless people. That would only mask and obscure the extent of the housing problem. Rather, we need to think in a new way about what we are doing.

Will We Ever Do What It Takes?

In many ways, the answer to "What will it take to end homelessness?" is pretty obvious. We need to make housing available and affordable. We can approach affordability in a variety of ways, through housing costs and household income. We need to provide more subsidies so households can gain access to existing housing, and we need to produce more housing, through subsidies, tax incentives, or other mechanisms, that will be affordable to low-income households. We also need to increase the ability of people to earn enough to keep themselves housed, again through a variety of mechanisms, including both human capital and job development. That being said, we must discuss why we have not done so and probably will not. This brings us to the issue of norms and expectations that govern views of personal, familial, community, and societal responsibility for individual security and well-being. We cannot talk about either the causes of or the solutions to homelessness without grappling with values, especially about who deserves what from whom, and who owes what to whom.

We start with the four "value tenets" articulated by David Ellwood (1988) in his analysis of American attitudes toward and feelings about welfare. They have certain parallels with American ideas of what to do about people who become homeless. These are (1) the autonomy of the individual; (2) the virtue of work; (3) the primacy of family; and (4) the desire for and sense of community. Ellwood describes these tenets in a fairly benign way, but he is focusing *only on families with children*, who, among the poor, elicit the most sympathy and compassion. For instance, Ellwood describes the autonomy tenet as follows: "Americans believe that they have a significant degree of control over their destinies and, at a minimum, that people can provide for themselves if they are willing to make the necessary sacrifices" (1988, p. 16). Implicit, but not stated, is a rather more-negative corollary, growing out of both the Calvinist origins of much American social thought and its Social Darwinist extension. That is that if one is poor, it is one's own fault, and that poor people are somehow *less worthy, less blessed, less "chosen," and also less "fit"* than those with money. This corollary applies most particularly in attitudes toward many homeless people.

The tendency to focus on the individual problems of homeless people, as a way of ascertaining whether they have done something that contributes to being homeless, develops directly from this corollary to the autonomy tenet. We are more willing to support people who clearly *cannot* provide for themselves *through no fault of their own*, than those whose inability is seen as a result of choice or will, or those who will not though they appear able to. This insistence on self-help, and self-responsibility for failure, is a strong theme in American thought.

On the work tenet, Ellwood discusses the moral imperative we as a society place on work. He expresses this tenet as, "People ought to work hard not only to provide for their families, but because laziness and idleness are seen as indications of weak moral character" (1988, p. 16). Phrased thus, it reflects the extreme emphasis that Americans place on the volitional aspects of behavior (wanting to), and their relatively little regard of capacity (being able to). The autonomy tenet shares this characteristic. Eisinger (1998) provides a highly detailed example of how both tenets operated in the area of hunger and hunger policy over most of the decades of the 20th century, resulting in a patchwork of programs that have not ended hunger for many Americans.

Public discourse about people receiving welfare, and, to a fairly great extent, homeless people, is usually heavily laden with assumptions that welfare recipients and homeless people simply do not want to work, and that if they did, they could not only find a job that would support them, but also their families, if they had them. Rarely is recognition given to significant and well-documented levels of disabling conditions among either population that preclude significant levels of working. Or, if disabilities *are* recognized, they are viewed simplistically and globally, as well as being assumed to characterize the whole homeless population (Baum and Burnes 1993; Torrey 1989). The two extremes of response are either to do nothing and perceive the individuals as responsible for their own situation, or to *take over and take care of* the people affected.

The value tenet of relying on family first is, likewise, problematic for people with the highest risk of homelessness. Many have no family, being products of the child welfare system and having spent considerable time in foster care. Others have "run out of" family, having relied on them already for as long as possible. Still others are homeless *because* of family, as in the case of women, with or without children, fleeing domestic violence. Still others have been long-estranged from family, often because of extended involvement with mental health or criminal justice systems, but sometimes because they left home to find work and never returned.

Finally, many of the same homeless people who have no family, or no available family, as well as many other homeless people, do not belong to a community that is willing or able to take responsibility for helping them. While this is possible to some extent even for people who become homeless in the locality where they reside, one of the biggest problems of transient homeless people (those without place) is that they are always "them" and not "us" to the residents of any particular location. As "them," they are to a large measure excluded from the social support and assistance that the fixed residents might proffer each other.

This exclusion from the social-welfare functions of a community is long-standing. To the extent that placeless migrants of past eras were self-sufficient, they posed little problem to fixed communities, as they made no demands for care or support. However, if, while resident in a particular place, they needed help sometime with some problems, they would have run up against this fundamental barrier in public welfare policy—that of being outsiders to, not members of, a community. In this country, we have a long history of unwillingness to help people who are "not us," however "us" is defined. Going back to the Puritans, when each community was expected to provide for temporarily destitute *community members* but not outsiders, local communities and jurisdictions have established policies and programs that exclude outsiders. More-recent examples include the Great Depression, when the federal government had to assume responsibility for transient homeless people because local communities would look after only "their own," and attempts in the past few years in several states to renew one-year residency requirements as a condition of eligibility for welfare. One of the first questions politicians ask about local homeless populations is, "Where do they come from? Are they from here?" Most are convinced that "they" are not "from here," and, therefore, have no call on community resources. They usually are wrong.

Ellwood's first, third, and fourth value tenets, in combination, depict a relatively extreme ambivalence, sometimes verging on antipathy, about the role of government in assuring individual and collective well-being. The premises of self-reliance first, reliance on family second, and a wispy sentimentality about wanting community third, do not form the basis of a strong commitment to sustained public action. Political rhetoric on the right, gaining ascendancy with Ronald Reagan and still a strong conservative theme, maintains that "the less government the better." Few in recent years have been speaking forcefully for the need for government and government's importance in organizing and supplying, or providing the resources for, those goods and services that are in no one's self-interest to supply for others, but without which everyone suffers.

None of the foregoing discussion, however, denies for a minute the incredible levels of effort that private charity contributes to the well-being of homeless people, and the immediate sense of community that these efforts may produce. The vast majority of emergency food programs in this country run on volunteer labor and are heavily dependent on donated goods (Ohls and Saleem-Ismail 2000). Homeless shelters also depend on volunteers to keep the doors open. But these programs are only necessary to the extent that collective action of a stronger and more stable sort—that is, government action—has left sufficiently large cracks in the safety net that upwards of half a million people a day need to rely on charity to get enough to eat, and even more to have a place to sleep. These arrangements leave everyone begging. The programs beg for money, space, food, and other goods; program clients must acknowledge their need and ask for assistance day after day. This is not a good way to "solve" a significant social problem that shows no signs of abating.

Possible Alternative Approaches

There *are* other alternatives, however, even ones known to work on the basis of concrete demonstrations. On the welfare front, some states have enacted programs under federal welfare reform legislation (the Personal Responsibility and Work Opportunity Reconciliation Act of 1996), and earlier waivers, that are predicated on *public (and therefore state agency) responsibility to help people overcome* barriers to work. These programs insist on work, but recognize that some people are not ready for it right away. Instead, they *invest public funds* in helping those people resolve difficulties and overcome barriers until they are able to hold a viable job. These programs cost some money, *but they work* (Knox, Miller, and Gennetian 2000).

Evaluations of programs serving severely disabled homeless people show that they can achieve a condition of stable housing. But, first, they need the housing, without which nothing helps. Then, in addition, they also may need some supportive services to achieve stability (Oakley and Dennis 1999; Shern 1989; Shinn and Baumohl 1999). Even working is not out of reach. For example, many programs have found that people with severe mental illnesses place the same value on work as most Americans do. They want to work, and will work if it can be structured to accommodate their disability (Beard, Probst, and Malamud 1982).

Another example of forward-looking analysis and action comes from the Community Shelter Board (CSB) of Franklin County (Columbus), Ohio. CSB was created in 1986 through the joint efforts of many Franklin County civil jurisdictions, service organizations, and foundations. Its initial goal was to coordinate collaborative planning and develop solutions to the problems of homelessness. All public and most private funds for homeless services flow through it. In turn, it distributes them according to comprehensive plans. Information was one of CSB's highest priorities, and, to ensure an adequate source, CSB created a county-wide data system used by all shelters. In recent years, information from the system has been used to set up an outcomes-based management system for shelters, and to develop a plan to prevent revolving-door homelessness and ensure that homeless clients are assisted into permanent housing solutions (General Accounting Office 1999). A moratorium was declared on expansion of emergency shelter accommodation, based on the premise that it, indeed, was not a solution. Existing emergency shelters took on the concrete goal of helping people achieve successful housing outcomes. Their continued funding is dependent in part on reaching established benchmarks toward this goal. Using system information to identify emergency shelter users who were least likely to return to stable housing on their own (single men), CSB developed a plan to produce and maintain 800 units of supportive housing that would meet such a desperate need (Community Shelter Board 1998). CSB has worked with the local public housing authority, the Corporation for Supportive Housing, and local nonprofit housing developers to make the plan a reality. Some units already are in operation, and demand for emergency shelter from the affected population already has begun to decline. Sadly, this progress in both thinking and acting is all too rare. It represents extensive community-wide planning, cooperation, and execution of plans to *change* the actual nature of the system of homeless assistance.

European Contrasts

Ellwood, of course, was speaking strictly in an American context. He was trying to devise an approach to helping families that would both not be "welfare" and also potentially "sell" as public policy in the United States.

This is undoubtedly a reasonable tack. But it does not challenge any American assumptions and, therefore, runs the risk of remaining stuck in existing "solutions" that do not solve the problem. As an alternative, we think some stimulus to creative thinking may come from juxtaposing the values or views that form the basis of social policy in other countries.

The social problem of homelessness is viewed quite differently in different countries. In contrast to many other developed countries, we have little, or no, concept in this country of a collective responsibility, through government, to assure everyone of a certain minimal standard of living, including housing.[2] Examining how some of the fully developed countries of Europe think about and deal with homelessness is very instructive. The particular nature of American assumptions about individual responsibility is starkly revealed when set against how other countries and cultures view the matter of who or what bears responsibility for individual well-being.

For example, "social housing" (meaning housing for which the government subsidizes rents) comprises more than 20 percent of the housing stock of Austria, Sweden, the Netherlands, and the United Kingdom, and more than 10 percent in Ireland, Finland, France, and Denmark (Daly 1999). These percentages are far higher than for the United States. Thus, in these countries, it is far more likely that people without the means to pay for their housing in whole or in part will still be housed. Most of these countries also provide universal access to publicly supported health care, and many also offer a wide variety of cash and non-cash supports for families and children, reducing the probability that paying for these necessities will absorb funds needed for housing. Under such circumstances, it is harder to lose one's housing, at least if one is a citizen or permanent resident and thus entitled to benefits. When loss of housing does happen, even with all these supports, one can truly consider individual characteristics as the last explanatory factor (Koch-Nielsen 1999; Kristensen 1999).

European discussions of the causes of homelessness, it is noteworthy, usually start from the premise that root causes are high housing cost and reduced availability, often coupled with high unemployment/low wages. Personal vulnerabilities are sometimes not mentioned at all. At other times, they follow only after housing costs and earning power have been given their due (Daly 1999; Koch-Nielson 1999; Kristensen 1999). Proposed solutions focus on supplying housing first, and then looking to compensate for individual vulnerabilities.

The Programs American Assumptions Have Created

In this country, virtually all federal programs related to homelessness focus on serving people who are already homeless. Few offer housing. This approach began under the Reagan administration, which was at some pains to focus on individual vulnerabilities, rather than structural factors, and on local rather than federal responsibility for solutions (to the extent that government action was thought necessary at all). But whether under Republican or Democratic administrations, and with both Democratic and Republican control of Congress, federal funding has continued to be restricted. Republicans have offered somewhat less money, and preferred to focus on personal problems. Democrats have offered somewhat more money, and sometimes allow the possibility of more systemic causes. But neither party has been willing to reverse the stagnation and decline in federal housing subsidies. Nor has either been willing to invest in even strictly targeted prevention. We think it essential to pursue an approach that combines the two, subsidies and targeted prevention.

In addition, both parties have assumed that federal leadership would stimulate localities to provide necessary ancillary services (as for the Shelter Plus Care program) and fund new programs, once their effectiveness had been demonstrated. Often, however, this has not happened. For example, three-fourths of the job training for the homeless demonstration programs funded under McKinney are no longer operating, because they failed to secure local funding to replace terminated federal resources. Further, a convenient myth persists that localities have adequate levels of needed homeless assistance and related services. Federal legislation admonishes, forbids duplication, and requires coordination and interagency referrals. These legislative provisions repeatedly ignore the obvious fact that *there are not enough services to go around*, even if a local system were perfectly coordinated. In particular, additions to the stock of affordable housing are few and far between, either physically or through voucher/subsidy programs. Further, many state and local governments have rushed even faster than federal actors to reduce programs or drop them entirely. The idea that devolution would put programs in the hands of state and local actors who would take up the cause and want to solve problems has been wishful thinking in many cases.

So, as noted earlier in this chapter, we need to make housing affordable, through both subsidies (e.g., to all households with worst-case housing needs) and production. After ensuring that supplies of housing are adequate, we should do everything we can to ensure that people can earn enough to afford it. For the poorest of the poor, from whom the ranks of homeless people inevitably come, this means different things for adults and children. For adults, we should be investing in literacy and education, job training, and supported work. For children, we should be making absolutely sure that their schools succeed in teaching them to read, write, calculate, think, and use computers. In addition, we need to be creating an economy in which they can see a future for themselves. We should also be thinking about how to make working pay, including an expansion of the Earned Income Tax Credit to reduce the poverty of working people, and subsidies for child care and other expenses that reduce the payoff from working. These are *general* approaches, and will obviously affect many more people than will become homeless during a year. The recommendation to ensure that the next generation of poor children has a lowered risk of homelessness is also long-term. In addition to contributing the resources to prevent homelessness among specific households, these recommendations also will strengthen the ability of remaining households to help people in their family and friendship networks who are experiencing short-term crises, and thus reduce the likelihood of widespread homelessness in the next generation.

We should take prevention seriously, in both the short and long term. Two aspects of prevention should attract policy attention. First, we should structure and invest in services to prevent homelessness among populations known to be at very high risk, as in Franklin County, Ohio. This approach can be shown to be cost-effective, if one considers costs for *all* public systems of care and support (health, mental health, chemical dependency, and corrections, as well as housing). Second, we should commit societal resources to eliminating the conditions in which people grow up that increase their vulnerability to homelessness as adults. Many of these conditions are quite clear from the research evidence. The remainder of this discussion considers these approaches in turn.

Preventing homelessness among high-risk populations could have considerable payoff. Episodically and long-term homeless individuals with severe and chronic disabilities use extensive amounts of homeless service resources, but, even so, usually remain homeless. They also repeatedly pass through and use extensive and expensive resources in other systems, including health, mental health, substance abuse, and corrections agencies (Bray, Dennis, and Lambert 1993; Robertson, Zlotnick, and Westerfelt 1997). We could, quite literally, *end homelessness for this group,* as is happening in Franklin County, Ohio, by investing in the types of supported housing arrangements that have been proven to work (Shinn and Baumohl 1999), with critical housing-related services in addition to health and mental health services. Critical housing-related services are negotiating with landlords and neighbors, handling situations in which a person's mental illness or substance abuse symptoms get out of hand, ensuring that the rent is being paid and the housing kept clean, and supplying tangible goods when necessary, such as furniture, transportation, and food (Burt 1997; Fosburg et al. 1996).

To implement this policy, each agency that routinely deals with these segments of the homeless population would have to commit resources and create service structures to ensure that no one leaves a residential treatment or corrections institution without a place to live *and* the financial and other supports necessary to keep them there. Agencies could limit such services, given scarce resources and the desirability of targeting, to people who already have had one recent homeless episode and clearly do not have the means to maintain themselves in housing without help. In addition, services located close to dwellings, such as SRO housing and boarding/lodging houses, that serve disproportionate numbers of this population (Bray, Dennis, and Lambert 1993) could reach those who currently are not institutionalized.

Above all, we do not have to think that every severely disabled homeless person is a lifelong burden on the public purse. Some people, it is true, will need long-term support, but they have conditions that *should* prompt us to offer it, such as chronic and severe mental illness. The systems with official responsibility for people with these conditions should be made to fulfill those responsibilities, with housing as the core component. For many others, including long-term substance abusers, some program experiences have shown that people can and do return to productive lives, with appropriate encouragement and support.

Another high-risk population that would benefit from serious prevention efforts is youth aging out of foster care. Many have no personal support system and little capacity to maintain themselves economically. Foster care placement is a major predictor for future homelessness. We saw in chapter 5 that the youngest homeless adults disproportionately have recent foster care experience. Chapter 6 showed that these young people probably have a future similar to that of the episodically homeless group unless significant intervention occurs. Transitional living arrangements of adequate duration, with ancillary supports and education- or work-oriented activities, could help these youth avoid future homelessness.

"Deep" prevention, in its most global interpretation, would involve eliminating the conditions of extreme childhood poverty and deprivation that are forerunners of homelessness and a variety of other ills. Focusing on today's homeless families and, especially, their children, the political commitment might be generated to take a more focused approach to "deep" prevention, although, as a society, we have consistently failed to provide the resources to pursue this ultimate objective.

It is pretty obvious that the characteristics of today's homeless families are the very characteristics that show up repeatedly in research on childhood antecedents of adult homelessness. They include histories of foster care and other out-of-home placement, physical and sexual abuse (which often precede out-of-home placement), parental substance abuse, and residential instability and homelessness with one's family as a child. Therefore, one of the most direct ways of preventing future homelessness among the children of today's homeless families is to help them achieve housing stability and, better yet, some real capacity to function independently. Remember that, over a year, these children may comprise 6 to 9 percent of poor children in this country. Thus, one could conclude that such an approach could make an appreciable dent in future homelessness, as well as in other problems associated with troubled youth. Thought about this way, the benefits of prevention for the next generation lend support to maintaining some of the most damaged families in housing, receiving cash benefits, and participating in mental health and substance abuse recovery programs until their children are grown—even if there is no expectation that the parent(s) ever will be self-sufficient. The possible benefits of success in helping homeless families might stimulate funders of research to initiate comprehensive demonstration and evaluation agendas to learn as much about how to help homeless families as we already have learned about how to help people whose chronic disabilities have led to their long-term homelessness.

Above all, our policies should not make things worse. Income support programs such as SSI, Food Stamps, and General Assistance helped some people avoid homelessness or return to stable housing. But federal and state governments began to cut these programs in the mid-1990s, by imposing time limits, restricting eligibility, or both. These cuts have continued. At first, they affected mostly single people. But the very families who were most likely to experience homelessness *while they still had Aid to Families with Dependent Children* are least likely to succeed under the strictures of federal welfare reform. They are, therefore, most likely to be sanctioned for noncompliance with state welfare regulations, to hit time limits without having achieved self-sufficiency, and to be left without cash assistance—even though they could not make it with cash assistance. As a set-up for intergenerational transmission of homelessness, this scenario is truly remarkable.

NOTES

1. These sources rely on several assumptions: A unit is "affordable" if it costs 30 percent or less of a household's earnings; a household is "struggling (low-income)" if its income is less than 30 (50) percent of the median household income in its community; the "fair market rent" is a figure that HUD calculates for jurisdictions throughout the country, based on analysis of local housing costs, and is the amount up to which a federal housing subsidy will cover. It is important to understand that these concepts are all *relative* to the community in which a person lives, not *absolute* in the manner of the federal poverty level. Thus, a household whose income qualifies it as "low-income" in one community would be classified as "struggling" if, with the same income, it lived in a community with a higher median income. And an apartment that rented for $800 a month could be well over the fair market rent in one community but under it in another. Fair market rent is as good a single-variable proxy for a community's cost of living as one is likely to find.
2. We do have Social Security for the elderly, but that is justified in the public eye as a "return on investment" and therefore earned, even though the system returns far more to the recipient than the recipient ever contributed, and also has a strong redistributive component, with low earners receiving proportionately more in relation to their input than high earners.

References

Alperstein, G., Rappaport, C., and Flanigan, J.M. 1988. "Health Problems of Homeless Children in New York City." *American Journal of Public Health* 78: 1232–1233.

Anderson, N. 1940. *Men on the Move.* Chicago: University of Chicago Press.

———. 1923. *The Hobo: The Sociology of the Homeless Man.* Chicago: University of Chicago Press. Reprinted 1975.

Arce, A., and Vergare, M. 1984. "Identifying and Characterizing the Mentally Ill among the Homeless." In *The Homeless Mentally Ill: A Task Force Report of the American Psychiatric Association,* edited by Lamb, H.R. (75–90). Washington, D.C.: American Psychiatric Association.

Avramov, D., ed. 1999. *Coping with Homelessness: Issues to Be Tackled and Best Practices in Europe.* Aldershot, UK: Ashgate.

Bahr, H.M., and Caplow, T. 1974. *Old Men: Drunk and Sober.* New York: New York University Press.

Basen-Engquist, K., Edmundson, E.W., and Parcel, G.S. 1996. "Structure of Health Risk Behavior among High School Students." *Journal of Consulting and Clinical Psychology* 64: 764–775.

Bassuk, E.L., Buckner, J.C., Weinreb, L.F., Browne, A., Bassuk, S.S., Dawson, R., and Perloff, J.N. 1997. "Homelessness in Female-Headed Families: Childhood and Adult Risk and Protective Factors." *American Journal of Public Health* 87 (2): 241–248.

Bassuk, E.L., and Rosenberg, L. 1990. "Psychosocial Characteristics of Homeless Children and Children with Homes." *Pediatrics* 85: 783–787.

Baum, A.S., and Burnes, D.W. 1993. *A Nation in Denial.* Boulder, CO: Westview Press.

Beard, J.H., Propst, R., and Malamud, T.J. 1982. "The Fountain House Model of Psychiatric Rehabilitation." *Psychosocial Rehabilitation Journal* 5 (1): 47–53.

Bogue, D.B. 1963. *Skid Row in American Cities.* Chicago: Community and Family Study Center, University of Chicago.

Bray, R.M., Dennis, M.L., and Lambert, E.Y. 1993. *Prevalence of Drug Use in the Washington, D.C., Metropolitan Area Homeless and Transient Population: 1991.* Rockville, MD: National Institute on Drug Abuse, Division of Epidemiology and Prevention Research.

Buckner, J., and Bassuk, E.L. 1997. "Mental Disorders and Service Utilization among Youths from Homeless and Low-Income Housed Families." *Journal of the American Academy of Child and Adolescent Psychiatry* 36: 508–524.

Bureau of the Census. 1997. *Statistical Abstract of the United States: 1997.* Washington, D.C.: U.S. Department of Commerce.

Burt, M.R. 1997. "Future Directions for Programs Serving the Homeless." *Understanding Homelessness: New Policy and Research Perspectives.* Washington, D.C.: Fannie Mae Foundation.

———. 1995. *Findings and Implications of RECD's Rural Homelessness Conferences.* Washington, D.C.: U.S. Department of Agriculture, Rural Economic, and Community Development Administration.

———. 1994. "Comment on Dennis P. Culhane, Edmund F. Dejowski, Julie Ibañez, Elizabeth Needham and Irene Macchia's 'Public Shelter Admission Rates in Philadelphia and New York City: The Implications of Turnover for Sheltered Population Counts.'" *Housing Policy Debate* 5 (2): 141–152.

———. 1991. "What to Look for in Studies That Try to Count the Homeless." In *Enumerating Homeless Persons: Methods and Data Needs,* edited by C. M. Taeuber. Washington, D.C.: U.S. Department of Commerce, Bureau of the Census.

Burt, M.R., and Cohen, B.E. 1989. *America's Homeless: Numbers, Characteristics, and the Programs that Serve Them.* Washington, D.C.: Urban Institute Press.

———. 1988. *Feeding the Homeless: Does the Prepared Meals Provision Work?* Washington, D.C.: Urban Institute.

Burt, M.R., and Taeuber, C.M. 1991. "Overview of Seven Studies That Counted or Estimated Homeless Populations." In *Enumerating Homeless Persons: Methods and Data Needs,* edited by C. M. Taeuber. Washington, D.C.: U.S. Department of Commerce, Bureau of the Census.

Burt, M.R., Resnick, G., and Novick, E. 1998. *Building Supportive Communities for At-Risk Adolescents: It Takes More than Services.* Washington, D.C.: American Psychological Association Press.

Burt, M.R., Aron, L.Y., Douglas, T., Valente, J., Lee, E., and Iwen, B. 1999. *Homelessness—Programs and the People They Serve: Summary and Technical Reports.* Washington, D.C.: Interagency Council on the Homeless/Department of Housing and Urban Development.

Caton, C.L.M., Shrout, P.E., Eagle, P.F., Opler, L.A., Felix, A., and Dominguez, B. 1994. "Risk Factors for Homelessness among Schizophrenic Men: A Case-Control Study." *American Journal of Public Health* 84: 265–270.

Committee on Ways and Means. 1998. *1998 Green Book: Background Material and Data on Programs within the Jurisdiction of the Committee on Ways and Means.* Washington, D.C.: U.S. House of Representatives.

Community Shelter Board. 1998. *Rebuilding Lives.* Columbus, OH: Author.

Crouse, J.M. 1986. *The Homeless Transient in the Great Depression: New York State, 1929–1941.* Albany, NY: SUNY Press.

Culhane, D.P. 1992. "The Quandaries of Shelter Reform: An Appraisal of Efforts to 'Manage' Homelessness." *Social Service Review* 66 (3): 428–440.

Culhane, D.P., and Kuhn, R. 1998. "Patterns and Determinants of Shelter Utilization among Single Adults in New York City and Philadelphia." *Journal of Policy Analysis and Management* 17 (1): 23–43.

Culhane, D.P., Dejowski, E., Ibañez, J., Needham, E., and Macchia, I. 1994. "Public Shelter Admission Rates in Philadelphia and New York City: Implications for Sheltered Population Counts." *Housing Policy Debate* 5 (2): 107–140.

Daly, M. 1999. "Regimes of Social Policy in Europe and the Patterning of Homelessness." In *Coping with Homelessness: Issues to Be Tackled and Best Practices in Europe*, edited by Avramov, D. (Chapter 14). Aldershot, UK: Ashgate.

Dennis, M.L., Bray, R.M., Iachan, R., and Thornberry, J. 1999. "Drug Use and Homelessness." In *Drug Use in Metropolitan America*, edited by R.M. Bray and M.E. Marsden (Chapter 4). Thousand Oaks, CA: Sage Publications.

Dennis, M.L., and McGeary, K.A. 1998. "Adolescent Alcohol and Marijuana Treatment: Kids Need It Now." *SCAT's TIE Communique Newsletter.* Rockville, MD: SAMSHA.

Department of Housing and Urban Development. 2000. *Rental Housing Assistance—The Worsening Crisis. A Report to Congress on Worst-Case Housing Needs.* Washington, D.C.: Office of Policy Development and Research.

———. 1999. *The Widening Gap: New Findings on Housing Affordability in America.* Washington, D.C.: Office of Policy Development and Research.

———. 1989. *A Report on the 1988 National Survey of Shelters for the Homeless.* Washington, D.C.: Office of Policy Development and Research.

Dolbeare, C. 1999. *Out of Reach: The Gap between Housing Cost and Income of Poor People in the United States.* Washington, D.C.: National Low Income Housing Coalition.

Eisinger, P. 1998. *Toward an End to Hunger in America.* Washington, D.C.: Brookings Press.

Ellwood, David T. 1996. *Poor Support.* Boston: Harvard University Press.

English, D.J. 1998. "The Extent and Consequences of Child Maltreatment." *The Future of Children, Protecting Children from Abuse and Neglect* 8 (1).

First, R.J., Toomey, B.G., Rife, J.C., and Stasny, E.A. 1994. *Outside of the City: A Statewide Study of Homelessness in Nonurban/Rural Areas.* Final report for NIMH Grant # RO1MH46111. Columbus, OH: College of Social Work, The Ohio State University.

Fosburg, Linda B., and Dennis, Deborah L., eds. 1999. *Practical Lessons: The 1998 National Symposium on Homeless Research.* Washington, D.C.: U.S. Department of Housing and Urban Development and U.S. Department of Health and Human Services.

Fosburg, L., Locke, G., Peck, L., and Finkel, M. 1996. *National Evaluation of the Shelter Plus Care Program.* Cambridge, MA: Abt Associates.

Foscarinis, M. 1996. "The Federal Response: The Stewart B. McKinney Homeless Assistance Act." In *Homelessness in America*, edited by Baumohl, J. (Chapter 15). Phoenix, AZ: Oryx Press.

Fureman, B., Parikh, G., Bragg, A., and McLellan, A.T. 1990. *Addiction Severity Index: Fifth Edition*. Philadelphia, PA: University of Pennsylvania/Veterans Administration Center for Studies of Addiction.

Garfinkel, I., and Piliavin, I. 1994. *Trends in the Size of the Nation's Homeless Population in the 1980s: A Surprising Result.* Madison, WI: Institute for Research on Poverty. Discussion Paper 1034–1094.

General Accounting Office. 1999. *Integrating and Evaluating Homeless Assistance Programs.* Washington, D.C.: Government Printing Office.

Herman, D.B., Susser, E.S., Struening, E.L., and Link, B.L. 1997. "Adverse Childhood Experiences: Are They Risk Factors for Adult Homelessness?" *American Journal of Public Health* 87 (2): 249–255.

Hoch, C.A., and Slayton, R.A. 1989. *New Homeless and Old: Community and the Skid Row Hotel.* Philadelphia: Temple University Press.

Hopper, K. 1991. "Homelessness Old and New: The Matter of Definition." *Housing Policy Debate* 2 (3): 757–814.

Hopper, K., and Baumohl, J. 1996. "Redefining the Cursed Word: A Historical Interpretation of American Homelessness." In *Homelessness in America,* edited by Baumohl, J. (Chapter 1). Phoenix, AZ: Oryx Press.

———. 1994. "Held in Abeyance: Rethinking Homelessness and Advocacy." *American Behavioral Scientist* 37: 522–525.

Hopper, K., Jost, J., Hay, T., Welber, S., and Haugland, G. 1997. "Homelessness, Severe Mental Illness, and the Institutional Circuit." *Psychiatric Services* 48 (5): 659–665.

HUD. *See* Department of Housing and Urban Development.

Humphreys, K., and Rosenheck, R. 1995. "Sequential Validation of Cluster Analytic Subtypes of Homeless Veterans." *American Journal of Community Psychology* 23: 75–98.

Institute of Medicine, Committee on Health Care for Homeless People. 1988. *Homelessness, Health, and Human Needs.* Washington, D.C.: National Academy Press.

Kentucky Housing Corporation. 1993. *Kentucky Homeless Survey Preliminary Findings.* Lexington, KY: Kentucky Housing Corporation.

Knox, V., Miller, C., and Gennetian, L.A. 2000. *Reforming Welfare and Rewarding Work: The Final Report on the Minnesota Family Investment Program.* New York: Manpower Demonstration Research Corporation.

Koegel, P., Burnam, M.A., and Baumohl, J. 1996. "The Causes of Homelessness." In *Homelessness in America,* edited by Baumohl, J. (Chapter 3). Phoenix, AZ: Oryx Press.

Koegel, P., Melamid, E., and Burnam, M.A. 1995. "Childhood Risk Factors for Homelessness among Homeless Adults." *American Journal of Public Health* 85 (12): 1642–1649.

Kuhn, R., and Culhane, D.P. 1998. "Applying Cluster Analysis to Test a Typology of Homelessness by Patterns of Shelter Utilization: Results from the Analysis of Administrative Data." *American Journal of Community Psychology* 12 (2): 207–232.

Jencks, C. 1994. *The Homeless.* Cambridge, MA: Harvard University Press.

Koch-Nielsen, I. 1999. "Conclusions and Policy Implications." In *Coping with Homelessness: Issues to Be Tackled and Best Practices in Europe,* edited by Avramov, D. (Chapter 18). Aldershot, UK: Ashgate.

Kristensen, H. 1999. "Housing Policy and Homelessness: The Danish Case." In *Coping with Homelessness: Issues to Be Tackled and Best Practices in Europe,* edited by Avramov, D. (Chapter 16). Aldershot, UK: Ashgate.

Lamison-White, L. 1997. *Poverty in the United States: 1996.* Series P60–198. Washington, D.C.: Department of Commerce.

Lindberg, L.D., Boggess, S., and Williams, S. 2000. "Multiple Threats: The Co-Occurrence of Teen Health Risk Behaviors." In *Trends in the Well-Being of America's Children and Youth: 2000.* Washington, D.C.: Office of the Assistant Secretary for Planning and Evaluation, Department of Health and Human Services.

Link, B. Phelan, J., Bresnahan, M., Stueve, A., Moore, R., and Susser, E. 1995. "Lifetime and Five-Year Prevalence of Homelessness in the United States: New Evidence on an Old Debate." *American Journal of Orthopsychiatry* 65 (3): 347–354.

Link, B., Susser, E., Stueve, A., Phelan, J., Moore, R., and Struening, E. 1994. "Lifetime and Five-Year Prevalence of Homelessness in the United States." *American Journal of Public Health* 84: 1907–1912.

Mangine, S.J., Royse, D., and Wiehe, V.R. 1990. "Homelessness among Adults Raised as Foster Children: A Survey of Drop-In Center Users." *Psychological Reports* 67: 739–745.

McAllister, W., and Berlin, G. 1994. "Prevention and Population Dynamics: One Works, the Other Doesn't." Paper presented at the Association for Public Policy Analysis and Management Annual Conference, October 27–29.

Milofsky, C., Butto, A., Gross, M., and Baumohl, J. 1993. "Small Town in Mass Society: Substance Abuse Treatment and Urban-Rural Migration." *Contemporary Drug Problems* 20 (3): 433–470.

Molnar, J., and Rath, W. 1990. "Constantly Compromised: The Impact of Homelessness in Children." *Journal of Social Issues* 46: 109–124.

Oakley, D., and Dennis, D.L. 1996. "Responding to the Needs of Homeless People with Alcohol, Drug, and/or Mental Disorders." In *Homelessness in America,* edited by Baumohl, J. (Chapter 17). Phoenix, AZ: Oryx Press.

Office of Applied Studies, SAMSHA. 1997. *Methodological Sourcebook, 1996.* Rockville, MD: U.S. Department of Health and Human Services, Public Health Service.

Office of Juvenile Justice Programs. 1995. *Delinquency Prevention Works.* Washington, D.C.: U.S. Department of Justice.

Ohls, J., and Saleem-Ismail, F. 2000. "Providing Food for the Poor: Findings from the Provider Survey of the Emergency Food System Study." Draft Report. Princeton, NJ: Mathematica Policy Research.

Parker, R., Rescorla, L., Finklestein, J.A., Barnes, N., Holmes, J.H., and Stolley, P.D. 1991. "A Survey of the Health of Homeless Children in Philadelphia Shelters." *American Journal of Adolescent and Child Psychiatry* 145: 520–526.

Piliavin, I., Wright, B.R.E., Mare, R.D., and Westerfelt, H. 1996. "Exits from and Returns to Homelessness." *Social Service Review* 70 (N1): 33–57.

Piliavin, I., Sosin, M., and Westerfelt, A.H. 1993. "The Duration of Homeless Careers: An Exploratory Study." *Social Service Review* 67: 576–598.

Rafferty, Y., and Shinn, M. 1991. "The Impact of Homelessness on Children." *American Psychologist* 46: 1170–1179.

Resnick, M.D., Harris, L.J., and Blum, R.W. 1993. "The Impact of Caring and Connectedness on Adolescent Health and Well-Being." *Journal of Paediatrics and Child Health* 29 (Suppl. 1): S3–S9.

Ringwalt, C.L., Greene, J.M., Robertson, M.J., and McPheeters, M. 1998. "The Prevalence of Homelessness among Adolescents in the United States." *American Journal of Public Health* 88: 1325–1329.

Robertson, M.J., and Toro, P.T. 1999. "Homeless Youth: Research, Intervention, and Policy." In *Practical Lessons: The 1998 National Symposium on Homelessness Research,* edited by Fosburg, L.B., and Dennis, D.L. Washington, D.C.: U.S. Departments of Housing and Urban Development and Health and Human Services.

Robertson, M.J., Zlotnick, C., and Westerfelt, A. 1997. "Drug Use Disorders and Treatment Contact among Homeless Adults in Alameda County, California." *American Journal of Public Health* 87 (2): 217–220.

Rosenheck, R.A., Bassuk, E.L., and Salomon, A. 1999. "Special Populations of Homeless Americans." In *Practical Lessons: The 1998 National Symposium on Homelessness Research,* edited by Fosburg, L.B., and Dennis, D.L. Washington, D.C.: U.S. Departments of Housing and Urban Development and Health and Human Services.

Rossi, P.H. 1989. *Down and Out in America: The Origins of Homelessness.* Chicago: University of Chicago Press.

Rossi, P.H., Fisher, G.A., and Willis, G. 1986. *The Condition of the Homeless in Chicago.* Amherst, MA: Social and Demographic Research Institute, University of Massachusetts; Chicago: National Opinion Research Center.

Royse, D., and Wiehe, V.R. 1989. "Assessing the Effects of Foster Care on Adults Raised as Foster Children: A Methodological Issue." *Psychological Reports* 64: 677–678.

SMS Research. 1990. *Hawaii's Homeless.* Honolulu, HI: Author.

Second Harvest. 1997. *Hunger 1997: The Faces and Facts.* Chicago: Author.

Shern, D.L., Felton, C.J., Hough, R.L., Lehman, A.F., Goldfinger, S., Valencia, E., Dennis, D., Straw, R., and Wood, P.A. 1997. "Housing Outcomes for Homeless Adults with Mental Illness: Results from the Second-Round McKinney Program." *Psychiatric Services* 48: 239–241.

Shinn, M., and Baumohl, J. 1999. "Rethinking the Prevention of Homelessness." In *Practical Lessons: The 1998 National Symposium on Homelessness Research,* edited by Fosburg, L.B., and Dennis, D.L. Washington, D.C.: U.S. Departments of Housing and Urban Development and Health and Human Services.

Shinn, M., Weitzman, B.C., Stojanovic, D., Knickman, J.R., Jimenez, L., Duchon, L., James, S., and Krantz, D.H. 1998. "Predictors of Homelessness among Families in New York City: From Shelter Request to Housing Stability." *American Journal of Public Health* 88: 1651–1657.

Simpson, G.A., and Fowler, M.G. 1994. "Geographic Mobility and Children's Emotional/Behavioral Adjustment and School Functioning." *Pediatrics* 93: 303–309.

Substance Abuse and Mental Health Services Administration. 1998. *NHSDA Public Release Codebook, 1996.* Rockville, MD: U.S. Department of Health and Human Services, Public Health Service.

Susser, E.S., Struening, E.L., and Conover, S.A. 1987. "Childhood Experiences of Homeless Men." *American Journal of Psychiatry* 144: 1599–1601.

Susser, E.S., Lin, S.P., Conover, S.A., and Struening, E.L. 1991. "Childhood Antecedents of Homelessness in Psychiatric Patients." *American Journal of Psychiatry* 148: 1026–1030.

Torrey, E.F. 1989. *Nowhere to Go: The Tragic Odyssey of the Homeless Mentally Ill.* New York: Harper and Row.

Uccello, C.E., McCallum, H.R., and Gallagher, L.J. 1996. *State General Assistance Programs, 1996.* Washington, D.C.: Urban Institute, *Assessing the New Federalism.*

Vernez, G., Burnam, M.A., McGlynn, E.A., Trude, S., and Mittman, B. 1988. *Review of California's Program for the Homeless Mentally Disabled.* Santa Monica, CA: The RAND Corporation.

Watson, V. 1996. "Responses by the States to Homelessness." In *Homelessness in America,* edited by Baumohl, J. (Chapter 16). Phoenix, AZ: Oryx Press.

Weinreb, L., Goldberg, R., Bassuk, E., and Perloff, J. 1998. "Determinants of Health and Service Use Patterns in Homeless and Low-Income Housed Children." *Pediatrics* 102 (3, part 1): 554–562.

Weitzman, B.C., Knickman, J.R., and Shinn, M. 1992. "Predictors of Shelter Use among Low-Income Families: Psychiatric History, Substance Abuse, and Victimization." *American Journal of Public Health* 82: 1547–1550.

White, R.W. 1992. *Rude Awakenings.* San Francisco: ICS Press.

Wigton, A., and D'Orio, D. 1999. "Income and Hardship: Affordability of Housing." *Snapshots of America's Families.* Washington, D.C.: Urban Institute, *Assessing the New Federalism.*

Wiseman, J.P. 1970. *Stations of the Lost: the Treatment of Skid Row Alcoholics.* Englewood Cliffs, N.J.: Prentice-Hall.

Wong, Y.I., and Piliavin, I. 1997. "A Dynamic Analysis of Homeless-Domicile Transitions." *Social Problems* 44 (3): 408–423.

Wood, D.L., Halfon, N., Scarlata, D., Newacheck, P., and Nessim, S. 1993. "Impact of Family Relocation on Children's Growth, Development, School Function, and Behavior." *Journal of the American Medical Association* 270 (11): 1334–1338.

Wood, D., Valdez, R.B., Hayashi, T., and Shen, A. 1990. "Homeless and Housed Families in Los Angeles: A Study Comparing Demographic, Economic, and Family Function Characteristics." *American Journal of Public Health* 80: 1049–1052.

Zanis, D.A., McLellan, A.T., Cnaan, R.A., and Randall, M. 1994. "Reliability and Validity of the Addiction Severity Index with a Homeless Sample." *Journal of Substance Abuse Treatment* 2: 541–548.

Ziesemer, C., Marcoux, L., and Marwell, B.E. 1994. "Homeless Children: Are They Different from Other Low-Income Children?" *Social Work* 39: 658–668.

Zima, B.T., Wells, K.B., and Freeman, H.E. 1994. "Emotional and Behavioral Problems and Severe Academic Delays among Sheltered Homeless Children in Los Angeles County." *American Journal of Public Health* 84: 260–264.

Zlotnick, C., Robertson, M.J., and Lahiff, M. 1999. "Getting Off the Streets: Economic Resources and Residential Exits from Homelessness." *Journal of Community Psychology* 27 (2): 209–224.

Zweig, J., Lindberg, L.D., and Alexander, K. 2000. "Adolescent Profiles of Risk: The Co-Occurrence of Risk Behaviors for Males and Females." Washington, D.C.: Urban Institute. Prepared for the Office of the Assistant Secretary for Planning and Evaluation, Department of Health and Human Services.

Appendix

NSHAPC DESIGN

Sample Design

NSHAPC was designed to provide nationally representative samples of homeless and other people who use homeless assistance programs, and of the programs themselves.[1] The study drew information from programs and their clients in 76 primary sampling areas, listed in the box on page 345. The 76 areas were chosen to include:

- The 28 largest metropolitan statistical areas (MSAs) in the United States;
- 24 small and medium-sized MSAs, selected at random to be representative of geographical region (northeast, south, midwest, west) and size;
- 24 rural areas (groups of counties), selected at random from a sampling frame defined as the catchment areas of Community Action Agencies, and representative of geographical regions. In New England, the actual areas sampled were parts of counties.

Data Collection

The study began by identifying and collecting information about *all* the programs within each of the 76 primary sampling areas that met its definition of a homeless assistance program. Such programs had to *have a focus* on serving homeless people (although they did not have to serve homeless people exclusively). They also had to offer direct service, and be within the geographical boundaries of the sampling area. In rural areas, the study's definition of a program was expanded to include programs that *served* homeless people but may not have had this population as a focus. Sixteen types of homeless assistance programs were defined:[2]

- Emergency shelters
- Transitional housing programs
- Permanent housing programs
- Programs distributing vouchers to obtain emergency accommodation
- Programs accepting vouchers in exchange for giving emergency accommodation
- Food pantries
- Soup kitchens
- Mobile food programs
- Physical health care programs
- Mental health programs
- Alcohol/drug programs
- HIV/AIDS programs
- Outreach programs
- Drop-in centers
- Migrant labor camps used to provide emergency shelter for homeless people
- Other programs

NSHAPC's Primary Sampling Areas

28 Largest Metropolitan Areas

- Atlanta, GA
- Baltimore, MD
- Boston, MA–NH
- Chicago, IL
- Cleveland–Lorain–Elyria, OH
- Dallas, TX
- Denver, CO
- Detroit, MI
- Houston, TX
- Kansas City, MO–KS
- Los Angeles–Long Beach, CA
- Miami, FL
- Minneapolis–St. Paul, MN–WI
- Nassau–Suffolk, NY
- New York, NY
- Newark, NJ
- Oakland, CA
- Orange County, CA
- Philadelphia, PA–NJ
- Phoenix–Mesa, AZ
- Pittsburgh, PA
- Riverside–San Bernardino, CA
- St. Louis, MO–IL
- San Diego, CA
- San Francisco, CA
- Seattle–Bellevue–Everett, WA
- Tampa–St. Petersburg–Clearwater, FL
- Washington, DC–MD–VA–WV

24 Smaller Metropolitan Areas

- Bangor, ME
- Bergen–Passaic, NJ
- Birmingham, AL
- Boise City, ID
- Bremerton, WA
- Dover, DE
- Enid, OK
- Indianapolis, IN
- Jackson, MI
- Kenosha, WI
- Las Cruces, NM
- Lincoln, NE
- Melbourne–Titusville–Palm Bay, FL
- Norfolk–Virginia Beach–Newport News, VA–NC
- Oklahoma City, OK
- Redding, CA
- Sacramento, CA
- Salt Lake City–Ogden, UT
- Savannah, GA
- Shreveport–Bossier City, LA
- Springfield, MA
- Utica–Rome, NY
- York, PA
- Youngstown–Warren, OH

NSHAPC's Primary Sampling Areas (*Continued*)

24 Rural Areas (Non-Metropolitan Areas)

- Lassen County, Modoc County, CA
- Chester town, Deep River town, Essex town, Lyme town, Westbrook town, CT
- Bradford County, Columbia County, Dixie County, Hamilton County, Lafayette County, Madison County, Suwannee County, Taylor County, Union County, FL
- Crisp County, Dooly County, Macon County, Marion County, Schley County, Sumter County, Taylor County, Webster County, GA
- Christian County, Clay County, Effingham County, Fayette County, Montgomery County, Moultrie County, Shelby County, IL
- Buena Vista County, Clay County, Dickinson County, Emmet County, O'Brien County, Osceola County, Palo Alto County, Pocahontas County, IA
- Bath County, Menifee County, Montgomery County, Morgan County, Rowan County, KY
- Union Parish, LA
- Caldwell County, Daviess County, Grundy County, Harrison County, Linn County, Livingston County, Mercer County, Putnam County, Sullivan County, MO
- Hall County, Hamilton County, Merrick County, NE
- Esmeralda County, Mineral County, NV
- Chaves County, Lea County, NM
- Cibola County, McKinley County, NM
- Iredell County, NC
- Hancock County, Hardin County, Putnam County, Wyandot County, OH
- Haskell County, Latimer County, Le Flore County, Pittsburg County, OK
- Douglas County, OR
- Bedford County, Fulton County, Huntingdon County, Juniata County, Mifflin County, PA
- Abbeville County, Greenwood County, Laurens County, McCormick County, Newberry County, Saluda County, SC
- Houston County, Humphreys County, Stewart County, TN
- Aransas County, Bee County, Live Oak County, Refugio County, TX
- Accomack County, Northampton County, VA
- Burnett County, Clark County, Rusk County, Sawyer County, Taylor County, Washburn County, WI
- Johnson County, Sheridan County, WY

The study collected information in three ways:

HOMELESS ASSISTANCE PROGRAMS—BASIC DESCRIPTION

- *Telephone interviews with representatives of 6,307 service locations offering 11,983 homeless assistance programs.*
  - A **service location** is the physical location at which one or more programs operate.
  - A **homeless assistance program** is a set of services offered to the same group of people at a single location and focused on serving homeless persons as an intended population (although not always the only population).
  - Program directors or other staff knowledgeable about the program(s) offered at a particular location were interviewed by telephone. Basic descriptions of all homeless assistance programs offered at that location were obtained.

**HOMELESS ASSISTANCE PROGRAMS—
DETAILED INFORMATION ABOUT SERVICES**

- *Mail surveys from 5,694 programs.*
  - Surveys were completed by a staff person who knew the program and its clients well. Detailed information was collected about client needs, the extent to which these needs were met, and whether services to meet these needs were available at their own program or other programs in the community.
  - A **service** is any good or activity offered to people using a *program,* but not qualifying on its own as a *program.*

CLIENTS OF HOMELESS ASSISTANCE PROGRAMS

- *Client interviews with 4,207 clients.*
  - A ***client*** is someone who uses a *program,* whether he or she is homeless or not. Interviews were conducted with clients of any age as long as they were *not* accompanied by a parent or guardian. Virtually all clients interviewed were adults; fewer than 1 percent were age 17, with the rest being 18 or older.
  - In each sampling area, the study selected a sample of the programs identified through the telephone interviews, taking into consideration program type and program size. Interviews with clients were conducted during each of about 700 program visits. Census Bureau staff worked with the programs selected to establish the best times

and methods to select and interview clients, and methods to pay clients once interviews were completed. The programs handled these payments.

- Six to eight clients were selected randomly from among all clients using the program at the time of data collection. They were interviewed in person by trained interviewers from the Census Bureau. Most interviews took place at the program location. Clients selected through outreach programs or programs operating in the evening or at night were sometimes interviewed the next day at locations arranged in advance. Every effort was made to ensure privacy during the interview. Clients completing the interview received $10 for their time.

Definitions

Definitions of NSHAPC Programs

A **program** was defined for NSHAPC as a set of services offered to the same group of people at a single location. To be considered a program, a provider had to offer services or assistance that were managed or administered by the agency (i.e., the agency provides the staff and funding); designed to accomplish a particular mission or goal; offered on an ongoing basis; focused on homeless persons as an intended population (although not always the only population); and not limited to referrals or administrative functions.

This definition of "program" was used in metropolitan areas. However, because rural areas often lack homeless-specific services, the definition was expanded in rural areas to include agencies serving some homeless people even if this was not a focus of the agency. About one-fourth of the rural programs in NSHAPC were included as a result of this expanded definition.

NSHAPC covered 16 types of homeless assistance programs, defined as follows:

Emergency shelter programs provide short-term housing on a first-come first-served basis, where people must leave in the morning and have no guaranteed bed for the next night, OR provide beds for a specified period of time, regardless of whether or not people leave the building. Facilities that provide temporary shelter during extremely cold weather (such as churches) and emergency shelters or host homes for runaway or neglected children and youth and victims of domestic violence were also included.

Transitional housing programs allow clients to stay a maximum of two years and offer support services to promote self-sufficiency and to help clients obtain permanent housing. These programs may target any homeless subpopulation, such as persons with mental illnesses or AIDS, runaway youths, victims of domestic violence, homeless veterans, etc.

Permanent housing programs for homeless people provide long-term housing assistance with support services for which homelessness is a primary requirement for program eligibility. Examples include the Shelter Plus Care Program, the Section 8 Moderate Rehabilitation Program for Single-Room Occupancy (SRO) Dwellings, and the Permanent Housing for the Handicapped Homeless Program administered by the Department of Housing and Urban Development (HUD). These programs also include specific set-asides of assisted housing units or housing vouchers for homeless persons by public housing agencies or others as a matter of policy or in connection with a specific program (e.g., the HUD-VA Supported Housing Program, "HUD-VASH"). A permanent housing program for homeless people does NOT include public housing, Section 8, or federal, state, or local housing assistance programs for low-income persons that do not include a specific set-aside for homeless persons, or for which homelessness is not a basic eligibility requirement.

Voucher distribution programs provide homeless persons with a voucher, certificate, or coupon that can be redeemed to pay for a specific amount of time in a hotel, motel, or other similar facility.

Programs that accept vouchers for temporary accommodation provide homeless persons with accommodation, usually in a hotel, motel, board-and-care, or other for-profit facility, in exchange for a voucher, certificate, or coupon offered by a homeless assistance program.

Food pantry programs are programs that distribute uncooked food in boxes or bags directly to low-income people, including homeless people.

Soup kitchen programs include soup kitchens, food lines, and programs distributing prepared breakfasts, lunches, or dinners. These programs may be organized as food service lines, bag or box lunches, or tables where people are seated, then served by program personnel. These programs may or may not have a place to sit and eat the meal.

Mobile food programs are programs that visit designated street locations for the primary purpose of providing food to homeless people.

Physical health care programs provide health care to homeless persons, including health screenings, immunizations, treatment for acute health problems, and other services that address physical health issues. Services are often provided in shelters, soup kitchens, or other programs frequented by homeless people.

Mental health care programs provide services for homeless persons to improve their mental or psychological health or their ability to function well on a day-to-day basis. Specific services may include case management, assertive community treatment, intervention or hospitalization during a moment of crisis, counseling, psychotherapy, psychiatric services, and psychiatric medication monitoring.

Alcohol/drug programs provide services to assist homeless individuals to reduce their level of alcohol or other drug addiction, or to prevent substance abuse among homeless persons. Such programs may include services such as detoxification services, sobering facilities, rehabilitation programs, counseling, treatment, and prevention and education services.

HIV/AIDS programs provide services for homeless persons where the services provided specifically respond to the fact that clients have HIV/AIDS or are at risk of getting HIV/AIDS. Services may include health assessment; adult day care; nutritional services; medications; intensive medical care when required; health, mental health, and substance abuse services; referral to other benefits and services; and HIV/AIDS prevention and education services.

Drop-in center programs provide daytime services primarily for homeless persons, such as television, laundry facilities, showers, support groups, and service referrals, but do not provide overnight accommodations.

Outreach programs contact homeless persons in settings such as on the streets, in subways, under bridges, and in parks to offer food, blankets, or other necessities; to assess needs and attempt to engage them in services; to offer medical, mental health, and/or substance abuse services; and/or to offer other assistance on a regular basis (at least once a week) for the purpose of improving their health, mental health, or social functioning, or increasing their use of human services and resources. Services may be provided during the day or at night.

Migrant housing is housing that is seasonally occupied by migrating farm workers. During off-season periods it may be vacant and available for use by homeless persons.

Other programs: Providers could describe other programs they offered, as long as the programs met the basic NSHAPC definition of a homeless assistance program. Types of programs actually identified through the survey include housing/financial assistance (e.g., from Community Action, county welfare, or housing agencies); Emergency Food and Shelter Program agencies; job training for the homeless, clothing distribution, and other programs.

Definitions Used with the Client Data

DEFINING HOMELESS STATUS. Because NSHAPC sampled all clients of homeless assistance programs, whether homeless or not, it was necessary to classify clients as currently, formerly, or never homeless based on the answers they gave to survey questions. The following specific conditions were used to classify clients as ***currently homeless***:

- The client stayed in any of the following places on the day of the survey or during the seven-day period prior to being interviewed for NSHAPC:
  1. An emergency or transitional shelter, or
  2. A hotel or motel paid for by a shelter voucher, or
  3. An abandoned building, a place of business, a car or other vehicle, or anywhere outside.
- Or:
  4. Reported that the last time they had "a place of [their] own for 30 days or more in the same place" was more than seven days ago, or
  5. Said their last period of homelessness ended within the last seven days, or
  6. Were identified for inclusion in the NSHAPC client survey at an emergency shelter or transitional housing program, or
  7. Reported getting food from "the shelter where you live" within the last seven days, or
  8. On the day of the interview, said they stayed in their own or someone else's place but that they "could not sleep there for the next month without being asked to leave."

Use of the first criterion (shelter use) classifies 34.9 percent of the sample as currently homeless. Criteria two (voucher use) and three (places not meant for habitation) add 1.7 percent and 10.0 percent, respectively, for a total of 46.4 percent. The five remaining criteria together add another 7.1 percent, for a final total of 53.5 percent of the sample classified as currently homeless. All but the final criterion meet the McKinney Act definition of homelessness; the last criterion adds only 0.3 percentage points to the final proportion classified as currently homeless, and was included because the survey itself treats clients in this situation as homeless.

Many clients who were not literally homeless reported having been homeless at some earlier time in their lives (22 percent of the sample). The circumstances used to classify clients as formerly homeless also meet the McKinney Act definition of homelessness. Clients were classified as ***formerly homeless*** if they:

- Did not meet any of the conditions qualifying them as currently homeless but at some point in their lives had stayed in any of the following:
  1. An emergency or transitional shelter, or
  2. A welfare/voucher hotel, or
  3. An abandoned building, a place of business, a car/other vehicle, or anywhere outside, or
  4. A permanent housing program for the formerly homeless, or
- Said they had previously had a period when they were without regular housing.

The remaining 24 percent of NSHAPC clients had never been homeless at the time of the survey, according to the criteria used here, and also said they had never been homeless. They are referred to throughout this book as ***never homeless***.

DEFINING FAMILY STATUS. Family statuses used in chapter 3 include:

- "Clients with children" = clients who reported that at least one of their own minor children was living with them;
- "Single clients" = clients who reported that they were alone;

- "Other clients" = clients who reported being with one or more persons, none of whom were their own minor children.

In chapters other than chapter 3, statistics are often reported for the proportion of different subgroups who are "in a homeless family." This is equivalent to "clients with children."

DEFINING URBAN/RURAL STATUS. A number of analyses focus on the geographic location where clients were found, including central cities, suburban and urban fringe areas, and rural areas. In these analyses, *central cities* were defined as the main or primary cities of metropolitan statistical areas (MSAs). *Suburban and urban fringe areas* were defined as what is left of MSAs after taking out the central cities, and may include smaller cities, suburbs, towns, and even open land if it is in the counties making up the MSA. *Rural areas* were defined as all areas outside of MSAs, and may include small cities (under 50,000), towns, villages, and open land.

DEFINING ALCOHOL/DRUG/MENTAL HEALTH STATUS. Responses to relevant NSHAPC questions were combined to create three variables each for alcohol problems, drug problems, and mental health problems. The three variables reflect different time periods during which a client might have had the problem: within the 30 days before being interviewed for NSHAPC (past month), within the year before the interview (past year), and in the person's whole lifetime (lifetime). Presence of each problem within the three time periods was defined as follows.

> Clients were classified as having a ***past-month alcohol use problem*** if *any* of the following conditions were met: (1) they scored 0.17 or higher on a modified Addiction Severity Index[3] (ASI) measure, (2) they reported drinking to get drunk three or more times a week within the past month, (3) they reported being treated for alcohol abuse within the past month, or (4) they reported ever having been treated for alcohol abuse *and* drinking three or more times a week within the past month. Clients were classified as having a ***past-year alcohol use problem*** if they met these same criteria within the past year (including the past month), and as having a ***lifetime alcohol use problem*** if they met these same criteria in their lifetime or if they

reported ever having had three or more of the following eight alcohol-related difficulties at some time in their lives: passing out, blackouts, tremors, convulsions, not being able to stop drinking when you wanted to, problems with close family members due to drinking, arrests because of behavior due to drinking, and attending an Alcoholics Anonymous meeting.

Clients were classified as having a ***past-month drug use problem*** if *any* of the following conditions were met: (1) they scored 0.10 or higher on a modified ASI measure, (2) they reported being treated for drug abuse within the past month, (3) they reported using drugs intravenously (shooting up), or (4) they reported using any of the usual variety of specific illicit drugs three or more times a week within the past month. Clients were classified as having a ***past-year drug use problem*** if they met these same criteria within the past year (including the past month), and as having a ***lifetime drug use problem*** if they met these same criteria in their lifetime or if they reported three or more of the following eight drug-related problems at some time in their lives: using more than one drug at a time, blackouts or flashbacks, had friends or relatives know or suspect you of using drugs, lost friends because of your drug use, neglected family or missed work because of drug use, had withdrawal symptoms, engaged in illegal activities to get money for drugs, or had medical problems as a result of drug use (e.g., hepatitis, convulsions, bleeding).

Clients were classified as having a ***past-month mental health problem*** if *any* of the following conditions were met: (1) they scored 0.25 or higher on a modified *Addiction Severity Index (ASI)* measure, (2) they reported receiving treatment or counseling or being hospitalized for emotional or mental problems within the past month, (3) they reported on the ASI taking prescribed medications for psychological or emotional problems within the past month, (4) they reported that a mental health condition was the single most important thing keeping them from getting out of homelessness, or (5) they reported receiving treatment or counseling or being hospitalized for emotional or mental problems at some point in their lives *and* having one or more of the ASI's seven emotional or psychological conditions within the past month (serious depression; serious anxiety or tension; hallucinations; trouble understanding, concentrating, or remembering; trouble controlling violent behavior; serious thoughts of suicide; attempted suicide).[4] Clients were classified as having a ***past-year***

mental health problem if they met these same criteria within the past year (including the past month), and as having a ***lifetime mental health problem*** if they met these same criteria in their lifetime or if they reported ever having stayed in an adult group home, crisis residence, or other housing for the mentally ill.

SPECIFYING TIME FRAMES. For clients, all time periods referred to in this book are in relation to the day a client was interviewed for the study (between October 18 and November 14, 1996). Thus "past week" or "past seven days" refers to the week before the interview; "past month" or "past 30 days" refers to the month before the interview; and "past year" refers to the year before the interview. "Lifetime" refers to the client's life up to the time of the interview. For homeless assistance programs, the time frame is "an average week in February 1996."

NOTES

1. A full treatment of study methodology may be found in Burt et al., *Homelessness—Programs and the People They Serve: Technical Report, Appendixes A to E.*
2. Full program definitions appear later in this appendix under "Definitions."
3. The Addiction Severity Index is an instrument developed by the National Institute on Drug Abuse (Fureman, Parikh, Bragg, and McLellan 1990). Its subscales measure a client's level of problems with alcohol, drugs, and mental or emotional problems. Cutoff levels used here are slight modifications of the means reported in Zanis, McLellan, Cnaan, and Randall (1994). For alcohol and drugs, the ASI measures amount and recency of use. For mental health it measures the eight items reported in the text. For both, it measures self-reported level of problems with use/disturbance at symptoms, and desire for treatment.
4. The eighth ASI item, "taking prescribed medications for psychological or emotional problems," was a criterion in its own right (criterion 3) for classifying a client as having a mental health problem.

Index

Addiction Severity Index (ASI), 100–101, 134n2, 354
age, 173. *See also* children; homeless clients, young adult
  at which clients were first without regular housing/place to stay, 172
Aid to Families with Dependent Children (AFDC), 74, 78, 119, 200. *See also* welfare
alcohol, drug, and mental health (ADM) problems, 97–100, 102–105, 131–132, 172, 174, 231
  among men and women heads of families, singles, and other clients, 105–106
  attitudes toward, 97–98
  characteristics of homeless clients with various patterns of, 111–131
  community types and, 203, 206–209
  comorbidity, 102, 105
  definitions/criteria, 100–102
  in low-income housed adults *vs.* homeless clients, 106–111
  sources of data on, 98–99
alcohol, drug, and mental health (ADM) treatment, 109–111
  implications regarding, 111
  programs, 350
alcohol/drug/mental health status, defining, 100–102, 353–354
America's Homeless (Burt and Cohen), 322

battered women, 66, 292
Bush administration, George (Sr.), 12

Census Bureau, 4
child abuse and neglect, 86–88, 128, 153–155
childhood experiences
  and adult homelessness, 85–92, 183, 231–232. *See also* out-of-home placement
  and alcohol, drug, and mental health status, 122, 126–129
children, 93, 137–140, 158. *See also* "clients with children"; family status
  characteristics and living situations, 140–149
  "homeless," 139
  in homeless families using homeless assistance programs, 33, 34
  homelessness experienced before age 18, 129, 130
  living with homeless clients, 33–34
  living with "the other parent," 148
  not living with their homeless parent, 144, 147

projections for number of homeless clients plus, 48–49
chronic homelessness. *See* homelessness, patterns/typologies of
cities, central, 36–37, 217n1. *See also* metropolitan statistical areas; urban/rural location
client, defined, 53n7
"clients with children," 56, 352. *See also* family status
Clinton administration, 12
community, social-welfare functions of, 325–326
Community Shelter Board (CSB), 328
community type(s), 187–188, 212, 215–217, 282–283
adverse experiences and out-of-home placement, 206, 210–214
alcohol, drug, and mental health problems, 203, 206–209
demographic characteristics, 190–193
homeless assistance programs, program contacts, and, 253–255
homeless histories and use of homeless assistance programs, 193–198
income levels and sources, 198–202
physical health and food insecurity, 202–205
comparison groups, 133–134, 188–189
crisis homelessness. *See* homelessness, patterns/typologies of
"currently homeless," 18–19, 32, 223, 351. *See also* homeless status; *specific topics*

data sources, 16–20
Democrats, 330
demographic characteristics, 57–63
of children of homeless clients, 142, 143
community types and, 190–193
of currently, formerly, and never homeless clients, 224–225, 229, 234
of homeless clients with alcohol, drug, and mental health problems, 112–115
of young adult homeless clients, 150–152
disabled persons, programs for, 327–328
diversity among homeless people, 93
domestic violence, 66, 292. *See also* child abuse
drop-in center programs, 350
drug use, 66. *See also* alcohol, drug, and mental health (ADM) problems
early initiation of, 128–129
in low-income housed adults *vs.* homeless clients, 107–109

education, 62, 172. *See also* school problems
emergency shelters. *See* shelters
employment. *See* income level, employment, and income source
episodic homelessness. *See* homelessness, patterns/typologies of
eviction, 66

family households, 30, 36
family status, 56, 232
and alcohol, drug, and mental health status, 102–104
childhood experiences, adult homelessness, and, 85–92
and conditions of homelessness, 63–70
defining, 352–353
and demographic characteristics, 57–62
differences by, among women and among men, 62–63
and incarceration, 92–93
income, employment, income sources, and, 74–77
and physical health and nutrition, 80–85
and reasons for leaving last residence, 66–68
and use of homeless assistance programs, 70–74
family(ies), 93–94, 149, 173–174, 333
aid/assistance for, 33, 34, 74, 78, 79, 119, 200
being without, 3–4
male- *vs.* female-headed, 94
relying on one's, 325–326
using homeless assistance programs, 33, 34
"familyness" among homeless people, 149

federal poverty level (FPL), 79, 116, 119, 122, 133, 134
food programs, 197–198, 260, 262, 275, 291, 349. *See also* homeless assistance programs; soup kitchens
mobile, 350
Food Stamp program, 78
"formerly homeless," 19, 188–189, 224–227, 229, 234, 352. *See also* homeless status
differentiating currently homeless from, 233–235
foster care, 129, 130, 138, 148, 174, 332–333. *See also* out-of-home placement

government, role of, 326–327
government response to homelessness, 11–12, 14. *See also specific topics*
new policy orientations, 12–14
weakness of safety net, 15–16
government-supported assistance, 6
Great Depression, 3

health and nutrition problems, 66–68, 80–85, 235
alcohol, drug, and mental health status and, 119, 122–125
health (care) programs, 260, 262, 275, 291, 350
high school graduation, 172
HIV/AIDS programs, 350
"home"
children being forced to leave, 129, 130
meanings of, 4
homeless
factors associated with ever being, 229–231
factors that promote exit from, 162
housed situations while
number of, 179–180
time spent in, 178–179
number of times, 64–66
homeless assistance "industry," 264
homeless assistance programs, 32, 93–94, 241–243, 246, 263–264. *See also* homeless service systems; public benefit programs
community type, homeless histories, and use of, 193–198
funding sources, 259–262, 268. *See also* McKinney Homeless Assistance Act
NSHAPC, 246, 248, 249, 263, 348–351
number of clients, 32, 50
estimating, 32–35
in February *vs.* October/November, 37–44
number of program contacts, 20, 31–33, 39, 249–250, 252, 271–273
expected, 250, 251, 253–259
percent allocated to different types of services, 306–307
in various cities, 303–315
operating agencies, 259, 260
program size, 255–259
service growth by 1996, 243
shelter/housing capacity, 243–245
soup kitchen/meal capacity, 244, 245
that American assumptions have created, 329–334
types of, 259–262
urban *vs.* rural location, 246, 248, 249, 255, 279, 282–283, 288–289
use of, 70–74, 94–95, 264
community types and, 196–198
by homeless *vs.* nonhomeless households, 40
homeless clients, 32
current living situation, 68–73
young adult, 149–150
demographic characteristics, 150–152
early signs of difficulty, 156–157
homeless histories, 152
"homeless count," 27
homeless histories, 193–196
homeless people. *See also specific topics*
assessing the number of, 23–24, 50–52
changes since 1987, 40–44
estimates produced by NSHAPC data, 28–50
going from weekly to annual estimate, 44–50
projections for future, 46–51
types of numerical estimates, 24–27
units of analysis, 30–31
demographic characteristics, 57–63
diversity among, 93
where they spend most of their time, 178–179
"homeless plans," 16

homeless service systems, 3, 267–268
  capacity and variety in local, 270–274
    distribution of contacts with different types of shelter/housing programs, 276–278, 308–311
    distribution of services by program type, 274–276
    implications for development of continuums of care, 282–283
    implications of service patterns, 278–280
    soup kitchen meals relative to population in poverty, 280–282, 316n5
  continuity of care, 300–301
    first efforts toward, 269–270
    need for, 268–269
  service location specialization, 291–292
    program clustering and service offerings, by program type and, 292–300
  service locations
    geographic and other characteristics of, 288–289
    organization of programs into, 288
    organization of programs within, 289–291
  services availability
    implications, 287
    program reports of, 283–286
    provider perceptions of, 283–285
  services not available or available only off-site, 286–287
  variations by program and community type, 286
homeless-specific *vs.* generic services, 15–16
homeless spell(s), 175–176, 193
  length, 193. *See also* homelessness, length of period of
    base, 175–178, 181
    net, 175–176, 180–181
  number of, 193–195
homeless status
  defining, 351–352
  factors associated with, 216, 219, 223–224, 228, 229–232. *See also specific factors*
    data analysis, 222–223, 228–229
    identified by previous research, 219–222
  risk factors and, 224, 226–227
  terminology and definitions, 18–19
homelessness, 1–2. *See also specific topics*
  causes
    individual factors, 7, 8
    primary, 322
    structural factors, 7–11, 322
  conditions of, 63–70
  definitions and meanings, 2–7, 23–24, 52, 53n12
  efforts to end, 324–327, 329–334
    alternative approaches, 327–328
    European contrasts, 328–329
  elements of, 2–5
  experienced before age 18, 129, 130. *See also* children
  historical overview, 2–5
  length of period of, 63, 64, 66, 94, 152, 174–175. *See also* homeless spell(s), length
  new evidence for an old phenomenon, 14
  patterns/typologies of, 161–165, 181–184
    and alcohol, drug, and mental health status, 112, 116–118
    cluster analysis, 166–170
    comparing results to those of other studies, 170–171
    cross-tabulation analysis, 165–166
    grouping method, 171–175
households, 53n7
  homeless, 37
housing, being without, 4–5
housing affordability, 8, 322, 323
Housing and Human Development Department (HUD), 11–13
  national surveys, 241–243
housing facilities, 52
housing market and scarcity, 10
housing programs, 260–262. *See also* homeless service systems; transitional shelter/housing programs
  permanent, 297–299, 349
  stand-alone, 291
"housing" *vs.* "home," 4

illness. *See* health
incarceration, 92–93, 231

income level, employment, and income source, 74–77, 120–121, 216–217. *See also* federal poverty level; *specific social programs*
  and alcohol, drug, and mental health status, 106–111, 116, 119
  community types and, 198–202
  family status and, 74–77
  job loss and, 66
  NSHAPC findings, 79–80
  structure of public benefit programs, risk of homelessness, and, 74, 78–79

job loss, 66

Kentucky studies, 53n4

legal problems, 129–131. *See also* incarceration
low-income housed adults, drug and mental health problems of, 106–111

married *vs.* single clients, 61. *See also* family status
McKinney Homeless Assistance Act, Stewart B. (McKinney Act), 11–12, 97, 183, 244, 268, 269, 302
Medicaid, 84, 122
mental health care programs, 350
mental health problems. *See* alcohol, drug, and mental health (ADM) problems
methodologies. *See under* homelessness, patterns/typologies of
metropolitan statistical areas (MSAs), 36, 37, 42, 187, 237n1, 279, 282, 283. *See also* cities
migrant housing, 351
mothers of homeless children. *See also* children; parenting status
  importance of, 140
movers, 37

National Household Survey on Drug Abuse (NHSDA), 99
National Household Survey on Drug Abuse (NHSDA) sample, 99, 132–133
  defining the appropriate comparison group, 133–134
National Survey of Homeless Assistance Providers and Clients (NSHAPC), 16–20, 56, 189, 217n2, 222–224, 237n1, 243. *See also specific topics*
  data collection, 344, 347–348
  limitations, 188, 237n1, 321
  primary sampling areas, 345–346
  sample design, 343
National Survey of Homeless Assistance Providers and Clients (NSHAPC) programs
  definitions of, 348–351
  definitions used with client data, 351–355
"never homeless," 19, 188–189, 223, 352. *See also* homeless status
nongovernment agencies, 259–261, 327
nonprofit agencies, 259–261
nutrition. *See* health and nutrition problems

"other clients," 56, 95, 353
out-of-home placement/living experiences in childhood, 88–92, 129–131, 153–155, 174
  community types and, 206, 210–214
outreach programs, 350

pantries/pantry programs. *See* food programs
parenting status of homeless clients, 140–142
parent(s)
  children living with the "other," 148
  children not living with their homeless, 144, 147
  sex of, and children's living situation, 144–148
permanent housing programs, 297–299, 349
place, being without, 2–3
point-in-time numbers and studies, 44, 45, 163–164
population in poverty, 272, 280–282, 316n5

poverty, 320, 322. *See also* low-income housed adults
  homeless program contacts among people living in, 271–273
  population in, 272
poverty level, federal, 79, 116, 119, 122, 133, 134
prevention, 331–333. *See also* homelessness, efforts to end
  "deep," 333
private agencies, 259–261, 327
public benefit programs. *See also* homeless assistance programs
  structure of, and risk of homelessness, 74, 78–79

race/ethnicity, 171–172
Reagan administration, 12
religious nonprofit agencies, 259–261
Republicans, 330
research methodologies. *See under* homelessness, patterns/typologies of
residence, reasons for leaving last, 66–68
residual homelessness. *See* homelessness, patterns/typologies of
risk factors
  among currently, formerly, and never homeless clients, 224, 226–227
  individual-level, 320–321
running away from home, children, 129, 130, 153–155
rural areas, 29, 42. *See also* urban/rural location
Rural Economic and Community Development (RECD), 13

school problems in childhood, and adult homelessness, 86, 87, 126–128
seasonal differences, 37–44
self-reliance, 326
service availability *vs.* need, 53n5
service locations. *See also under* homeless service systems
  defined, 288
sex, differences by
  within family status, 61–62
sex differences, 172–173, 232–233. *See also* demographic characteristics; parent(s), sex of
  in alcohol, drug, and mental health status, 102–104
  among young adult homeless clients, 150–151
  in childhood experiences and adult homelessness, 85–92
  in conditions of homelessness, 63–70
  in incarceration rates, 92–93
  in income, employment, and income sources, 74–77
  in physical health and nutrition, 80–85
  in reasons for leaving one's last residence, 66–68
  in use of homeless assistance programs, 70–74, 94–95
sex subgroups, and demographic characteristics, 57–61
shelter tracking database, 26
shelter use, level of, 26
shelters, 52, 218n5, 248, 249, 279, 328
  programs and services attached to, 293–296, 348–359
"single clients," 56, 352. *See also* family status
"social housing," 329
Social Security, 198, 201
Social Security Disability Insurance (SSDI), 119, 122, 201
soup kitchen meals, relative to population in poverty, 280–282, 316n5
soup kitchens, 244, 245. *See also* homeless assistance programs
  programs and services attached to, 297, 300, 349
    program contacts, 312–315
stand-alone programs, 290–291
"street people," 28
suburban/urban fringe areas, 42–44
Supplemental Security Income (SSI), 78–79, 119, 122, 198, 201–203

telephone surveys, 26
Temporary Assistance for Needy Families (TANF), 78, 79
transitional shelter/housing programs, 94, 275, 296–298, 349. *See also* shelters
  in various cities, 308–311

Urban Institute, 32, 65, 143, 177, 181, 225, 275, 277, 281, 291
  1987 study, 24–25, 40–43, 55, 162, 170
urban/rural location, 29, 42–44. *See also* community type(s)
  of homeless assistance programs, 246, 248, 249, 255, 279, 282–283, 288–289
urban/rural status, 36–37, 172
  defining, 353

value tenets regarding welfare, 324–325
victimization while homeless, 65, 69–70
violence, domestic, 66, 292. *See also* child abuse
voucher (distribution) programs, 243–245, 349
"voucher theory," 278
vouchers, programs that accept, 349

wanderers, 3
Washington, D.C., 52n3
welfare. *See also* Aid to Families with Dependent Children
  attitudes toward and feelings about, 324–325
welfare reform, 135n7, 327

About the Authors

Martha Burt is the director of the Social Services Research Program at the Urban Institute. She has been involved in research and evaluation pertaining to a wide variety of populations and issues. Her work has included the first national survey of homeless individuals, conducted in 1987 and reported in *America's Homeless: Numbers, Characteristics, and Programs that Serve Them* (Urban Institute Press, 1989). She is the author of a number of books and reports on homelessness, including *Over the Edge: The Growth of Homelessness in the 1980s* (Fannie Mae, 1992), and both editions of *Practical Methods for Counting Homeless People: A Manual for State and Local Jurisdictions* (Urban Institute, 1992 and 1994). She is also the author of the federal report based on the National Survey of Homeless Assistance Providers and Clients, *Homelessness: Programs and the People They Serve* (Urban Institute, 1999).

Laudan Y. Aron is a research associate at the Urban Institute's Labor and Social Policy Center. Her work has covered a wide range of social welfare issues, including child welfare and child support; health, disability, and family planning; education; employment and training; and homelessness. She is currently studying health insurance coverage among child support–eligible children and is working on a national evaluation of the Adult Education and Family Literacy Act. Prior to joining the Urban

Institute, Ms. Aron worked as a senior associate in the economic analysis and evaluation practice area of Lewin-ICF.

Edgar Lee was a researcher at the Urban Institute, where he specialized in issues related to homelessness, workforce development programs, and low-skill labor markets, when this book was written. He is currently pursuing graduate studies at the John F. Kennedy School of Government at Harvard University, and is a researcher at the Civil Rights Project at Harvard Law School.

Jesse Valente, now at Abt Associates in Boston, was a research assistant at the Urban Institute from 1998 through 2000. During that time he conducted much of the basic analysis for this book. He also worked on *Homelessness: Programs and the People They Serve* (Urban Institute, 1999), and participated in a variety of other research projects focused on welfare reform. His primary research is in the area of poverty policy.